D1563833

Consorting
with Saints

Tympanum of the Last Judgment, west facade of the Abbey Church of
Conques, Aveyron. © 1994 ARS, New York/SPADEM, Paris.

Consorting with Saints

PRAYER FOR THE DEAD IN EARLY MEDIEVAL FRANCE

Megan McLaughlin

Cornell University Press

ITHACA AND LONDON

First published 1994 by Cornell University Press.

Printed in the United States of America

Library of Congress Cataloging-in-Publication Data

McLaughlin, Megan, 1954–
    Consorting with saints : prayer for the dead in early Medieval
France / Megan McLaughlin.
        p.   cm.
    Includes bibliographical references and index.
    ISBN 0-8014-2648-0 (alk. paper)
    1. Dead—Religious aspects—Catholic Church—History of doctrines—
Middle Ages, 600–1500. 2. France—Church history—To 987.
3. Funeral rites and ceremonies—France—History. 4. Catholic
Church—France—Liturgy—History. I. Title.
BX2170.D5M375   1994
264'.020985'094409021—dc20   93-34803

⊗The paper in this book meets the minimum requirements
of the American National Standard for Information Sciences—
Permanence of Paper for Printed Library Materials, ANSI Z39.48-1984.

CONTENTS

ACKNOWLEDGMENTS

My thanks to the librarians, archivists, and staffs of the Bibliothèque Nationale, the Bibliothèque Municipale of Boulogne-sur-Mer, and the Archives Départementales d'Ille-et-Vilaine, de Maine-et-Loire, and de Saône-et-Loire for their assistance and advice. I am especially grateful to M. Jean Delmas and his staff at the Archives Départementales de l'Aveyron, who, in the midst of preparing for a *déménagement,* arranged for me to see the documents I needed. The Institut de Recherche et d'Histoire de Textes gave prompt attention to my many demands for information and microfilm, while the Caisse Nationale des Monuments Historiques provided the frontispiece photograph. The people who work at the library of the University of Illinois, Urbana–Champaign have occasionally been bewildered by my requests, but have always done their best to honor them. Special thanks are due to Martha Friedman and Jody Seibold of the History Library, and to Ann Ricker and her staff at Inter-Library Borrowing for their patience and expertise.

Grants from the Fondation Georges Lurcy, the Margaret C. Whiting Foundation, and the UIUC Research Board supported the research for this book. The Research Board also provided a publication subvention. I appreciate their generosity.

I am grateful to many other scholars for sharing their enthusiasm and specialized knowledge with me. Alan E. Bernstein, Marcia Colish, Sharon Farmer, Patrick J. Geary, Thomas Head, Anne D. Hedeman, Martha Newman, Frederick S. Paxton, and Barbara H. Rosenwein provided references, advice, and encouragement. Faculty and graduate students at the University of Illinois contributed in particularly important ways to this project. Members of the "Social History Group" read and commented on several chapters in progress; Carol and Mark Leff reviewed the entire manuscript and made many helpful suggestions; Louis Haas and Daniel Peris verified bibliographical references.

Although my graduate adviser, Gavin I. Langmuir, had relatively little to do with this book, I hope his influence is apparent in its pages. He continues to serve as a model of scholarly integrity for me, as for many of his other students, past and present.

I deeply appreciate the friendly advice and encouragement provided by John Ackerman of Cornell University Press over the last few years. Thanks are also due to Kate Gilbert for her firm (but tactful) editing, and to Kay Scheuer for her skillful management of the production process.

This book was written under circumstances of great difficulty, which often slowed my work, and occasionally brought it to a complete halt. At those times, only the remarkable generosity of my friends made it possible for me to continue. They gave me advice, encouragement and support, sympathy and realism, laughter, anger, and tears in appropriate measure. Most important of all, they gave me hope, in a period when that commodity was in very short supply in my life. It is trite, but entirely true, to say that without their help the project would never have been completed. In all affection and gratitude, then, I offer what I have written to them, as a small return for their many gifts to me.

Consorting with Saints is dedicated to Jenny Barrett, Jim Barrett, Howard Berenbaum, Louise Fitzgerald, Caroline Hibbard, Carol Leff, Mark Leff, Lissa McLaughlin, Beth Matthias, Debbie Merritt, Bob Murphy, and Ron Toby: *amicis et familiaribus meis.*

MEGAN MCLAUGHLIN

Urbana, Illinois

ABBREVIATIONS

AA. SS.	J. Bollandus, et al., eds., Acta sanctorum
Arch. Dép.	Archives Départementales
BM	Bibliothèque Municipale
BN	Bibliothèque Nationale
CC, CM	Corpus christianorum, continuatio mediaevalis
CC, SL	Corpus christianorum, series latina
CSEL	Corpus scriptorum ecclesiasticorum latinorum
DACL	F. Cabrol and H. Leclercq, eds., *Dictionnaire d'archéologie chrétienne et de liturgie*
DTC	A. Vacant and E. Mangenot, eds., *Dictionnaire de théologie catholique*
FS	*Frühmittelalterliche Studien*
Mansi	G. D. Mansi, ed., *Sacrorum conciliorum nova et amplissima collectio*
MGH	Monumenta Germaniae Historica
EPP	Epistolae
LC	Libri confraternitatum
LM	Libri memoriales
LMN	Libri memoriales et necrologiae
PP	Poetae latini medii aevi
SRM	Scriptores rerum merovingicarum
SS	Scriptores

NCE	*New Catholic Encyclopedia*
PG	J. P. Migne, ed., Patrologiae cursus completus, series graeca
PL	J. P. Migne, ed., Patrologiae cursus completus, series latina
SRG	Scriptores rerum germanicarum in usum scholarum ex Monumentis Germaniae Historicis recudi

Consorting
with Saints

INTRODUCTION

In the summer of 875 a man named Deurhoiarn and his wife, Roiantken, came to visit the little monastery of Saint-Maxent in eastern Brittany. They wanted to see where they would be buried when they died, so Abbot Liosic and the monks took them to the church porch to point out the exact spot. Then the whole party moved into the sanctuary, where husband and wife made separate donations "to St. Maxent, in honor of the Savior, and to the monks serving God in that place" by placing a glove representing their gifts on the altar. When Deurhoiarn died in January 876, Roiantken and their son Iarnwocon had his body taken to Saint-Maxent. The monks came out to meet them in solemn procession, carrying the relics of their saints, and brought the body back to the monastery, where Deurhoiarn was buried "in keeping with his dignity"—for he was a member of the local aristocracy. After the funeral Iarnwocon confirmed his parents' gifts in the presence of his mother and a large crowd of nobles. Roiantken died soon after her husband and was buried "with great honor" next to him. On the Sunday after her funeral Iarnwocon came to Saint-Maxent to visit his parents' grave and made a new donation to "Maxent and the monks" for his mother's soul. Later he came again and gave yet another gift to the saint for the souls of his parents.[1]

1. *Cartulaire de l'abbaye de Redon en Bretagne,* ed. Aurélien de Courson (Paris, 1863), no. 236 (875–78). In references to documents from the Redon cartulary, I have corrected de Courson's dates, where necessary, in keeping with the findings of Arthur de la Borderie, "La Chronologie du cartulaire de Redon," *Annales de Bretagne* 5 (1889–90), 535–630; 12

This account, drawn from a contemporary charter, of the negotiations between a noble family and a monastery in late ninth-century
Brittany poses some intriguing problems. Why were Deurhoiarn and
Roiantken so interested in seeing the spot where they would be
buried? Why were the relics of the saints included in Deurhoiarn's
funeral procession? What was the nature of the relationship between
this family and the monks of Saint-Maxent, and what role did the
monks' prayers play in that relationship? Finally, what did Deurhoiarn, Roiantken, and Iarnwocon hope to gain from their dealings
with the monastery? Within the last few decades questions such as
these have begun to exercise a growing number of scholars in Europe
and in North America. By unearthing new evidence and reinterpreting old texts, these scholars have exponentially increased our knowledge of the practice and meaning of rituals for the dead in early
medieval Europe. And in the process, they have revolutionized a field
of study whose foundations were laid long ago.

The expansion of scholarship has done much more than explain
how particular liturgical institutions and beliefs developed. It has also
made it possible to trace the configurations within which they flourished, and this has revealed that rituals for the dead were practiced and
understood in a special way in the period from the mid-eighth century to the end of the eleventh century. Of course, some early medieval
institutions and beliefs had their roots in Christian antiquity, and
some endured into the later middle ages. There are, then, many similarities of detail between early medieval prayer for the dead and that
of earlier and later periods. However, the thesis of this book is that
prayer for the dead followed a distinctive "pattern" in the early middle
ages, a pattern that reflected the distinctive social, economic, and
cultural structures of early medieval society.

The Growth of Scholarship on Prayer
for the Dead

Modern historiography on Christian rituals for the dead has its
roots in the age of the Reformation. By the sixteenth century prayer

---

(1896–97), 473–522; 13 (1897–98), 11–42, 263–79, 430–58, 590–611. On Deurhoiarn's
status, see Wendy Davies, *Small Worlds: The Village Community in Early Medieval Brittany*
(London, 1988), pp. 178–79. Here and throughout, all translations are mine, unless otherwise noted.

for the dead had become a divisive issue in western Christendom, with Protestants rejecting the practice and many of the beliefs associated with it, and Catholics defending it as a charitable act of great utility to the departed faithful. Apologists on both sides mustered historical arguments in support of their positions. Protestant scholars denied that the earliest Christians had prayed for the dead; they described the practice as a superstition that had grown up since the age of the Apostles. Catholic scholars asserted the biblical origins of prayer for the dead and the continuity of what they considered a sacred tradition from the first days of the church to their own time. Thus, the apologetic debates of the sixteenth century gave rise to the first historical sketches of Christian burial practices and commemorative institutions.[2]

For a long time thereafter scholarly attention remained fixed on the practices and beliefs of the paradigmatic early Christian centuries and—to a lesser extent—on those that existed on the eve of the Reformation. The history of prayer for the dead in the early middle ages remained largely uncharted territory.[3] Only in the middle of the nineteenth century did some of the pioneers of positivist history—most notably the great French scholar Léopold Delisle—become interested in confraternity books, mortuary rolls, and other documents associated with prayer for the dead as sources of information on early medieval politics and society.[4] Over the next few decades, many of these documents and a number of works devoted to their criticism and interpretation were published. This flurry of scholarly activity culminated in 1890 with the appearance of Adalbert Ebner's *Die klösterlichen Gebets-verbrüderungen*, the first extended study of early medieval commemorative practices.[5]

Something of a hiatus followed in the first part of the present century. Not only did the series of editions of confraternity books and necrologies projected by the Monumenta Germaniae Historica in

2. See, for example, Martin Luther, *Ein Widerruf vom Fegefeuer*, ed. O. Clemen and O. Brenner, in *D. Martin Luthers Werke: Kritische Gesamtausgabe*, sect. 1, vol. 30, pt. 2 (Weimar, 1909), pp. 360–90. The Catholic historian Onofrio Panvinio's *De ritu sepeliendi mortuos apud veteres christianos* (Cologne, 1568) was composed in direct response to Lutheran polemics.

3. Before the nineteenth century, only the monks of the Congregation of Saint-Maur, in their great collections of documents in aid of the history of the liturgy, and the Italian liturgical historian Giuseppe Tommasi devoted much attention to the subject.

4. Delisle's work on the liturgy is summarized by André Wilmart, "Delisle (Léopold)," *DACL* 4: 1, especially cols. 515–31.

5. Adalbert Ebner, *Die klösterlichen Gebets-Verbrüderungen bis zum Ausgang des karolingischen Zeitalters* (Regensburg, 1890).

Germany and by the Académie des Inscriptions et Belles-Lettres in France come to a halt, but interest in the study of early medieval prayer for the dead seems to have declined. The influence of late nineteenth-century scholarship ensured that some attention would continue to be paid to the early middle ages in general works on the afterlife and prayer for the dead. In particular, Albert Michel discussed early medieval liturgical practices and the work of early medieval theologians in his important monograph-length article on the doctrine of Purgatory, published in 1936.[6] Yet very few scholars were producing important works devoted specifically to early medieval rituals for the dead. The most notable achievement of this period was the series of studies published by Georg Schreiber and his students between the 1910s and the 1930s, which examined the role of prayer in negotiations between noble patrons and religious houses in the tenth and eleventh centuries.[7] But these studies had, at first, little influence outside of Germany.

The real flowering of scholarship on early medieval rituals for the dead has occurred since World War II, and especially since the late 1960s. It is the work of three distinguishable, if not entirely distinct, groups of scholars. The first is made up of Catholics engaged in the movement for a more critical history of the liturgy. This movement, which led up to the liturgical reforms of the Second Vatican Council and continued with even greater vigor through the 1970s and 1980s, has been dominated by the towering figure of Josef Jungmann. However, most of the crucial work on the early medieval liturgy, including the liturgy of death, has been done by other scholars. Some of these scholars have focused on a crucial issue raised by Jungmann: the transformation of the eucharistic gathering of the early Christians into the medieval mass. Otto Nussbaum, Angelus Häussling, Cyrille Vogel, and Arnold Angenendt have all explored the growth of *missae speciales* (masses for special intentions, including masses for the dead) in the early middle ages, and the relationship of these masses both to more public celebrations and to the development of the so-called private mass.[8] Others have turned their attention to burial rituals. In a

6. Albert Michel, "Purgatoire," *DTC* 13: 1163–1326.
7. See Schreiber's collected essays: *Gemeinschaften des Mittelalters: Recht und Verfassung, Kult und Frömmigkeit* (Münster, 1948); see also Willibald Jorden, *Das cluniazensische Totengedächtniswesen, vornehmlich unter den drei ersten Äbten Berno, Odo, und Aymard (910–954)* (Münster, 1930).
8. Otto Nussbaum, *Kloster, Priestermönch, und Privatmesse: Ihr Verhältnis im Westen von den Anfängen bis zum hohen Mittelalter* (Bonn, 1961); Angelus Häussling, *Mönchskonvent und Eucharistiefeier: Eine Studie über die Messe in der abendländischen Klosterliturgie des frühen Mit-

path-breaking work published in 1978, Damien Sicard traced the evolution of Christian funerals in the West from late antiquity to the end of the eighth century.[9] Still more recently, the work of Catholic historians of the liturgy has begun to dovetail with that of anthropologically minded historians interested in the study of ritual in society and culture. One of these historians, Frederick Paxton, has recently revised some of Sicard's findings and carried the study of funerary ritual through the end of the ninth century, in an effort to explain the formation of a coherent Christian "rite of passage" from life to death.[10]

Anthropology has also shaped the thinking of a second group of scholars, who draw on ethnographic studies to illuminate the cultural significance of prayer for the dead in early medieval Europe. Some of these cultural historians, including Jacques Le Goff and Franz Neiske, have traced the development of ideas about the afterlife and the ways in which prayer was believed to help the dead in the next world.[11] Others have explored the relationship between the living and the dead as it was imagined in the early middle ages. Karl Schmid and Joachim Wollasch (whose work is discussed more fully below) discussed the liturgical aspects of that relationship in an influential article published in 1967.[12] Philippe Ariès devoted parts of his fascinating, though often unreliable works on the history of death to the physical and emotional links between the living and the dead.[13] Otto Gerhard Oexle has summarized and elaborated on this earlier scholarship in his

telalters und zur Geschichte der Meßhäufigkeit (Münster, 1973); Cyrille Vogel, "Une Mutation cultuelle inexpliquée: Le passage de l'Eucharistie communautaire à la messe privée," *Revue des sciences religieuses* 54 (1980), 231–50; idem, "La Multiplication des messes solitaires au moyen âge: Essai de statistique," *Revue des sciences religieuses* 55 (1981), 206–13; Arnold Angenendt, "Missa specialis: Zugleich ein Beitrag zur Entstehung der Privatmessen," *FS* 17 (1983), 153–221.

9. Damien Sicard, *La Liturgie de la mort dans l'église latine des origines à la réforme carolingienne* (Münster, 1978).

10. Frederick S. Paxton, *Christianizing Death: The Creation of a Ritual Process in Early Medieval Europe* (Ithaca, 1990).

11. Jacques Le Goff, *La Naissance du Purgatoire* (Paris, 1981), trans. Arthur Goldhammer as *The Birth of Purgatory* (Chicago, 1984); Franz Neiske, "Vision und Totengedenken" *FS* 20 (1986), 137–85. See also the important study by Arnold Angenendt, "Theologie und Liturgie der mittelalterlichen Toten-Memoria," in Karl Schmid and Joachim Wollasch, eds., *Memoria: Der geschichtliche Zeugniswert des liturgischen Gedenkens im Mittelalter* (Munich, 1984), pp. 79–199.

12. Karl Schmid and Joachim Wollasch, "Die Gemeinschaft der Lebenden und Verstorbenen in Zeugnissen des Mittelalters," *FS* 1 (1967), 365–405.

13. Philippe Ariès, *Western Attitudes toward Death from the Middle Ages to the Present*, trans. Patricia M. Ranum (Baltimore, 1974), pp. 14–25; idem, *L'Homme devant la mort* (Paris, 1977), pp. 37–96, trans. Helen Weaver as *The Hour of Our Death* (New York, 1981).

important essay on the "presence" of the dead in medieval society, published in 1983.[14] His insights have been further developed by Patrick Geary, in an article on "exchanges" between the living and the dead in the early middle ages.[15] Together, Oexle and Geary have demonstrated the strength of the sense of obligation that bound the living to the dead in the early middle ages. They have also shown how the imagined relationship of the living and the dead reflected the realities of relationships among the living in early medieval society.

The third group responsible for the growth of scholarship on early medieval rituals for the dead is made up of social historians interested in tracing relationships among religious communities, and between religious communities and lay society, in the early and high middle ages. European and North American scholars have conducted a tremendous amount of research on these relationships in recent years, much of which at least touches upon the role of prayer for the dead. However, within this general expansion of scholarly activity, the work of Karl Schmid of the University of Freiburg im Breisgau, and his student Joachim Wollasch, who is now at the University of Münster, deserves special attention. They and their colleagues in what has come to be known as the Münster-Freiburg School have produced an extremely important body of research on early medieval commemorative practices and the sources associated with those practices. Their writings appear in the pages of the journal *Frühmittelalterliche Studien*, in the series Münstersche Mittelalter-Schriften, and in the editions and studies published by the Monumenta Germaniae Historica.

Probably the most lasting contribution of this group of scholars has been the publication, in critical editions of a new kind, of the name-lists used in early medieval rituals for the dead.[16] Traditional

14. Otto Gerhard Oexle, "Die Gegenwart der Toten," in Herman Braet and Herman Verbeke, eds., *Death in the Middle Ages* (Louvain, 1983), pp. 19–77.

15. Patrick Geary, "Échanges et relations entre les vivants et les morts dans la société du haut moyen âge," *Droit et cultures* 12 (1986), 3–17.

16. The new editorial techniques were developed in response to the problems presented by the publication of the *Liber memorialis* of Remiremont, the first volume in the new series "Libri memoriales" (later "Libri memoriales et necrologiae") of the Monumenta Germaniae Historica: *Liber Memorialis von Remiremont*, ed. Eduard Hlawitschka, Karl Schmid, and Gerd Tellenbach (Zurich, 1970). By the late 1970s those techniques had been largely perfected, and a series of editions with associated studies followed. These include *Das Verbrüderungsbuch der Abtei Reichenau (Einleitung, Register, Faksimile)*, ed. Johanne Autenrieth, Dieter Geuenich, and Karl Schmid (Hanover, 1979); *Der Liber vitae der Abtei Corvey*, ed. Karl Schmid and Joachim Wollasch (Wiesbaden, 1983); *Die Totenbücher von Merseburg, Magdeburg, und Luneburg*, ed. Gerd Althoff and Joachim Wollasch (Hanover,

editions of these documents simply reproduced all or part of a name-
list in print, sometimes using different typefaces to indicate different
hands in the original manuscript. Users were obliged to rely not only
on the editor's reading of the text, but also on his or her identification
and dating of the sometimes numerous scribal hands that occur in
documents used over the course of centuries. Moreover, even when
indexes were provided, it was often very difficult to locate a particular
name among the hundreds or even thousands recorded in these lists.
The new editions being produced by the Schmid-Wollasch research
group are much more usable, although initially daunting in appearance. Computer-generated indices, organized by *lemmata* or "key-
spellings," make it possible to locate individual names, despite variant
spellings, wherever they occur in one or even in several related manuscripts.[17] The volumes published by the Monumenta Germaniae Historica also include photographic reproductions of the manuscript
sources, so that users may identify and date the different hands for
themselves.

Karl Schmid began his career as a historian by studying the early
medieval nobility and its social relationships. He first turned to the
sources associated with liturgical commemoration as a way of getting
at early medieval prosopography; his colleagues and students have

---

1983); *Die Altarplatte von Reichenau-Niederzell*, ed. Dieter Geuenich, Renate Neumullers-
Klauser, and Karl Schmid (Hanover, 1983); *Das Martyrolog-Necrolog von St. Emmeram zu
Regensburg*, ed. Eckhard Freise, Dieter Geuenich, and Joachim Wollasch (Hanover, 1986).
See also Karl Schmid, ed., *Die Klostergemeinschaft von Fulda im früheren Mittelalter*, 3 vols.
(Munich, 1978); Otto Gerhard Oexle, *Forschungen zu monastischen und geistlichen Ge-
meinschaften im westfränkischen Bereich* (Munich, 1978); *Synopse der cluniacensischen Necrologien*,
ed. Joachim Wollasch, with Wolf Dieter Heim et al., 2 vols. (Munich, 1982); Michael
Borgolte, Dieter Geuenich, and Karl Schmid, eds., *Materialien und Untersuchungen zu den
Verbrüderungsbüchern und zu den älteren Urkunden des Stiftsarchivs St. Gallen* (St. Gall, 1986).

17. The editorial techniques are discussed by Karl Schmid, "Zum Interdisziplinären
Ansatz, zur Durchführung und zum Anliegen des Fulda-Projekts," in Schmid, *Die
Klostergemeinschaft von Fulda*, 1: 11–36. On the use of computers to analyze these sources,
see Karl Schmid and Joachim Wollasch, "Zum Einsatz der EDV im Quellenwerk 'Societas et
Fraternitas'," in Karl Ferdinand Werner, ed., *L'Histoire médiévale et les ordinateurs/ Medieval
History and Computers* (Munich 1981), pp. 69–76; Karl Schmid, "Zum Einsatz der EDV in
der mittelalterliche Personenforschung," *FS* 22 (1988), 53–69. On the differences between
traditional editions and those of the Münster-Freiburg School, see Jean-Loup Lemaître, "La
Commémoration des défunts et les obituaires dans l'occident chrétien," *Revue d'histoire de
l'église de France* 71 (1985), 131–45. Important studies of medieval name-lists and related
documents have also been conducted by scholars not directly associated with the Münster-
Freiburg School. Among general works, see especially Nicholas Huyghebaert, *Les Documents nécrologiques* (Turnhout, 1972); Jean-Loup Lemaître, ed., *Repertoire des documents nécrologiques français*, 2 vols. (Paris, 1980), with *Supplément* (Paris, 1987).

maintained that interest.[18] Indeed, one of the major goals of the new editions of name-lists has been to facilitate prosopographical studies. In addition to their computer program for identifying variant forms of the same name by key-spellings, the Schmid-Wollasch research group has created another set of computer programs designed to identify recurring groups of names, even when they appear in a slightly different order in different places. The *Gruppensuchprogramm* makes it possible to study the relationships between similar groups of names occuring in different manuscripts, thereby clarifying the relationships between the different groups of clerics that produced and preserved those manuscripts (as for example in the recent synoptic edition of the Cluniac necrologies).[19] The *Gruppensuchprogramm* can also be used to identify groups of people whose names were all entered on the lists at the same time. The potential of these research tools for the study of family ties, political affiliations, and religious movements is only now being realized.[20]

The historians of the Münster-Freiburg School share a common interest in early medieval commemorative institutions. In other re-

18. Already in 1965 Schmid had noted the connection between the nobility's family relationships and their spiritual relationships: Karl Schmid, "Religiöses und sippengebundenes Gemeinschaftsbewusstsein in frühmittelalterliche Gedenkbucheinträgen," *Deutsches Archiv für Erforschung des Mittelalters* 21 (1965), 18–81, reprinted in Karl Schmid, *Gebetsgedenken und adliges Selbstverständnis im Mittelalter: Ausgewählte Beiträge* (Sigmaringen, 1983), pp. 532–97. On the Münster-Freiburg prosopographical research group, see Karl Schmid and Joachim Wollasch, "Societas et Fraternitas: Begründung eines kommentierten Quellenwerkes zur Erforschung der Personen und Personengruppen des Mittelalters," *FS* 9 (1975), 1–48. Wollasch discussed the use of name-lists as a source for the study of monastic history in "Neue Methoden der Erforschung des Mönchtums in Mittelalter," *Historische Zeitschrift* 225 (1977), 529–71.

19. On the GSP, see Friedrich-Wilhelm Westerhoff, "Gruppensuche: Ein Verfahren zur Identifizierung von Personen und Personengruppen in mittelalterlichen Namen-Quellen," in *Dokumentationsband zum EDV-Kolloquium, 1985* (Münster, 1985), pp. 67–77; see also Maria Hillebrandt, "The Cluniac Charters: Remarks on a Quantitative Approach for Prosopographical Studies," *Medieval Prosopography* 3 (1982), 3–25.

20. For studies of noble families and political groupings by members of the Münster-Freiburg School, see Karl Schmid, "Die Sorge der Salier um ihre Memoria," in Schmid and Wollasch, *Memoria*, and his collected essays, *Gebetsgedenken und adliges Selbstverständnis*; Gerd Althoff, *Adels- und Königsfamilien im Spiegel ihrer Memorialüberlieferung: Studien zum Totengedenken der Billunger und Ottonen* (Munich, 1984); idem, *Verwandte, Freunde, und Getreue: Zum politischen Stellenwert der Gruppenbindungen im früheren Mittelalter* (Darmstadt, 1990); idem, *Amicitiae und Pacta: Bündnis, Einung, Politik und Gebetsgedenken im beginnenden 10. Jahrhundert* (Hanover, 1992). For studies of clerical groups, see Joachim Wollasch, *Mönchtum des Mittelalters zwischen Kirche und Welt* (Munich, 1973); Oexle, *Forschungen zu monastischen und geistlichen Gemeinschaften;* Dieter Geuenich, Otto Gerhard Oexle, Karl Schmid, *Die Listen geistlicher und monastischer Kommunitäten aus dem früheren Mittelalter* (Munich, 1989).

spects, though, it is difficult to generalize about their work, for they approach prayer for the dead in widely varied ways.[21] Some study the liturgy itself, others focus on the early medieval understanding of commemoration, and still others look at the individuals and groups associated with a particular religious community and its liturgy at any given time, and the specific religious, political, and social factors that affected such affiliations. Finally, there are those who examine commemoration of the dead from the point of view of more enduring economic, social, and cultural structures. Regardless of their individual interests, however, the members of the Münster-Freiburg School have carried the study of prayer for the dead in the early middle ages to an entirely new level of critical scholarship, through their meticulous examination of individual texts and comparative analysis of groups of documents from the same religious communities.

CHANGING MODELS

The combined efforts of liturgical, cultural, and social historians over the last twenty-five years have produced a vast body of new information on the practice and meaning of prayer for the dead in early medieval Europe. But these historians have done much more than simply fill in the blanks. Their work has also brought into question the model of intercession for the dead which has dominated most modern scholarship on this subject, a model that—like the historiographical tradition itself—has its roots in the later middle ages and in the age of the Reformation.

Whether they accepted or rejected prayer for the dead, the sixteenth-century apologists assumed that it had always been what it was in their own day. Catholic writers, arguing for the antiquity of the practice, believed that it must have taken the same basic shape throughout Christian history, since it was that shape which they were anxious to preserve. Protestant writers, asserting the relative novelty of prayer

21. The varied interests of the group are evident in these essay collections: Schmid and Wollasch, *Memoria*; Karl Schmid, ed., *Gedächtnis, das Gemeinschaft Stiftet* (Munich, 1985); Gerd Althoff et al., eds., *Person und Gemeinschaft im Mittelalter* (Sigmaringen, 1988). See also the bibliographical reports published after the research group at Münster was disbanded: "Der Münsterer Sonderforschungsbereich 7: 'Mittelalterforschung (Bild, Bedeutung, Sachen, Wörter, und Personen)'," *FS* 19 (1985), 543–47; "Mittelalterforschung in Münster in der Nachfolge des Sonderforschungsbereichs 7," *FS* 24 (1990), 397–410.

for the dead, nevertheless believed that the defects they observed in
their own day were inherent in the institution: when prayer for the
dead arose it must already have had the same (unsatisfactory) form
and meanings it had in the sixteenth century. What were those forms
and meanings? To begin with, in the fifteenth and sixteenth centuries
there was often little or no direct connection between the dead and the
clerics who prayed for them. Many services for the dead were performed privately, outside of the formal liturgy offered by churches on
a regular basis, and by clerics hired for the purpose or supported by
an endowed chantry. As a result, attention came to be focused on the
services themselves, which were abstracted from the context of the
liturgy as a whole and reified. In the Reformation debates, both Catholics and Protestants understood prayer for the dead less as a reflection
of the social and spiritual relationships that bound together the intercessor, the interceded-for, and the divine than as a series of distinct
intercessory acts, which could be weighed, compared, accumulated—
and purchased.[22] Both sides also held similar views on the intended
function of prayer for the dead. Catholics, of course, asserted that
prayer could liberate the dead from their purgatorial sufferings, while
Protestants rejected the doctrine of purgation after death and denied
that prayer had any effect at all on the condition of the dead in the
next world. Nevertheless, all concerned assumed that prayer for the
dead was at least intended to propel souls out of a Purgatory that
might or might not exist.[23] This is clearly an oversimplified treatment

22. Popular funerary customs are described by A. N. Galpern, *The Religions of the
People in Sixteenth-Century Champagne* (Cambridge, 1976), pp. 20–29. Compare Ralph E.
Giesey, *The Royal Funeral Ceremony in Renaissance France* (Geneva, 1960); Colette Beaune,
"Mourir noblement à la fin du moyen âge," in *La Mort au moyen âge* (Strasbourg, 1977),
pp. 125–43. On the growing demand for masses in the fourteenth and fifteenth centuries,
see Jacques Chiffoleau, *La Comptabilité de l'au-delà: Les hommes, la mort, et la religion dans la
région d'Avignon à la fin du moyen âge (vers 1320–vers 1480)* (Rome, 1980); idem, "Sur l'usage
obsessionnel de la messe pour les morts à la fin du moyen âge," in *Faire croire: Modalités de la
diffusion et de la réception des messages religieux du XIIe au XVe siècle* (Rome, 1981), pp. 235–56;
Marie-Thérèse Lorcin, *Vivre et mourir en Lyonnais à la fin du moyen âge* (Paris, 1981), pp. 135–
46; Michel Vovelle, *La Mort et l'occident de 1300 à nos jours* (Paris, 1983). On chantries, see
Jean Quéguiner, "Recherches sur les chapellenies au moyen âge," Thesis, École Nationale
des Chartes, 1950; K. L. Wood-Legh, *Perpetual Chantries in Britain* (Cambridge, 1965); Alan
Kreider, *English Chantries: The Road to Dissolution* (Cambridge, 1979).
23. Some historians have recently questioned whether belief in Purgatory was very
widespread among ordinary people before the seventeenth century: see Philippe Ariès, "Le
Purgatoire et la cosmologie de l'au-delà," *Annales* 38 (1983), 155–56. Clearly, however, the
scholars involved in apologetic debates in the sixteenth century associated prayer for the
dead with Purgatory. The main outlines of these debates are traced by Michel, "Purgatoire," *DTC* 13: 1264–82; on the debate in England, see Kreider, *English Chantries*,
pp. 93–153. See also Vovelle, *La Mort et l'occident*, pp. 190–212, 225–36.

of a complex set of practices and beliefs, but it provides at least a rough map of the ground upon which the sixteenth-century battles over prayer for the dead were waged.

These battles have deeply influenced modern western historiography on the subject. Until very recently, most historians who studied prayer for the dead were themselves believers, with an interest in attacking "medieval superstition" or defending the "immemorial tradition of the church." Even those with no particular religious bone to pick were strongly influenced by the writings of the partisans, from which they drew evidence and interpretations. The apologetic debates focused the historical gaze for a long time on the paradigmatic early Christian and problematic later medieval periods. But even when historians began to turn their attention to the early middle ages, they still generally looked for the antecedents of fifteenth- and sixteenth-century liturgical practices and interpretations, ignoring or discounting as "curiosities" other aspects of early medieval prayer for the dead.[24] Moreover, they tended to interpret early medieval evidence using a model of intercession based on later medieval practices and beliefs. Only very recently have scholars begun to recognize the problems this traditional model presents when applied to the very different ritual, social, and cultural practices of the early middle ages.

The thrust of much liturgical scholarship in this century has been to document the decline of the community worship practiced in the early Christian era and the growth of liturgical practices directed at providing special benefits for specific individuals or groups within the church—including the departed faithful. Liturgical historians have long regarded late antiquity and the early middle ages as the period in which such practices began to develop, laying the foundation for the abuses eventually condemned by reformers in the fifteenth and sixteenth centuries.[25] Many scholars have assumed that the liturgy of death was already envisioned in the early middle ages as a series of distinct ritual acts—masses for the dead, offices of the dead, anniversaries, and so on—which were only loosely connected with the rest of

24. This is true even of such scholarly works as Adolph Franz, *Die Messe im deutschen Mittelalter: Beiträge zur Geschichte der Liturgie und des religiösen Volkslebens* (Freiburg, 1902): see pp. 218–67. A striking example of this anachronistic tendency is the unreliable book by A. Molien, *La Prière pour les défunts* (Avignon, 1928).

25. This is apparent in the great surveys of Gregory Dix, *The Shape of the Liturgy* (2d ed., London, 1945), especially pp. 589–94; and Josef Jungmann, *The Mass of the Roman Rite: Its Origins and Development*, trans. Francis A. Brunner, 2 vols. (New York, 1951–55), especially 1: 212–33. See also Cyrille Vogel, "An Alienated Liturgy," in Herman Schmidt, ed., *Liturgy: Self-Expression of the Church*, Concilium, 72 (New York, 1972), pp. 11–25.

the liturgy. They have further assumed that early medieval Christians, like their successors in the later middle ages, were anxious to accumulate as many of these reified "units of intercession" as possible.

An important recent contributor to this scholarly tradition is Arnold Angenendt of the University of Münster. In 1983 he published a richly documented and persuasive study of *missae speciales* or votive masses, including masses for the dead.[26] Angenendt attributes the development of these masses for special intentions to the spread of the Irish system of "tariffed" penance, which presupposed that every sin could be expiated through the performance of a specific number of spiritual acts. While at first satisfaction was made for sin through fasting, the recital of psalms, or almsgiving, by the eighth century it had become possible to arrange for the performance of masses as a substitute for other forms of satisfaction. Angenendt traces the creation of special masses for both living and dead sinners, the development of contractual agreements—which might involve specific payments to the clergy—for their performance, and the rapid growth in the frequency with which votive masses were performed in the eighth and ninth centuries. He also discusses the logic behind these practices: the idea that each mass had a specific expiatory value, that many masses had more value than one, and that a mass offered specifically for an individual would be more effective on his or her behalf than a mass offered for all of the faithful.

Angenendt offers the most convincing explanation to date of the development of the *missae speciales*. However, like many earlier liturgical historians, he focuses on their long-term implications. He believes that these masses represented a corruption of the early Christian understanding of the eucharist, and argues that they inevitably led to the kind of problems denounced by the sixteenth-century reformers.[27] Other recent scholars, more concerned with the special character of the early medieval liturgy than with the origins of later abuses, have understood the *missae speciales* in a rather different way. In particular, they have noted the survival of the ancient ideal of collective worship into the middle ages, despite the changing structure of the liturgical community. Angelus Häussling, for example, asserts that the many masses performed for special intentions in early medieval cathedrals and monasteries were understood as different

26. Angenendt, "Missa specialis." This study is explicitly presented as a development of Jungmann's ideas, and as a response to the work of Angelus Häussling: see p. 153.
27. Angenendt, "Missa specialis," especially pp. 175–81, 212–21.

parts of a single liturgy, in which the whole clerical community was united. For Häussling, then, votive masses represent not a "threat" to the collective liturgy of the church, but an elaboration of it.[28] In a recent article he has discussed the prayer associations (*Gebetsge-meinschaften*) made up of clerics from various churches, who promised to perform a certain number of masses for each other after death. Whereas Angenendt sees in this development the triumph of "numbers" over community, Häussling views the *Gebetsgemeinschaft* as a liturgical community in its own right, with a complex but integrated liturgy.[29] In the same vein, Franz Neiske has pointed out that what was important to early medieval Christians was not the total number of masses performed, but the spiritual community's collective effort on behalf of the dead.[30] The work of Häussling, Neiske, and other recent scholars has thus undermined traditional assumptions about the relationship of rituals for the dead to the rest of the liturgy in the early middle ages.[31]

In positing the reification of prayer, the traditional model of intercession turns rituals for the dead into the object of negotiations between those who prayed and those who wished to be prayed for. This aspect of the subject has been of special interest to social historians concerned with the nature of the relationship between the clergy and the laity in the early middle ages. Some of these scholars have interpreted that relationship in terms of a commercial transaction: in their work, prayer becomes a commodity, "purchased" by the laity with their gifts to the clergy who pray.[32] Such an interpretation has some validity for the later middle ages, when prayer was, in fact, often

28. Häussling, *Mönchskonvent und Eucharistiefeier*; idem, "Missarum Sollemnia: Beliebige Einzelfeiern oder integrierte Liturgie?" in *Segni e riti nella chiesa altomedievale occidentale*, 2 vols. (Spoleto, 1987), 2: 559–78.

29. Häussling, "Missarum Sollemnia," p. 566.

30. Franz Neiske, "Frömmigkeit als Leistung? Uberlegungen zu grossen Zahlen im mittelalterlichen Totengedenken," *Zeitschrift für Literaturwissenschaft und Linguistik* 80 (1990), 35–48.

31. The continuing importance of community bonds in the early medieval liturgy has been noted by a number of other scholars: see especially Jean Leclercq, "Culte liturgique et prière intime dans le monachisme au moyen âge," *La Maison-Dieu* 69 (1962), 39–55. On the role of community in the liturgy of death see Otto Gerhard Oexle, "Memoria und Memorialüberlieferung im früheren Mittelalter," *FS* 10 (1976), 70–95; Sicard, *La Liturgie de la mort*, pp. 254–57, 414–18.

32. See, for example, Elisabeth Magnou-Nortier, *La Société laïque et l'église dans la province ecclésiastique de Narbonne (zone cispyrénéenne) de la fin du VIIIe à la fin du XIe siècle* (Toulouse, 1974), p. 442; Dominique Iogna-Prat, "Les Morts dans la comptabilité céleste des Clunisiens de l'an Mil," in Dominique Iogna-Prat and Jean-Charles Picard, eds., *Religion et culture autour de l'an mil: Royaume capétien et Lotharingie* (Paris, 1990), p. 67.

treated as a kind of commodity. However, it becomes problematic when applied to the early middle ages, a period in which commerce played only a limited role, and the economy was dominated by other forms of exchange. The need for a different interpretation of the lay/clerical relationship in the early middle ages was recognized long ago by Georg Schreiber, who chose to describe the negotiations between nobles and monasteries in terms of gift-exchange rather than commerce.[33] Following Schreiber's lead, most recent social historians have viewed grants of liturgical privileges as clerical "return-gifts" for noble donations to religious communities.[34]

There remains, however, the problem of determining the exact role of liturgical services in the lay/clerical relationship during the early middle ages. Were they the primary focus of that relationship, as they were in the later middle ages, when services were often performed for the dead by priests hired specifically for that purpose, and whose only connection with those for whom they prayed was their stipend? Did the early medieval laity offer their gifts to clerical communities simply in order to ensure that they would be prayed for when they died? This was Schreiber's assumption, and it has continued to influence the work of many scholars.[35] However, recent research indicates that early medieval Christians understood rituals for the dead not just as desirable commodities, but as reflections of deeper social relationships. Otto Gerhard Oexle, for example, has shown how liturgical commemoration served to both express and create

33. See Schreiber, "Kirchliches Abgabenwesen an französischen Eigenkirche aus Anlass von Ordalien: Zugleich ein Beitrag zur gregorianisch-cluniazensische Reform und zur Geschichte und Liturgik der Traditionsnotizen," *Zeitschrift der Savigny-Stiftung für Rechtsgeschichte* 36, Kanonistische Abteilungen, 5 (1915), 414–83; reprinted in Schreiber, *Gemeinschaften des Mittelalters*, pp. 151–212; idem, "Cluny und die Eigenkirche: Zur Würdigung der Traditionsnotizen des hochmittelalterlichen Frankreich," *Archiv für Urkundenforschung* 17 (1942), 359–418, reprinted in Schreiber, *Gemeinschaften des Mittelalters*, pp. 81–138; Jorden, *Das cluniazensische Totengedächtniswesen*, especially pp. 21–33, 94–95.
34. These historians have also drawn upon the work of the early twentieth-century sociologist Marcel Mauss, who studied gift-exchange in nonwestern societies: see Mauss's "Essai sur le don: Forme et raison de l'échange dans les sociétés archaïques," *L'Année sociologique* 1 (1923), 30–186; published in English as *The Gift: Forms and Functions of Exchange in Archaic Societies*, trans. I. Cunnison (New York, 1967). Mauss's ideas have been applied to prayer for the dead by, among others, Oexle, "Memoria und Memorialüberlieferung," pp. 87–95, and Geary, "Échanges et relations entre les vivants et les morts."
35. E.g., Herbert Edward John Cowdrey, "Unions and Confraternity with Cluny," *Journal of Ecclesiastical History* 16 (1965), 152–62; Heinrich Dormeier, *Montecassino und die Laien im 11. und 12. Jahrhundert* (Stuttgart, 1979).

religious community in the early middle ages.[36] Other scholars have examined the ways in which secular affiliations were reflected in rituals for the dead.[37]

Within the last decade, three American historians have published studies which explore the full range of interactions between the lay nobility and elite religious communities, and suggest new ways of understanding those interactions. In her study of nobles and the church in Burgundy, Constance Bouchard demonstrates how closely the first two orders of society were connected with each other in the central middle ages.[38] She traces the kinship relationships between Burgundian church leaders and the great noble families of the area, the role of the nobility in promoting monastic reform, and lay generosity to religious houses in general, as well as donations specifically associated with grants of prayer. Her work thus places the negotiations that resulted in prayer for the dead within their proper context—that of the generally "intimate" relationships between nobles and religious communities. Stephen White focuses on a particular aspect of noble dealings with monasteries in western France between 1050 and 1150: the *laudatio parentum*, or approval of gifts by the donor's relatives. White argues that donations to monasteries in this period were not simple legal acts, but simultaneously "economic, juridical, moral, aesthetic, religious, mythological and socio-morphological" transactions.[39] The main parties involved were not individuals but complex groups—noble kindreds and monastic communities—and the transactions were not completed quickly, but took shape over a long period of time. Whereas Bouchard demonstrates the "intimacy" of the ties between nobles and clergy, White elucidates the complicated character of those ties and—although this is not a central theme in his book—the role of rituals for the dead in confirming them.

Barbara Rosenwein also makes an important contribution to this growing body of literature.[40] Her book focuses on the meaning

---

36. Oexle, "Memoria und Memorialüberlieferung." See also the very important study by Dietrich Poeck, "Laienbegräbnisse in Cluny," *FS* 15 (1981), 68–179.

37. See the works listed in notes 18 and 20 above.

38. Constance Brittain Bouchard, *Sword, Miter, and Cloister: Nobility and the Church in Burgundy, 980–1198* (Ithaca, 1987).

39. Stephen D. White, *Custom, Kinship, and Gifts to Saints: The Laudatio Parentum in Western France, 1050–1150* (Chapel Hill, 1988), p. 4. White draws his list of adjectives from E. E. Evans-Pritchard's introduction to Mauss, *The Gift*, p. vii.

40. Barbara H. Rosenwein, *To Be the Neighbor of Saint Peter: The Social Meaning of Cluny's Property, 909–1049* (Ithaca, 1989).

of property transactions in the tenth and eleventh centuries; like
Bouchard and White, Rosenwein is only tangentially interested in
prayer for the dead. Nevertheless, she has done the most of any recent
historian to clarify the place of such prayer in the negotiations between nobles and religious communities. Rosenwein disputes the
long-established view that donors gave to the famous Burgundian
monastery of Cluny in order to obtain prayers for themselves. "Natu-
rally, Cluny's prayers and commemoration of the dead remain important for understanding why laymen wanted to associate themselves
with the monastery. But they are not the complete explanation."[41] In
the tenth and early eleventh centuries, she argues, property exchanges
were primarily intended to create close relationships between St. Peter, the patron saint of Cluny, and his lay neighbors. While liturgical
commemoration was one expression of these relationships, the emphasis in these transactions was on the creation of social bonds, not
the acquisition of prayer.

The negotiations that resulted in prayer for members of the lay
nobility are, then, coming to be understood as part of complex transactions, sometimes conducted over long periods of time, and centered
not on the exchange of goods (primarily land) and services (prayer),
but rather on the formation of enduring bonds between social groups.
But what about non-nobles? Did they deal with the clergy and their
rituals in similar ways? The ways in which the poor and powerless
were prayed for has hitherto received little attention from historians.
Joachim Wollasch and Michael Borgolte have considered the poor in
their role as beneficiaries of almsgiving and of manumissions associated with the commemoration of the more privileged members of
society, but not as individuals who were themselves commemorated
after death.[42] This is an area in which much research still remains to
be done.

If recent scholarship has altered traditional views of the negotiations that resulted in the performance of prayers, it has also begun to
transform our understanding of the meanings attributed to prayer for
the dead in the early middle ages. Historians have traditionally sought

41. Rosenwein, *To Be the Neighbor of Saint Peter*, p. 41, responding to the views of
Schreiber, Jorden, Cowdrey, Poeck, and many other recent scholars (see nn. 7, 35, and 36,
above).

42. Joachim Wollasch, "Gemeinschaftsbewusstsein und soziale Leistung im Mittelalter," *FS* 9 (1975), 268–86; idem, "Les Obituaires, témoins de la vie clunisienne," *Cahiers de
civilisation médiévale* 22 (1979), 139–71; Michael Borgolte, "Freigelassene im Dienst der
Memoria," *FS* 17 (1983), 234–50.

the meaning of prayer for the dead in the medieval West within the theological tradition, as formulated in the later middle ages and debated during the Reformation. In other words, prayer for the dead has been associated primarily with the doctrine of purgation after death.[43] Indeed, many of the most important scholarly discussions of the subject have occurred in works on Purgatory. A notable example is the long article on Purgatory in the *Dictionnaire de théologie catholique*, in which Albert Michel attempted to present a defense of the doctrine, using the tools of modern critical scholarship. Michel, writing in 1936, rejected some of the arguments used by earlier Catholic apologists, admitting in particular that no explicit reference to Purgatory could be found in Scripture. He asserted instead that the strongest argument for the existence of Purgatory was the tradition of the church. In order to demonstrate the continuity of that tradition, he reviewed not only patristic texts but also the evidence for prayer for the dead in the early Christian period. For so closely did Michel associate prayer for the dead with the doctrine of Purgatory, that he believed he could demonstrate the existence of the latter from the practice of the former. Prayer for the dead was "the most solid basis for Christian belief in Purgatory."[44] Throughout the article, he reverted to discussion of liturgical developments as a means of demonstrating continuity of belief in Purgatory.

Within the last few decades, however, the idea that belief in Purgatory has been continuous from the earliest Christian centuries has been criticized not only by Protestant apologists, but also by secularized scholars and even by a few Catholic ones. The issue has achieved new prominence since the publication in 1981 of Jacques Le Goff's controversial book *La Naissance du Purgatoire*. Le Goff is con-

---

43. This is true of the most important recent treatment of the ideas associated with prayer for the dead in the early middle ages, Arnold Angenendt's "Theologie und Liturgie," in Schmid and Wollasch, *Memoria*, pp. 79–199. The title of this essay is somewhat misleading, since in fact Angenendt is concerned with the ways in which the commemoration of the dead was understood during the period of theological decline between the death of Gregory the Great in the seventh century and the revival of theology in the twelfth. Angenendt attributes the growing importance of prayer for the dead in this period to the triumph of crude assumptions about divine justice over theological subtlety. Nevertheless, his essay still focuses on those early medieval beliefs that fed into the theological tradition. He argues that the scholastics of the later middle ages were obliged to find justifications for liturgical practices which had grown up during the earlier period of theological decline; in the process they paved the way for the controversies of the sixteenth century: see p. 199. Thus, as in his article on *missae speciales*, Angenendt sees in early medieval developments the roots of later problems.

44. Michel, "Purgatoire," *DTC* 13: 1198.

cerned in this work with the emergence of Purgatory as a place, an intermediate space in the other world between heaven and hell. While he admits that belief in the possibility of purgation after death can be traced back to the first centuries of Christianity, he asserts that Purgatory—the place—came into being only in the late twelfth century. As proof of this, Le Goff cites linguistic evidence: the appearance of the substantive *purgatorium* (Purgatory), which eventually replaced earlier phrases such as *purgatorius ignis* (purging fire) or *purgatoriis locis* (places of purgation) in discussions of the afterlife.[45] He argues that the substantive form first appeared between 1160 and 1180, and that this linguistic development signals the "birth" of Purgatory as a place. In the tradition of the *Annales* school, he associates this change in *mentalités* with the general transformation of feudal society in the twelfth century.

Le Goff has been roundly attacked for this book—by theologians for his "sociological" approach, by students of popular culture for his emphasis on theology, and by specialists of various stripes for his treatment of particular texts.[46] Many reviewers have questioned his assertion that the term *purgatorium* first appeared in the late twelfth century.[47] Some scholars have also questioned the significance of this development, arguing that the appearance of the substantive form represented a clearer definition of existing belief, not the kind of revolutionary change that Le Goff suggests.[48] But while he has certainly overstated his case at many points in *La Naissance du Purgatoire*, Le Goff is, in my view, essentially correct. While individual early medieval writers (notably the Venerable Bede) may have described something very like Purgatory in their works, there was certainly no shared notion of a single place of purgation in the next world before

45. This is not an original observation, although Le Goff interprets it in a new way. Critics have failed to note that in insisting that the word *purgatorium* first appeared in the twelfth century, Le Goff was following Michel ("Purgatoire," col. 1228).
46. See, for example, Adriaan H. Bredero, "Le Moyen Age et le Purgatoire," *Revue d'histoire ecclésiastique* 78 (1983), 429–52; Aron J. Gurevich, "Popular and Scholarly Medieval Cultural Traditions: Notes in the Margin of Jacques Le Goff's Book," *Journal of Medieval History* 9 (1983), 71–90; Graham Robert Edwards, "Purgatory: 'Birth' or Evolution?" *Journal of Ecclesiastical History* 36 (1985), 634–46; Brian Patrick McGuire, "Purgatory, The Communion of Saints, and Medieval Change," *Viator* 20 (1989), 61–84.
47. E.g., Bredero, "Le Moyen Age et le Purgatoire," pp. 443–46; Gurevich, "Popular and Scholarly Medieval Cultural Traditions," p. 79.
48. Alan E. Bernstein, review of *La Naissance du Purgatoire* in *Speculum* 59 (1984), 179–83; Jean-Pierre Massaut, "La Vision de l'au-delà au moyen âge: A propos d'un ouvrage récent," *Le Moyen Age* 91 (1985), 75–86.

the twelfth century.[49] Moreover, I believe that the popularization (if not necessarily the first appearance) of the term *purgatorium* in the late twelfth century reflected the new importance that purgation after death was taking on at this time both in works on eschatology generally, and in discussions of prayer for the dead. Other images and ideas associated with prayer for the dead in the early middle ages were gradually discarded in the twelfth and early thirteenth centuries.[50]

More important for our purposes, the controversy over Le Goff's book has thrown into prominence the related issue of the meaning of prayer for the dead. For if Purgatory was "born" only in the twelfth century, then what was the significance of prayer for the dead in the early middle ages? Le Goff devotes some space in his book to early medieval liturgical developments. However, he treats them as preparatory to the "birth" of Purgatory rather than as significant in their own right; as a result, his discussion of the subject is cursory at best. In fact, he never really explains what prayer for the dead might have meant before Purgatory was "born"—as Philippe Ariès pointed out in his critique of Le Goff's thesis.[51] Le Goff's great contribution to our subject has been to clear away some of the "purgatorial underbrush," facilitating exploration of the other meanings associated with prayer for the dead in the early middle ages. A few intrepid scholars have undertaken such exploration, yet here, too, much still remains to be done.[52]

The new research of the last few decades has, then, done much more than add to our knowledge of the ways in which early medieval Christians cared for their dead. It has gradually undermined the validity of the traditional model of intercession when applied to the early middle ages, as well as suggesting new ways of thinking about rituals

49. See below, Chapter 5.
50. Megan McLaughlin, "Consorting with Saints: Prayer for the Dead in Early Medieval French Society," Ph.D. diss., Stanford University, 1985, pp. 413–65.
51. Ariès, "Le Purgatoire et la cosmologie de l'au-delà," 151–53.
52. Scholars who study the early Christian period have long recognized that in the first few centuries of the church prayer for the dead may have served functions other than that of liberating souls from purgation or ameliorating purgatorial sufferings. See, for example, Franz J. Dölger, "Antike Parallelen zum leidenden Dinocrates in der *Passio Perpetuae*," *Antike und Christentum: Kultur- und religiongeschichtliche Studien* 2 (1930), 1–40. The most important study of the meaning of prayer for the dead in the early Christian period is that of Joseph Ntedika, *L'Évocation de l'au-delà dans la prière pour les morts: Étude de patristique et de liturgie latines (IVe–VIIIe s.)* (Louvain, 1971); see also Nancy Gauthier, "Les Images de l'au-delà durant l'antiquité chrétienne," *Revue des études augustiniennes* 33 (1987), 3–22. On the early middle ages, see especially A. Cabassut, "La Mitigation des peines de l'enfer d'après les livres liturgiques," *Revue d'histoire ecclésiastique* 23 (1927), 65–70.

for the dead. The time has now come to pull together the many
threads that have been spun out of this research. In the chapters that
follow, I attempt to analyze and integrate the work of earlier scholars,
and to supplement that work with my own research (especially on the
ritual treatment of the poor, long-term trends in the commemoration
of the wealthy, and the meanings associated with rituals for the dead)
in order to present a coherent picture of the practice and meaning of
prayer for the dead in the early middle ages.

I argue that early medieval rituals for the dead were primarily
"associative" in character. By this I mean that they were full of
social—more specifically, ecclesiological—symbolism, which was
designed to emphasize the complex network of relationships that
bound together the intercessor, the dead, and the divine. Individual
men and women came to be prayed for after death because of their
close ties to the clerical communities that prayed, and the forms of
commemoration they enjoyed were intended to dramatize those ties:
to associate the dead with those who prayed, with their patron saints,
and, ultimately, with their promised reward. In Chapter 5, I also
propose a new model of intercession, a model that I believe accounts
in a more satisfactory way than the traditional one for this associative
"pattern" of prayer.

Prayer for the Dead in Early Medieval France

The first section of this book describes the liturgy of death performed in early medieval churches. It relies primarily on the evidence
of sacramentaries, *ordines*, and customaries to answer questions about
what services were offered for the dead, and how those services coexisted with the other rituals performed by the clergy. Chapter 1 is
devoted to funerary ritual, that is, the ceremonies precipitated by the
death of an individual. Chapter 2 deals with nonfunerary prayer for
the dead: the ceremonies performed for the dead in general within the
ordinary round of prayer. The continuing commemoration of individuals after their funerals were over will also be considered in this
chapter. The central section of the book, based largely on narrative
texts and legal documents, deals with prayer for the dead in its broader social context. In this section I consider how members of the laity

came to be prayed for by clerical communities, and the impact of social and economic structures on the source and nature of their commemoration. The first part of Chapter 3 sketches the relationship of the laity to the various liturgical communities that arose between late antiquity and the end of the eleventh century, noting, in particular, the diverging situations of *humiles* and *potentes* from the eighth century on. The commemoration of ordinary people is also explored in Chapter 3, while Chapter 4 focuses on the commemoration of more powerful individuals, such as Deurhoiarn and Roiantken. Finally, Chapter 5 draws on material from a wide variety of sources, including theological texts, vision literature, miracle stories, and preambles to charters, in order to enumerate and classify the meanings attributed to prayer for the dead in the early middle ages.

This book examines prayer for the dead as it was practiced and interpreted in one area of Europe, the area that corresponds to modern France, from the middle of the eighth century through the end of the eleventh century. The geographical parameters of the study are determined largely by practical considerations, related to the number and distribution of the surviving sources. On the one hand, certain kinds of sources, primarily those having to do with the meanings attributed to prayer for the dead in the early middle ages, are distributed very unevenly. If I had concentrated on a much smaller area, it would have been impossible to get an adequate idea of how the people in that area understood the prayers they performed for the dead. As it is, I have sometimes looked beyond France for relevant material, although in such cases I have tried to make the provenance of that material very clear.

On the other hand, when dealing with other kinds of sources, primarily those having to do with the actual practice of prayer for the dead, we are faced with an overabundance of material. In order to do justice (insofar as possible) to the specific social setting within which the liturgy was carried out, I have restricted my study to France, rather than trying to cover all of western Europe. One might argue that France was an extremely varied territory socially, economically, culturally, and politically in the early middle ages, and that by casting my net so wide I have missed many local variations. My choice was admittedly a compromise and so necessarily unsatisfactory in some respects. However, it offered the best means possible of addressing the questions with which I was concerned.

The temporal parameters of the book are defined by important

changes in liturgical practice and—not coincidentally—by important
points in the continuum of social and cultural change. The liturgical
reforms of the eighth and early ninth centuries, which included, as we
shall see, important changes in the liturgy of death, reflect the political centralization and social transformations of that period. They
must also be seen as part of the literary revival—the so-called Carolingian Renaissance—which resulted in the preservation not only of
classical texts, but also of the far less glamorous sources used in this
book. It would be impossible to study the actual practice of prayer for
the dead in early medieval France had it not been for the preservation
of "documents of practice," notably charters, in increasing numbers
from the second half of the eighth century on. To some extent, then,
the starting point for this study is determined by the availability of
sources as well as by the historical facts of liturgical and social change.

Because they are less clearly associated with identifiable figures,
the liturgical reforms of the late eleventh century are less well known
than those of the eighth century. They are, however, equally important. Not only did the new religious orders that arose in this period
worship in ways very different from their predecessors in the early
middle ages, but both the old and the new clergy were affected by
subtle but significant changes in the understanding and practice of
liturgical prayer, which reflected the profound economic, social, political, and cultural changes that occurred in the period from 1050 to
1150. Not surprisingly, the transformation of the liturgy as a whole
left its mark on the liturgy of death. Indeed, as I shall argue in the
epilogue, it was in this period that the early medieval pattern of prayer
for the dead finally began to give way to a new one.

A NOTE ON TERMINOLOGY

A project like this presents special problems of periodization.
Readers have the right to expect some easily recognizable signposts to
guide them through a discussion that ranges over more than a thousand years of history. Yet familiar signposts do not always correspond
with crucial moments in the chronology of liturgical change. I have
tried to resolve these problems by using some conventional chronological terms in slightly unconventional ways. Thus, in the chapters
that follow, "the early Christian era" refers to the time before the

Peace of the Church, while "late antiquity" extends from the fourth century to the middle of the eighth century. "The early middle ages" run from the mid-eighth century to the end of the eleventh century and are followed by "the high middle ages." I should make it clear, however, that the chronological boundaries of "the early middle ages" should really be understood as falling somewhere within two long transitional periods, the first corresponding roughly to the eighth century and the second to the century from about 1050 to 1150. The dates 750 and 1100, which are used throughout this book to mark off the early middle ages, simply represent the approximate mid-points of these two transitional periods.

1   THE BURIAL OF THE DEAD

Early medieval rituals for the dead present a rich and, at first glance, bewildering array of meanings. The texts of prayers touch on the joys of heaven, the terrors of hell, and the dangers of this world. They describe the unworthiness of those praying and the fidelity of those prayed for, the sufferings of Job and the triumph of the martyrs, the justice and the mercy of God. Ritual actions serve to cleanse bodies awaiting burial; align them with other bodies near the walls of churches, in doorways, or near altars; and make tombs sacred with incense. Often it is difficult to understand the connections between the many different ideas found in liturgical texts, let alone between texts and ritual actions. The same diversity of meanings is evident in the writings of the theologians, church leaders, and even those few ordinary Christians who have left us written interpretations of prayer for the dead.[1]

Yet at a deeper level, beneath the widely disparate images presented by early medieval rituals for the dead, there runs a common theme, which structured those rituals and, to a large extent, determined the ways in which they were used. This is the theme of spiritual relationship—both the vertical relationship between the individual Christian and God, and the horizontal relationships within the Christian community. These might be understood in terms of ritual kinship, ties of patronage between saints and ordinary men and women,

---

1. See Chapter 5 below.

or membership in the liturgical community which represented on earth the community of the elect in heaven. The ties between God and the individual have often been explored in studies of the liturgy, including the liturgy of death. One purpose of this book is to demonstrate the significance of horizontal relationships—the importance of "consorting with saints"—in early medieval prayer for the dead.

Rituals for the dead could, of course, both reflect and affect ordinary social relationships as well as spiritual ones. Social and ecclesiological themes resonated strongly with one another in the early middle ages. Ritual structures both reinforced and cut across social structures, in ways which will be explored more fully in later sections of this book. However, in this and in the following chapter, I focus on the ways in which ideas of spiritual relationship, expressed in ecclesiological symbolism, shaped the development of Christian rituals for the dead from antiquity through the end of the eleventh century.

CHRISTIAN FUNERARY RITUAL BEFORE THE MIDDLE OF THE EIGHTH CENTURY

Ecclesiological statements and symbolism played a role in Christian funerary ritual from the earliest times. This was the natural outcome of the circumstances in which the early churches found themselves. Christianity—at least Pauline Christianity—is a social religion, in the sense that salvation is attained by unity not only with Christ but also with the body of Christ, the church (however that may be interpreted) which gathers together "in his name" for worship. Assumptions about the collective nature of salvation found expression in the doctrine of the communion of saints, first elaborated in late antiquity and developed further over the course of the middle ages.[2] A sense of community was also experienced very concretely in the liturgy.

In the first few centuries, the church was made up of a number of relatively small, tightly knit groups, bound together not only by mutual faith but also quite frequently by outside persecution. The body of Christ was closely identified at this time with a specific

2. P. Bernard, "Communion des saints (son aspect dogmatique et historique)," *DTC* 3: 429–54; Émilien Lamirande, *The Communion of Saints*, trans. A. Manson (New York, 1963), pp. 15–30.

human community, the gathering of Christians known as the *ecclesia*.[3] But since the purpose for which the ecclesia came together was worship and the celebration of the communal meal, it can be said that the body of Christ constituted itself primarily through the liturgy.[4] The collective action of the eucharist was the raison d'être of the church and the center of the Christian life. Hence the urgency of the need to keep up the regular worship of the church even when to do so would be dangerous. The ecclesia of Abitina, for example, was decimated during the persecution under Diocletian because its members insisted on meeting for worship on Sundays. When asked why they exposed themselves to arrest in this way, the reply was: "We cannot survive without the Lord's gathering. . . . The Lord's celebration cannot be superseded."[5] The powerful sense of corporate unity which ultimately allowed the churches to survive persecution was thus expressed in, and created by, the act of worship.

In this earliest period of Christianity, the community that saved was also the community that prayed. This was true not in an abstract way but in a very concrete sense. Baptism in that period brought with it not only membership in a spiritual community, but also the right and the obligation to participate in a specific liturgical community, the ecclesia. Through baptism, one entered the order of the laity, an order with its own special part in the eucharistic service, its own "liturgy" in fact, which fit together with the "liturgies" of the other, clerical orders to form the liturgy of the ecclesia as a whole.[6] Without the active participation of all the orders, there could be no worship, and without worship there was no church. Conversely, the person who did not participate by adding his or her liturgy to that of the rest of the ecclesia was no Christian. This was why regular Sunday communion was almost universal among both clergy and laity in the early Christian period, for it was believed that the salvation that was begun

3. Bernard Botte, "Christian People and Hierarchy in the Apostolic Tradition of St. Hippolytus," in *Roles in the Liturgical Assembly: The Twenty-Third Liturgical Conference Saint-Serge (Paris, 1976)*, trans. Matthew J. O'Connell (New York, 1981), pp. 23–24; Jean Daniélou, *The Origins of Latin Christianity*, vol. 3 of *A History of Early Christian Doctrine before the Council of Nicea*, ed. John A. Baker, trans. David Smith and John A. Baker (Philadelphia, 1977), p. 461.

4. Henri de Lubac, *Corpus mysticum: L'eucharistie et l'église au moyen âge*, 2d ed. (Paris, 1949), pp. 23–24.

5. Josef Jungmann, *The Early Liturgy, to the Time of Gregory the Great*, trans. Francis A. Brunner (Notre Dame, Ind., 1959), p. 13; Dix, *The Shape of the Liturgy*, pp. 151–53.

6. Jungmann, *The Early Liturgy*, pp. 18–19; Dix, *The Shape of the Liturgy*, pp. 141–55.

in baptism could be maintained only through participation in the liturgy.[7] Even after death the faithful kept up their roles in the liturgical assembly, through the efforts of the living on their behalf.

It is difficult, given the limitations of the sources, to determine what the funerals of the earliest Christians were like. In all probability, they combined some traditional practices, centered on the family, with some specifically Christian rites, which reflected the dead person's religious identity. Presumably the mixture varied from place to place and from era to era.[8] It seems clear, however, that ecclesiological ideas and symbolism played a role in the Christian aspects of these "mixed" funerals from a very early date.

At the approach of death, the faithful would receive the viaticum, the eucharist for the dying, which constituted a final act of communion with Christ and with the ecclesia.[9] But even after death it was assumed that Christians would continue to participate in the ritual activities of the liturgical assembly. Indeed, some of the early fathers suggested that the departed faithful might be personally present at the assembly. Tertullian, for example, describes a miracle in which a corpse awaiting burial took on the *orans* position, the traditional posture of prayer, with arms outstretched, during the prayer of the priest, and maintained that position until the congregation exchanged the kiss of peace.[10] Others believed that the dead would maintain their role in the liturgy through the actions of the living. The ecclesia made it a point to pray as a community during the funerals of its members. On the other hand, the leaders of the church asserted that those who died outside its communion were not entitled to commemoration in its collective prayers.[11]

What distinguished Christian from pagan funerals, in the view of

7. Ene Braniste, "The Liturgical Assembly and its Functions in the *Apostolic Constitutions*," in *Roles in the Liturgical Assembly*, p. 91; see also Kenneth Hein, *Eucharist and Excommunication: A Study in Early Christian Doctrine and Discipline* (Frankfurt, 1973).

8. Alfred C. Rush, *Death and Burial in Christian Antiquity* (Washington, D.C., 1941); Paul-Albert Février, "Le Culte des morts dans les communautés chrétiennes durant le IIIe siècle," in *Atti del IX congresso internazionale di archeologia cristiana (Roma, 21–27 settembre, 1975)*, 2 vols. (Rome, 1978), 1: 211–74; Victor Saxer, *Morts, martyrs, reliques en Afrique chrétienne aux premiers siècles: Les témoignages de Tertullien, Cyprien, et Augustin à la lumière de l'archéologie africaine* (Paris, 1980).

9. Rush, *Death and Burial in Christian Antiquity*, pp. 92–99.

10. *De anima*, 51: 6, ed. J. H. Waszink, in Tertullian, *Opera*, 2 vols. (Turnhout, 1954), 2: 857–58; and see Origen, *De oratione*, 33 (PG 11: 553).

11. E.g., Cyprian, *Epistulae*, 1, in *S. Thasci Caecili Cypriani opera omnia*, ed. Wilhelm Hartel, 3 vols. (Vienna, 1868–71), 2: 465–67; text discussed in Saxer, *Morts, martyrs, reliques*, pp. 103–4. On this rule, see Ntedika, *L'Évocation de l'au-delà*, pp. 31–35.

the earliest Christian apologists, was their triumphal character. The faithful accompanied the bodies of their departed brothers and sisters to the cemetery, singing psalms and hymns of praise, rather than weeping and lamenting in the traditional way.[12] This psalmody remained a major feature of Christian burials for centuries to come. However, the central rite of the church—the celebration of the eucharist—was also associated with the funerals of Christians from at least the second century on. What part it played in those funerals is less clear. There is little evidence from the first three centuries of celebrations conducted in the presence of the body before it was buried. However, the practice of offering the eucharist for the dead after they were laid to rest is well attested. It seems to be related to pre-Christian customs, common throughout the Mediterranean region, which called for sacrifices at the tomb of a dead person on set days after the burial. The Christian communities substituted eucharistic sacrifices for these traditional ones at an early date.[13]

The end of the persecutions and the developments within the Christian communities associated with the Peace of the Church mark the beginning of a new stage in the history of prayer for the dead. Important changes occurred in both funerary ceremonies and nonfunerary prayer for the dead from the fourth century on. The traditional belief that the departed faithful were still members of the church and hence entitled to participate in its liturgy remained in force and shaped the new institutions as they emerged.[14] However, the role of the dead in the community that prayed had to be both emphasized and reinterpreted over the next few centuries, as the structure of the ecclesia and the pattern of liturgical prayer began to change, and as new ideas about the status of the dead began to influence their treatment in the liturgy.

This was the period when the liturgy of the Christian churches became "clericalized." For reasons that will be discussed more fully in a later chapter, the laity began to lose their active role in the services of the ecclesia from the fourth century on. They retained some liturgical functions, but as time passed their presence was no longer necessary for the performance of the liturgy. Gradually, then, liturgical

12. Rush, *Death and Burial in Christian Antiquity*, pp. 231–35; Paxton, *Christianizing Death*, pp. 39–43.
13. Emil Freistedt, *Altchristliche Totengedächtnistage und ihre Beziehung zum Jenseitsglauben und Totenkultus der Antike* (Münster, 1928).
14. Ntedika, *L'Évocation de l'au-delà*, pp. 30–44.

prayer became an activity that the clerical orders performed on behalf of the Christian community, rather than in concert with the order of the laity.[15] But as active participation in the liturgy lessened overall, it may have seemed important to reaffirm the individual Christian's participation in the liturgical community through the use of ecclesiological symbolism.

As the church found a recognized place in society and attracted a growing number of converts, a new pessimism became evident in the writings of church leaders and in the prayers of the liturgy. Awareness of the sin to be found within a larger and in some ways more worldly church grew, and as a result confidence in the salvation of the faithful slowly began to give way to anxiety about the fate of individual Christians after death.[16] But as their fate began to seem less certain, their need to be remembered in the liturgy began to seem more urgent. It is no accident that visions in which the dead appear asking for prayers became increasingly common in late antiquity. The anxiety expressed in such visions led to a redoubling of liturgical efforts on behalf of the departed faithful. The development of prayer for the dead can, then, be seen as a response to the now keener perception that the dead needed help.[17] And the prominence of ecclesiological symbolism in prayer for the dead can be viewed as an effort to reaffirm their membership in the saving community of the church.

As might be expected, the changes described above had important effects on Christian funerary ritual. "Clericalization" was the most important factor in a general liturgical expansion, which began in late antiquity and continued throughout the early middle ages. As the clergy began to perceive themselves as liturgical specialists, they devoted more and more time to the fulfillment of their liturgical functions, with the not-unexpected result that those functions expanded. Services of all kinds, including those for the burial of the dead, were formalized and elaborated in this period. Gradually the "mixed" funerals of the early Christian period began to give way to more fully "Christianized" funerals, until in the end liturgical prayer performed by the clergy accompanied every step in the process of death, burial, and mourning.

Ecclesiological statements and symbolism played a very promi-

15. See Chapter 3 below.
16. Paul-Albert Février, "La Mort chrétienne," in *Segni e riti*, 2: 901, 935–36; and see below, Chapter 5.
17. See Chapter 5 below.

nent role in rituals of death and burial as they evolved between the fourth and the eighth centuries. For example, the viaticum emerged in this period as a potent symbol of membership in the church, and great controversies arose over who was entitled to receive it. This issue had first come up during the persecutions of the third century, when certain rigorists refused to grant the viaticum to "lapsed" Christians—those who had agreed to sacrifice to the gods under the threat of death—even if they later repented and asked for forgiveness. Also at issue was the treatment of catechumens and unshriven penitents. In the fourth and fifth centuries, most church councils adopted moderate positions on these questions. Arrangements were made to allow those who were very ill to be baptized or reconciled with the church on short notice if necessary. Every effort was made to ensure that those who asked for these services would be granted them, for in this way they could be given the viaticum before they died.[18] However, the councils also ordered communion to be withheld from heretics and those who died unrepentant. Heretics, excommunicates, and suicides were also denied the processional psalmody and prayers with which Christians normally accompanied their dead to the grave.[19]

In late antiquity, the ecclesiological symbolism of funeral services was enhanced by their new setting—a specifically Christian building, the church. In the first three centuries, funeral processions had apparently moved directly from the home or the place of death to the cemetery.[20] However, after the persecutions came to an end and it became possible to build permanent, sometimes sumptuous settings for the Christian cult, funeral processions were directed into these new basilicas for part of the burial service.[21] The more privileged members of the Christian community were sometimes even buried inside churches, in order to be close to the relics they contained. From the fourth century on, such "privileged" burials occurred in the suburban basilicas built over the tombs of the martyrs. By the fifth century, the relics of the saints were being transferred into urban basilicas, and the bodies of the dead followed.[22] Church councils

18. Paxton, *Christianizing Death*, pp. 34–37.

19. Charles A. Kerin, *The Privation of Christian Burial: An Historical Synopsis and Commentary* (Washington, D.C., 1941), pp. 8–9, 16. Compare Council of Braga (563), c. 16 and 17 (Mansi 9: 779); *Liber sacramentorum Augustodunensis*, ed. O. Heiming (Turnhout, 1984), p. 307.

20. Rush, *Death and Burial in Christian Antiquity*, p. 155; and see the description of Cyprian's funeral in Saxer, *Morts, martyrs, reliques*, pp. 91–92.

21. Rush, *Death and Burial in Christian Antiquity*, p. 160.

22. Yvette Duval, *Auprès des saints corps et âme: L'inhumation "ad sanctos" dans la chrétienté d'Orient et d'Occident du IIIe au VIIe siècle* (Paris, 1988), pp. 54–56.

repeatedly legislated against the practice of burial in churches. They were, however, unable to prevent the wealthy and powerful from seeking entombment *ad sanctos*, near the altars and relics that they believed would afford them protection while they awaited the resurrection.

Even those who were not to be buried in the churches were taken there for a service of prayer before being carried to the cemetery. Prayer vigils for the dead date back at least to the fourth century. It seems likely, however, that in late antiquity there was as yet no special office of the dead to be recited during those vigils. The funeral party joined the clergy who served the church in the office of the hours, continuing with their own prayers around the corpse between the hours. There are also some indications that the bodies of the dead awaiting burial were sometimes present during the celebration of the eucharist.[23] However, there seems to have been some disagreement within Christian communities about whether this was appropriate. In 393, the Council of Hippo forbade the custom of celebrating the eucharist in the presence of the dead, and even giving communion to "inanimate cadavers."[24] This suggests that the dead not only were present during eucharistic celebrations in some North African churches, but were actually being allowed their accustomed roles in the proceedings. A diocesan synod in Gaul in the late sixth century warned against giving communion or the kiss of peace to the dead, suggesting that similar practices were current there.[25] Many church leaders were willing to accept the presence of the dead, so long as a corpse was not treated like a living member of the assembly. As late as the early eighth century, however, some people seem to have believed that the eucharist was not an appropriate part of ordinary burials. At Rome, according to the pseudo-Theodoran penitential, the eucharist was offered only during the funerals of monks and ascetics; the first mass for members of the laity was performed on the third day

23. Damien Sicard states that no ancient text refers explicitly to a mass celebrated during the burial service or in the presence of the dead: *La Liturgie de la mort*, p. 174. However, he does not consider the conciliar texts discussed here. Février asserts that the dead were sometimes present when the eucharist was celebrated: "La Mort chrétienne," in *Segni e riti*, 2: 903–5.

24. *Concilia Africae, A. 345-A. 525*, ed. C. Munier (Turnhout, 1974), p. 21. The rule against giving the eucharist to the dead was repeated in later collections of canons from this area: ibid., pp. 34, 123, 139, 264.

25. Synod of Auxerre (561–605), c. 12, in *Concilia Galliae, A. 511-A. 695*, ed. Carlo de Clercq (Turnhout, 1963), p. 267. On the presence of the dead during masses for the living, see Megan McLaughlin, "On Communion with the Dead," *Journal of Medieval History* 17 (1991), 23–34.

after death.[26] Clearly, then, while some Christian funerals in late antiquity may have included something like a "funeral mass," this was not always the case.

The eucharist continued to be offered on set days after the burial in late antiquity. In the West, the most common days for celebrations came to be the third, seventh, and thirtieth after burial, and the anniversary of death.[27] These offerings were public events within the Christian community, at which a great many people might be present.[28] Sometimes, too, the eucharist would be celebrated even more often for the recently deceased. In the sixth century, Gregory of Tours described a wife making daily offerings for her husband during the first year after his death, without suggesting that this was in any way unusual.[29] However, these daily celebrations were probably less solemn than the celebrations on the third, seventh, and thirtieth days. In fact, it is not clear whether we are dealing here with special celebrations for the dead, or simply offerings made for the dead during the ordinary eucharistic celebration.[30]

The ritual of death and burial thus underwent a long evolution in late antiquity, which culminated in several efforts at consolidation during the early middle ages. Between the middle of the eighth century and the late ninth century traditional elements were gradually synthesized into a unified rite, which began with the care of the sick and dying, continued with the funeral service proper, then stretched into the days and weeks of the year after death. Two scholars, Damien Sicard and Frederick Paxton, have recently studied this process of synthesis in great detail.[31] My intention in the remainder of this chapter is not to go over the ground which they have covered so well. Rather, I propose to describe briefly the basic structure of the funeral as it was performed in France between the mid-eighth century and the end of the eleventh century, and to point out how the ancient themes of participation, inclusion/exclusion, and community—in short, of spiritual relationship—were developed in its prayers and in the directions for ritual action. In the last section of this chapter I examine the

---

26. *Canones Theodori*, "U" Text, II, 5: 3, 5 and 6, in *Die Canones Theodori Cantuariensis und ihre Überlieferungformen*, ed. Paul Finsterwalder (Weimar, 1929), pp. 318–19.
27. Freistedt, *Altchristliche Totengedächtnistage*, pp. 27–46.
28. Gregory of Tours, *Vitae patrum*, 15:4 (PL 71: 1074).
29. Gregory of Tours, *De gloria confessorum*, 65 (PL 71: 875–76).
30. See Häussling, *Mönchskonvent und Eucharistiefeier*, pp. 256–58.
31. Sicard, *La Liturgie de la mort*; Paxton, *Christianizing Death*.

ways in which monastic communities elaborated on that basic structure, while still maintaining the traditional emphasis on community.

THEMES OF SPIRITUAL RELATIONSHIP IN
EARLY MEDIEVAL FUNERARY PRAYER

Many of the prayer texts employed during early medieval funerals
had actually been composed in late antiquity.[32] Their continued popularity suggests that the ecclesiological themes they expressed remained important to the faithful throughout the early middle ages.
And indeed, the same themes continued to sound in new texts composed between 750 and 1100. In the following pages, I consider some
of the social images and ideas found in texts used for funerals between
the mid-eighth century and the end of the eleventh century, regardless of their date of composition.

The primary relationship expressed in the liturgy was always that
between the dead person and God, to whom, of course, most of the
prayers were directed.[33] It is worth noting that the God described in
early medieval funerary texts is generally a distant and often a frightening one: "Indeed it is an act of temerity, Lord, that a man should
dare to commend a man, a mortal [dare to commend] a mortal, ashes
[dare to commend] ashes to you, our Lord God. . . ."[34] In the liturgy,
as in theology, God the Father was always depicted as the creator and
almighty ruler of everything in heaven, on earth and in hell. He did
offer mercy to the faithful after death, but always within the context
of his justice.

The departed faithful were always represented in the early medieval liturgy as the servants of God, as his devoted followers and the
subjects of his tremendous power. They were also very often represented as sinners, threatened with eternal damnation unless God forgave their faults. This had not been the case during the early Christian
era. Early Christian apologetic writings and prayers had sometimes

32. See Paxton, *Christianizing Death*, passim, on the reuse (and occasional rewriting)
of earlier texts in the ninth century.
33. The liturgy of death did include some invocations of the angels and saints, which
will be discussed below.
34. *Le Sacramentaire grégorien: Ses principales formes d'après les plus anciens manuscrits*, ed.
Jean Deshusses, 3 vols. (Fribourg, 1971–82), 1:462, no. 1414.

depicted humanity as sinful and lost without God's mercy. However, in the first few centuries, while Christians remained a minority group within Roman society, the emphasis had been on redemption offered through faith in Christ and baptism. Those who remained faithful to the redeemer despite the threat of persecution, it had been argued, could anticipate an assured reward in heaven.[35] Such assurance began to fade, however, in late antiquity, with the end of the persecutions and the growth in conversions. Gradually the focus shifted from the sinful unbeliever cleansed through baptism, to the sinful Christian, who must repent or forfeit the redemption Christ had offered.

In the early middle ages, it was no longer assumed that those who died in the faith deserved to be welcomed into heaven. Only if their faults were forgiven or purged away could they hope to enter the company of the elect. Thus, early medieval funerary prayers freely acknowledged the sins of the dead, even as they asked for those faults to be remitted:

> Do not enter into judgment with your servant N., Lord, for no one is justified before you, unless through you remission of all sins is granted. Therefore we ask that your judicial sentence not bear hard on one whom the true supplication of Christian faith commends to you. Rather, with the help of your grace, let one who was marked in life with the sign of the Trinity deserve to evade avenging judgment.[36]

Early medieval funerary prayer is by no means despairing. However, the tone of these services has clearly became darker, their character more penitential, compared to those of the first three centuries of our era.

Liturgical representations of Christ had also been transformed in late antiquity, the Son being reconstructed after the model of his Father. Josef Jungmann has attributed this change to the fear of Arianism, which became keener in the western churches with the advent of tribes like the Goths who professed an unorthodox form of Christianity. Threatened by the presence of Arians in their midst, western churchmen felt compelled to emphasize the divinity of Christ, often at the expense of his humanity. In early medieval prayers and

35. Février, "La Mort chrétienne," in *Segni e riti*, 2: 899–901; Gauthier, "Les Images de l'au-delà;" and see below, Chapter 5.
36. *Le Sacramentaire grégorien*, 1:458, no. 1401.

other religious texts the redeemer increasingly came to be treated as an awe-inspiring figure, who triumphed rather than suffered on the cross.[37] Here was no mere man, but—in the words of a tenth-century offertory for the mass for the dead—"Lord Jesus Christ, king of glory."[38]

This view of Christ could not fail to have its effect on the spiritual relationships depicted in the rites of burial. In funerary inscriptions from the first centuries of the church it had been common to emphasize the personal identification of the faithful with their redeemer.[39] Early medieval funerary ritual continued to identify the dead with Christ, but the identification became at once more tentative and more labored, for now Christ was always presented as far above ordinary men and women.[40]

Uncertain about the ultimate fate of the dead and constantly aware of the chasm that divided sinful humanity from a distant and frightening God, the authors of late antique and early medieval liturgical texts stressed the collective context within which salvation might still be achieved—the communion of saints. The early medieval funerary liturgy thus focuses sharply on the relationship between the dead and the rest of the Christian community. The texts of funerary prayers establish the dead person's identity as one of the servants of God, but that identity is defined in ecclesiological terms, through frequent references to the saints, the angels, and the elect in general. The dead are associated with the community of those who serve God, for only within that community can safety and salvation be found.

The liturgy associated the dead above all with the particular liturgical community that performed the funeral. The dead person was the "beloved brother" or "sister" of those who prayed, a fellow ser-

---

37. Josef Jungmann, *Pastoral Liturgy* (New York, 1962), pp. 38–47; and see R. W. Southern, *The Making of the Middle Ages* (New Haven, 1953), pp. 237–38.

38. On the *Domine Jesu Christe*, see Mary Cecilia Hilferty, *The Domine Jesu Christe, Libera Me, and Dies Irae of the Requiem: A Historical and Literary Study* (Washington, D.C., 1973), pp. 1–111. On the diffusion of this offertory in the early middle ages, see Claude Gay, "Formulaires anciens pour la messe des défunts," *Études grégoriennes* 2 (1957), especially pp. 96–97, 101.

39. See, for example, *Inscriptiones latinae christianae veteres*, ed. Ernst Diehl, 3 vols. (Berlin, 1924–31), nos. 1050, 1235, 1705, 1706, 2193, 2217, 2219, 2219A, 2225 (vol. 1, pp. 201, 240, 331, 433–35).

40. This identification is not evident in the liturgical texts, but only in such ritual actions as the final communion, the reading of the passion, and—in the monastic rites—the presentation of the crucifix and the placing of the dying person on a cross sprinkled in ashes on a piece of sackcloth. See below.

vant in the household of God. If he belonged to one of the clerical
orders, special texts described his role as a bishop, priest, or abbot.
Participation in the liturgical community anticipated, if it did not
guarantee, participation in the company of the elect in heaven:

> Grant this mercy, we pray, Lord, to your departed servant N., that
> he who upheld your will in his mind not receive in suffering the
> recompense of his deeds. Just as the true faith bound him here to
> the company of the faithful, so let your pity join him there with the
> angelic choirs.[41]

Or, from a mass for a dead priest:

> God—who made your servant N. flourish with pontifical dignity
> among the apostolic priests—we ask that you also join him to their
> perpetual fellowship.[42]

As we shall see later in this chapter, the ritual actions of the funeral
service also emphasized the dead person's role in the community that
prayed, which represented on earth the community that saved.

Liturgical texts associate the dead person not only with the concrete community of the servants of God present at the funeral, but
also with the servants of God throughout time. One prayer expresses
the hope that God will treat the dead person as he has treated a whole
series of Old and New Testament saints.[43] It calls on him to free the
soul,

> as you freed Enoch and Elias from the world's common death,
> . . . as you freed Lot from Sodom and the flames of fire, . . .
> as you freed Moses from the hand of Pharaoh, king of Egypt,
> . . . as you freed Isaac from the sacrifice . . . [44]

41. *Le Sacramentaire grégorien*, 1:459, no. 1402.
42. A formula from the eighth-century Gelasian sacramentary, e.g., *Liber sacramentorum Augustodunensis*, p. 246, no. 1939. ·It remained in use in later centuries. See, for
example, *Le Sacramentaire grégorien*, 2:198, no. 2812, and the eleventh-century mis-
sal/sacramentary from Amiens, Paris, BN, Latin 17306, fol. 204v.
43. Louis Gougaud, "Étude sur les '*ordines commendationis animae*,'" *Ephemerides Liturgicae* 49 (1935), 13–14; see also Marie Pierre Koch, *An Analysis of the Long Prayers in Old
French Literature with Special Reference to the "Biblical-Creed-Narrative" Prayers* (Washington,
D.C., 1940).
44. Many variants of this prayer occur in early medieval liturgical manuscripts. This
version comes from a sacramentary of Troyes, Paris, BN, Latin 818, fol. 183v.

Nor was it only the patriarchs and martyrs with whom the dead were associated in the funeral liturgy: "May the chorus of angels receive you, and may you have eternal rest with Lazarus, once a pauper."[45] Through such invocation of figures from the past as well as the present, the dead were linked with the community of the elect beyond time.

Most early medieval funerary prayers were directed at God himself, the just and merciful judge who would ultimately determine the fate of the dead. Sometimes, however, they were directed at other supernatural figures, the saints and the angels, who were believed to have the power to help the faithful in the next world. Such a belief is reflected in the practice of burial ad sanctos, which had its origins in late antiquity, but remained current throughout the early middle ages. But it also finds direct expression in the texts of the funeral liturgy. The litany recited at the deathbed called on the saints by name to help the dying. After the litany came the response *Subvenite*: "Come help, saints of God; hasten, angels of the Lord, receiving his soul, offering it before the highest one. . . ."[46] The belief that when one of the elect died, angels and saints were present to conduct the soul to its reward is reflected not only in the early medieval liturgy, but also in a wide variety of hagiographical, historical, and even secular literary texts.[47]

If the dead were not as holy or as powerful as the saints, still they shared a goal with them, a goal frequently evoked in the texts of funerary prayers:

Incline your ear, Lord, to our prayers, by which we humbly implore your mercy. Establish the soul of your servant N., which you have commanded to leave this world, in a place of peace and light, and decree that it shall be an associate of your saints [*sanctorum tuorum . . . consortem*].[48]

Through the mercy of God and the intercession of others, the departed faithful could hope to enter into the joys of heaven, to "rejoice with the joyful, be wise with the wise, sit down with the martyrs, be useful with the patriarchs and prophets, study to follow Christ with

45. On this anthem, see Sicard, *La Liturgie de la mort*, pp. 66, 69–71.
46. Sicard, *La Liturgie de la mort,* p. 66.
47. See Chapter 5 below.
48. *Le Sacramentaire grégorien,* 1:459, no. 1403.

the apostles."[49] They could, in short, hope to enter into the company of saints (*in consortio sanctorum*), or, as it was often put, into the bosom of Abraham, where their weary souls could lie, safe at last.

THE STRUCTURE OF THE EARLY MEDIEVAL FUNERAL SERVICE

The Christian funeral service of the early middle ages was both more elaborate than that performed in the ancient ecclesiae and more strictly regulated, for now it was recorded in liturgical books rather than being performed *ad libitum*.[50] The solemn celebration of the liturgy required the use of a number of books—the *ordines* (which supplied the *ordo* or ritual directions), the sacramentary (which contained the prayers of the celebrant), the lectionary (for the lessons), and so forth. More than one book was needed because each was used for a different ritual function, and each function was performed by a different minister.[51] In practice, the various liturgical books were beginning to be combined in the eighth and ninth centuries, in order to facilitate the performance of the rituals they described. Many sacramentaries, for example, contained at least rough outlines of the ordines for frequently performed services such as funerals. This allowed the presiding priest to coordinate the activities of the various ministers more effectively.[52] Most of what we know about the structure of early medieval funerals actually comes from the ordines recorded in sacramentaries.

The ordines and the celebrant's prayers were still recorded on separate pages, however, even though they were now both included in the same book. And the sacramentaries did not yet contain the full texts of the lessons and chants as the later plenary missal would.[53]

49. This prayer for the washing of the corpse from the eighth-century Gelasian Sacramentary remained in use through the eleventh century. See *Liber sacramentorum Augustodunensis*, p. 243; *Le Sacramentaire grégorien*, 3:157, no. 4051; and compare Paris, BN, Latin 818, fols. 184v–185r.

50. On the move from improvised prayers to the use of formulae, see Cyrille Vogel, *Medieval Liturgy: An Introduction to the Sources*, rev. and trans. William G. Storey and Niels Krogh Rasmussen, with John K. Brooks-Leonard (Washington, D.C., 1986), pp. 31–59.

51. Vogel, *Medieval Liturgy*, pp. 4–5.

52. Vogel, *Medieval Liturgy*, p. 64.

53. Vogel, *Medieval Liturgy*, p. 105. The statement found on this page that plenary missals were becoming more numerous than sacramentaries "by the second half of the IX century" is a typographical error. That it should read "by the second half of the XI century"

These structural features of early medieval liturgical books are significant, for they show that the liturgy was still viewed as an essentially collective activity, to be performed by the whole Christian community—or at least the various clerical representatives of that community.[54] It was not viewed as a collection of rituals that could be performed by a single celebrant on behalf of a larger community. The prescribed form of the funeral demanded the presence of not only a priestly (or sometimes episcopal) officiant, but the proper assistants from the other orders. Even the laity had its part, albeit a somewhat limited one, in the early medieval liturgy of burial.

The funeral ritual proper was described in an ordo usually known as the *ordo commendationis animae*, that is, the ordo for commending the soul to God.[55] By the late ninth century, this ordo was closely associated in the liturgical books with a service for the visitation and anointing of the sick, which now included a final confession, reconciliation, and communion. The whole transition from life to death had thus been Christianized.[56] The *ordo commendationis animae* proper, however, began after the dying sinner had been reconciled with the church and received the viaticum. Several versions of this ordo were in use during the early middle ages.[57] The following description of the service is based on the ordo found in the influential sacramentary copied in the late ninth century at the monastery of Saint-Amand for the monks of Saint-Denis.[58]

"When a soul in the dissolution from its body is seen to labor in

---

is apparent from the notes (p. 134, n. 288) and from the text of the French edition (see Cyrille Vogel, *Introduction aux sources de l'histoire du culte chrétien au moyen âge* [Spoleto, 1965], pp. 87–88).

54. On the clericalization of the liturgy, see Chapters 2 and 3 below.

55. On the terms used to describe this ordo, see Gougaud, "Étude sur les '*ordines commendationis animae*,'" pp. 3–10; Sicard, *La Liturgie de la mort*, pp. 2–27; Paxton, *Christianizing Death*, pp. 116–17.

56. Paxton, *Christianizing Death*, pp. 162–200.

57. The funeral ordines developed in the eighth century and recorded in Gelasian sacramentaries such as that of Gellone declined markedly in popularity in the ninth century, but were still being copied as late as the twelfth century. (See, for example, the mixed ordo with a strong Gelasian flavor in Paris, BN, Latin 823, fols. 332v–339r.) The "reform" ordo developed by Benedict of Aniane was widely diffused in the early ninth century and continued to appear in later liturgical books. (See Paxton, *Christianizing Death*, pp. 154–56; compare the late twelfth-century missal of Saint-Gervais de Fos, Paris, BN, Latin 2298, fols. 102v–107r.) The synthetic rites developed at Saint-Denis and Lorsch in the late ninth century eventually came to be accepted as authoritative. However, they continued to compete with other ordines for several centuries. (See Paxton, *Christianizing Death*, pp. 192–94, 207–9.)

58. Paris, BN, Latin 2290, fols. 160r–166v. On this ordo see Paxton, *Christianizing Death*, pp. 173–79; the translation is also Paxton's: ibid., pp. 176–77.

the death agony," the Saint-Denis ordo directs, the clergy and "others of the faithful" should "make every effort to attend." The clergy were to sing the seven penitential psalms and a litany. Then came the response *Subvenite*, which has already been discussed, and prayers of commendation by the presiding priest. At the moment of death, the clergy intoned an antiphon which expressed the hope that Christ would receive the soul that he had called, and that angels would lead it to the bosom of Abraham. This was followed by the psalm *In exitu Israel*. After further prayers by the clergy and by all those assembled at the deathbed, the preparation of the body for the grave began.

After the corpse was washed and dressed and placed on a bier, the presiding priest said a further prayer. Then the body was carried in solemn procession to the church, as the clergy chanted responses, psalms, and antiphons. This procession was the dramatic center of the funeral, just as it had been in antiquity. Many early medieval texts describe this moment in the funeral, focusing on the gestures of respect shown to the dead as they were borne to their final resting place.[59] Sometimes the clergy of the burial church would go out in a body to meet the procession; sometimes, as in the funeral of Deurhoiarn described earlier, the relics of the saints would be carried out as well, to welcome the dead into their precincts.[60] This was also seen as the moment for earthly society to pay its homage to the departed, by joining in the procession or gathering to witness it and lamenting the loss being suffered.[61]

According to the ordo in the Saint-Denis sacramentary, the body was to remain in the church until the funeral mass was sung. While this ordo does not describe what was to happen in the meantime, it seems likely that continuous prayers were offered for the soul of the dead person. This had been the practice in many churches from late antiquity on, and other early medieval funeral ordines do call for such vigils around the body.[62] It is also likely that a special office of the dead was performed as part of this service of continuous prayer. Such

59. On descriptions of the funeral processions in saints' lives, see Michel Lauwers, "La Mort et le corps des saints: La scène de la mort dans les *Vitae* du haut moyen âge," *Le Moyen Âge* 94 (1988), 44–45.

60. In a charter of the abbey of La Trinité of Vendôme, the act of going out to meet the funeral procession is treated as a great favor, granted only to very important people: *Cartulaire de l'abbaye cardinale de la Trinité de Vendôme*, ed. Charles Métais, 5 vols. (Paris, 1893–1904), no. 374 (1040–1100). On Deurhoiarn's funeral, see above, Introduction, n. 1.

61. This is most clear in the case of royal funerals. See Alain Erlande-Brandenburg, *Le Roi est mort: Étude sur les funérailles, les sépultures, et les tombeaux des rois de France jusqu'à la fin du XIIIe siècle* (Geneva, 1975), pp. 5–12.

62. Sicard, *La Liturgie de la mort*, pp. 147–74.

an office had been developed in Rome in the seventh century, apparently as an addition to the daily office performed there.[63] By the ninth century it had become part of the daily round of prayer in some places, and that usage spread in the tenth and eleventh centuries.[64] Even where this office was not celebrated daily, it may have been used during funerals. It should be emphasized, however, that while the office of the dead performed during the funeral modified the ordinary services of the liturgical community in some places, it did not simply replace those services. The prayers of the burial service were, rather, intermingled with and integrated into the regular round of prayer.[65] The dead awaiting burial were "present" in the liturgy, in a very concrete sense.

In the Saint-Denis ordo, the performance of the funeral mass was the central feature of the service in the church. As we have seen, the bodies of the dead were already sometimes present at eucharistic celebrations in late antiquity. In the eighth century, some church leaders thought that a mass should be performed during the burial service only for monks and ascetics, not for ordinary sinful Christians. Those reservations were soon overcome, however, and by the ninth century it was apparently the normal practice in the Frankish realm for a mass to be celebrated at every funeral except under special circumstances.[66] This was the moment for all those present to exercise their special liturgical roles on behalf of the dead. The ordo in the Saint-Denis sacramentary calls for the mass to be offered "by all who wish to participate."[67]

63. Camillus Callewaert, "De officio defunctorum," in his *Sacris Erudiri: fragmenta liturgica collecta a monachis Sancti Petri de Aldenburgo in Steenbrugge ne pereant* (Steenbrugge-The Hague, 1940), pp. 169–77.

64. Callewaert, "De officio defunctorum," in his *Sacris Erudiri*, pp. 173–74; Paxton, *Christianizing Death*, p. 135; and see Chapter 2 below.

65. That this was the case is most obvious from the monastic sources discussed below.

66. Damien Sicard, "The Funeral Mass," in Johannes Wagner, ed., *Reforming the Rites of Death* (New York, 1968), p. 47. When the funeral fell on a Sunday, there was some concern about the funeral mass detracting from the solemnity of the mass of the day. If the funeral had to take place on Sunday (it was not usually possible to wait very long to bury the dead), the best solution was to put off the funeral mass until after the mass of the day: see *De missis secundum usum romanum celebrandis*, ed. J. Semmler, in *Initia consuetudinis Benedictinae: Consuetudines saeculi octavi et noni*, ed. Kassius Hallinger (Siegburg, 1963), p. 72; compare Ivo of Chartres, *Decretum*, 2: 119 (PL 161: 193). Some clerics suggested putting off the funeral, relying on Christ to give those who died on Sundays repose: see the texts cited by Edmund Bishop, "On the Early Texts of the Roman Canon," in his *Liturgica Historica* (Oxford, 1918), p. 111; Michel Andrieu, "L'Insertion du 'Memento' des morts au canon romain de la messe," *Revue des sciences religieuses* 1 (1921), 152–53.

67. Paxton, *Christianizing Death*, p. 176. Is this a reference to true concelebration, that is, the joint consecration of the host by several priests? The practice was known in the

With the mass, the ritual of burial had almost reached its end. Before the funeral party left the church, the presiding priest recited a series of prayers with responses from the rest of the clergy, and invited the rest of those present to pray. Then a second cortege bore the body to the grave, as the clergy chanted "Open the gates of justice to me, so that I may enter within and proclaim God." A number of prayers were said at the grave. (Some tenth-century liturgical books include a special prayer for all those resting in the cemetery.[68] By this time, as we shall see, burial in consecrated ground, in an exclusively Christian cemetery, had finally become the rule in France. [69] Thus, by the tenth century, the liturgy made note of the bonds of faith uniting the person who had just been buried with those who lay nearby.) Finally the body was placed in the grave, and the assembled priests recited further prayers, ending with this one:

> Lord, absolve the soul of your servant N. from every bond of sin, so that he may breathe again, revived, among your saints in the glory of the resurrection.[70]

The early medieval funeral outlined in the sacramentary of Saint-Denis required the active participation of a whole group of people, whose presence was ritually as well as socially important. Not only the officiating priest, but the rest of the clergy and even the laity had a part to play in the ceremony. We know from other sources that the activities of this liturgical community did not stop with the burial. On the Sunday after the funeral, the person who had just died was remembered by the whole congregation in the "bidding prayers" of the mass. These prayers, too, had ancient roots.

In the liturgy of the early church, when the first part of the eucharistic celebration (including the readings and the sermon) was over, and the catechumens and general public had been dismissed, the faithful who remained behind joined in a series of prayers for those with special needs: bishops, the rulers of the state, the sick, travelers,

---

Carolingian period: see Archdale A. King, *Concelebration in the Christian Church* (London, 1966), pp. 25–28. However, this phrase in the Saint-Denis ordo might simply mean that all those who wished to do so could make an offering during the funeral mass.

68. Sicard, *La Liturgie de la mort*, p. 234.

69. See below, Chapter 3.

70. Paxton, *Christianizing Death*, p. 177; *Le Sacramentaire grégorien*, 1:459, no. 1404.

and so forth. Sometimes the dead were among those prayed for.[71] These intercessory prayers consisted of an exhortation by a priest or deacon, to which the laity responded with a silent prayer or a Kyrie eleison. This was the "universal prayer," an integral part of the liturgy. More specifically, it was part of the liturgy of the laity, and thus only the baptised, those who had entered the order of the laity, were allowed to take part.[72] By the fifth or sixth century, as the importance of the clergy's role in the liturgy increased and the laity became less active, this prayer lost its place in the more "clericalized" ritual of the mass. It was not mentioned in the liturgical books of the early middle ages.[73]

Still, the tradition hung on, or was revived, in the northern European churches. There is evidence that something like the ancient "universal prayer" was practiced in the East Frankish realm and England in the tenth century.[74] In the eleventh century, Ivo of Chartres described the practice in France as follows: "It is fitting that on Sundays or feasts, after the sermon preached during mass, the priest admonish the people to pour out prayers to the Lord, all together, according to the apostolic institution, for various needs: for the king, and the bishops and rectors of the churches, for peace, for the plague, for those who lie ill in the parish, and for those recently dead. In these prayers, each shall say the Lord's Prayer silently."[75] In these prayers not just the clergy, but the whole Christian community remembered those who had just died. Like the office and mass performed during the funeral, the bidding prayers were actually part of the ordinary round of church services. They were carried on from day to day, and

71. At least this was the case in Jerusalem in the fourth century: see Cyril of Jerusalem, *Catéchèses mystagogiques*, 5: 9, ed. Auguste Piédagnel, trans. (into French) by Pierre Paris (Paris, 1966), pp. 158–59. It is not clear whether the dead were mentioned in the early "universal prayers" of the West; by the late fifth century, they were mentioned in the kyrie-litany at Rome: Jungmann, *The Mass of the Roman Rite*, 1: 333–37.

72. Jungmann, *The Mass of the Roman Rite*, 1: 480–83; Dix, *The Shape of the Liturgy*, pp. 42–45; Pierre-Marie Gy, "La Signification pastorale des prières du prône," *La Maison-Dieu* 30 (1952), 126–27. Paul de Clerck has suggested using the term "universal prayer" to describe the various intercessory prayers of this type practiced in the ancient churches: *La "Prière universelle" dans les liturgies latines anciennes: Témoignages patristiques et textes liturgiques* (Münster, 1977), p. xvii.

73. Gy, "La Signification pastorale des prières du prône," pp. 127–28.

74. Jungmann, *The Mass of the Roman Rite*, 1: 483–90; J. B. Molin, "L'*Oratio communis fidelium* au moyen âge en occident du Xe au XVe siècle," in *Miscellanea liturgica in onore di Sua Eminenza il Cardinale Giacomo Lercaro*, 2 vols. (Rome, 1966–67), 2: 321–30.

75. Ivo of Chartres, *Decretum*, 2: 120 (PL 161: 193).

from week to week, regardless of whether anyone had died or not. A good deal of early medieval funerary ritual, then, actually consisted of the integration of the dead into ordinary services. The same is true of nonfunerary prayer for the dead, which will be considered at greater length in the next chapter.

The eucharist was still celebrated on the third, seventh, thirtieth, and anniversary days in the early middle ages, as it had been in late antiquity. And these celebrations still retained their public character. Donatus, the eighth-century author of the *Life of St. Trond*, relates how crowds came to church on the thirtieth day after the saint's death.[76] In the ninth century, the liturgist Amalar of Metz also emphasized that the masses of the third, seventh, and thirtieth days were publicly celebrated, with some solemnity.[77] He distinguished these more solemn (*celebrius*) celebrations from the simpler masses offered for the dead on other days.[78]

What is new in the early middle ages is the remarkable multiplication of these simpler masses. As we have seen, in late antiquity some of the faithful had made offerings or had the eucharist celebrated for their dead frequently, sometimes even daily, during the first year after death. That practice was formalized and generalized from the mid-eighth century on. Eventually, whole series of masses came to be performed during the funerals of many ordinary people. But because the development of the mass series is closely associated with monastic institutions and practices, it is considered more fully in the following section.

MONASTIC BURIAL

The various early medieval funeral ordines survive today in liturgical books written and preserved at important churches such as monasteries and cathedrals. They outline the services performed for members of the elite clerical communities at those churches. However, as Frederick Paxton has shown, those services were never the

---

76. Donatus, *Vita Trudonis confessoris Hasbaniensis*, 22, ed. Bruno Krusch and Wilhelm Levison, MGH, SRM, 6, p. 292.

77. Amalar of Metz, *Liber officialis*, 3: 44, in his *Opera liturgica omnia*, ed. I. M. Hanssens, 3 vols. (Vatican City, 1948–50), 2: 383.

78. Amalar of Metz, *Liber officialis*, 4: 42 (2: 535).

exclusive province of the clergy. In principle, at least, the funerary rituals described in the ordines were meant to be performed for all of the faithful. Certainly church leaders and Christian rulers strove to make them available to ordinary women and men in the period from the mid-eighth century to the end of the eleventh century. It is not clear how much success they had in that endeavor.[79]

The ordines sketch the outline of a ritual which was supposed to be performed for all Christians when they died. But the elite clerical communities who developed and recorded them went far beyond that outline when they gathered to conduct their own members into the grave. The active participation of a whole community of liturgical specialists led to an extreme elaboration of the ceremonies of death, burial and commemoration—especially in the monasteries.[80] It also intensified the ecclesiological symbolism of those ceremonies. Not only did prayer in the period after death become more concentrated and ritual actions more solemn, as more people took an active part in them, but the dead person's "place" in the community was also more clearly marked.

The ordines only hint at the complexity of the services performed for the dead in these elite houses, and the richness of their ecclesiological symbolism. For further information we must turn to other sources. The most important of these are the customaries, practical descriptions of the liturgical customs that prevailed in the great Benedictine monasteries. Unfortunately, we have only sketchy accounts of monastic practices in the Carolingian period. Detailed customaries first began to make their appearance around the year 1000.[81] The following account is based on these eleventh-century documents of practice, and on the evidence of narrative sources such as saints' lives.

The monastic community's care for the dead began, as usual,

79. Paxton, *Christianizing Death*, pp. 4–5, 128–31, 163–69, 194–200; compare Jean Chélini, *L'Aube du moyen âge: Naissance de la chrétienté occidentale* (Paris, 1991), pp. 479–80, on the clergy's failure to extend the rite of extreme unction to all the faithful in the ninth century. See also Chapter 3 below.

80. We are much better informed about monastic practices than about those of cathedral chapters. However, whenever comparison is possible, prayer for the dead does seem to have been more elaborate at the monasteries than at any secular church, including the cathedrals. See below, Chapter 2.

81. See Kassius Hallinger's introduction to *Initia consuetudinis Benedictinae*, especially pp. xxii–xlix; Joachim F. Angerer, "Consuetudo und Reform," in Raymond Kottje and Helmut Maurer, eds., *Monastische Reformen im 9. und 10. Jahrhundert* (Sigmaringen, 1989), pp. 107–16; Joachim Wollasch, "Reformmönchtum und Schriftlichkeit," *FS* 26 (1992), 274–86.

before death had occurred. Those who fell seriously ill confessed their sins, were annointed with holy oil, and were given the viaticum in the presence of the whole community. The passion was read from one or more of the Gospels. Then, laid out on the ground on a piece of sackcloth sprinkled with ashes, they waited for death. Usually a crucifix was placed before the eyes of the dying, to remind them of their relationship with the Savior.[82] But other relationships also played a prominent part in these proceedings. When Abbot Gervin of Saint-Riquier lay dying in 1075, the monks placed a little sack containing relics around his neck, as they chanted litanies asking the saints to help him. Although he was almost helpless at this point, Gervin managed to join in the litany, beseeching St. Mary and especially St. Riquier to pray for him.[83]

Delegated attendants kept watch around the dying person, praying constantly. When it became clear that a sick person was dying, bells were rung, community members dropped their tasks and ran to the infirmary chanting the Credo.[84] Even if the call came during mass or one of the canonical hours, those outside the choir and those charged with the care of the dead had to go to the infirmary. The urgency of the command emphasizes how important the community's presence at the death was considered: "for while it is completely prohibited for a man of our order ever to exceed a grave and temperate pace, no matter what the reason, yet the precept is that he run for a dying man and for a fire. . . ."[85] The constant repetition of the Credo established the identity of the dying person as a believer. At the same time, it established his or her identity as a member of a group of believers who recited the creed together. It was chanted, according to Ulric of Cluny, "so that fraternal faith might be of help to the one about to die."[86] Members of the early medieval monastic communities were expected to die surrounded and assisted by their fellows.

82. *Liber tramitis aevi Odilonis abbatis*, 2: 32–33, ed. Peter Dinter (Siegburg, 1980), pp. 269–72; Ulric of Cluny, *Consuetudines Cluniacenses*, 3: 28–29 (PL 149: 770–72); William of Hirsau, *Constitutiones Hirsaugienses*, 2: 62 (PL 150: 1132–34); *Redactio Virdunensis*, 18, ed. Maria Wegener and Kassius Hallinger, in *Consuetudinum saeculi X/XI/XII: Monumenta non-Cluniacensia*, ed. Kassius Hallinger, 4 vols. (Siegburg, 1984–86), 3: 422–23.
83. Hariulf, *Chronicon Centulense*, 4: 35, ed. Ferdinand Lot (Paris, 1894), p. 272.
84. *Liber tramitis*, 2: 33 (pp. 272–73); Ulric of Cluny, *Consuetudines Cluniacenses*, 3: 29 (PL 149: 772); William of Hirsau, *Constitutiones Hirsaugienses*, 2: 64 (PL 150: 1134); Lanfranc, *Decreta monachis Cantuariensibus transmissa*, 112, ed. David Knowles (Siegburg, 1967), p. 99.
85. Ulric of Cluny, *Consuetudines Cluniacenses*, 3: 29 (PL 149: 772).
86. Ulric of Cluny, *Consuetudines Cluniacenses*, 3: 29 (PL 149: 772).

The early medieval monastery was an independent liturgical community. As far back as the sixth century, western monastic houses had already included members of all the orders necessary for the performance of the liturgy under most circumstances. By the eleventh century, the great Benedictine monasteries saw themselves and were seen by others as the most perfect liturgical communities of their day, in which the work of God was carried out more splendidly than anywhere else.[87] It is not surprising, then, that the monastic funeral rites laid so much emphasis on the dead person's status within the liturgical community. For example, in the monasteries the corpse was often washed and dressed by *similes*, those who belonged to the same ecclesiastical order as the dead person. Moreover, the body was to be dressed for burial in monastic garb, but with the liturgical vestments appropriate to its owner's order in the church.[88]

The round of daily prayer in the Benedictine houses of the eleventh century was often extremely complex and time-consuming. Outside the regular hours of service, moreover, the members of these houses often devoted their time to private prayer and the performance of masses.[89] As a result, when the corpse was washed and dressed, and brought into the monastery church, the dead person could benefit not only from the unusually solemn and full services of prayer performed there by the community every day, but also from the extra prayers performed by individual members of the house. In the monastic funeral, the continuous vigil around the body before burial included not only the office, but additional psalms—sometimes whole psalters—and masses by the priests of the house.[90] The funeral mass was generally a conventual mass, one of those celebrated every day by the whole convent. All the monks or nuns were expected to

87. John van Engen, "The 'Crisis of Cenobitism' Reconsidered: Benedictine Monasticism in the Years 1050–1150," *Speculum* 61 (1986), 292–96.

88. Sicard, *La Liturgie de la mort*, pp. 108–11; *Liber tramitis*, 2: 33 (p. 276); Ulric of Cluny, *Consuetudines Cluniacenses*, 3: 29 (PL 149: 773); William of Hirsau, *Constitutiones Hirsaugienses*, 2: 65 (PL 150: 1136–37); *Redactio Virdunensis*, 19–20, in *Consuetudinum saeculi X/XI/XII*, 3: 424. See also Simon of Saint-Bertin's description of the funeral of abbot John in 1095: "Ablutoque et induto veste sacerdotali, *pro more*, corpusculo, lacrimis hoc deducentibus psalmisque comitantibus, in ecclesia deponitur" (in *Cartulaire de l'abbaye de Saint-Bertin*, ed. Benjamin Guérard [Paris, 1840], p. 209).

89. See Chapter 2 below.

90. *Liber tramitis*, 2: 33 (p. 274); Ulric of Cluny, *Consuetudines Cluniacenses*, 3: 29 (PL 149: 773–74); William of Hirsau, *Constitutiones Hirsaugienses*, 2: 65 (PL 150: 1138–39); Lanfranc, *Decreta*, 113 (pp. 101–2). And see Hariulf, *Chronicon Centulense*, 4: 36 (p. 273), on the masses said at Abbot Gervin's funeral.

attend this mass and to make an offering.[91] Finally, the whole congregation joined in the candlelit procession to the grave, and in the singing of the seven penitential psalms that followed the burial.[92]

The body was buried among the bodies of other members of the community. By the sixth century, if not earlier, many monasteries in Gaul had their own cemeteries, and that remained the normal practice throughout the early middle ages.[93] Sometimes, of course, physical seclusion from the world made this only practical, but ideas about the nature of the monastic community also lay behind this development. Those whom the bonds of charity united in life, it was believed, should lie together in death.[94] And while the unity of the dead was maintained by a common burial-place, the ties of the living members of the community with their dead were maintained by the masses and annual feasts celebrated for those buried in the community's cemetery.[95]

By the same token, those who breached monastic discipline were denied burial in the monastic cemetery. Pope Gregory the Great (d. 604), in his *Dialogues*, describes his treatment of a monk who had kept some money for himself, in defiance of the monastery's rules against private property. Gregory refused to allow him burial in the monks' cemetery, but had the corpse thrown onto a dungheap.[96] By the eleventh century, such disciplinary denial of burial had been enshrined in legislative texts.[97] It was widely accepted that burial within the monastery's cemetery symbolized the dead person's membership in the monastic community. The privilege was to be refused to those who, by breaking the rules, had forfeited their membership.[98]

91. *Liber tramitis*, 2: 33 (pp. 274–75); Ulric of Cluny, *Consuetudines Cluniacenses*, 3: 29 (PL 149: 774); William of Hirsau, *Constitutiones Hirsaugienses*, 2: 65 (PL 150: 1139).

92. Ulric of Cluny, *Consuetudines Cluniacenses*, 3: 29 (PL 149: 774); William of Hirsau, *Constitutiones Hirsaugienses*, 2: 65 (PL 150: 1139); *Liber tramitis*, 2: 33 (pp. 275–76). When Abbot John of Saint-Bertin was buried in 1095, the priests of the house acted as pallbearers: *Cartulaire de l'abbaye de Saint-Bertin*, p. 209.

93. Luce Pietri, "Les Sépultures privilégiées en Gaule d'après les sources littéraires," in Yvette Duval and Jean-Charles Picard, eds., *L'Inhumation privilégiée du IVe au VIIIe siècle en Occident* (Paris, 1986), pp. 138–39; and see Émile Lesne, *Histoire de la propriété ecclésiastique en France*, 6 vols. in 7 (Lille, 1910–43), 3: 129–31.

94. Pseudo-Isidore, *Regula monachorum*, 23 (PL 103: 572); and see Pascal II, *Epistolae et privilegia*, 76 (PL 163: 95).

95. See below, Chapter 2.

96. Gregory the Great, *Dialogi*, 4: 57, ed. Umberto Moricca (Rome, 1924), pp. 317–18.

97. See, for example, the decree of the Council of London (1075), at which Lanfranc presided (Mansi 20: 453).

98. See, for example, the early twelfth-century work of Guibert of Nogent, *Monodiae de vita sua*, 1: 22, ed. Georges Bourgin (Paris, 1907), p. 84.

Thus the whole convent participated in the funerals of former members, demonstrating ritually its spiritual relationship with the dead person. The same pattern can be traced in the services that followed the burial proper. For monastic communities used their liturgical resources to elaborate on the services traditionally offered during the first year after death, while at the same time emphasizing the dead person's place in the community. Sometimes these arrangements were made ad hoc. Before the monks of Saint-Bertin buried Abbot John in 1095, for example, they agreed upon the masses, alms, and commendations they would offer for him.[99] More often, however, the shape of these services was dictated by established custom. Part of the community's regular round of services would be performed for the benefit of a dead monk or nun for seven or sometimes thirty days after the funeral. During that period one of the daily masses, certain psalms or prayers from the ordinary *cursus* (round) of prayer, or part of the alms ordinarily given to the poor every day, would be devoted to the dead person.[100] In this way he or she remained personally involved in the community's collective activities during the period just after death.

An important aspect of care for the dead in early medieval monasteries was ritualized almsgiving. Joachim Wollasch has shown how significant a role alms given for the dead played in the "social welfare system" of the early middle ages.[101] It is important to remember, however, that the lavish almsgiving associated with monastic funerals was carefully structured so as to express the identity of the dead person and his or her ties to the community. Both the source of the alms and the importance attributed to them betray the ecclesiological meaning of the practice. The almoner did not take the alms to be given from a communal source of revenue. They came instead from the dead monk or nun's own prebend or personal allotment of food, drink, and clothing. A monk from one of the Cluniac houses, for example, could expect to have his share of bread and wine and the rest of his stipend given to the poor for thirty days after his death.[102]

99. *Cartulaire de l'abbaye de Saint-Bertin*, p. 209: "Pacta ergo missarum frequentatione, elemosinarumque distributione, et stationaria anime commendatione, . . . ad tumulum defertur."
100. *Liber tramitis*, 2: 33 (p. 277); Ulric of Cluny, *Consuetudines Cluniacenses*, 3: 29 (PL 149: 775); William of Hirsau, *Constitutiones Hirsaugienses*, 2: 66 (PL 150: 1140); *Redactio Virdunensis*, 20, in *Consuetudinum saeculi X/XI/XII*, 3: 424–25.
101. Wollasch, "Gemeinschaftsbewusstsein und soziale Leistung;" see also Otto Gerhard Oexle, "Mahl und Spende im mittelalterlichen Totenkult," *FS* 18 (1984), 401–20.
102. *Liber tramitis*, 2: 33 (p. 277); Ulric of Cluny, *Consuetudines Cluniacenses*, 3: 29 (PL

The significance of such practices is apparent in a story related by the eleventh-century German monk, Othlo of St. Emmeram. A monk of Fulda had drowned accidentally, but his body was recovered and carefully buried. The usual prebend was to be given for him, but after a few days the cellarer, who was in charge of distributing alms in this house, refused to give it any more. He claimed that the dead monk should have "no communion" with the other brothers, because he had died by throwing himself in the water (in other words, by committing suicide). Soon, however, the dead monk appeared to the cellarer in a dream, demanding to know why he had been denied the common prebend which was decreed for all dead brothers of the house. Accusing the official of presumption, the ghost proceeded to beat him soundly.[103] In this story the dead monk was enraged—and justly—because the cellarer had presumed not only to deny him alms, but to deny him what was due to a brother of the house, for the alms served as a symbol of his communion with the others.

The most striking development in monastic funerary ritual during the early middle ages, however, was the increase in the number of masses performed for the dead. For in the monasteries the traditional practice of celebrating masses during the first year after death underwent a breathtaking expansion, which began perhaps as early as the sixth century, but accelerated sharply from the eighth century on. The real novelty of this development lay not in the practice of having the eucharist celebrated frequently for the dead—for, as we have seen, even layfolk sometimes arranged for such celebrations in late antiquity—but rather in the formalization of the process, and the careful distribution of effort throughout a whole community of liturgical specialists, so as to mark their relationship with the dead.

Most historians of the liturgy have considered Pope Gregory the Great the founder of the mass series, because he reports in his *Dia-*

149: 775); William of Hirsau, *Constitutiones Hirsaugienses*, 2: 66 (PL 150: 1140). See also "Documents sur la mort des moines," ed. Jean Leclercq, *Revue Mabillon* 45 (1955), 166, n. 6.

103. Othlo of St. Emmeram, *Liber visionum*, 16 (PL 146: 371–72). A similar story appears in a twelfth-century collection from Marmoutier: *De rebus gestis in Majorimonasterio saeculo 11.*, 10, in *Acta sanctorum ordinis Sancti Benedicti*, ed. Jean Mabillon and Luc d'Archery, 9 vols. (Venice, 1733–38), Saec. VI, pt. 2: 400; on this text, see Sharon Farmer, "Personal Perceptions, Collective Behavior: Twelfth-Century Suffrages for the Dead," in Richard C. Trexler, ed., *Persons in Groups: Social Behavior as Identity Formation in Medieval and Renaissance Europe* (Binghamton, N.Y., 1985), pp. 231–39; Farmer, *Communities of Saint Martin: Legend and Ritual in Medieval Tours* (Ithaca, 1991), pp. 134–50.

logues that he eventually decided to have a series of thirty masses performed over the course of thirty days for the soul of the sinful monk whose body had been thrown onto a dungheap.[104] However, Gregory himself treats this as an unusual expedient, and there is no evidence that the practice was immediately imitated. There are certainly references to the performance of masses for the dead in the monasteries during the seventh and early eighth centuries, but I have found no references to specific numbers of masses in the sources from that period. The real move toward the mass series seems to have come during the late eighth century. Even at this point there are virtually no references to such a practice in the sketchy accounts of monastic customs.[105] The best evidence for this period comes from the records of prayer associations and confraternities, which will be considered in Chapter 2. By the ninth century, however, the mass series seems to have become a normal part of funerals in some monasteries. The custom at this time seems to have been for every member of the community to recite a certain number of masses (those who were not priests could recite psalters) during the period just after death.[106]

We are better informed about the performance of mass series during funerals in the eleventh century. The series most often mentioned in the customaries of this period seem to have developed out of the masses traditionally performed on the seventh and thirtieth days after death; monastic communities simply extended these single masses into a series. Thus, a *septennarium* was a series of seven masses offered during the first seven days after death; the *tricennarium* was a series of thirty masses offered during the first thirty days.[107] The labor of performing these masses was sometimes distributed in a slightly different way in the eleventh century than it had been in the ninth century. In some religious houses, priests specially delegated for the

104. Gregory the Great, *Dialogi*, 4: 57 (pp. 317–18).

105. The only such reference I have found comes from a letter written by an Italian abbot, Theodomar of Monte Cassino, sometime between 778 and 797. Theodomar describes the funerals of his monks, noting that after the burial, the ordinary monks each recite two psalters for their departed brother, while the monk-priests say twelve masses: Theodomar, *Epistula ad Theodoricum gloriosum*, ed. J. Winandy and K. Hallinger, in *Initia consuetudinis Benedictinae*, p. 136.

106. See, for example, Oexle, "Memorialüberlieferung und Gebetsgedächtnis in Fulda," in Schmid, *Die Klostergemeinschaft von Fulda*, 1: 150–52, on the internal "prayer association" established at Fulda in 863. A similar distribution of effort can be found in the confraternity agreements from this period. See below, Chapter 2.

107. Lanfranc, *Decreta*, 113 (p. 102); Ulric of Cluny, *Consuetudines Cluniacenses*, 3: 29 (PL 149: 775).

task performed these additional masses.[108] Presumably this new arrangement was a response to the practical difficulties that arose in large monasteries such as Cluny, where funerals must have been frequent occurrences. It would be difficult for individual monks to keep track of and perform a set number of masses for every one of their brothers who died, let alone the members of other, "associated" communities.[109] Far simpler to make a single monk-priest responsible for the masses of a single funeral.

The multiplication of masses for the dead during the early middle ages is often cited as one of the important factors behind the appearance of the "private" mass, in which the traditional collective rite of the eucharist was reduced to the action of a single priest. Anxious about the condition of the dead in the next world, and convinced that every offering of the mass would help to expiate their sins, early medieval monks are assumed to have focused obsessively on the number of masses they could celebrate. Participation by all the members of the liturgical community began to seem less important than the frequency with which the host was consecrated. As a result, more and more masses for the dead and for other special intentions came to be celebrated at side altars in a simplified rite centered on the action of an individual priest. The ancient meaning of the liturgy as a collective celebration by the whole Christian community was obscured.[110]

There are several problems with this picture. In the first place, it is now recognized that while the masses performed in series during the year after death were less solemn than the "public" masses of the third, seventh, thirtieth, and anniverary days, they were not "private" celebrations in the modern sense. The celebrating priest always had assistants to represent the different clerical orders in their traditional roles and to respond to his biddings.[111] Neither were early medieval monks so preoccupied with the frequency of celebrations that they ignored their quality. In the eleventh century, the monks of Cluny

108. *Liber tramitis*, 2: 33 (pp. 276–77); Ulric of Cluny, *Consuetudines Cluniacenses*, 3: 29 (PL 149: 775); William of Hirsau, *Constitutiones Hirsaugienses*, 2: 6 (PL 150: 1140); Lanfranc, *Decreta*, 113 (p. 102).
109. On "associated" communities and individuals, see below, Chapter 2.
110. Jungmann, *The Mass of the Roman Rite*, 1: 217–19; Vogel, "Une mutation cultuelle inexpliquée," p. 240; Angenendt, "Missa specialis," pp. 195–203.
111. Others may have been present as well. For example, in the tenth century the canons of Saint-Martin of Tours were required to attend each of the thirty masses performed after the death of one of their brothers: see Farmer, *Communities of Saint Martin*, p. 219, n. 70.

prided themselves not only on the number of masses performed in their monastery every day for the dead, but also on the "angelic" manner in which these rituals were carried out.[112]

It is clear, moreover, that a strong sense of community endeavor was at work in the ways monastic communities structured the celebration of masses in conjunction with funerals. Certainly the monks were concerned about the state of the dead and eager to offer them all the help possible. However, their efforts were not uncoordinated or idiosyncratic. In the late eighth and ninth centuries, every member of the community was expected to perform the same number of masses (or an equivalent number of psalters) for the dead within the same period of time. By the eleventh century, if not before, the practical difficulties presented by this arrangement had become obvious and we find the masses of the septennarium or tricennarium delegated to a single priest for performance. But this did not mean that the rest of the community simply forgot their departed brother or sister. For as we have seen, during the period when the septennarium or tricennarium was being performed, part of the community's ordinary round of prayer and almsgiving was also devoted to the dead person. What we see in these arrangements is not the breakdown of the ancient tradition of collective celebration, but the creation of what Häussling has called an "integrated" liturgy.[113] Conventual services and special masses were not separate rites, but different aspects of this liturgy. Both helped to mark the dead person's enduring place in the community that prayed.

Members of monastic communities spent a good part of their lives carrying out their assigned roles in the liturgy. When they died, they continued to participate in the collective prayers of the liturgical community through the efforts of others on their behalf. Because the liturgy played an especially prominent role in the lives of monks and nuns, ecclesiological symbolism played an especially prominent role in monastic funerals. As we have seen, such symbolism is evident in the burial rite proper and in the ordering of the services performed in the monasteries during the days and weeks after death. But if ecclesiological symbolism was especially prominent in the monastic realm, it was present in all early medieval death rituals. Funerary rites

112. Jotsald, *De vita et virtutibus sancti Odilonis abbatis*, 2: 13 (PL 142: 927).
113. On the "integrated" liturgy, see Häussling, "Missarum Sollemnia," in *Segni e riti*, 2: 564, 578. On the meaning of funerary masses, see idem, *Mönchskonvent und Eucharistiefeier*, pp. 256–58, 278–80.

served as mirrors for the ecclesiastical community that performed them and for the cosmic community of the servants of God toward which they pointed. Reflected in these ritual mirrors, the dead appeared as members of the liturgical community on earth and thus as potential members of the community of the saints in heaven.

2 COMMEMORATION

During the funeral, when grief was fresh and concern for the
well-being of the dead at its height, the corpse and the tomb became
centers for a flurry of ritual activity. After the corpse had been buried
this intense activity began to taper off until, with the mass of the first
anniversary of death, the funerary rites proper came to an end. This
did not mean that the dead were forgotten, however. One of the most
striking features of late antique and early medieval liturgical history is
the growth of nonfunerary prayer for the dead, prayer performed
whether a death had occurred recently or not. Such services were not
simple acts of intercession, independent of the other ritual activities of
the church. They developed as part of the general expansion of the
liturgy that began in late antiquity; throughout the early middle ages
they were treated as an integral part of the regular round of prayer.

The Expansion of the Liturgy in Late Antiquity

At the center of early Christian worship lay the celebration of the
eucharist, the ritual meal within which Christ's redemptive sacrifice
was reenacted. At first this seems to have been a deeply serious, but
still relatively informal ceremony, conducted in a domestic setting
with improvised prayers. In the first two centuries, it took place

chiefly on Sundays; it is not clear whether there were solemn celebrations on other occasions. By the beginning of the third century, however, there is evidence that the "Lord's gathering" occurred more often. The ecclesia (or at least a good part of it) came together on other days of the week—on Saturday in many places, on Wednesday and Friday in others.[1] The "birthdays" (i.e., anniversaries of the deaths) of the martyrs were also solemnized with eucharistic celebrations at which the whole Christian community gathered.

Between the fourth and the eighth century, celebrations of the eucharist became much more formal. Small groups of Christians still sometimes met in homes or other places, but from the fourth century on the ecclesia as a whole gathered in a public setting, in its own basilica. The celebrations led by bishops were now conducted in a much more ceremonious manner, which eventually affected even the less solemn celebrations led by priests.[2] Moreover, improvised prayer was gradually replaced with set formulae. In the liturgical books that begin to appear in this period we find recorded not only the "ordinary," the invariable part of the service, but also a whole system of "proper" prayers, lessons, and chants. These "propers" were what fitted the service to the occasion. Separate propers were established for the great feasts, for each Sunday throughout the year, and for a variety of special intentions.[3] The significance of these changes has been hotly debated by liturgical historians, but it is now generally agreed that they launched a trend which would gradually become more pronounced over the course of the next thousand years. The celebration of the eucharist was being transformed from the collective action of the people of God into a rite, a fixed set of actions and prayers—in short, a "mass."[4] To put it another way, what we see in

    1. Robert Taft, "The Frequency of the Eucharist throughout History," in Mary Collins and David Power, eds., *Can We Always Celebrate the Eucharist?*, Concilium, 152 (Edinburgh-New York, 1982), p.14. P. Jounel dated this development to the sixth century: "Le Dimanche et la semaine," in Aimé-Georges Martimort, ed., *L'Église en prière: Introduction à la liturgie* (Paris, 1961), p. 688. However, Tertullian seems to have referred to eucharistic celebrations on Wednesday and Friday in the third century: *De oratione*, 19, ed. G. F. Diercks, in Tertullian, *Opera*, 1: 267–68.
    2. Theodor Klauser, *A Short History of the Western Liturgy: An Account and Some Reflections*, trans. John Halliburton, 2d ed. (Oxford, 1979), pp. 32–37.
    3. Dix, *The Shape of the Liturgy*, pp. 360–69, 527–45; Vogel, *Medieval Liturgy*, pp. 31–36.
    4. On the development of the term "mass," see Christine Mohrmann, "Missa," *Vigiliae Christianae* 12 (1958), 67–92; Josef A. Jungmann, "Von der 'Eucharistia' zur 'Messe,'" *Zeitschrift für katholische Theologie* 89 (1967), 29–40. On the hotly debated subject of the "private" mass, see the literature reviewed in Vogel, *Medieval Liturgy*, pp. 156–59.

the period from the fourth to the eighth century is the beginning of a reification of Christian prayer.[5]

The creation of propers contributed to the perception that there were different "kinds" of masses, characterized by different prayer texts and eventually by differences in the accompanying rituals, depending on the use to which the service was to be put. Distinctions in practice were related to the imagined distinctions between the needs of different groups within the Christian community, including the living, the dead, and the saints.[6] Each group now required its own type of service, and so a tension was created between the desire to serve special needs and the ancient vision of the church united in the liturgy. Hence all the problems of establishing priority of services, of regulating the relationship between masses, and between eucharistic and non-eucharistic services, which would begin to occupy writers on the liturgy in the ninth century.

The eucharist also came to be celebrated much more frequently in late antiquity, albeit in various settings and with various degrees of solemnity. Several factors seem to have contributed to this development. One was the clericalization of the liturgy. By the fourth century the laity were beginning to abandon their active role in the assembly, leaving the liturgy in the hands of the clergy.[7] But the clericate was also becoming a full-time profession, which meant that those responsible for the liturgy now had much more time to devote to it.[8] These changes made it possible to offer the eucharist more frequently, but several factors made more frequent celebrations seem desirable as well.[9] One was the tradition of personal devotion to the eucharist. Individual Christians had long had the habit of taking communion privately with "presanctified" hosts on days when the eucharist was not offered publicly. They had also gathered in small groups to offer the eucharist on various special occasions. These essentially private practices helped lay the groundwork for more regular offerings in a

5. On the reification of prayer, see Cyrille Vogel, "Symboles cultuels chrétiens—les aliments sacrés: Poisson et refrigeria," in *Simboli e simbologia nell'alto medioevo*, 2 vols. (Spoleto, 1976), 1: 221–23.

6. Häussling, *Mönchskonvent und Eucharistiefeier*, pp. 255–71; Angenendt, "Missa Specialis," pp. 177–80; see also Vogel, *Medieval Liturgy*, p. 163.

7. See below, Chapter 3.

8. Gregory Dix, "The Ministry in the Early Church," in Kenneth E. Kirk, ed., *The Apostolic Ministry: Essays on the History and the Doctrine of Episcopacy* (London, 1946), pp. 284–85.

9. The subject is discussed most fully by Angelus Häussling: *Mönchskonvent und Eucharistiefeier*, pp. 226–88.

public setting. Another important factor at work here was the desire to honor the saints with celebrations at their shrines, not only on their anniversaries but on many other occasions. The development of the cult of the saints had a tremendous impact on liturgical practice from the fourth century on. Finally, an important shift in the interpretation of the eucharist occurred between the fourth and eighth centuries. The mass increasingly came to be seen not only as the Christian community's remembrance of Christ's redeeming sacrifice, but as a renewed sacrifice, which could help to ensure the salvation of individual men and women. There was, in other words, a shift in emphasis toward instrumentality. Eventually some people came to believe that many masses must be more efficacious than one mass, and as this belief spread celebrations for various special intentions increased. The notion was not accepted everywhere; indeed, several church leaders argued against it.[10] However, it certainly affected liturgical practice in late antiquity and, as we shall see, in the early middle ages, to some extent.

As these factors came into play, the eucharist was celebrated more and more often. By the end of the fourth century, solemn daily celebrations had become the rule in a number of cities in the West.[11] In some cities, these solemn services were always held in the same church, the cathedral where the bishop had his permanent seat. In other cities, however, a stational system developed, in which the bishop presided at mass in a different basilica each day. These solemn celebrations, together with the less solemn masses offered on other days by the priests assigned to those basilicas, made up a single complex liturgy for the whole city. The stational system made it possible for the now very large Christian communities of the more important urban areas to preserve some sense of ritual unity.[12] In Gaul, the stational system seems to have been employed at Tours in the late fifth century. It was introduced at a few other places in the Frankish realm in the eighth century by reformers apparently influenced by the Roman model.[13] However, these efforts had little lasting success, and

10. Häussling, *Mönchskonvent und Eucharistiefeier*, pp. 280–87.
11. Taft, "The Frequency of the Eucharist," in Collins and Power, *Can We Always Celebrate the Eucharist?*, p. 14.
12. On the Roman stational liturgy, see Jungmann, *The Mass of the Roman Rite*, 1: 59–60, 67–74; Klauser, *A Short History of the Western Liturgy*, pp. 60–71; Häussling, *Mönchskonvent und Eucharistiefeier*, pp. 182–98.
13. Klauser, *A Short History of the Western Liturgy*, pp. 78–80; Häussling, *Mönchskonvent und Eucharistiefeier*, pp. 198–201, 207–10. On the early liturgy at Tours see also Luce

the Frankish bishops eventually reverted to the practice of celebrating solemn episcopal masses in the cathedral church. The monasteries which began to spread throughout Christendom in late antiquity were not, at first, centers of eucharistic devotion. In the fourth and fifth centuries the religious seem to have joined in the celebration of the local ecclesia on Sundays and feasts; sometimes the community had its own priest to offer mass within the monastic precincts on those occasions.[14] More frequent celebrations were not yet the rule in the monasteries. By the sixth century, however, probably for the reasons cited above, the desire for more frequent celebrations began to affect monastic practices. By the seventh century, a daily conventual mass had become a common feature of monastic life. By the eighth century, two conventual masses were sometimes performed.[15] Side altars, dedicated to various saints, began to appear in monastic churches, and the number of small-group celebrations held at these altars increased. Some priests celebrated in these less solemn settings several times a day.[16] Häussling has suggested that these developments reflect the influence of the urban stational liturgy on monastic communities. The monastery became a "city," with a complex, yet fully integrated liturgy, now conducted within the walls of a single church.[17]

Just as the eucharistic liturgy underwent important developments and rapid expansion in late antiquity, so, too, did the non-eucharistic liturgy. In the first three centuries, many of the faithful attempted to direct their daily lives toward God by praying regularly at certain hours of the day and night.[18] We know very little about these prac-

---

Pietri, *La Ville de Tours du IVe au VIe siècle: Naissance d'une cité chrétienne* (Rome, 1983), pp. 430–520.

14. Nussbaum, *Kloster, Priestermönch, und Privatmesse*, pp. 124–25; Häussling, *Mönchskonvent und Eucharistiefeier*, pp. 18–31.

15. Nussbaum, *Kloster, Priestermönch, und Privatmesse*, pp. 125–32. Häussling associates the double conventual mass with the influence of the Roman stational liturgy: *Mönchskonvent und Eucharistiefeier*, pp. 323–25.

16. Jungmann, *The Mass of the Roman Rite*, 1: 216–23; Nussbaum, *Kloster, Priestermönch, und Privatmesse*, pp. 78–81; Vogel, "La Multiplication des messes solitaires." Side altars were already being built in cathedrals in Gaul by the late sixth century: Jungmann, *The Mass of the Roman Rite*, 1: 223.

17. Häussling, *Mönchskonvent und Eucharistiefeier*, pp. 150–59, 299–329.

18. Pierre Salmon, *L'Office divin: Histoire de la formation du bréviaire* (Paris, 1959), pp. 12–18; idem, "La Prière des heures," in Martimort, *L'Église en prière*, pp. 793–805; Robert Taft, *The Liturgy of the Hours in East and West: The Origins of the Divine Office and Its Meaning for Today* (Collegeville, Minn., 1986), pp. 13–29.

tices, from which the later office of the canonical hours grew. It is generally agreed, however, that they became more complex and more highly organized from the fourth century on. Some of the most important developments took place in the monastic communities that came into being in this period, as groups of pious men and women began to retire from the world in order to give their lives over entirely to the service of God. For the ascetics of the fifth and sixth centuries, regular prayer was an obligation, one of the spiritual activities that characterized their new way of life. As monastic life became more organized, monastic leaders planned how the office should be carried out and what part it should play in the monastic life as a whole.[19] In St. Benedict of Nursia's rule for monks, the communal prayer of the hours was called the *opus Dei*, literally "God's work." Nothing took precedence over this daily round of prayer; rather it governed and sanctified the lives of the monks.[20]

The office celebrated in the monasteries of the Merovingian realm consisted of psalms and lessons, recited with the addition of various prayers and chants at each of the canonical hours. There was considerable variation from place to place in the way these elements were combined. In some monasteries, the office was very elaborate, providing virtually continuous prayer day and night. The monks of Agaune, for example, prided themselves on their *laus perennis* or "perpetual praise" of God. The monks who followed the rules of Caesarius of Arles and Columban also had, in the words of Robert Taft, "staggering" liturgical obligations.[21] Elsewhere, however, the services were much simpler. It has been estimated, for example, that the early Benedictines spent only about three and a half hours a day in communal prayer, and in other churches the services may have been even shorter.[22]

Regular daily prayer also went on in the urban churches of late antiquity, led by the bishop and priests and attended by the more

19. Salmon, *L'Office divin*, pp. 18–22; Taft, *The Liturgy of the Hours*, pp. 57–140.
20. Benedict of Nursia, *Regula monachorum*, 43, ed. A. de Vogüé, trans. (into French) by J. Neufville, 7 vols. (Paris, 1971–77), 2: 586.
21. Taft, *The Liturgy of the Hours*, pp. 110, 115. On the *laus perennis*, see C. Gindele, "Die gallikanischen 'Laus Perennis'-Klöster und ihr 'Ordo Officii'," *Revue Bénédictine* 69 (1959), 32–48; Jean Leclercq, "Prière incessante: A propos de la *laus perennis* du moyen âge," in his *La Liturgie et les paradoxes chrétiens* (Paris, 1963), pp. 230–35.
22. Cited by Philibert Schmitz, "La Liturgie de Cluny," in *Spiritualità cluniacense: Convegno del Centro di Studi sulla Spiritualità Medievale, 12–15 ottobre, 1958* (Todi, 1960), p. 85.

devout members of the laity.[23] In some cities this office was conducted at the cathedral. In others, however, the hours of prayer were distributed throughout the various urban basilicas, like the stational eucharistic liturgy. In the city of Vienne, for example, matins and nocturns were recited at the cathedral, terce and sext at the basilica of St. Stephen, none at St. Lawrence's, vespers and duodecima (the final service of the day in many Gallican churches) at St. Alban's, outside the city walls.[24] Here again, the intent was to promote the ritual unity of a growing Christian community.

In Gaul, as in much of the West, the cathedral offices were strongly influenced by monastic traditions. Presumably, the cathedral offices never approached the complexity of the services performed at Agaune or the Columban monasteries, but they were fairly elaborate in some places, even to the point of having the psalmody performed by two choirs.[25] Eventually, however, the liturgical and pastoral ideals came into conflict. As the number of converts to Christianity and the burden of pastoral care grew, some of the clergy—especially priests assigned to service in the countryside—had difficulty keeping up.[26] Yet so closely had the office become identified with the true service of God by the eighth century that reformers such as Chrodegang of Metz sought to impose some form of regular daily prayer on those secular clerics who had not accepted it on their own.[27]

Just as the development of the office "sanctified" the Christian day, so the development of the calendar, in which a series of annual festivals commemorated the great events of Christian history, made the year holy. Between the fourth and the eighth centuries, a large number of festivals in honor of events in the life of Christ or in commemoration of the deaths of saints came into being.[28] The most important of these—Christmas, Easter, Pentecost, the feasts of the most prominent saints—were celebrated everywhere. But otherwise

23. Jungmann, *The Early Liturgy*, pp. 280–87.

24. According to a seventh-century life of the fifth-century saint Severius, a priest of Vienne: cited in Taft, *The Liturgy of the Hours*, p. 145.

25. Taft, *The Liturgy of the Hours*, pp. 145–56. The traditional view has been that the cathedral clergy offered a much simpler office and only accepted the office as an obligation in the eighth century: e.g., Salmon, *L'Office divin*, pp. 206–8; idem, "La Prière des heures," in Martimort, *L'Église en prière*, pp. 808–10. However, Taft provides convincing evidence to the contrary.

26. Taft, *The Liturgy of the Hours*, pp. 298–99.

27. Salmon, *L'Office divin*, pp. 27–29; idem, "La Prière des heures," in Martimort, *L'Église en prière*, pp. 808–33.

28. Dix, *The Shape of the Liturgy*, pp. 370–84.

the annual cycle varied widely from place to place.[29] Because each church kept its own calendar, all sorts of peculiar celebrations and commemorations of local saints flourished in late antiquity, and festivals were created rather more freely than in later centuries.

Between the fourth and eighth centuries, then, the liturgy expanded tremendously, as clerical communities devoted more and more time to the celebration of solemn masses and offices on Sundays and the growing number of feast-days, to the performance of less elaborate public services on ordinary days, and to masses and prayers by small groups or individuals at all times. Prayer for the dead played a part in all these developments, for the clergy believed that the departed faithful had the right to participate in the liturgy, and they were increasingly conscious that the dead needed prayer. As a result, they integrated services designed specifically for the dead into the mass, the office, and the calendar, and those services expanded along with the rest of the liturgy.

Our earliest evidence concerning the commemoration of the dead in the eucharistic celebration dates from the third century, although it is possible that the practices described in the sources from this period date back to earlier times. In the mid-third century, Cyprian of Carthage refers to the practice of naming the dead in the prayer of the bishop who presided over the assembly.[30] Serapion of Alexandria and Cyril of Jerusalem described similar customs in their respective churches.[31] This is why, in the fifth century, Augustine could write that it was by the authoritative custom of the universal church that "the commendation of the dead has its place in the prayers of the celebrant which are offered to the Lord God at his altar."[32]

These prayers might name individuals, but they were also intended to commemorate the Christian dead in general. For, as Augustine noted in *The City of God*, the faithful remained members of the ecclesia and retained their right to participate in the liturgy even after death: "The souls of the pious dead are not separated from the church, which is indeed the kingdom of Christ at present. Other-

29. Dix, *The Shape of the Liturgy*, pp. 380–83; Jungmann, *The Early Liturgy*, pp. 184–87; P. Jounel, "Le Culte des saints," in Martimort, *L'Église en prière*, pp. 768–84.

30. Cyprian, *Epistulae*, 1 (2: 466–67).

31. Dix, *The Shape of the Liturgy*, p. 499.

32. Augustine, *De cura pro mortuis gerenda*, 1, ed. Joseph Zycha, in Augustine, *Opera, Sectio 5, pars 3* (Vienna, 1900), pp. 623–24.

wise, they would not be remembered at the altar in the commemoration of the Body of Christ. . . . For why are these things done, unless it is because the faithful are still members [of that Body] even when they are dead?"[33]

The dead were also sometimes mentioned in the "universal prayer." After the service of readings which made up the first part of the eucharistic rite, a priest or deacon would go through a list of people or groups with special needs, exhorting the congregation to pray for each in turn. Although this practice was already well established in the second century,[34] the dead do not seem to have been commemorated in the "universal prayer" at this point. The earliest reference we have to the commemoration of the dead in this part of the eucharistic service comes from fourth-century Jerusalem.[35] In the West, the dead first appear in the lists in the fifth century.[36] The "universal prayer" soon fell into disuse, however,[37] at which point the dead came to be commemorated in a different part of the mass.

As eucharistic celebrations increased in frequency in late antiquity, prayer for the dead increased as well. For the dead continued to be commemorated in the prayers of the celebrant, although the specifics of that custom varied from place to place. In seventh-century Gaul, the dead and the living were mentioned together in the prayer that followed the offertory procession. The wording of the prayer and the rubric *post nomina* assigned to it suggest that it was associated with a reading of the names of those who were "offering" at the mass. The dead were included among these *offerentes*, presumably because the living offered "for" them—in their name or in their memory. Thus, the image of the dead as active participants in the liturgy lies behind their commemoration in the Gallican mass.[38]

At Rome, a prayer specifically for the dead was inserted in the canon of the mass, following the consecration. There has been some

33. Augustine, *De civitate Dei*, 20: 9, ed. Bernard Dombart and Alphonse Kalb, in Augustine, *Aurelii Augustini Opera, pars 14*, 2 vols. (Turnhout, 1955), 2: 717.
34. de Clerck, *La "Prière universelle,"* p. 12.
35. Cyril of Jerusalem, *Cathéchèses mystagogiques*, 5: 9 (pp. 158–59).
36. de Clerck, *La "Prière universelle,"* p. 302.
37. The "universal prayer" disappeared in the fifth or sixth century: see de Clerck, *La "Prière universelle,"* p. 298.
38. Jungmann, *The Mass of the Roman Rite*, 2: 162. He cites a *post nomina* prayer from the feast of the Circumcision, which reads: "Auditis nominibus offerentum, fratres dilectissimi, Christum Dominum deprecemur . . . ut haec sacrificia sic viventibus proficiant ad emendationem, ut defunctis opitulentur ad requiem."

controversy, however, about when this insertion took place. The wording of the *Memento* (as it is called from the first word of the Latin text) suggests that it was composed at a fairly early date:

> Be mindful, Lord, of your male and female servants and of those who have gone before us with the sign of faith, and who sleep the sleep of peace. To them and to all those resting in Christ, we pray that you grant a place of refreshment, light and peace.[39]

However, it does not appear in the earliest Roman sacramentaries. Most liturgical historians now agree that this prayer was created for use in masses for the dead. It was not needed in the solemn papal mass so long as the dead were still commemorated in the "universal prayer." Only after the "universal prayer" fell out of common use in the fifth or sixth century did the *Memento* become a normal part of the Roman canon.[40]

The early Christians clearly remembered the dead within the regular eucharistic liturgy, both in the celebrant's prayer and, for a time at least, in the "universal prayer." It is less clear whether they commemorated the dead during the hours of the office. Presumably when a body was brought to church for the vigil before burial many of the prayers recited during that vigil were directed towards the needs of the dead. Prayers may also have been recited on the third, seventh, and thirtieth days after a death, and on the anniversary. In the seventh century, a special "office of the dead" was composed at Rome, possibly for use in conjunction with funerals or the services of the first year after death.[41] However, we do not know whether this office or other prayers for the dead were used on a regular basis when a death had not recently occurred. The earliest evidence of prayer for the dead as a regular element in the office comes from the early middle ages.

Finally, there are the services—specifically, masses—performed annually for the dead. Cyprian, again, offers some of the earliest concrete testimony to this practice. In a letter to the Christian community at Carthage he wrote: "We always offer sacrifices for them, as

39. *Le Sacramentaire grégorien*, 1: 90, no. 13 bis.
40. See Bishop, "On the Early Texts of the Roman Canon," in his *Liturgica Historica*, pp. 100–103; Andrieu, "L'Insertion du '*Memento*' des morts," pp. 151–54; Dix, *The Shape of the Liturgy*, pp. 499, 507–8; Jungmann, *The Mass of the Roman Rite*, 2: 238–39; N. Denis-Boulet, "Analyse des rites et des prières de la messe," in Martimort, *L'Église en prière*, pp. 408–9.
41. Callewaert, "De officio defunctorum," in his *Sacris Erudiri*, pp. 169–77.

you recall, whenever we celebrate the days of the martyrs' passions
with anniversary celebrations."[42] Cyprian refers here, of course, to
the eucharist celebrated for the anniversaries of the martyrs. However, the early Christians made a much smaller distinction than medieval people did between the status of "martyr" and that of any person
who died in the faith. There is certainly every reason to think that the
eucharist was offered annually in commemoration of ordinary Christians as well as martyrs in the third century.[43] The chief difference
between the cult of the martyrs and the cult of the dead in this period
seems to have been that the service offered for a martyr every year on
the anniversary of his or her death was treated as an important community celebration, which was kept up by the ecclesia even after the
martyr's close friends and relatives had themselves died or after they
could no longer arrange to have masses said for their dead.[44]

With the end of the persecutions in the fourth century, sacrifices in
memory of the martyrs came to be carried out in the new basilicas
built above their tombs. These celebrations were often orchestrated
by the bishops to ensure the unity of the growing Christian community. As belief in the miraculous powers of the martyrs spread, and as
their anniversary services and the buildings within which they were
carried out became more splendid, they attracted larger and larger
crowds.[45] The cult that developed out of the commemoration of the
martyrs in the fourth century provided the nucleus around which the
medieval liturgy for saints' days would form.[46]

At around the same time clearer distinctions began to be made
between the saints and the ordinary dead. These distinctions were
reflected in the propers composed for services performed in their
memory. The propers of the saints in the early liturgical books trium-
phantly affirmed the power of faith and the promise of salvation.
Here, for example, is a prayer from a mass for the feast of a virgin
martyr:

42. Cyprian, *Epistulae*, 39 (2: 583). For two different interpretations of this text, see
Ntedika, *L'Évocation de l'au-delà*, p. 28; Saxer, *Morts, martyrs, reliques*, pp. 106–7.
43. Tertullian, *De monogamia*, 10: 4, ed. Eloi Dekkers, in Tertullian, *Opera*, 2: 1243;
and see Saxer, *Morts, martyrs, reliques*, pp. 70–73.
44. On this point, see B. de Gaiffier, "Réflexions sur les origines du culte des martyrs," *La Maison-Dieu* 52 (1957), 19–44; Jounel, "Le Culte des saints," in Martimort,
L'Église en prière, p. 768; Saxer, *Morts, martyrs, reliques*, pp. 104–7.
45. Peter Brown, *The Cult of the Saints: Its Rise and Function in Latin Christianity*
(Chicago, 1981), especially pp. 23–49.
46. Jungmann, *The Early Liturgy*, pp. 179–80.

God who, among the other marvels of your power, has even conferred on the fragile sex the virtue of martyrdom, grant pro-
pitiously that by the example of the one whose "birthday" we
celebrate here, we may approach you.[47]

Services for the dead, on the other hand, apparently influenced by
church leaders' growing perception of the sin to be found within the
Christian community, became more somber in tone and more anxious in their petitions. A mass for those lying in a cemetery, for
example, included the following prayer:

Omnipotent and eternal God, grant what we ask in our prayers,
and give to all those whose bodies rest here a place of refreshment,
the blessedness of peace, [and] the brightness of light, so that the
supplication of the church may commend [to you] those who are
burdened by the weight of their sins.[48]

The cult of the saints and the cult of the dead were not yet completely
independent. As late as the eighth century, and even beyond, sacramentaries included prayers under the rubric *ad missa in natale sanctorum
sive agenda mortuorum*, "for a mass on saints' days or in commemoration of the dead."[49] In fact, the two cults remained closely connected
throughout the early middle ages.[50]

However, those responsible for the organization of the liturgy
were increasingly concerned to offer services appropriate to the special status of each group. Hence the spectacular development of feasts
for the anniversaries, inventions, and translations of the saints between the fourth and eighth centuries. But hence, too, the appearance
of a feast of the dead in a monastic rule which was attributed to the
seventh-century bishop Isidore of Seville, and which is in any case
earlier than the ninth century. This rule calls for a mass to be offered
each year "for the spirits of the dead" on the next day but one after

47. *Liber sacramentorum Augustodunensis*, p. 137, no. 1192.
48. *Liber sacramentorum Augustodunensis*, p. 253, no. 2000.
49. Antoine Chavasse, *Le Sacramentaire gélasien (Vaticanus Reginensis 316): Sacramentaire
presbytérale en usage dans les titres romains au VIIe siècle* (Paris, 1957), pp. 494–95; and see *Liber
sacramentorum Augustodunensis*, p. 248.
50. This connection is suggested by Oexle, "Die Gegenwart der Toten," in Braet and
Verbeke, *Death in the Middle Ages*, p. 30, and by van Engen, "The 'Crisis of Cenobitism'
Reconsidered," p. 296. Thomas Head points out, however, that the exact relationship
between the two has yet to be fully explored: *Hagiography and the Cult of Saints: The Diocese
of Orléans, 800–1200* (Cambridge, 1990), p. 196.

Pentecost.[51] There is not much information here to go on, but this text does at least show that precedents existed for the annual commemorations of the dead established in early medieval monasteries.

The Commemoration of the Dead in the Early Middle Ages

Around the year 790, Charlemagne gave the monastery of Saint-Riquier to his friend, the courtier Angilbert. The new lay abbot took his position very seriously indeed, devoting himself to improving the monastery library, building a new main abbey church with two smaller churches nearby, and, most important of all, bringing numerous relics of the saints to be housed in the thirty altars he established in those churches. Angilbert also drew up a description of the liturgy he hoped would be carried out in his magnificent new churches. The adult monks and the boys being trained in the monastery's school were divided into three choirs, of one hundred monks and thirty-three or thirty-four boys each. These three choirs were responsible for maintaining an elaborate office, reminiscent of the earlier *laus perennis*, which was to be carried out throughout the day and night. Two conventual masses were to be offered every day "most solemnly" (*sollemnissime*), in the morning and at noon. Moreover, the monks were to let no day pass in which they did not celebrate at least thirty masses at the thirty altars which Angilbert had endowed with the relics of the saints. These thirty masses were the collective responsibility of the choirs, and together with the conventual masses they made up the eucharistic liturgy of the abbey.[52]

Angilbert's *Institutio* for Saint-Riquier does not describe a "typical" monastic liturgy. What we see in this document is one man's

---

51. Pseudo-Isidore, *Regula monachorum*, 23 (PL 103: 572).

52. Hariulf, *Chronicon Centulense*, 2: 6–11 (pp. 51–72). Angilbert of Saint-Riquier, *Institutio de diversitate officiorum*, 17, ed. Kassius Hallinger, Maria Wegener, and Hieronymus Frank, in *Initia consuetudinis Benedictinae*, pp. 291–303, is a critical edition of the liturgical section of this text. On the significance of this arrangement, see Häussling, *Mönchskonvent und Eucharistiefeier*, pp. 54–58. On the abbey church and its altars, see especially Edgar Lehmann, "Die Anordnung der Altäre in der karolingischen Klosterkirche zu Centula," in Wolfgang Braunfels, ed., *Karl der Grosse: Lebenswerk und Nachleben*, 5 vols. (Düsseldorf, 1965), 3: 374–83; Carol Heitz, "Symbolisme et architecture: Les nombres et l'architecture religieuse du haut moyen âge," in *Simboli e simbologia*, 1: 391–97.

image of what that liturgy should be. Nevertheless, the *Institutio* does give us some idea of the complex round of prayer carried out in large monastic communities between the mid-eighth century and the end of the eleventh century. The relatively simple round of prayer outlined in the rule of St. Benedict was not adopted by the Frankish monasteries, even after that rule was imposed on them by Louis the Pious and Benedict of Aniane in the early ninth century. Apparently its modest proportions did not appeal to the sensibilities of the age. Carolingian monasteries generally offered an elaborate eucharistic liturgy and a much more extensive office than the first St. Benedict had ordained. Moreover, the monastic liturgy continued to expand in various directions over the course of the next two and a half centuries.

We are much less well informed about the liturgy conducted in the cathedrals and other secular churches during the early middle ages. While there are occasional references in narrative and diplomatic sources to the services offered by the secular clergy, there are no sources equivalent to the monastic customaries for most of this period. Fairly detailed accounts of the liturgies performed in cathedrals and communities of canons become available only in the late eleventh century. It is not clear whether the practices they describe were traditional or new outgrowths of the reform movement usually associated with Pope Gregory VII.[53] In the following discussion, therefore, I have focused on the monastic liturgy, while including whatever information is available concerning other rites.

The tendency to reify prayer that first became apparent in late antiquity is reflected more clearly in the customaries and liturgical commentaries of the early middle ages. Indeed, customaries and commentaries came into existence in the early middle ages precisely because the liturgy had become alienated to some extent from the life of the Christian community, and had taken on a life of its own.[54] These sources distinguish between different kinds of services, performed for different purposes, and often associate numbers with prayers—as in Angilbert's instructions for the performance of at least thirty masses a day at the thirty altars of Saint-Riquier.

It would be a mistake, however, to see behind the liturgical arrangements of this period nothing more than a desire to multiply

53. On the liturgical aspects of the eleventh-century reform, see Enrico Cattaneo, "La vita comune dei chierici e la liturgia," in *La vita comune del clero dei secolo XI e XII*, 2 vols. (Milan, 1962), 1: 241–72.

54. Vogel, "Symboles cultuels chrétiens," in *Simboli e simbologia*, 1: 223.

special services for special intentions. While some people did apparently believe that special needs could best be served through the performance of special services, this view was never accepted by the leaders of the early medieval church. In the ninth century, the great scholar Walahfrid Strabo ridiculed those who thought that

they cannot make a full commemoration of those for whom they offer unless they offer individual offerings for each . . . [and that] an offering cannot be made at the same time for the living and for the dead. But truly we know that One died for all, and it is one bread and blood which the universal church offers. If it pleases anyone to offer individually for individual [needs], for the sake of great devotion alone or out of a delight in increasing prayer, let him do so—but not because of the foolish opinion that the one sacrament of God is not a general antidote.[55]

The anonymous author of a tenth-century homily for the office of the dead similarly reminded his audience that "[someone] who labors for all does better [than someone who labors for one]; prayer for all is always better than prayer for special needs, although both are good."[56] While these early medieval writers were aware of the emphasis some of their contemporaries placed on special services, they rejected the argument that those services were really "better" or more effective.[57] Descriptions of practice in early medieval customaries and liturgical commentaries also suggest that the different kinds of services performed by clerical communities were still understood in this period as different aspects of a single liturgy, within which all of the faithful were commemorated.

This understanding of the liturgy clearly lies behind the early medieval practice of prayer for the dead. Services for the dead expanded in the early middle ages, along with the rest of the liturgy. Indeed, these services achieved much greater prominence in the early

---

55. Walahfrid Strabo, *De exordiis et incrementis rerum ecclesiasticarum*, 23, in *Capitularia regum Francorum*, 2, ed. Alfred Boretius and Victor Kraus (MGH, Leges, sect. 2, pt. 2) (Hanover, 1897), p. 500.

56. "Un Ancien Recueil de leçons pour les vigiles des défunts," ed. Jean Leclercq, *Revue Bénédictine* 54 (1942), 34.

57. Their views on this point differ radically from those of the scholastic theologians of the high middle ages, who generally accepted the greater effectiveness of special services as a given, and attempted to explain it: see Angenendt, "Missa specialis," pp. 213–14; Artur Landgraf, *Dogmengeschichte der Frühscholastik*, 4 vols. (Regensburg, 1952–56), 4: 321–50.

middle ages than they had enjoyed in late antiquity. Concern about the well-being of the departed faithful appears to have reached new heights in this period. It is reflected both in the increased reporting of visions in which the dead appeared asking for prayer, and in the pronouncements of those responsible for the organization of the liturgy.[58] Significantly, though, those pronouncements were more often couched in terms of entitlement than in terms of need. Early medieval church leaders, like their predecessors in late antiquity, believed that the departed faithful had the right to be mentioned in the liturgy. And so continual efforts were made to ensure that they would be fully represented in every aspect of the regular round of prayer.

The clergy assembled at the Council of Chalon-sur-Saône in 813, for example, proclaimed that: "In all masses, at a suitable place, the Lord should be invoked for the spirits of the dead. Just as the Lord is invoked every day, without exception, for the living and for various necessities, so prayers should be poured out to the Lord in masses every day without exception for the souls of the faithful."[59] It is likely, although not certain, that the council was referring here to the *Memento*. Roman liturgical books and Roman practices were exerting increasing influence in the Frankish realm at this time, as a result of Charlemagne's reform efforts.[60] As a result, the traditional Gallican practice of commemorating the living and the dead together after the offertory, which had been losing ground for some time, finally disappeared altogether. It seems to have been in the late eighth century that the clergy in France began reciting the *Memento* during the canon of the mass. Moreover, they no longer seem to have restricted its use to masses for the dead. The *Memento* became an invariable part of the canon, to be recited even on Sundays.[61]

As we have seen, a large number of masses were now being

58. On visions of the dead from this period, see Neiske, "Vision und Totengedenken," pp. 152–72.

59. Council of Chalon-sur-Saône (813), c. 39, ed. Albert Werminghoff in *Concilia aevi Karolini* (MGH, Leges, sect. 3, pt. 2), 2 vols. (Hanover, 1906–08), 1:281.

60. See Cyrille Vogel, "La Réforme liturgique sous Charlemagne," in Braunfels, *Karl der Grosse*, 2: 215–32.

61. Florus of Lyons, writing in the early ninth century, treats the *Memento* as an invariable part of the canon: *De expositione missae* (PL 119: 61–63). Some early medieval documents suggest that the *Memento* was not used on Sundays: see Bishop, "On the Early Texts of the Roman Canon," in his *Liturgica Historica*, pp. 100–103, 109–15; Andrieu, "L'Insertion du '*Memento*' des morts," pp. 151–54. However, this seems to have gradually become a minority view: see Jungmann, *The Mass of the Roman Rite*, 2: 238–39 and nn. 7, 9, 10, and 11.

offered every day in the monasteries. The use of the *Memento* turned them all into sacrifices for the dead as well as for the living faithful. One characteristic of the liturgical developments of late antiquity, however, had been the creation of fixed texts for different kinds of services. Propers had been composed from at least the fifth century on for use in masses for the dead. Those recorded in the earliest surviving liturgical books were probably intended for use during the services of the third, seventh, and thirtieth days after the funeral and on the anniversary of a death.[62] They would have been celebrated publicly, with some solemnity. The same texts may also have been used for votive masses for the dead, performed by a single priest with only a few assistants. These masses were performed in conjunction with funerals, as we have seen, or whenever special "aids" (*suffragia*) for the dead seemed to be called for.

However, early medieval churches also offered masses for the dead on a regular basis, regardless of whether someone had recently died or not. In churches where more than one conventual mass was celebrated each day, the custom arose in the eighth century of devoting one of them to the dead.[63] This practice remained common throughout the early middle ages. While the "principal" mass (*missa maior*) would use propers for the day (if it were a feast) or derived from those of the preceding Sunday's mass, the morning mass (*missa matutinalis*) was frequently a mass for the dead. At the abbey of Remiremont in the ninth century, this mass was apparently offered each day in a chapel in the cemetery, in commemoration of those buried there.[64] Elsewhere, the celebration took place in the main church.

The service was, in any case, often carried out by the entire monastic community with all due ceremony. At Cluny in the eleventh century the daily mass for the dead was performed "solemnly" (*solemnius*). The celebrant recited as many as ten collects at this mass, and all the brothers made offerings.[65] The solemn daily mass for the dead

62. *Sacramentarium Veronense (Cod. Bibl. Capit. Veron. LXXXV [80]),* 2d ed., ed. Leo Cunibert Mohlberg, with Leo Eizenhöfer and Petrus Siffrin (Rome, 1966), pp. 144–46, nos. 1138–60; Chavasse, *Le Sacramentaire gélasien,* pp. 61–71.
63. Nussbaum, *Kloster, Priestermönch, und Privatmesse,* pp. 126–27.
64. *Liber Memorialis von Remiremont,* pp. 41–42.
65. Ulric of Cluny, *Consuetudines Cluniacenses,* 1: 7 (PL 149: 652–53). The collect is the prayer the celebrant says when he first steps before the assembled congregation and summons them to join in his prayer: see Jungmann, *The Mass of the Roman Rite,* 1: 359–61. Originally only one prayer was recited at this point, but from the late eighth century on the number of collects recited at each mass began to grow: ibid., pp. 386–87.

was also a feature of some cathedral liturgies in the same period. Bishop John of Avranches contrasted the practice of other churches, where the mass for the dead was offered "in a festive way" (festive) only for funerals and at the beginning of the month, with the practice of his own cathedral, where it was so offered every day.[66] The mass for the dead was, then, an important event in the daily round of communal prayer in many early medieval churches.[67]

Much of the additional prayer added to the office between the late eighth and eleventh centuries was also devoted specifically to the departed faithful. To begin with, the office of the dead came to be recited more and more often in this period; eventually it was integrated fully into the regular round of prayer. A modern historian of the liturgy has argued from the peculiarities of its structure that this office must have developed in Rome, probably before the end of the seventh century. Callewaert suggests that it was first used in conjunction with funerary ritual. By the ninth century, however, the office of the dead was recited on a regular basis—once a day in some churches and once a month in others—whether a death had occurred recently or not.[68] Angilbert, for example, states that "through every day and night . . . [the monks of Saint-Riquier] offer vespers, nocturns, and matins in memory of all the departed faithful."[69]

At first, when it was part of the funerary prayers for an individual, the office of the dead was probably celebrated as a simple addition to the daily office. Although technically divided into "hours," it would have been sung not in sections, but straight through, just before the nocturns of the day.[70] The pattern, in other words, went like this:

vespers	office	nocturns	matins	
of the day	of the dead	of the day	of the day	and so forth.

In the early ninth century, it was apparently still performed in this way, even after it became part of the regular round of prayer.[71] The

66. John of Avranches, De officiis ecclesiasticis (PL 147: 38).
67. Jungmann, The Mass of the Roman Rite, 1: 204–5; see also Häussling, "Missarum sollemnia," in Segni e riti, 2: 567–68.
68. Amalar of Metz, Liber officialis, 4: 42 (2: 537).
69. Angilbert of Saint-Riquier, Institutio, 17, in Initia consuetudinis Benedictinae, p. 302.
70. Callewaert, "De officio defunctorum," in his Sacris Erudiri, p. 172.
71. At least this seems to be what some texts from this period describe: see Angilbert of Saint-Riquier, Institutio, 17, in Initia consuetudinis Benedictinae, p. 302; Supplex libellus monachorum Fuldensium Carolo imperatori porrectus, 1, ed. Joseph Semmler, ibid., pp. 321–22.

innovation of the late ninth and tenth centuries would be the integration of the office of the dead into the office as a whole. As its celebration became more common, an effort was made to divide up the hours of the office of the dead and fit them alongside the regular hours of the daily office.[72] Since the office of the dead was rather long, this task was not particularly easy, but the customaries of the eleventh century show that monastic communities made the best compromises they could. Eventually a fairly common pattern developed.[73] In the winter, when nights were longer, the hours were arranged according to this scheme:

vespers	vespers	nocturns	matins	nocturns	matins
of the	of the	of the	of the	of the	of the
day	dead	day	day	dead	dead.

In summer, it was more convenient to arrange them as follows:

vespers	vespers	nocturns	nocturns	matins	matins
of the	of the	of the	of the	of the	of the
day	dead	dead	day	day	dead.

The office of the dead was celebrated daily not only in the monasteries but also at some cathedrals, including those of Avranches and Chartres, in the eleventh century. Apparently the cathedral canons arranged the hours in much the same way.[74] It is significant that despite the need for such a complicated arrangement, the clerical communities of the early middle ages persisted in fitting the office of the dead as best they could into the pattern of their ordinary services. The attempt was, perhaps, only partially successful, but it shows the influence of the idea that prayer for the dead should have its own place in the opus Dei. In his description of the office performed at Saint-Riquier, Angilbert noted that ". . . the brothers in this monastery sacred to God, fighting in the love of God and of their neighbor, take

72. *Capitula in Auvam directa*, 11, ed. Hieronymus Frank, in *Initia consuetudinis Benedictinae*, p. 336.
73. Ulric of Cluny, *Consuetudines Cluniacenses*, 1: 4 (PL 149: 647–48). My reconstruction of Ulric's liturgical schedule differs somewhat from that of Barbara Rosenwein: "Feudal War and Monastic Peace: Cluniac Liturgy as Ritual Aggression," *Viator* 2 (1971), 134–36. Compare *Redactio Virdunensis*, 17, in *Consuetudinum saeculi X/XI/XII monumenta*, 3: 422.
74. John of Avranches, *De officiis ecclesiasticis* (PL 147: 40); *Un Manuscrit chartrain du XIe siècle*, ed. René Merlet and M. Clerval (Chartres, 1893), pp. 238–39.

care every day and night to celebrate vespers, nocturns, and matins most devoutly, not only for ourselves and themselves, but actually for the salvation of all the living and in memory of all the dead. . . ."[75] The office was the prayer of the whole Christian community. Early medieval clerics believed that the dead as well as the living were entitled to share in it.

In the eighth century, some monks and nuns began performing extra psalms between the regular hours of prayer, as a private devotional exercise. Over the course of the next three centuries, these "supplementary" psalms gradually became part of the collective worship of monastic communities.[76] In most places, however, they were devoted to various special purposes, including the needs of the dead. In the ninth century, Benedict of Aniane established the practice of reciting the fifteen gradual psalms before matins or prime. In many monasteries, five or ten of these psalms were specifically intended for the dead.[77] In one tenth-century nunnery, where the seven penitential psalms were chanted at nocturns, three were said for the dead sisters of the house, two for the abbess and congregation, and two for the nuns who were reciting them.[78] Often the same seven psalms were recited again after chapter for the sake of the dead whose names had been read from the necrology that day.[79] It also became customary in some places to say one or two psalms after each of the daytime hours, for the dead or for the benefactors of the house.[80] By the late eleventh century some cathedral chapters had also added special psalms after

75. Angilbert of Saint-Riquier, *Institutio*, 16, in *Initia consuetudinis Benedictinae*, pp. 301–2.

76. Edmund Bishop, "On the Origin of the Prymer," in his *Liturgica Historica*, pp. 211–37; Salmon, "La Prière des heures," in Martimort, *L'Église en prière*, p. 835.

77. *Ordo diurnis Anianensis*, ed. C. Molas and Maria Wegener, in *Initia consuetudinis Benedictinae*, p. 314; *Legislationis monasticae Aquisgranensis collectio sancti Martialis Lemovicensis*, 76–78, ed. Joseph Semmler, ibid., p. 561; Ulric of Cluny, *Consuetudines Cluniacenses*, 1: 5 (PL 149: 648–51). In other houses only psalms for the dead were said at this time: *Consuetudines Floriacenses antiquiores*, ed. A. D'Avril et al., in *Consuetudinum saeculi X/XI/XII monumenta*, 3: 51. On Benedict of Aniane's liturgical reforms, see Philibert Schmitz, "L'Influence de saint Benoît d'Aniane dans l'histoire de l'ordre de saint Benoît," in *Il monachesimo nell'alto medioevo e la formazione della civiltà occidentale*, 2 vols. (Spoleto, 1957), 2: 404–7.

78. *Memoriale qualiter (II)*, 1, ed. Claudius Morgand, in *Initia consuetudinis Benedictinae*, p. 267.

79. *Memoriale qualiter (II)*, 3, in *Initia consuetudinis Benedictinae*, p. 271; Ulric of Cluny, *Consuetudines Cluniacenses*, 1: 3 and 5 (PL 149: 646–47, 648–51). On the necrology, see below.

80. Ulric of Cluny, *Consuetudines Cluniacenses*, 1: 2 (PL 149: 645).

the hours, categorized as *pro defunctis*, "for the dead."[81] Customs varied widely from house to house, but everywhere these psalms were divided among the various hours and interspersed with prayers for the living, for the congregation, and so forth. In other words, like the office of the dead, the psalms for the dead were fully integrated into the daily cursus of prayer.

Just as prayer for the dead had its place in the office of the hours, so it became part of the calendar of the Christian year during the early middle ages. Annual feasts for the dead were celebrated in many early medieval monastic houses. In the early ninth century the abbeys of Saint-Gall and Reichenau shared an annual feast, celebrated for the dead of both houses. This celebration was more elaborate than that described in the pseudo-Isidoran rule mentioned earlier. It included masses and psalters recited by each member of the community privately, as well as a conventual vigil and probably a mass.[82] The combination of private prayers by each member of the community and public services, reminiscent of monastic funerary ritual, was typical of monastic feasts for the dead. By the eleventh century it had become common for monasteries to celebrate feasts for the dead brothers and sisters of the house, for those buried in their cemeteries, or for the relatives and friends of the monks or nuns. Sometimes several such services would be held each year. At Cluny, for example, a tricennarium was performed three times a year for the *familiares*—the friends and benefactors of the house.[83]

The only early medieval feast for the dead to have endured and found a place in the calendar of the modern Catholic church is that of All Souls, celebrated on November 2. Because a number of texts describing its establishment by Abbot Odilo of Cluny have survived, and because of its later success, the importance of the feast of All Souls when it first appeared has sometimes been exaggerated. In fact, like most early medieval feasts of the dead it was largely a local affair. In the eleventh century it was celebrated only at Cluniac houses and a few other churches, primarily those with close ties to Cluny and its abbots. Not until the twelfth century did the idea of celebrating a feast for all the departed faithful really seize the imagination of the world

81. John of Avranches, *De officiis ecclesiasticis* (PL 147: 46).

82. *Libri confraternitatum sancti Galli, Augiensis, Fabariensis*, ed. Paulus Piper, MGH, LC (Berlin, 1884), p. 140.

83. Bernard of Cluny, *Ordo Cluniacensis*, 2: 32, in *Vetus disciplina monastica*, ed. Marquard Herrgott (Paris, 1726), p. 354.

outside Cluny.[84] Nevertheless, because of the relatively large amount of information available on All Souls, it merits a closer look.

It is important to remember that All Souls was not simply the occasion for offering a large amount of extra prayer for the dead. It really was a feast, with many of the same elements as feasts for the saints or for events in the life of Christ. At Cluny All Souls was celebrated "in a festive way" (*festivo more*).[85] The bells were rung on the evening of November 1 before the office of the dead was performed, and again the next day before the morning mass of the dead. That mass was celebrated "most solemnly" (*solemnissime*) with special chants and an offering by all the monks. In addition to these public services, each of the monks said masses or psalms privately for the dead, and alms were given to the poor.[86]

In the eleventh-century customs for All Souls used at several monasteries influenced by, but not formally affiliated with Cluny, the celebration was even more festive.[87] These customs describe a special office, unlike the ordinary office of the dead and apparently created specifically for the feast of November 2. It included a service of compline for the dead, and very long and elaborate services for vespers, nocturns, and matins (lauds) of the dead, which seem to have completely replaced, rather than simply complementing, the ordinary night offices.[88] There were also hymns, and prayers for the daytime hours—elements of other festive offices, but ones not usually included in the office of the dead.[89] In addition, the community took part in processions to the high altar, where the saints were invoked on behalf of the dead, and to the cemetery.[90] The monks also prayed privately for the dead, but these houses, even more than Cluny, emphasized the solemn and elaborate public services which commemo-

84. The feast appears in the calendars of many French churches only in the late twelfth and early thirteenth centuries. On the close association of all souls with Cluniac "propaganda" in the eleventh century, see below, Chapter 5.

85. *Statutum "S. Odilonis" de defunctis* (PL 142: 1037–38). This text is actually a decree of the chapter of Cluny, probably from after 1024, confirming Odilo's foundation: see Henri Leclercq, "Mort," *DACL* 12: 37.

86. Ulric of Cluny, *Consuetudines cluniacenses*, 1: 42 (PL 149: 689); compare Bernard of Cluny, *Ordo cluniacensis* 2: 32, in *Vetus Disciplina monastica*, pp. 353–54.

87. "Un Office monastique pour le 2 novembre," ed. André Wilmart and L. Brou, *Sacris Erudiri* 5 (1953), 247–330.

88. "Un Office monastique," pp. 261–75; and see pp. 289–91.

89. "Un Office monastique," pp. 263, 265, 274–75, 276–78.

90. "Un Office monastique," pp. 273, 278–80.

rated the departed faithful, much as the saints were commemorated on their feast days.

The feast of All Souls was designed, then, not simply to provide prayer for the dead, but to give the dead their rightful place within the Christian calendar. According to one of the biographers of Odilo, the founder of All Souls, "Venerable Father Odilo promulgated a general decree for all his monasteries that just as on the first day of November the solemnity of All Saints is performed by the rule of the whole church, so on the following day the commemoration of all those resting in Christ should be celebrated with psalms and almsgiving and chiefly with masses."[91] In other words, Odilo chose November 2 as the date for All Souls because the feast of All Saints fell on November 1. If the saints were to be remembered in the liturgy, so too should the departed faithful. The date of All Souls served as a reminder of that fact.

Many early medieval texts refer to the bonds of charity uniting the faithful in life and after death, and to the obligation they had to pray for one another. A tenth-century collection of lessons for the office of the dead presents the image of the members of the church throughout time, united in the act of offering prayer and good works for one another, and in the expectation of being prayed for themselves after death:

> we are obliged to celebrate vigils and masses, and to perform faithfully psalmody, fasting, alms, hymns, and sacred songs for those who went before us and lived faithfully and had a just end. They did the same for those who went before them and sleep the sleep of peace; we enter into their labors. Therefore we should imitate their good deeds, and what they did for their dead we should do for ours, so that we be found not unequal to them in good works, but equal sharers. By the same token, too, those who come after us should carry out the same office prudently and devoutly for us, since they owe it to us to do these things for us, so that they will not appear shameful, but faithful in the sight of God.[92]

A sense of obligation toward "those who had gone before" led the

91. Peter Damian, *Vita sancti Odilonis* (PL 144: 936–37); compare Jotsald, *De vita et virtutibus sancti Odilonis abbatis*, 2: 13 (PL 142: 927).
92. "Un Ancien Recueil de leçons," pp. 33–34.

living members of the Christian community to offer prayer for its
dead. And so, services for the dead came to be performed every day in
most early medieval churches. Many monastic churches actually offered prayer for the dead at every hour of the day. Services originally
designed for use during the funeral (the mass and the office of the
dead) came to be part of the daily round of prayer. On the other hand,
certain prayers which had originally been said for devotional purposes, and had no particular association with the cult of the dead (the
supplementary psalms), came to serve special needs, including the
needs of the dead, when they were added to the public liturgy.

But despite the designation of certain masses, offices, and psalms
as "for the dead," in practice these rituals were an integral part of the
liturgy, the worship which sanctified the life of an ecclesiastical community and symbolized its relationship with God. The morning mass
of the dead brought the whole clerical congregation together. The
hours of the office of the dead were distributed between the everyday
hours. Psalms for the dead followed and were followed by psalms for
the living. The feast of All Souls corresponded to the feast of All
Saints. So intertwined, in other words, were prayer for the dead and
the praise of God and the saints, that the one served for the other. By
praying for the dead, as the text cited above reminds us, the members
of the liturgical community would appear "faithful in the sight of
God."

The same idea underlies a miracle story recounted by the Italian
cardinal Peter Damian in the eleventh century. There was, he says, a
certain monk who did not like to say the daily office or the special
offices for saints' days. He was, however, devoted to the office of the
dead. When the brother died, demons were waiting to carry him off,
since he had neglected the rule and scorned to carry out what he had
vowed to God. But the saints, led by the Virgin, rushed to his rescue,
claiming him as their chaplain and minister: in always attending services for the dead, he had served them as well. The demons were thus
defeated, and the monk gained admission to the heavenly host.[93] In
this tale, the office of the dead actually serves as the opus Dei, as the
labor of prayer which sanctified the monk's life.

The emphasis that early medieval churches gave to integrating the
commemoration of the dead into their ordinary round of prayer rath-

93. Peter Damian, *De variis miraculosis narrationibus (opusculum 34)*, 5 (PL 145: 588–90).
This text has not yet been published in Reindel's new edition of the letters and short
treatises: *Die Briefe des Petrus Damiani*, ed. Kurt Reindel, 3 vols. to date. (Munich, 1983–).

er than simply increasing the number of services for the dead whenever convenient is significant. It shows that the reification of prayer
begun in late antiquity was not yet complete. The general expansion
of the liturgy, and the growing emphasis on using services tailored to
special needs, had increased the amount of prayer performed "for the
dead." However, it never broke the connection between that prayer
and the rest of the liturgy. Services for the dead were beginning to be
seen as fixed rituals—an "office of the dead," a "mass for the dead"—
but they were also still seen as the collective activity of the community that prayed.

SOCIETAS ORATIONUM

The clerical communities of the early middle ages offered their
prayers for all the living and all the departed faithful. But they also
offered them for specific individuals or groups of people. Most often
mentioned in masses, offices, psalms, and feasts for the dead were the
former leaders and members of the communities that prayed: abbots,
abbesses, bishops, monks, nuns, and canons. There were often services for relatives of the clergy and for *familiares*, people closely associated with them in other ways. There might also be supplementary psalms for those who had given alms to the community and
special masses for those buried in its cemetery. Most of the prayers
offered for the dead in early medieval churches, then, were either for
the abstract group of "all the departed faithful," or for the clergy who
actually performed the liturgy and those personally associated with
them. Other considerations—for example, the relationship of the secular clergy to the laity for whom they were responsible—do not seem
to have come into play. Cathedral clergy seldom mentioned their
flocks directly in their prayers.[94] At the cathedral of Chartres in the
eleventh century, for example, the daily office of the dead included
prayers for former bishops, for the canons of the cathedral, for those
whose anniversaries were being celebrated that day, for the benefactors of the clergy, and finally, for all the departed faithful. No special
mention was made of the people of Chartres or of the diocese.[95]

94. The obligations of parish priests toward their parishioners will be considered in the
following chapter.
95. *Un Manuscrit chartrain*, pp. 238–39.

The practice of praying only for the dead who belonged to the clerical community or for those who had specific ties with it was not simply a form of elitism, although this may have played a role in the organization of the liturgy in some churches. Mostly, this practice reflects the early medieval clergy's assumptions about where salvation was to be found. In the first few centuries of Christianity, the members of the ecclesiae had envisioned themselves as a community of saints, standing together in defiance of the sinful world around them. In the early middle ages, the members of clerical communities came to see themselves in much the same light. They were the true servants of God and the saints; their liturgical activities and their special way of life marked them off from the world—still viewed as sinful even though it was now largely Christian.

The changes in liturgical practice and in the organization of the church that began in late antiquity had gradually broken down the ancient unity of the ecclesia.[96] By the eighth century a distinction of function had appeared within the Christian community. The *saeculares*, whose business was the defense and support of the church, were set apart from the *spirituales*, whose business it was to intercede for the rest of the community.[97] The *spirituales* were also distinguished by special practices such as tonsuring and the taking of vows, and sometimes by their ascetic way of life as well. In any case, it was the clergy, much more than the laity, who were seen as the servants of God in the early middle ages.[98] It was therefore entirely appropriate for the clergy to pray primarily for themselves and for the layfolk who defended and supported them.

Moreover, in the fragmented social world of the early middle ages, it was not the church hierarchy or the clergy as a whole, but rather the local clerical community, the group gathered around the shrine of the local saint for collective prayer, that was viewed as the locus of salvation. That community was identified metonymically with the church as a whole and figuratively with the community of the saints in heaven. It provided the gateway through which individual men and women could enter into those wider communities.

96. The implications of these changes for the laity are discussed in the following chapter.

97. Jean Chélini, "Les Laïcs dans la société ecclésiastique carolingienne," in *I laici nella "societas christiana" dei secoli XI e XII* (Milan, 1968), pp. 23–28.

98. On the transformation of the ideal of sanctity in this period, see Frantisek Graus, *Volk, Herrscher, und Heiliger im Reich der Merowinger: Studien zur Hagiographie der Merowingerzeit* (Prague, 1965), pp. 90–120.

In this context it is worth noting a special use of the word *societas* which developed in the early middle ages. This word had long been used by Christian writers to refer to the community of the elect in heaven—*societas sanctorum, societas electorum*. In ancient and in early medieval usage, people sought to "associate" (*associare*) themselves with the saints through burial near their relics.[99] *Societas* had also long been used to refer to the community of the elect on earth, and especially to that community as it was united in the liturgy. Thus, Augustine had written in the fifth century that prayers were to be said in the mass for all those who died "in Christian and Catholic society" (*in christiana et catholica societate*).[100] In the ninth century, Florus of Lyons, drawing on Augustine's work, wrote that all those who were not separated from the "unity and society of Christ and the church" (*ab unitate et societate Christi et ecclesiae*) could be remembered in the mass.[101] In each case, while *societas* could be taken in an abstract sense to refer to the church as a whole, it also had a more concrete meaning, which referred to the local community of Christians united in the liturgy, the microcosm of the community of the faithful. For Augustine, writing in the fifth century, this was still the ecclesia, but for Florus, writing in the ninth, it was the clerical community. In the early middle ages, the word *societas* came to be used to refer to this clerical community and all those "associated" with it. The people commemorated in its liturgy were the members of its *societas orationum*.[102]

Long association and close friendship with a liturgical community —*familiaritas*—might lead, almost casually, to inclusion in its societas orationum.[103] A late eleventh-century sacramentary of Saint-Martin of Tours includes prayers for all those whose alms the canons had received or who were joined to them by bonds of "familiarity and consanguinity" (*familiaritate ac consanguinitate*).[104] Many monastic houses offered some of their supplementary psalms for the familiares of the house. These became known, in fact, as the *psalmi familiares*.

99. Duval, *Auprès des saints*, pp. 145–54.
100. Augustine, *De cura pro mortuis gerenda*, 4 (p. 631).
101. Florus of Lyons, *De expositione missae*, 68 (PL 119: 61).
102. In the following pages I use the modern terms "liturgical community" and "community that prayed" to refer to a group of clerics who performed the liturgy together. In the absence of a satisfactory modern equivalent, I use the early medieval term *societas orationum* (literally: "community of prayers") to refer to the extended group of people associated with a particular liturgical community and commemorated in its prayers.
103. See below, Chapter 4.
104. Paris, BN, Latin 9434, fol. 338r.

At Cluny in the eleventh century there were special collects for the living familiares in the mass and office of the day, and for the dead familiares in the mass and office of the dead.[105] Annual feasts were also celebrated for the friends, relatives and familiares of clerical communities.[106]

Many people, however, entered into a more formal relationship with the clerical community, a relationship that allowed them to participate fully, if vicariously, in all its spiritual activities. These men and women might still be known as familiares, but they were also often referred to as *confratres* or *consorores*, for they had in effect become members of the community, through entry into its societas orationum.[107] A useful blanket term for these relationships, which took various forms and which were known under various names in the early middle ages, is confraternity (*confraternitas*).[108]

One form of confraternity was that which united individual clerics in an association of mutual prayer. Often these associations were formed at synods, where clerics from a diocese, a province, or an even larger area gathered. At the synod of Attigny (ca. 760), the assembled bishops and abbots agreed

> that each of those whose names are found written below on this notice will, when any [of them] leaves this world, recite one hundred psalters and have his priests recite one hundred special masses. Let each bishop perform thirty masses personally, unless he is prevented by illness or some other impediment. Then let him ask another bishop to perform them for him. Let the abbots who are not bishops ask bishops to perform those thirty masses in their

105. Ulric of Cluny, *Consuetudines Cluniacenses*, 1: 5–7 (PL 149: 650–53).
106. Bernard of Cluny, *Ordo Cluniacensis*, 2: 32, in *Vetus disciplina monastica*, p. 354.
107. There are no English equivalents for these terms. The Latin words for "brother" and "sister" (*frater, soror*) were often used in the early middle ages not only for blood relationships, but also for relationships of "spiritual" kinship, such as those that bound together the members of a monastic community. Sometimes people affiliated with such a community, the members of its societas orationum, were also referred to simply as *fratres* or *sorores*. More often, however, a distinction was made between the clerical members of the community that prayed (*fratres, sorores*), and associated outsiders (*confratres, consorores*). The addition of the prefix "con-" (related to the English "co-") underlined the fact that this kinship relationship was socially created, and was probably intended to suggest a somewhat more tenuous bond than "real" kinship.
108. On the different terms used for these relationships, see Karl Schmid and Otto Gerhard Oexle, "Voraussetzungen und Wirkung des Gebetsbundes von Attigny," *Francia* 2 (1974), 80–81.

place, and let them remember to have their priests perform one hundred masses and their monks one hundred psalters.[109]

Similarly, in 840 Bishop Aldric summoned the clergy of Le Mans to a synod, in order to determine how they should pray for one another in life and after death. The members of the confraternity established at this synod agreed to offer regular prayers for Aldric and for "the people committed to his care," that is, presumably, for the whole diocese. Most of their liturgical efforts, however, were directed towards their own good. Every year the clerics present at this synod were to offer twelve masses for their living confratres. Whenever one of them died, the others were to offer twelve masses and a vigil for him.[110] At the very end of the eighth century, a second type of confraternity appeared. These associations were created by agreements between whole clerical communities rather than individual clerics. In 800, for example, the abbeys of Reichenau and Saint-Gall established a prayer association (*conventio et unanimitas precum*), each promising to offer funerary services whenever a monk of the other house died. On the day when the death was announced, all the priests were to offer three masses, and the other monks were to recite a psalter. The community would also celebrate vigils (presumably some form of the office of the dead?) and a conventual mass for the dead brother. On the seventh day after death, they would recite thirty psalms for him, and on the thirtieth day, all the priests would celebrate one mass and the other monks fifty psalms. The two monasteries also agreed to perform the office of the dead on the first day of every month and a special commemorative service every year on November 13 or 14, for all the dead brothers of both houses.[111] During the early ninth century whole networks of houses' bound together by this type of arrangement were created.[112] They remained an important feature of the religious landscape throughout the early middle ages.

109. Synod of Attigny (ca. 760), in *Capitularia regum Francorum*, 1, ed. Alfred Boretius, (MGH, Leges, sect. 2, pt. 1) (Hanover, 1883), pp. 221–22; and see Schmid and Oexle, "Voraussetzungen und Wirkung des Gebetsbundes von Attigny," especially pp. 85–86.
110. Council of Le Mans (840), in *Concilia aevi Karolini*, 2: 784–88.
111. *Libri confraternitatum sancti Galli*, p. 140; and see Oexle, "Memorialüberlieferung und Gebetsgedächtnis in Fulda," in Schmid, *Die Klostergemeinschaft von Fulda*, 1, especially pp. 136–54.
112. The best known is that which left its traces in the famous *liber memorialis* of

Finally, it was possible for an individual cleric or a member of the laity to form a personal association with a clerical community, by joining its *societas orationum* or confraternity. The earliest references to this practice date back to the eighth century; in the late tenth century the number of individuals seeking formal association with the more prestigious monasteries began to grow, reaching a peak in the late eleventh century.[113] Tenth- and eleventh-century charters of donation often refer to the *societas orationum* of a church, to which the donors hope to belong. In the late eleventh century, for example, Gilduin and his father Hamelin were offered the benefit of the *societas orationum* of the abbey of Marmoutier, in recognition of the concessions they had made to the monastery.[114] Likewise, the customs of monastic houses like Cluny sometimes refer to outsiders who obtained the *societatem et fraternitatem* of the house.[115]

Adalbert Ebner, the first modern scholar to study these phenomena, argued that prayer confraternities were a novel kind of institution which originated in Britain and then spread to the Continent with the Anglo-Saxon monks.[116] Most scholars now believe, however, that confraternities were not necessarily of insular origin. Neither were they entirely new when they first appeared in the sources in the eighth century. They seem to have been closely related to other social institutions which had been in existence for a long time and which were found throughout much of Europe.[117] For example, some clerical confraternities show remarkable similarities to the drinking and burial societies known as gilds.[118] A curious document of the ninth century

Reichenau, compiled around 825: see *Das Verbrüderungsbuch der Abtei Reichenau*. A map of this network, which included dozens of associated houses, appears in Hubert Jedin, Kenneth Scott Latourette, and Jochen Martin, eds., *Atlas zur Kirchengeschichte: Die christlichen Kirchen in Geschichte und Gegenwart* (Freiburg, 1970), p. 34. On its background, see Schmid and Wollasch, "Die Gemeinschaft der Lebenden und Verstorbenen," pp. 373–76; Karl Schmid, "Bemerkungen zur Anlage des Reichenauer Verbrüderungsbuches: Zugleich ein Beitrag zum Verständnis der 'Visio Wettini,'" in his *Gebetsgedenken und adliges Selbstverständnis*, pp. 514–31. On *libri memoriales*, see below.

113. See Appendix B.

114. *Marmoutier: Cartulaire blésois*, ed. Charles Métais (Blois, 1889–91), no. 70 (1096–1104).

115. Ulric of Cluny, *Consuetudines Cluniacenses*, 3: 33 (PL 149: 777).

116. Ebner, *Die klösterlichen Gebets-Verbrüderungen*, pp. 32–33, 35–42.

117. On this point see especially Schmid and Oexle, "Voraussetzungen und Wirkung des Gebetsbundes von Attigny," p. 81; and Herbert Edward John Cowdrey, "Legal Problems Raised by Agreements of Confraternity," in Schmid and Wollasch, *Memoria*, p. 234.

118. On the wide diffusion of these societies, see Otto Gerhard Oexle, *"Conjuratio* et *ghilde* dans l'antiquité et dans le haut moyen âge: Remarques sur la continuité des formes de

describes the customs of a community of clerics who called themselves the *Societas duodecim apostolorum*, the Society of the Twelve Apostles. They seem to have lived separately in the world, but came together at regular intervals to share a meal, celebrate mass, and offer alms to the poor. As with the gilds, however, this community's other important obligation was the burial and commemoration of its members. A special meal, like that mentioned in gild records, was part of this group's burial customs.[119]

The existence of gilds in early Frankish society probably provided a structure for the growth of this kind of association. However, the development and spread of clerical confraternities from the middle of the eighth century on may have received its impetus from the Irish and Anglo-Saxon missionaries. As strangers, far from home, they would have been especially eager to establish spiritual bonds with the members of other churches.[120] Confraternities were probably also encouraged by the Carolingian monarchs, as part of their effort to create political and spiritual unity within their realm with the assistance of the clergy.[121]

The Carolingians understood what they were about. For in fact, these voluntary associations did help to maintain the unity of the Frankish realm and of western Christendom in the early middle ages. During the long centuries of transition from the ancient ecclesia to the more centralized and encompassing church of the high middle ages,

---

la vie sociale," *Francia* 10 (1982), 1–19; Susan Reynolds, *Kingdoms and Communities in Western Europe, 900–1300* (Oxford, 1984), pp. 67–78. On the connection between gilds and confraternities, see Schmid and Oexle, "Voraussetzungen und Wirkung des Gebetsbundes von Attigny," p. 81. Gilles Gerard Meersseman also notes the connection, but argues that the two types of organization were ultimately different: Gilles Gerard Meersseman, with Gian Piero Pacini, *Ordo fraternitatis: Confraternite e pietà dei laici nel medioevo* (Rome, 1977), pp. 8–10.

119. Meersseman, *Ordo fraternitatis*, pp. 150–69; Meersseman linked a text from a manuscript in the Vatican Library with another text, from a manuscript in Berne, published earlier by André Wilmart, "Le Règlement ecclésiastique de Berne," *Revue bénédictine* 51 (1939), 49–51. The members of this clerical society did not allow layfolk to join (Meersseman, p. 162: "nullam laicam personam inter vos adhibite"), but they did pray for members of the laity (ibid., p. 151). On their services for dead brothers, see ibid., pp. 164–65.

120. See Ebner, *Die klösterlichen Gebets-Verbrüderungen*, p. 35; Joachim Wollasch, "Die mittelalterliche Lebensform der Verbrüderung," in Schmid and Wollasch, *Memoria*, pp. 218–20.

121. On the growth of confraternities, see Schmid and Wollasch, "Die Gemeinschaft der Lebenden und Verstorbenen," pp. 371–77; Schmid and Oexle, "Voraussetzungen und Wirkung des Gebetsbundes von Attigny," pp. 94–95; Schmid, "Bemerkungen zur Anlage des Reichenauer Verbrüderungsbuches," in his *Gebetsgedenken und adliges Selbstverständnis*, pp. 528–31.

confraternities of various kinds, ranging from the parish gild of a tiny rural church to the huge *societas orationum* of an important monastery, helped to create enduring ties between one clerical community and another, and between those communities and the rest of Christian society. They thus played an important role in the christianization of Europe.

By entering into the confraternity, the *societas orationum* of a religious house, outsiders actually became members of its congregation. This is clear from the ceremony of association itself. In the second half of the eleventh century Archbishop Lanfranc included a description of this ceremony in the customary he wrote for the monks of Canterbury, a customary based on the practices of the Norman monastery of Bec. According to Lanfranc, when one monastic community sought confraternity with another, the abbot and some of the monks of the first house were received in chapter by the second. They threw themselves down, begging for the privilege they wanted. If the abbot agreed to their request, he handed the visiting abbot the book containing the monastic rule, as a sign that he was accepted as a member of the *societas*, and showed him to a seat next to his own in the chapter-house. The visiting monks had to return to the place where they had first prostrated themselves and bow three times, but after chapter they exchanged ceremonial kisses with the brothers of the house, thus becoming *confratres*.

If a single monk wanted to be a *confrater*, he went through much the same ritual, accepted the rule in token of *societas*, kissed all the brothers, who bowed to him in return, and was finally given a place to sit in chapter. Secular men and women followed a similar ceremony, with fewer signs of humility. However, they were given a copy of the Gospels rather than the rule as a symbol of the grant of *societas*. Nor were women allowed to kiss their monastic *confratres*—a precautionary measure, no doubt.[122] The different books used suggests that layfolk were received as fellow Christians, whereas monks were received as fellow monks. In either case, however, the symbolism of book, kiss, and offer of a seat in chapter indicates that this ceremony, which I am calling "formal association," was seen as a form of entry into the community that prayed.

Confratres and *consorores* were entitled to many of the same privileges as the monks, nuns, or clerics who actually performed the

122. Lanfranc, *Decreta*, 108 (pp. 93–94).

liturgy together. It was not unusual for clerical confratres, at least, to be promised a seat in chapter, a place in the choir, and food in the refectory, whenever they visited the community with which they were associated. In the late eleventh century, for example, the canons of Saint-Denis of Doué formed a *societas* with the canons of the cathedral of Angers. The cathedral scribe who recorded the agreement noted that "we shall have communion in prayers for both the living and the dead with them, and they with us, like a canon of the chapter. Moreover, when they come here, they will share in our table, prayers, and chapter-meeting, and they will read the lessons and make responses in the choir like one of us."[123]

Confraternity could give rise not only to shared privileges, but also to various kinds of special assistance. In the eleventh century, a knight named Hugh, a confrater of the monastery of Montiérender, was wounded and captured in battle. He sent to the monks, asking them to ransom him and then make him a monk "for the sake of the fraternity which was between [them]." The community fulfilled his request.[124] Sometimes two associated religious houses would exchange favors. In the late ninth century, for example, the abbot of Saint-Amand sent one of his monks, named Hucbald, to the monastery of Saint-Bertin, where he served as a teacher. In 889, the monks of Saint-Bertin granted their "beloved confrater Hucbald" a piece of property, to support him while he stayed at Saint-Bertin. They set up an agreement with Saint-Amand, according to which each community would offer fifty psalms and a special mass with an offering by all the monks on behalf of the other community every Wednesday during Lent. Finally, it was arranged for Hucbald to use the resources of the property he had been given to prepare a special meal for the monks every year on the feast of his own patron, St. Amand. Presumably the idea was that the monks would then show more devotion to that saint.[125]

123. *Cartulaire noir de la cathédrale d'Angers*, ed. Charles Urseau (Angers, 1908), no. 118 (1063–93). On the material benefits of confraternity, see Cowdrey, "Legal Problems Raised by Agreements of Confraternity," in Schmid and Wollasch, *Memoria*, pp. 238–54. On the problems the presence of lay and clerical confratres posed for monastic communities, see Karl Schmid, "Von den 'fratres conscripti' in Ekkeharts St. Galler Klostergeschichten," *FS* 25 (1991), especially pp. 116–22.

124. *Cartulaire de l'abbaye de la Chapelle-aux-Planches, chartes de Montiérender, de Saint-Étienne et de Toussaints de Châlons, d'Andecy, de Beaulieu et de Rethel*, ed. Charles Lalore (Paris-Troyes, 1878), Montiérender no. 57 (1088).

125. *Cartulaire de l'abbaye de Saint-Bertin*, pp. 131–32 (889).

Confraternity agreements could be the first step in the creation of formal ties of dependency between two houses. In 942, for example, Abbot Odo of Cluny, who was then reforming the monastery of Fleury, sent four monks of that house to Limoges, to establish a confraternity with the monks of Saint-Martial. The arrangement was that "from that day on for the remainder of the age, there would be no difference between the monks of this place and the servants of the blessed Benedict of Fleury, but when they pass back and forth, let the common intercourse of both in all things be recognized, and let them be held as one congregation."[126] This was not simply a pious statement of unity in charity. It actually represented a move toward affiliation. For within a century, Saint-Martial, like Fleury, had become a member of the great network of monasteries institutionally linked with Cluny, the *Cluniacensis ecclesia*.[127]

It is clear that early medieval confraternity agreements created real social bonds, which had implications in many different areas of life.[128] This fact is reflected in the promise of liturgical privileges which lay at the heart of these accords. For what was promised was not just a certain number of prayers. Early medieval confraternity agreements, like early medieval funeral ordines and customaries, describe services carefully structured so as to create an "integrated" liturgy, within which an expanded liturgical community commemorated its confratres and consorores.[129] This is already evident in the famous *Gebetsbund*, or prayer association, that came out of the synod of Attigny, which emphasized the personal involvement of the bishops and abbots in performing the promised services for the dead.

It is even more apparent in the arrangements for funerary prayer and continuing commemoration made by associated communities in the ninth century. The monks of Saint-Remi of Reims and Saint-Denis, for example, formed a confraternity in 840. They agreed

126. *Recueil des chartes de l'abbaye de Saint-Benoît-sur-Loire*, ed. Maurice Prou and Alexandre Vidier, 2 vols. (Paris, 1907–32), no. 49 (942): "ut ab ea die in reliquum aevum nulla esset differaencia inter monachos ejusdem loci et beati Benedicti Floriacensis famulos, sed utrique, dum ad se invicem transirent, communis agnosceretur in omnibus conversatio et quasi una haberetur congregatio."

127. See Wollasch, "Die mittelalterliche Lebensform der Verbrüderung," in Schmid and Wollasch, *Memoria*, p. 221.

128. On the relationship between formal association and the more general relationship of *familiaritas*, see below, Chapter 4.

129. See Häussling, *Mönchskonvent und Eucharistiefeier*, pp. 273–76; idem, "Missarum sollemnia," in *Segni e riti*, 2: 565–67.

that when any of them [the monks of the associated house], freed from his corporeal bonds, leaves this world, each of us will perform a complete psalter within thirty days, and our priests will strive to celebrate masses equivalent to that psalter for him, and we will perform three vigils, namely on the first and seventh and thirtieth day, collectively and most devoutly for him . . . and let the names of their dead be inserted among the names of ours, so that the sacrifice will be offered daily to the Lord for them as for us.[130]

Similar agreements, describing the prayers to be offered by each member of the community individually and by the whole community acting together, can be found in the tenth- and eleventh-century sources.[131] In the eleventh century, however, some religious communities simply agreed to treat the members of associated houses "like brothers" (or "like sisters") of their own house, promising them a share in all the prayers and good works performed there.[132]

Finally, there were the individual men and women who entered the *societas orationum* through the act of formal association. The clearest description of the privileges they were to enjoy comes from the customary of Cluny drawn up by Ulric in the late eleventh century.

There are, moreover, many of the faithful of Christ, both poor and rich, who, when they are brought into our chapter, ask that they also may be allowed to belong to our fraternity. This is granted and conferred on them with the book, so that they may have a share and communion in all the good works which are performed in any way, whether in prayers or in almsgiving, not only among us [at Cluny], but also in all the places which are under our law.[133]

The services performed for individual *confratres* and *consorores* at Cluny, then, marked their place not only in the community at Cluny,

130. *Les Obituaires de la province de Sens*, ed. Auguste Molinier and Auguste Longnon, 3 vols. (Paris, 1902–1906), vol. 1, pt. 2, p. 1023. On the use of names, see below.

131. Ulric of Cluny, *Consuetudines Cluniacenses*, 3: 33 (PL 149: 777). See also Odorannus of Sens, *Opera omnia*, ed. and trans. (into French) by Robert-Henri Bautier and Monique Gilles (Paris, 1972), p. 261, on the confraternity between the monks of Saint-Pierre-le-Vif and the priests of the province of Sens.

132. *Recueil des chartes de l'abbaye de Cluny*, ed. Auguste Bernard and Alexandre Bruel, 6 vols. (Paris, 1876–1903), no. 1947 (993); *Cartulaire de Saint-Vincent de Mâcon: Connu sous le nom de Livre Enchaîné*, ed. M.-C. Ragut (Mâcon, 1864), no. 12 (probably early 11th c.); *Recueil des chartes de l'abbaye de Saint-Benoît-sur-Loire*, no. 84 (1075).

133. Ulric of Cluny, *Consuetudines Cluniacenses*, 3: 33 (PL 149: 777–78).

but in the whole *Cluniacensis ecclesia.* Small wonder that this privilege was so eagerly sought in the late eleventh century.[134]

THE PRESENCE OF THE DEAD

Early medieval religious communities remembered the members of their societates orationum by name in their prayers. The use of names in the Christian liturgy can be traced back at least as far as the third century, for Cyprian of Carthage mentions it in one of his letters. He is discussing the case of a certain Geminius Victor, who had had a priest named as the executor of his will, contrary to the law of the church. Earlier bishops, Cyprian says, have established a penalty for anyone who acts in this way: "the sacrifice is not offered for him, nor celebrated for his repose; neither does he deserve to be named before the altar of God in the prayer of the priests—he who wanted the priests and ministers to be called away from the altar."[135] A century and a half later, Augustine also refers to the naming of the dead in the celebrant's prayer, as well as to a more general commemoration of the dead in which names were not mentioned.[136]

As we have seen, the eucharistic liturgy of seventh-century Gaul included a special mass prayer which followed the offertory procession. Because the names of the *offerentes* were recited at this point, this prayer came to be called the *oratio post nomina.*[137] In the early middle ages, its function was assumed by the two prayers which began with the word *Memento,* one recited for the living before the consecration, and one for the dead after it. In the *Memento* of the dead, the names were recited in the break between the two sentences of the prayer or,

134. On the demand for confraternity at Cluny in the late eleventh century, see Cowdrey, "Unions and Confraternity with Cluny," p. 160; Wollasch, "Les Obituaires, témoin de la vie clunisienne," pp. 151–52.
135. Cyprian, *Epistulae,* 1 (2: 466): "non offerretur pro eo nec sacrificium pro dormitione eius celebraretur. neque enim apud altare Dei meretur nominari in sacerdotum prece qui ab altari sacerdotes et ministros voluit avocari."
136. Augustine, *De cura pro mortuis gerenda,* 4 (p. 631). See also Saxer, *Morts, martyrs, reliques,* pp. 163–65.
137. Bishop, "On the Early Texts of the Roman Canon," in his *Liturgica Historica,* p. 114.

less frequently, in the middle of the first sentence after the word "servants."[138]

But if the names of individuals were to be read out during mass, they had to be recorded in some form. By the fourth century, the eastern churches had begun to record the names of both the living faithful and the dead on two tablets, hinged together—a diptych.[139] Generally there were several columns of names: one for bishops, another for priests, and a third for the laity. The word diptych (and sometimes the tablet form) was adopted by the western churches for their name-lists in the sixth or seventh century. Hence the rubric *super diptycha*, "at [the reading of] the diptych," still found in many early medieval sacramentaries before the *Memento*.[140]

By the eight century, a new kind of name-list had appeared in western Europe, apparently originating in the monasteries. The growing number of names to be remembered in the monastic liturgy were now recorded in codices known as *libri memoriales*. Usually the names were arranged, as in the earlier lists, by ecclesiastical order (bishops, priests, laity—with kings as a special category), but sometimes one finds the names arranged instead according to relationship with the monastery. Thus, for example, there might be a section for abbots of the house, for monks, and then for friends or familiares—in other words, for outsiders who were associated with the monastic community.

A further refinement of the liber memorialis, which appeared in the ninth century as confraternities between religious communities began to develop, was the *liber confraternitatum*. In this format, names were arranged in groups, according to the church to which their owners had owed their primary allegiance; individual confratres were listed separately.[141] The changing structure of these name-lists—the

138. Jungmann, *The Mass of the Roman Rite*, 2: 244–45. On the rule against reciting the names of the dead on Sundays, see the works cited in n. 61 above.

139. Jean-Charles Picard points out that even in antiquity the lists were sometimes kept on pieces of parchment rather than on tablets: *Le Souvenir des évêques: Sépultures, listes épiscopales, et culte des évêques en Italie du Nord des origines au Xe siècle* (Rome, 1988), pp. 522–23.

140. Dix, *The Shape of the Liturgy*, pp. 506–11; Jungmann, *The Mass of the Roman Rite*, 2: 245. On the famous Barberini diptych, with its list of the seventh-century Frankish kings, see Heinz Thomas, "Die Namenliste des Diptychon Barberini und der Sturz des Hausmeiers Grimoald," *Deutsches Archiv für Erforschung des Mittelalters* 25 (1969), 17–63.

141. Ebner, *Die klösterlichen Gebets-Verbrüderungen*, pp. 97–129; Schmid and Wollasch, "Die Gemeinschaft der Lebenden und Verstorbenen," especially pp. 366–70; Huyghebaert,

shift from a format which stressed ecclesiastical office to one which emphasized affiliation with a particular group of clerics—reflects the changing nature of the liturgical community in this period, the replacement of the ecclesia by the clerical community.

The libri memoriales were used as the earlier diptychs and namelists had been. That is, they were read from or (as the list became unwieldy) simply placed on the altar during the mass.[142] These documents, which included the names of both the living and the dead, served as concrete symbols of the liturgical community on earth and were believed to reflect the community of the elect in heaven as well. Indeed, the libri memoriales were often referred to in the early middle ages as *libri vitae*, in deliberate evocation of the heavenly "book of life" in which the names of the saved were supposedly recorded.[143] Through inscription in the book of the earthly community the living and the dead were to be inscribed in the book of the heavenly community. A prayer from an eleventh-century sacramentary expresses just this idea:

> Lord, to whom alone is known the number of the elect to be set in heavenly bliss, grant, I ask, that the names of those whom I have received for commendation in prayer and of all the dead faithful be kept written in the book of blessed predestination.[144]

In another prayer, the celebrant begged that those whose names had been recited or placed on the altar during mass be joined to the company (*consortio*) of the elect.[145]

In the middle of the ninth century a new type of name-list appeared. This was the necrology, a document arranged like a calendar, with the name of each person recorded next to a date—in theory that of his or her death. Unlike the earlier liber memorialis, the necrology

---

Les Documents nécrologiques, pp. 13–15; Oexle, "Memoria und Memorialüberlieferung," especially pp. 70–79. On the transition from diptych to liber memorialis, see especially Franz-Josef Jakobi, "Diptychen als frühe Form der Gedenk-Aufzeichnungen: Zum 'Herrscher-Diptychon' im Liber Memorialis von Remiremont," *FS* 20 (1986), 186–212.

142. Edmund Bishop, "Some Ancient Benedictine Confraternity Books," in his *Liturgica Historica*, pp. 352–53; Oexle, "Memoria und Memorialüberlieferung," pp. 73, 76–79.

143. On the heavenly book of life, see especially Rev. 20:12. On the use of this term in connection with the libri memoriales, see Bishop, "Some Ancient Benedictine Confraternity Books," in his *Liturgica Historica*, p. 352; Schmid and Wollasch, "Die Gemeinschaft der Lebenden und Verstorbenen," pp. 366–67.

144. Paris, BN, Latin 9434, fol. 337v.

145. Paris, BN, Latin 9434, fol. 338r.

was not meant to be used during mass. It was read in the monastic chapter-meeting each morning at prime, along with a selection from the rule and the appropriate entries from the calendar and martyrology.[146] The appearance of this new form of list was related to a form of commemoration which had earlier roots, but which became institutionalized in the monasteries at the beginning of the middle ages.

In the first few centuries of Christianity, both the saints and the ordinary dead were commemorated once a year on the anniversaries of their deaths. The anniversaries of the saints were public events, which became institutionalized in late antiquity as permanent feasts. The anniversaries of the ordinary dead, on the other hand, were essentially private events. Most Christians were remembered on their anniversaries only as long as their relatives and friends continued to arrange commemorative services for them.[147] In the eighth century, however, some monastic communities began to incorporate annual services for the more important members of the community into their liturgies, for performance in perpetuity. Once a year, on the appropriate date, a name would be announced during the office of prime and the prayers of the day would be dedicated especially to the memory of that person. In the ninth century, this practice became increasingly common. The reforming council held at Aix in 817 insisted that anniversaries be celebrated in the newly reformed monasteries for the abbots of those houses.[148] Continuing annual services were also introduced at about this time for the great benefactors of religious houses—bishops, kings, and a few important nobles.[149] Around the middle of the ninth century many monasteries instituted the practice of commemorating every member of the house once a year, on the anniversary of his or her death. This was the development which led to the creation of the necrology.

The first necrologies appeared in the ninth century; by the eleventh century this kind of name list had become very common, espe-

146. Ebner, *Die klösterlichen Gebets-Verbrüderungen*, pp. 130–40; Huyghebaert, *Les Documents nécrologiques*, pp. 33–41. See also Jean-Loup Lemaître, "Liber capituli: Le livre du chapitre, des orgines au XVIe siècle—l'exemple français," in Schmid and Wollasch, *Memoria*, pp. 625–48.

147. On anniversary celebrations in the African church from the third to the fifth century, see especially Saxer, *Morts, martyrs, reliques*, pp. 69–71, 104–5, 133–45, 157–59, 170–73.

148. *Collectio capitularis Benedicti levitae monastica*, ed. Joseph Semmler, 73, in *Initia consuetudinis Benedictinae*, p. 552.

149. On the anniversaries of kings, see Appendix A.

cially in the reformed Benedictine houses. The older libri memoriales, on the other hand, were falling into disuse.[150] This replacement of the liber memorialis by the necrology is the material sign of a change in practice: a move from the commemoration of all the living and dead members of the societas orationum during the mass, toward the commemoration of the dead on the anniversaries of their deaths.[151] The appearance of necrologies can, therefore, be seen as part of the general trend described above, in which prayer devoted specifically to the dead was integrated into the liturgy. Just as the dead faithful—as a group—came to be commemorated in the daily mass and office of the dead, and in the annual feasts of the dead during the early middle ages, so individuals came to be commemorated on the anniversaries of their deaths.

For a number of scholars, the development of the necrology also represents a move from "collective" to more "individualized" commemoration.[152] They note that while a person whose name was recorded in a liber memorialis would be commemorated every day in mass in the company of the hundreds or even thousands of other people whose names were also recorded there, a person whose name was recorded in a necrology would be commemorated every year alone or in the company of a few other individuals who had died on the same day. It would be a mistake, however, to assume that individualized commemoration on the anniversary of death in any way obscured the relationship between the individual being commemorated and the community that prayed. If anything, that relationship was

150. Schmid and Wollasch, "Die Gemeinschaft der Lebenden und Verstorbenen," p. 400. It is important to note, however, that the older form of commemoration, using a list of both the living and the dead during the celebration of the mass, was still practiced through the eleventh century in some places. See, for example, Orderic Vitalis, *Historia aecclesiastica*, 3, ed. and trans. Marjorie Chibnall, 6 vols. (Oxford, 1969–80), 2: 114. I have modified Chibnall's translations where necessary to clarify certain points of practice or meaning.

151. Most of the names listed in the libri memoriales were, of course, those of the dead, since the same book remained in use over a long period of time. However, a name was normally entered in a liber memorialis while its owner still lived, and that person would be prayed for before as well as after death. The necrology, on the other hand, was by definition a list of the dead: the names were entered on it according to the date of death. On this point see Ebner, *Die klösterlichen Gebets-Verbrüderungen*, p. 92; Schmid and Wollasch, "Die Gemeinschaft der Lebenden und Verstorbenen," p. 368.

152. E.g., Schmid and Wollasch, "Die Gemeinschaft der Lebenden und Verstorbenen," p. 400; Wollasch, "Les Obituaires, témoins de la vie clunisienne," pp. 143–44; Angenendt, "Theologie und Liturgie," in Schmid and Wollasch, *Memoria*, pp. 185–88, 198–99.

reinforced by the move from collective to more individualized commemoration. For now individuals became the focus of the community's efforts not only during their funerals, but again every year on their anniversaries.

Anniversary prayer was part of the regular round of prayer in monasteries and at least some cathedrals.[153] At Cluny, for example, some of the psalms recited after chapter, one of the collects in the office of the dead, and another in the mass of the dead were dedicated to those whose anniversaries were being celebrated that day.[154] The custom also arose at Cluny of giving a monk's own prebend as alms every year on the anniversary of his death.[155] It is not clear whether this custom, which placed a tremendous burden on the community's economic resources, was followed elsewhere.[156] However, it served to mark with particular clarity the rights former members of the community retained to a share in its resources.[157]

Annual commemoration linked the dead not only with the earthly community which performed the liturgy, but also with the community of the saints. As Amalar of Metz wrote in the ninth century: "Just as the anniversary days of the saints, [celebrated] in their honor, are brought back to our remembrance for our benefit, so are those of the dead performed, for their benefit and for our devotion, in the belief that they will at some time come to the community of the saints."[158] It is worth noting that some of the earliest records of these anniversaries were not separate documents—necrologies proper—but "necrological notes" in the margins of calendars that also recorded the feasts of the saints.[159] Only when the privilege of continuing annual commemoration was extended to the whole monastic community in the ninth century did the necrology develop into a separate docu-

153. On the celebration of anniversaries in eleventh-century cathedrals, see *Un Manuscrit chartrain*, pp. 238–39; John of Avranches, *De officiis ecclesiasticis* (PL 147: 38, 56).

154. Ulric of Cluny, *Consuetudines Cluniacenses*, 1: 3, 5, 7 (PL 149: 647, 649–51, 652–53).

155. Ulric of Cluny, *Consuetudines Cluniacenses*, 3: 29 (PL 149: 775): "Et de caetero, quoties venerit anniversarius ejus, iterum praebenda sua dabitur ad eleemosynam."

156. Wollasch, "Les Obituaires, témoins de la vie clunisienne," pp. 161–64.

157. This practice is closely related to that of the anniversary meal: see Oexle, "Der Gegenwart der Toten," in Braet and Verbeke, *Death in the Middle Ages*, pp. 48–53; idem, "Mahl und Spende im mittelalterlichen Totenkult," pp. 409–19. It may also be related to notions that the dead had given their inheritance to the living and had to be offered a "return-gift" in exchange: see Geary, "Échanges et relations entre les vivants et les morts," pp. 3–7.

158. Amalar of Metz, *Liber officialis*, 3: 44 (2: 386).

159. Huyghebaert, *Les Documents nécrologiques*, p. 33.

ment. Even then, it was still frequently bound in the same volume with the rule, the calendar, and the martyrology, and was often referred to as the "martyrology."[160] Like the term *liber vitae*, this term underlines the association between the departed faithful and the community of the elect in heaven.

The similarities between the early medieval cult of the dead and the cult of the saints are most obvious in the solemn anniversaries celebrated for especially important people. At Cluny, for example, when the anniversary of one of the abbots was to be celebrated, the bells were rung "for a long time." There was a procession before the office of the dead and special chants at the mass of the dead, which were performed "festively" (*festive*). Five candelabra burned on the altar throughout the service. Each member of the house also offered a mass or seven psalms on his own. Finally, there was unusually good food and wine in the refectory, and special alms for the poor.[161]

These solemn anniversaries were sometimes recorded separately in the calendar or at the beginning of the necrology.[162] They were more festive than ordinary anniversaries and, like the feasts of the saints, they sometimes stressed the special qualities of the person being honored. On the feast of a saint, selections from a *vita* or biographical legend, which recorded his or her unusual merits and miraculous powers, were normally read. In the same way, during the solemn anniversary selections from a vita of the dead person were sometimes read during the chief meal of the day in the refectory.[163] In the ninth century, for example, a vita of Abbot Sturm of Fulda was read at the monks' table during the anniversary celebrated for him and the dead brothers of the house.[164] I have as yet found no evidence for

160. Huyghebaert, *Les Documents nécrologiques*, p. 34; and see, for example, *Liber tramitis*, 2: 35 (p. 286); *Cartulaire de l'abbaye de Redon*, no. 356 (1021); *Cartulaire de la cathédrale d'Angers*, no. 66 (1096).

161. Bernard of Cluny, *Ordo Cluniacensis*, 1: 25, in *Vetus disciplina monastica*, pp. 199–200; Ulric of Cluny, *Consuetudines Cluniacenses*, 3: 32 (PL 149: 776).

162. *Liber tramitis*, 2: 35 (p. 286). Elsewhere, solemn anniversaries were recorded in the necrology, but distinguished by rubrics. See, for example, the early twelfth-century necrology of Saint-Jean-en-Vallée of Chartres, Paris, BN, Latin 991.

163. On the significance of the annual meal and its relationship with almsgiving to the poor, see Oexle, "Der Gegenwart der Toten," in Braet and Verbeke, *Death in the Middle Ages*, pp. 48–53; idem, "Mahl und Spende im mittelalterlichen Totenkult," 409–19; and see below, Chapter 4.

164. Candidus of Fulda, *Vita Eigilis abbatis Fuldensis*, 22, ed. Georg Waitz, MGH, SS, 15, p. 232. On this life and its relation to the commemoration of the dead at Fulda, see Oexle, "Die Gegenwart der Toten," in Braet and Verbeke, *Death in the Middle Ages*, pp. 28–29.

this practice during the tenth and eleventh centuries, but in the early twelfth century the monks of Pontoise read from a vita of their great benefactor, the lady Hildeburge, during the festive meal held on her anniversary.[165] Suger likewise composed his famous *Life of Louis VI* for use during the celebration of the king's anniversary at Saint-Denis.[166] It seems possible, then, that the use of vitae during anniversary celebrations was, if not the rule, at least known in the tenth and eleventh centuries.

This practice suggests, however, that the person whose anniversary was celebrated festively was remembered as someone of special virtue and even miraculous powers. The vita of Hildeburge, for example, ended with a reference to her miracles.[167] The solemn anniversary may sometimes have been the first step in the generally informal early medieval canonization process.[168] Sturm of Fulda, whose anniversary was originally celebrated in conjunction with a feast for all the dead brothers of the house, was later commemorated as a saint. It is also significant that all the early leaders of Cluny—where very elaborate anniversary services were customarily performed for dead abbots—eventually came to be regarded as saints. The solemn anniversary, with its many festive features, could easily have been transformed into a feast.

Early medieval churches went to elaborate lengths to ensure that each person who had a right to commemoration in the liturgy would actually be included in their lists of names.[169] Monastic records indicate that when a monk died, his name was immediately recorded in the necrology of his own house, and a notice of his death was sent out by special messenger to other houses.[170] This notice or *breve* was sometimes inscribed at the top of a long roll of parchment. When the messenger came to a church he gave the roll to the scribes there, who recorded the name of their community, the date of the messenger's

165. *Cartulaire de l'abbaye de Saint-Martin de Pontoise*, ed. Joseph Depoin (Pontoise, 1895–1909), no. 56 (no date), and see p. 231.
166. *Chronicon Morigniacensis*, 3, ed. Léon Mirot (Paris, 1912), p. 69. And see Suger, *Vita Ludovici grossi regis*, ed. Henri Waquet (Paris, 1929).
167. *Cartulaire de l'abbaye de Saint-Martin de Pontoise*, no. 56 (no date).
168. On the spontaneous creation of local saints' cults in the early middle ages, see Eric Waldram Kemp, *Canonization and Authority in the Western Church* (London, 1948), pp. 24–55; André Vauchez, *La Sainteté en Occident aux derniers siècles du moyen âge d'après les procès de canonisation et les documents hagiographiques* (Rome, 1981), pp. 15–26.
169. Oexle, "Memoria und Memorialüberlieferung," p. 78.
170. *Liber tramitis*, 2: 35 (pp. 286–87); Ulric of Cluny, *Consuetudines Cluniacenses*, 3: 33 (PL 149: 777).

arrival, and the names of their own dead. If they had an agreement of confraternity with the house which had sent out the notice, they would inscribe the name of the monk who had just died on their own liber memorialis or necrology for continuing commemoration.[171] These "mortuary rolls," full of the names of churches and of individuals who had died, along with pious verses on the meaning of death and the importance of mutual charity, bear witness to the early medieval liturgical community's determination to commemorate by name each individual who was entitled to participate in its prayers.

That determination is also evidenced in the libri memoriales and necrologies themselves. The famous liber memorialis of Reichenau, compiled around 825, was made up of lists of the living and dead members of dozens of associated monasteries and secular churches, as well as many individual confratres and consorores. In all, the book contains some 40,000 names of men and women who were to be commemorated in the prayers of the monks of Reichenau.[172] An equally staggering number of names appear, arranged in calendar form, in the surviving necrologies of Cluniac houses. While the necrology of Cluny itself has not survived, a computer-assisted comparison of the name-lists from communities dependent on Cluny has demonstrated that the Cluniacs did indeed exchange among themselves the names of all their dead monks and nuns, and perhaps the names of some lay confratres and consorores as well. Thus, these lists are monuments not just to the members of individual houses, but to the entire *Cluniacensis ecclesia*.[173]

The liber memorialis and the necrology were the two types of name-list most commonly used in the liturgy during the early middle ages. However, the names of the dead were recorded in many other

171. *Rouleaux des morts du IXe au XVe siècle*, ed. Léopold Delisle (Paris, 1866); E. Junyent, "Le Rouleau funéraire d'Oliba, abbé de Notre-Dame de Ripoll et de Saint-Michel de Cuixa, évêque de Vich," *Annales du Midi* 63 (1951), 249–63; L. Kern, "Sur les rouleaux des morts," *Études suisses d'histoire générale* 14 (1956), 139–47; Huyghebaert, *Les Documents nécrologiques*, pp. 26–29.

172. Schmid and Wollasch, "Die Gemeinschaft der Lebenden und Verstorbenen," pp. 373–76; and see Schmid, "Bemerkungen zur Anlage des Reichenauer Verbrüderungsbuches," in his *Gebetgedenken und adliges Selbstverständnis*, pp. 514–31.

173. *Synopse der cluniacensischen Necrologien*. In the eleventh century Ulric of Cluny claimed that confratres were commemorated at all the houses of the order: *Consuetudines Cluniacenses*, 3: 33 (PL 149: 777–78). However, Wollasch has recently argued, using the evidence of the necrologies, that lay familiares were only commemorated at their local Cluniac house: "Les Moines et la mémoire des morts," in Iogna-Prat and Picard, *Religion et culture autour de l'an mil*, p. 51.

ways during this period.[174] There were a variety of "official" name-lists, maintained by communities for use in their liturgies.[175] There were lists kept by individuals, which expressed their own special concerns. In the eleventh century, for example, Bishop Hugh of Besançon had a list of the bishops of his see—himself included—copied in the margin of his sacramentary, next to the *Memento* of the dead. Presumably Hugh wanted the bishops of Besançon to be commemorated in the mass, even though this was not yet the custom of the city.[176] Finally, there were lists, or one might better say "agglomerations" of names, created when individual women and men scribbled their own names in the margins of a liturgical book or even on the altar itself.[177]

In his remarkable study of commemoration in the early middle ages, Otto Gerhard Oexle discusses the significance of names in pre-modern cultures.[178] He points out that names were far more than just external referents; they were understood as an intrinsic part of the person to whom they referred. When someone was named, they were brought into the presence of the namer. In the early middle ages, Oexle argues, the absent and the departed faithful were made present among the living in the liturgy through the recording and ritual use of their names. Such commemoration was both an expression of and a means to religious community, for by naming its members within the round of collective prayer, the liturgical community constituted and reconstituted itself over time.[179]

The close connection between commemoration and community envisioned by Oexle is clearly reflected in a practice initiated at the Norman monastery of Saint-Évroul in the second half of the eleventh

174. Oexle, "Die Gegenwart der Toten," in Braet and Verbeke, *Death in the Middle Ages*, pp. 31–48.

175. At the east Frankish monastery of Fulda, the names of the dead were listed next to the year of death in what have come to be called "necrological annals." This type of list is not found in the west Frankish realm: Oexle, "Memorialüberlieferung und Gebetsgedächtnis in Fulda," in Schmid, *Die Klostergemeinschaft von Fulda*, 1: 136–37.

176. Picard, *Le Souvenir des évêques*, p. 529; the commemoration of bishops in the mass during the early middle ages is discussed on pp. 525–35.

177. Ebner, *Die klösterlichen Gebets-Verbrüderungen*, pp. 106–14; Oexle, "Die Gegenwart der Toten," in Braet and Verbeke, *Death in the Middle Ages*, pp. 46–47. See, for example, the sacramentary of Notre Dame of Paris, BN, Latin 2294, which has names in the margins of the canon, fols. 2v–4v, next to the *apologiae* on fol. 6r, and apparently in a list of those who contributed to the construction of the cathedral on fol. 7v.

178. This part of Oexle's article draws on the work of Rupert Berger, *Die Wendung "offerre pro" in der römischen Liturgie* (Münster, 1964), pp. 228–33.

179. Oexle, "Memoria und Memorialüberlieferung," especially pp. 79–86.

century. When someone became a monk at Saint-Évroul, his name
was inscribed on a long parchment roll, along with the names of his
mother, father, sisters, and brothers. The roll was kept on the altar all
year long, and those inscribed on it were commemorated at mass
when the priest prayed: "Deign to join the souls of your servants and
handmaidens, whose names appear here in writing before your holy
altar, to the company of your chosen ones."

On June 26, however, a special anniversary was held for the parents and siblings of the monks. All the bells were rung for a long time
in the evening and the morning before the hours of the dead; the roll
was then untied and laid out on the altar, and prayers were offered
first for the dead, then for the living relatives of the monks, and for
their benefactors, and all the departed faithful. The morning mass
was performed solemnly (*celebriter*) by the abbot. The almoner assembled as many poor people as there were monks, and fed them each
bread and drink and a main course in the guest house; after chapter
the whole convent washed the feet of the poor, as they did on Maun-
dy Thursday.[180]

The use of the roll of names at Saint-Évroul is especially interesting, because it seems to combine the features of the two main forms
of name-list: the liber memorialis and the necrology. Like the liber
memorialis, it was used in the mass every day to make the living and
the dead present among the group gathered around the altar—and
hopefully among the chosen ones. But, like the necrology, it was also
used for a special anniversary service—in this case a general anniversary for all the monks' relatives held on June 26. It is significant that
the name-list, which was usually kept rolled up, was opened and laid
out on the altar once a year. Even if the names were not actually read
from the list, the fact that it was unrolled must have made the dead
seem present in an especially concrete way on June 26. In this peculiar
local practice, then, we may find a further clue to the growing popularity of the necrology in eleventh-century religious houses. It had
long been impossible to read all the many names recorded in a liber
memorialis during mass. But it was possible to read a few names
from a necrology once a year, and to keep those names in one's
mouth and mind during the services of that day. The liber memorialis
represented the community that prayed in a distant and almost abstract way. But with the introduction of the necrology, the former

180. Orderic Vitalis, *Historia aecclesiastica*, 3 (2: 114).

members of the community once again became a living presence among those who served God and the saints.[181]

The point of all these lists, then, was not simply to preserve the names of certain individuals; it was, rather, to record them *among* other names. For as we have seen, early medieval rituals for the dead were essentially associative in character. That is, they were designed to express the relationship between the dead and the community within which salvation was to be found: the societas orationum. Themes of spiritual relationship structured nonfunerary prayer for the dead as well as funerary ritual in the early middle ages; ecclesiological symbolism played a prominent role in both "collective" and more "individualized" services, for it was within the context of their horizontal relationships with the community of the faithful that early medieval Christians understood their vertical relationship with God. The treatment of the body, before and after burial, could associate someone with a particular religious house. However, the best way to recognize someone's continuing presence in the liturgical community was to record his or her name in its register, and use that name in its prayers.

181. See Oexle, "Memoria und Memorialüberlieferung," p. 85.

3 THE LAITY AND THE
LITURGICAL COMMUNITY

It is easy to see why the early medieval clergy focused so sharply on the ecclesiological symbolism of rituals for the dead. They structured and then interpreted those rituals in terms of spiritual relationships which reflected very clearly the dominant social relationship in their lives—their membership in the liturgical community. It is less clear whether the early medieval laity shared this awareness of the ecclesiological symbolism in prayer for the dead. Unlike the earliest Christian layfolk, they did not participate actively in the activities of the liturgical community. One might reasonably assume, then, that the themes of spiritual relationship those activities presented would have been less obvious to them than they were to the clergy.

Nevertheless, there are indications that the laity shared the clergy's preference for associative forms of prayer for the dead, for services which emphasized the dead person's relationship with the community that prayed and hence with the community of the elect. Of course very little direct information about the lay understanding of the liturgy is available, since few members of the laity could read and write. However, we do have information from narrative and diplomatic sources about the kinds of lay behavior that resulted in commemoration after death in the period from the mid-eighth century to the end of the eleventh century. If we assume that actions which resulted in prayer were informed—at least to some extent—by the actors' ideas about prayer, we can use information about what the laity did as a guide to what they thought about the liturgy.

If it is to be interpreted correctly, however, this behavior must be seen within its social as well as its spiritual context. The relationship of the laity to the liturgical community underwent a series of important changes from late antiquity on, in response to a variety of political and economic as well as religious factors. The fourth through the eighth centuries were a time of increasingly tenuous liturgical loyalties. In the Carolingian period, partly through the initiative of the Carolingian rulers themselves, the bonds that linked the laity to the communities that prayed became tighter again. This process continued through the eleventh century. However, it affected different segments of the early medieval population in different ways. The dealings of the poor and powerless with the clergy were determined to a large extent by forces beyond their control. As a result, their behavior cannot be taken as a reliable guide to their understanding of prayer for the dead. On the other hand, because members of the elite formed largely voluntary relationships with the communities that prayed, their behavior is a much more useful indicator of their attitudes.

THE CLERICALIZATION OF THE LITURGY IN LATE ANTIQUITY

The earliest Christian laity, whether poor or powerful, certainly had relationships with the liturgical community very different from those of their successors in the early middle ages. As we have seen, during the first three centuries of the present era Christians commemorated the dead, as they prayed for the living, collectively. Both laity and clergy had essential roles to play when the faithful assembled to celebrate a funeral or remember the martyrs. As the close-knit liturgical community of the second and third centuries began to unravel from the fourth century on, however, the clergy gradually emerged as the primary intercessors for the rest of the faithful in life and after death.

A variety of factors contributed to this development. Attitudinal changes certainly played some role. There is considerable, though sometimes ambiguous, evidence that by the third century men and women were already becoming more aware of the disjunction between a troubled and transient world and the eternal realities of heaven, and that traditional religious practices were beginning to seem inadequate to bridge the gap.[1] Christian writings of the fourth and fifth centuries show a new and keen awareness of the sin to be found within the church and a loss of confidence in the spiritual status of all—or even most—Christians.

Membership in the church, as evidenced by baptism and participation in the liturgy, no longer seemed such a strong guarantee of salvation as it had in the past. Something more was needed. Hence the growing attraction of the ascetic life, which lay behind the development of monasticism, first in the deserts of Egypt and Syria, then in Europe as well.[2] Hence, too, the growing desire for intercessors, for friends and patrons with "good connections" in the other world, which gave rise to the cult of the saints, as Peter Brown has brilliantly demonstrated.[3]

But the "new mood" of this period may also help to explain the laity's increased reliance on earthly, clerical intercessors, who—in large part because they had separated themselves from the everyday world—were perceived as somehow closer to heaven than the average believer. In the first centuries of the church, bishops and priests had lived lives very similar to those of other Christians. However, that situation began to change in the fourth and fifth centuries. The Peace of the Church, the growing number of conversions, and the resulting financial gains made it possible—and, indeed, necessary—for clerics to devote all their time to their ecclesiastical obligations. The priesthood was becoming a profession.[4] This made it possible for the clergy to expand and elaborate the liturgy over the course of the next few centuries.

It was the ascetic movement, however, which gave the clerical profession its special character. Bishops urged their clergy to maintain chastity, to hold property in common, and to devote more time to prayer and meditation, in imitation of (and sometimes in conjunction with) the ascetics.[5] Soon church councils began to insist that

1. Peter Brown, _The World of Late Antiquity, A. D. 150–750_ (New York, 1971), pp. 49–57, 96–112; E. R. Dodds, _Pagan and Christian in an Age of Anxiety: Some Aspects of Religious Experience from Marcus Aurelius to Constantine_ (Cambridge, 1965), especially pp. 1–36.

2. Rudolf Lorenz, "Die Anfänge des abendländischen Mönchtums im 4. Jahrhundert," _Zeitschrift für Kirchengeschichte_ 77 (1966), 1–61; Derwas Chitty, _The Desert a City: An Introduction to the Study of Egyptian and Palestinian Monasticism under the Christian Empire_ (Oxford, 1966).

3. Brown, _The Cult of the Saints_, pp. 50–68.

4. Dix, "The Ministry in the Early Church," in Kirk, _The Apostolic Ministry_, pp. 284–85.

5. Peter Brown has sketched the influence of asceticism on the Christian congrega-

those who administered the sacraments must be "pure."[6] Thus a stricter standard of morality was established for the clergy than for the lay members of the ecclesia. Obviously, not every priest or bishop conformed to this standard, but its very existence gave the clergy as a group greater prestige and increased their credibility as intercessors. These tendencies in late antique Christianity were exaggerated still further in the early middle ages. The newly converted peoples of northern Europe often attributed magical powers to the Christian clergy, making them seem mysterious and powerful, essentially different from the rest of the faithful.[7]

By the same token, ordinary Christians, who continued to live what was now defined as a "worldly" life, lost status vis-à-vis the clergy in late antiquity. The laity came to be perceived, and apparently to perceive themselves, as unworthy to participate fully in the liturgy. As a result they began to withdraw from their hitherto active roles in the collective worship of the church. Frequency of communion declined steadily from the fourth century on, until, in the eighth century, church leaders had to insist that the faithful communicate at least three times a year.[8] As communion became less frequent, so too did the liturgical act of offering. The procession of lay *offerentes*, which had been such a central feature of the early liturgy, was gradually replaced by the clerical offertory. The laity now brought their gifts to the church before the service; they did not usually present them during mass.[9] In addition, the "universal prayer"—the intercessory prayer performed by the whole Christian community for those with special needs—was suppressed, surviving only in the liturgy of Holy Week.[10] From this point on, the clergy would serve as intercessors for the rest of the faithful.

---

tions of the late fourth century in *Augustine of Hippo: A Biography* (Berkeley and Los Angeles, 1967), pp. 198, 249.

6. Arnold Angenendt, "Die Liturgie und die Organisation des kirchlichen Lebens auf dem Lande," in *Cristianizzazione ed organizzazione ecclesiastica delle campagne nell'alto medioevo: espansione e resistenze*, 2 vols. (Spoleto, 1982), 1: 192–99. On the movement for clerical celibacy, see Roger Gryson, *Les Origines du célibat ecclésiastique du premier au septième siècle* (Gembloux, 1970).

7. E.g., Bede, *Historia ecclesiastica gentis anglorum*, 2: 5, ed. and trans. Bertram Colgrave and R. A. B. Mynors (Oxford, 1969), p. 152.

8. Dix, *The Shape of the Liturgy*, p. 18. On lay communion in the eighth century, see Jean Chélini, "La Pratique dominicale des läics dans l'église franque sous le règne de Pepin," *Revue d'histoire de l'église de France* 42 (1956), 161–74.

9. Dix, *The Shape of the Liturgy*, pp. 436–37. On lay offerings outside of mass, see Lesne, *Histoire de la propriété ecclésiastique*, 1: 178–81.

10. Gy, "La Signification pastorale des prières du prône," pp. 127–29; de Clerck, *La "Prière universelle,"* p. 298.

Ordinary Christians came to be separated from the clerics who prayed for them in space as well as in action. By the sixth century, if not earlier, laymen were forbidden to stand with the clergy in the sanctuary during vigils or masses.[11] The relationship of women to sacred spaces was even more ambiguous.[12] By the eighth century, the priest celebrating mass whispered the "secret" prayer of consecration to himself; by about the year 1000 he faced away from the congregation while doing so.[13] The laity were expected to observe from a discreet distance what were now essentially clerical mysteries.

The ideal of collective prayer by all of the faithful was never completely lost in the early middle ages. In northern Europe in the tenth and eleventh centuries, as we have seen, the laity were expected to pray for the living and the dead during the bidding prayers of the Sunday mass. Moreover, those members of the lay elite who could read sometimes joined in the prayers of the office. In the ninth century, Dhuoda urged her son to pray for his dead godfather in this context: "Pray often for his sins, above all in the company of many others during nocturns, matins, vespers and the other hours, at all hours and in all places, in case he has committed some injustice and not done penance for it in eternity. As much as possible, [pray] most often with those who are very good; as much as you can, through the prayers of holy priests. And, by giving alms to the poor, have the sacrifice [of the mass] offered frequently for him to the Lord."[14]

While Dhuoda urges her son to participate in the office, she also makes it clear that the prayers of the "very good" and those of "holy priests" are especially valuable. The laity can and should pray for the dead, but the clergy are still the most important intercessors in her eyes.

11. Council of Tours (567), c. 4, in *Concilia Galliae A. 511-A. 695*, p. 178.

12. Suzanne Fonay Wemple, *Women in Frankish Society: Marriage and the Cloister, 500 to 900* (Philadelphia, 1981), pp. 142–43.

13. Jungmann, *The Mass of the Roman Rite*, 2: 90–93; Klauser, *A Short History of the Western Liturgy*, pp. 98–101.

14. Dhuoda, *Liber manualis*, 8: 15, ed. Pierre Riché, trans. (into French) by B. de Vregille and C. Mondésert (Paris, 1975), p. 322. "Pluriora enim et speciali cum plurimis in nocturnis, matutinis, vespertinis, caeterisque oris, per orarum tempora et spatia locorum, pro eius delictis, si aliquid iniuste egit, et non aeterno poenituit, in quantum vales, cum valde bonis pluraliter, in quantum potes, per orationes sanctorum sacerdotum, et elemosinas in pauperibus erogando, Domino sacrificium pro eo offerre iubeas frequenter." The text in this passage is clearly corrupt; I have followed Riché (p. 323, n. 2) in interpreting "pluriora" as "pluri[es] ora."

THE DISPERSION OF LITURGICAL LOYALTIES
IN LATE ANTIQUITY

The increasingly attenuated relationship between the laity and the
liturgical community in the fourth to eighth centuries was a result not
only of the clericalization of the liturgy, but also of the rapid growth
of the church in this period. In the second and third centuries there
had generally been only one gathering of the Christian community in
each city, which all the baptized frequented. But with the acceptance
of Christianity as the official religion of the Empire and, later, of the
Frankish kings, the number of believers within each ecclesia grew
larger, and so, too, did the number of places where the liturgy was
celebrated. Basilicas built over the tombs of the martyrs in suburban
cemeteries attracted growing crowds not only on the feasts of the
saints but on a regular basis.[15] More churches were being built within
the city walls as well to accommodate the faithful.[16] There was still a
mother church for each urban center, over which the bishop presided,
and which retained its liturgical primacy. In principle, the whole
body of the faithful was supposed to assemble there on Sundays and
feasts.[17] However, the multiplication of cult sites in and around the
city now made it possible for urban Christians to choose where they
would pray to the saints and give alms, where they would attend the
eucharistic celebration and—on occasion—make their offerings and
take communion.

If this was the case in the older urban areas of Gaul, where the
tradition of unified community worship was deep-rooted, the situation was even more complex in the countryside, where Gallo-Roman
(and later Frankish) paganism was only slowly giving way to Christianity. It was only in the late fourth century, when most city-dwellers
had been converted to Christianity, that the leaders of the church
began sending out missionaries to preach the Gospel to the rural
population and destroy or reconsecrate the ancient shrines. This process moved more quickly in the south and west of Gaul, where Christianity had long been established in the cities, than in the north and

15. Paul-Albert Février et al., *La Ville antique des origines au IXe siècle* (Paris, 1980),
pp. 434–40; Jungmann, *The Early Liturgy*, pp. 186–87.
16. See, for example, Pietri, *La Ville de Tours*, pp. 355–63.
17. Michel Aubrun, *La Paroisse en France, des origines au XVe siècle* (Paris, 1986),
pp. 11–12. The cathedral church retained its ritual primacy in the towns until the eleventh
or twelfth century: Jean-François Lemarignier, Jean Gaudemet and Guillaume Mollat, *Institutions ecclésiastiques* (Paris, 1962), p. 198.

east, where newly established bishops were just beginning to organize religious life between the fourth and sixth centuries.[18] But even in the south it would be centuries before the new religion would have a firm institutional basis in the countryside. In the meantime, the relationship between the barely christianized rural population and the liturgical community was often very tenuous indeed.

As part of their efforts to evangelize the countryside, bishops built churches along major roads, near military encampments, in the market towns, wherever there was a sizable population to be served. Some landowners assisted in these efforts by establishing oratories on their estates.[19] In some of the new extra-urban churches, especially those located in the larger settlements, the liturgy was performed regularly by a group of clerks drawn from the clergy of the mother church in the city. The most important of these churches acquired their own baptisteries, and became the centers of a new ecclesiastical unit, the large rural parish, just as the cathedral church was the center of what we would call the diocese. But the liturgy performed in these "baptismal churches" was still not wholly independent of the cathedral liturgy. The clergy were expected to return to the mother church in the city from time to time to take part in services there. They were not permitted to perform certain functions, such as reconciling penitents, except in emergencies.[20] The smaller rural churches, simple oratories without baptisteries, enjoyed even less independence. The clergy assigned to these churches were at first not permitted to offer mass on Sundays and feasts, but only during the week.[21]

Thus, while the inhabitants of the country estates might be able to attend daily services at a nearby oratory, they were supposed to travel to the city or at least to the nearest baptismal church for Sunday mass and feast-days. This was clearly not possible for everyone, but the clergy assembled at Clermont in 535 insisted that citizens who be-

18. Charles Pietri, "Remarques sur la christianisation du nord de la Gaule (IVe-VIe siècles)," *Revue du Nord* 66 (1984), 55–68; Paul Fouracre, "The Work of Audoenus of Rouen and Eligius of Noyon in Extending Episcopal Influence from the Town to the Country in Seventh-Century Neustria," in Derek Baker, ed., *The Church in Town and Countryside* (Oxford, 1979), pp. 77–91.

19. Aubrun, *La Paroisse en France*, pp. 13–22. On the placement of the earliest rural churches, see Gabriel Fournier, "La Mise en place du cadre paroissial et l'évolution du peuplement," in *Cristianizzazione ed organizzazione ecclesiastica*, 1: 498–502.

20. E. Griffe, "Les Paroisses rurales de la Gaule," *La Maison-Dieu* 36 (1953), 48–49.

21. Council of Agde (506), c. 21, in *Concilia Galliae, A. 314-A. 506*, ed. C. Munier (Turnhout, 1963), pp. 202–3; Council of Clermont-en-Auvergne (535), c. 15, in *Concilia Galliae, A. 511-A. 695*, p. 109. See also Griffe, "Les Paroisses rurales," pp. 52–53.

longed to important families (*cives natu maiores*) be present in the urban church on the major feasts, on pain of excommunication.[22] The men and women who lived in the more important rural settlements could attend most services locally, but they might still have to travel to the nearest city to be reconciled with the church if they had fallen into sin. The situation was further complicated by the presence in the countryside of a growing number of monastic churches, which theoretically existed only for the benefit of the monks or nuns, but which sometimes offered services for the laity as well.[23] This is a somewhat simplified picture of the situation that existed in rural Gaul between the fourth and eighth centuries, but it offers some idea of the confusion of liturgical loyalties that was possible in this period.

This confusion was reflected in the treatment of the dead. In general, members of the small Christian communities of the first few centuries had tried to have themselves buried together, either in some section of the public cemeteries or in private burial plots that belonged to families of wealthy Christians. As a persecuted sect, however, they could not always manage to bury their dead as they wanted. The state sometimes left the bodies of those executed as Christians unburied, or had them dismembered or burned.[24] The cemeteries themselves were not always accessible. Under Valerian and Diocletian, some were apparently confiscated by the state.[25] So while burial with other Christians may have been thought desirable in the first few centuries, it was certainly not obligatory or even always possible.

With the end of the persecutions in the fourth century, Christian communities began to acquire burial grounds of their own, which were administered by the clergy or by appointed guardians.[26] These were located in the suburbs, in keeping with the ancient prohibitions

22. Council of Clermont-en-Auvergne (535), c. 15, in *Concilia Galliae, A. 511-A. 695,* p. 109.

23. Concilium incerti loci (after 614), c. 6, in *Concilia Galliae A. 511-A. 695,* p. 287; Giles Constable, "Monasteries, Rural Churches, and the *Cura Animarum* in the Early Middle Ages," in *Cristianizzazione ed organizzazione ecclesiastica,* 1: 354–58.

24. *The Letter of the Churches of Lyons and Vienne,* in *The Acts of the Christian Martyrs,* ed. Herbert Musurillo (Oxford, 1972), pp. 80–83; Augustine, *De cura pro mortuis gerenda,* 6 (pp. 633–34).

25. Henri Leclercq, "Cimetière," *DACL* 3: 1, col. 1637.

26. Leclercq, "Cimetière," cols. 1658–65. At Angers a new cemetery seems to have been established for Christians in the fourth century: Michel Provost, *Angers gallo-romain* (Angers, 1978), pp. 152–53. See also Council of Paris (556–73), c. 9, in *Concilia Galliae, A. 511-A. 695,* p. 209.

against the burial of corpses within the boundaries of a settlement.[27] Between the sixth and eighth centuries, cemeteries began to be established within settlements as well.[28] At about the same time, some of the more important rural churches established burial grounds for the faithful in their parishes.[29] Many monastic communities also laid out cemeteries for their members.[30]

It would be a mistake to assume, though, that because the Christian communities now had their own burial grounds, the members of those communities were always buried together. Church law did not yet dictate where the faithful would "normally" be buried; it was possible to chose among various, equally "Christian," burial sites. Urban Christians might be interred near the tomb of a saint in an old suburban necropolis, in one of the new cemeteries administered by the church, or inside an urban basilica.[31] By the same token, families might arrange for offerings to be made on behalf of their dead at any church, although it seems likely that their first choice was the burial church or the church where the person had attended services in life.[32] Moreover, religion was not the only factor that determined an individual's choice of burial site. Family and civic tradition might play a role as well. Some city-dwellers continued to be buried in their family burial grounds—or even in the ancient public cemeteries. In the fifth and sixth centuries, Christians as well as pagans were still being buried in the necropolis of Aliscamps, near Arles.[33]

In the countryside, a distinctive new pattern of burial began to appear between the fourth and sixth centuries. In some places, we

27. Aimé-Georges Martimort, "La Fidélité des premiers chrétiens aux usages romains en matière de sépulture," *Société toulousaine d'études classiques, Mélanges,* 1 (1946), 178–80; that this rule was still remembered in the sixth century is clear from the *Vita Vedastis episcopi Atrebatensis,* 9, ed. Bruno Krusch, MGH, SRM, 3: 412–13.

28. Edouard Salin, *La Civilisation mérovingienne d'après les sépultures, les textes, et le laboratoire,* 4 vols. (Paris, 1949–59), 2: 33–36; Gabriel Fournier, *Le Peuplement rural en basse Auvergne durant le haut moyen âge* (Paris, 1962), pp. 421–22.

29. Michel Aubrun, *Le Ancien Diocèse de Limoges des origines au milieu du XIe siècle* (Clermont-Ferrand, 1981), pp. 297–98; Fournier, *Le Peuplement rural en basse Auvergne,* pp. 415–23.

30. *Concilium incerti loci* (after 614), c. 6, in *Concilia Galliae, A. 511-A. 695,* p. 287; Gregory of Tours, *Historia Francorum,* 9: 42 (PL 71: 524); *Visio Baronti monachi Longoretensis,* 18, ed. Bruno Krusch and Wilhelm Levison, MGH, SRM, 5: 392.

31. Salin, *La Civilisation mérovingienne,* 2: especially 23–36, 42–51.

32. See the texts cited by Lesne, *Histoire de la propriété ecclésiastique,* 1: 180–83.

33. Henri Leclercq, "Aliscamps," DACL 1: 1, cols. 1211–18; Fernand Benoît, *Les Cimetières suburbains d'Arles dans l'antiquité chrétienne et au moyen âge* (Rome, 1935), pp. 62–72.

find existing cemeteries in which the newest graves are lined up in rows, with their orientation dictated by a dominant tomb or tombs. In other places, especially in the northeastern parts of Gaul, entirely new cemeteries appear, in which the graves are aligned in the same way. Many of these "row grave" cemeteries were eventually taken over by the church and transformed into parish cemeteries, but they seem to have originally reflected political, rather than religious affiliation.[34] The dominant tombs in the earliest of these cemeteries were those of Frankish chieftains, the leaders of bands of Germanic auxiliaries invited into the empire to protect its borders. The graves aligned with these "dominant" tombs belonged to the auxiliaries themselves, the members of the chieftains' retinues. As the Frankish chieftains gained political ascendancy in Gaul in the fifth and sixth centuries, many members of the indigenous population also came to be buried in the graves aligned in the same way.[35]

It used to be thought that the graves of pagans could be distinguished from those of Christians by the presence of grave goods. Since many of the burials in row grave cemeteries were associated with grave goods, it was assumed that the cemeteries themselves were pagan, and that Christians would have been buried elsewhere. Scholars now agree, however, that rich grave furnishings were associated not so much with paganism as with the culture of Frankish warriors in the migration period, when a display of newly acquired wealth promoted a warrior's prestige.[36] The church did not object to the practice of burying personal items of wealth with the dead. Consequently, burials that include grave goods may be Christian. Indeed, as late as the seventh and even the eighth century in some places, Christian warriors and their wives continued to be buried with fine weapons and rich jewelry.[37] The final abandonment of this practice seems to reflect not christianization per se, but the growing influence of monasticism, with its emphasis on simplicity and humility, on the Frankish nobility.[38]

34. On changing interpretations of the row grave cemeteries, and the problems presented by the term itself, see Laure-Charlotte Feffer and Patrick Périn, *Les Francs: A l'origine de la France* (Paris, 1987), pp. 133–36.
35. Feffer and Périn, *Les Francs*, pp. 136–38, 182–86.
36. Bailey Young, "Exemple aristocratique et mode funéraire dans la Gaule mérovingienne," *Annales: Economies, sociétés, civilisations* 41 (1986), 382.
37. Salin, *La Civilisation mérovingienne*, 2: 223–67; Bailey Young, "Paganisme, christianisation, et rites funéraires mérovingiens," *Archéologie médiévale* 7 (1977), 5–81.
38. This is suggested by the case of Gertrude of Nivelles presented in Young, "Exemple aristocratique et mode funéraire," pp. 379–81, 401.

Nevertheless, christianization did affect the burial practices of the Frankish nobility in significant ways. In the early sixth century, the Frankish kings and nobles began to seek burial ad sanctos, near the tombs of the saints. Presumably they were imitating in this the practices of the Gallo-Roman aristocracy.[39] However, the members of the new ruling dynasty shaped the practice in their own way. They began building new and sumptuous churches over the tombs of the saints, within which they, their families, and their retinues would be buried.[40] Often these royal foundations were served by monastic communities which were given the responsibility for performing the *laus perennis* in honor of the saints and in memory of the founder.[41]

Soon members of the nobility were establishing their own burial churches. The remaining Gallo-Roman aristocrats, who increasingly conducted their religious as well as their social life in the countryside, rather than in the decaying cities, built churches on their estates. (Presumably, these were the *cives natu maiores* about whom the Council of Clermont complained.) By the late sixth century, Frankish magnates were following their lead.[42] Sometimes the burial churches of the nobility were located in villages, and served as the nuclei around which the graves of the poorer members of rural society clustered.[43] In the seventh century, however, a growing number of nobles established monasteries, to serve as homes for some family members, and as burial churches. Often these "family monasteries" were lavishly endowed with property and hallowed by carefully acquired relic collections to increase the prestige of their patrons.[44] However, it was only among the wealthiest members of lay society that we find such close ties with a particular religious community. In death as in life, the vast majority of the laity had only loose ties to the clergy and their prayers in the period from the fourth to the eighth century.

39. Young, "Exemple aristocratique et mode funéraire," pp. 390–92.
40. Young, "Exemple aristocratique et mode funéraire," pp. 386–90.
41. On the burial churches of the Frankish and Burgundian royal families, see Karl H. Krüger, *Königsgrabkirchen der Franken, Angelsachsen, und Langobarden bis zur Mitte des 8. Jahrhunderts: Ein historischer Katalog* (Munich, 1971), pp. 30–250.
42. Young, "Exemple aristocratique et mode funéraire," p. 390; Feffer and Périn, *Les Francs*, pp. 63–71.
43. See the discussion of the cemetery at Hordain in Feffer and Périn, *Les Francs*, p. 174.
44. Friedrich Prinz, *Frühes Mönchtum im Frankenreich: Kultur und Gesellschaft in Gallien, den Rheinlanden, und Bayern am Beispiel der monastischen Entwicklung (4. bis 8. Jahrhundert)* (Munich, 1965), pp. 493–99; Feffer and Périn, *Les Francs*, p. 79.

HUMILES AND POTENTES

In the early middle ages the bonds tying the laity to the liturgical community grew tighter again. Even though they did not regain their active role in the liturgy, the laity entered into increasingly close relationships with those who did perform the rituals of the faith. It became easier to determine which church most Christians belonged to, where they would attend mass and make their offerings, where they would be buried and commemorated after death. Even the elite, who were often linked to more than one community, began to establish more intimate ties with the churches of their choice. This process, which began in the mid-eighth century, intensified in the tenth and eleventh centuries. By the year 1100 the bonds that linked the laity to the community that prayed were once again very strong. However, the nature of those bonds differed from one segment of the population to another.

Carolingian society was divided, de facto if not de jure, into two great classes of people. On one side stood the nobility of blood and function, wielders of great power, both political (through their exercise of public authority) and economic (through their ownership of great tracts of land). These were the *potentes*, the "powerful," increasingly identified with the military way of life, and—as Duby has put it—with the ability to eat "as much as they wished."[45] On the other side stood the *humiles*, the "weak," who lived by the labor of their hands, subject to great distress in hard times, and to the power of the potentes at all times. The great majority of the population belonged to this group. While the distinction *potens/humilis* does not by any means account for all the complexities of the early medieval class system, it is nevertheless a useful distinction for our purposes.[46] For in practice, if not in theory, the two classes developed two quite different types of relationship with the communities that prayed. Among the powers of the potentes was that of choosing where they wished to seek commemoration in the liturgy; the humiles, on the

45. Georges Duby, *Rural Economy and Country Life in the Medieval West*, trans. Cynthia Postan (Columbia, 1968), p. 35.
46. On the vocabulary of social distinction in the early middle ages see Karl Bosl, "*Potens* und *Pauper*: Begriffsgeschichtliche Studien zur gesellschaftlichen Differenzierung im frühen Mittelalter und zum 'Pauperismus' der Hochmittelalter," in his *Frühformen der Gesellschaft im mittelalterlichen Europa: Ausgewählte Beiträge zu einer Strukturanalyse der mittelalterlichen Welt* (Munich, 1964), pp. 106–34.

other hand, had a relationship with the clergy based largely, though not exclusively, on obligations imposed from above.

As the parochial system took shape in France from the mid-eighth century on, members of the lower class were tied—regardless of their own wishes in the matter—to the parish church. Rural sanctuaries multiplied greatly in this period. By 900, most of the inhabitants of the countryside had fairly easy access to a church and new churches were still being founded.[47] In the eleventh century, with the revival of towns, urban and suburban churches also became more numerous.[48] At the same time, these small churches were beginning to acquire more independence from the mother church of the diocese. Even the oratories which landowners built on their estates (the majority of the foundations in this period) began to assume the liturgical functions performed by the episcopal church and by the few large "baptismal" churches of the fourth through the eighth centuries. Many small churches had their own baptisteries and their own cemeteries by the ninth century. A body of clerks, presided over by a priest, was permanently attached to many of these churches, and was supported—at least in part—by its own patrimony. Consequently, not only weekday services, but masses for Sundays and feasts, and most of the other sacraments came to be celebrated there.[49]

The growing importance of these smaller, local churches was no accident. The leaders of Carolingian society saw the rural church as an instrument which could be used to ensure both the spiritual well-being of the populace and the *utilitas publica*.[50] Thus the kings of the late eighth and ninth centuries supported the reforming bishops in their efforts to ensure that churches would be adequately staffed and equipped to perform their functions. Among those efforts was the

47. Fournier, "La Mise en place du cadre paroissial," in *Cristianizzazione ed organizzazione ecclesiastica*, 1: 502–24; Aubrun, *La Paroisse en France*, pp. 33–36, 70–75.

48. Jean Gaudemet, "La Paroisse au moyen age: État des questions," *Revue d'histoire de l'église de France* 59 (1973), 11–15; Jean Becquet, "La Paroisse en France aux XI et XII siècles," in *Le istituzioni ecclesiastiche della 'societas christiana' dei secoli XI-XII: Diocesi, pievi, e parrocchie* (Milan, 1977), pp. 199–222; but see Fournier, "La Mise en place du cadre paroissial," in *Cristianizzazione ed organizzazione ecclesiastica*, 1: 532–34.

49. Émile Amann and Auguste Dumas, *L'Église au pouvoir des laïques (888–1057)* (Paris, 1948), pp. 265–73; Aubrun, *La Paroisse en France*, pp. 42–59. On parish cemeteries, see also Lesne, *Histoire de la propriété ecclésiastique*, 3: 124–29.

50. Rosamond McKitterick, *The Frankish Church and the Carolingian Reforms, 789–895* (London, 1977), pp. 9–10; Fournier, "La Mise en place du cadre paroissial," in *Cristianizzazione ed organizzazione ecclesiastica*, 1: 502–3; J. M. Wallace-Hadrill, *The Frankish Church* (Oxford, 1983), p. 287.

imposition of obligations on the people who lived around the church, obligations which arose from and reinforced their new status as "parishioners."

The payment of tithes, which had long been encouraged by religious leaders, was made mandatory by Pepin and Charlemagne in the second half of the eighth century. After some hesitation, it was determined that tithes were to be paid not to the episcopal church but directly to the local church, which would thus be assured of the income necessary to carry on its important work.[51] Bishops began to identify the lands which would tithe to a particular church, the basis of its parish. The people who lived on and farmed those lands became the parishioners of that church. Their produce would go to support it, and it was expected that they would benefit from its services.[52]

Over the next two centuries the weaker members of society were subjected to an increasing number of obligations, which bound them ever more tightly to the parish church. Some of these obligations—notably, the obligation to attend mass and receive the sacraments in one's own parish—were imposed by the church hierarchy, presumably for spiritual reasons. If the faithful were tied to the parish, they could receive religious instruction from a local priest who knew them well and who was responsible for their welfare. It would also be more difficult for recalcitrant sinners to neglect their assigned penance or evade a sentence of excommunication, if they were unable to turn to another church for the sacraments. Priests were thus instructed to check their congregations each week before Sunday mass, and to send any "outsiders" who were present back to their own parishes.[53]

Other "parochial" obligations, however, seem to have originated not with the church hierarchy, but with the proprietors of churches, a group which included lay landowners, as well as religious communities, bishops, and other members of the secular clergy. Many parish churches, and especially those established between the ninth and eleventh centuries, were founded by the wealthy for their dependents and

51. Paul Viard, *Histoire de la dîme ecclésiastique, principalement en France, jusqu'au Décret de Gratien* (Dijon, 1909), especially pp. 70–85.

52. Josef Semmler, "Zehntgebot und Pfarrtermination in karolingischer Zeit," in Hubert Mordek, ed., *Aus Kirche und Reich: Studien zu Theologie, Politik, und Recht im Mittelalter* (Sigmaringen, 1983), pp. 33–44.

53. *Capitula ecclesiastica* (810–13), in *Capitularia regum Francorum*, 1: 178; Regino of Prüm, *De ecclesiasticis disciplinis*, 1: 61 (PL 132: 203–4); Ivo of Chartres, *Decretum*, 2: 122 (PL 161: 194).

remained under their founders' protection and control.[54] Landowners
—both lay and clerical—may have been moved to found churches by
a pious wish to offer their people the benefits of the faith, but it soon
became clear that there were economic advantages to be reaped as
well. In theory, tithes and other parochial revenues were to be used at
the discretion of the bishop and the parish priest for the upkeep of the
church, the welfare of the poor, and other spiritual purposes. However, these revenues were diverted into seigneurial coffers with increasing frequency from the ninth century on, despite resistance from
the ecclesiastical hierarchy. The proprietor might even grant a share
in those revenues to other individuals, or to a monastery, a practice
which could lead to very complicated situations indeed for the parishioners.[55]

Clearly it was to the advantage of proprietors to increase parish
revenues as much as possible. Moreover, they had the power to ensure that their dependents paid as much as possible, and to the "right"
church. It thus seems reasonable to assume that the imposition of
some parochial obligations—notably those involving fees for specific
services, since these are particularly difficult to reconcile with church
law—resulted from seigneurial rather than from pastoral initiative.
Nor should it come as any surprise that the bishops accepted these
obligations, for they reinforced the disciplinary power of the church,
as well as increasing the revenues of churches under episcopal control. By about the year 1000 it had become very difficult for the
parishioner of one church to be baptized, shriven, or buried in another church.[56]

The growing ritual importance of the parish church in the lives of
the humiles was matched by its increasing social importance. The
parishioners who were obliged to pay tithes, attend services, and have

54. Fournier, "La Mise en place du cadre paroissial," in *Cristianizzazione ed organizzazione ecclesiastica*, 1: 502–5; Amann and Dumas, *L'Église au pouvoir des laïques*, pp. 273–
81. The importance of monasteries as proprietors of churches has recently been emphasized
by Giles Constable, "Monasteries, Rural Churches, and the *Cura Animarum*," in *Cristianizzazione ed organizzazione ecclesiastica*, 1: 366–70.

55. Viard, *Histoire de la dîme ecclésiastique*, pp. 134–39, 205–17; Amann and Dumas,
L'Église au pouvoir des laïques, pp. 285–89. Elisabeth Magnou-Nortier has argued that the
patrons of churches in the Midi disposed of ecclesiastical revenues in their role as "guardians," not as "proprietors": *La Société laïque et l'église*, p. 429. However, the effect was the
same: the diversion of revenues from the parish church to the guardian.

56. The obligatory nature of the bonds that existed between the parish church and its
parishioners was recognized by Gerbert, in a letter to the archbishop of Sens concerning the
unfair effects of an interdict: *Epistolae*, 203, ed. Jules Havet (Paris, 1889), pp. 192–94.

their children baptized at the local church gradually became associated with it in other ways. In earlier centuries ecclesiastical institutions had generally followed the population. Churches sprang up where there were large groups of people already in place—in market towns or in good-sized villages.[57] But from the ninth century on, the population began to follow the church. Patterns of settlement shifted according to the placement of ecclesiastical buildings. Villages grew up around some churches, while older settlements were even moved to bring them closer to a parish church. Some villages took the name of the church around which they were built.[58]

This development was not, of course, only the result of the parish church's growing ritual importance. In the troubles of the first feudal age, the immunities and asylum provided by ecclesiastical sites, as well as the defensive walls which had been erected around many of them, made these places increasingly attractive to the poor and powerless.[59] Some settlements actually moved into the cemeteries of churches in this period; houses were built and markets held among the graves.[60] Thus the rural community was becoming physically more closely identified with its parish church between the eighth and eleventh centuries, and this contributed to the strength of the bonds uniting the individual members of the community to the parish clergy and their liturgy.

Those bonds remained powerful even after death, for most members of the lower class were buried in the parish cemetery and prayed for by the parish clergy throughout this period. In part, this was a matter of convenience: the parish was generally the most accessible source of prayer for the dead. But by the late tenth century, if not before, obligation as well as convenience determined the humilis's final resting place. It should be noted here that the law of the church granted all Christians the right to choose where they wished to be

57. Fournier, "La Mise en place du cadre paroissial," in *Cristianizzazione ed organizzazione ecclesiastica*, 1: 498–99.

58. Fournier, *Le Peuplement rural en basse Auvergne*, pp. 448–53; Fournier, "La Mise en place du cadre paroissial," in *Cristianizzazione ed organizzazione ecclesiastica*, 1: 503–24.

59. Fournier, *Le Peuplement rural en basse Auvergne*, pp. 454–57; Lucien Musset, "'Cimiterium ad refugium tantum vivorum non ad sepulturam mortuorum'," *Revue du moyen âge latin* 4 (1948), 56–60; Aubrun, *La Paroisse en France*, pp. 97–101.

60. Antoine Bernard, *La Sépulture en droit canonique du Décret de Gratien au Concile de Trente* (Paris, 1933), p. 57; Lucien Musset, "Le Cimetière dans la vie paroissiale en Basse-Normandie (XIe-XIIIe siècles)," *Cahiers Léopold Delisle* 12 (1963), 16. See also *Cartulaire de Saint-Vincent de Mâcon*, no. 533 (no date); *Recueil des chartes de l'abbaye de Saint-Benoît-sur-Loire*, no. 75 (1065).

buried and commemorated when they died. Pope Leo III (795–816) established the principle of free choice in one of his decrees, and it continued to be recognized by canonists throughout the middle ages.[61] Neither was anyone legally subject to burial charges. A whole series of councils followed Pope Gregory the Great in insisting that the clergy were not to demand fees from the faithful for burial in their cemeteries, although they were permitted to accept voluntary offerings occasioned by a funeral.[62]

Reality, however, was often very different from the ideal proposed in legal texts. Even before the tenth century the poor seldom had any real choice about where their bodies would be buried. In the mid-ninth century Hincmar of Reims called for the establishment of cemeteries near rural oratories, so that those who were too impoverished to have their bodies carried elsewhere could still be laid to rest in consecrated ground.[63] It is also clear that some of the clergy were still demanding burial fees. This made it impossible for poor people to be buried in the church cemetery. Indeed, another ninth-century bishop, Jonas of Orléans, complained that some of the poor could not even find burial sites in the fields because landowners demanded payment for such sites.[64] Nevertheless, at this point poverty was the only restriction on one's free choice of burial. Those who had the wherewithal to have their bodies carried to the site they had chosen and to make an "offering" (if necessary), could be buried wherever they wished—in the cathedral or parish cemetery, near an oratory, or in a monastery. Burial at the church where one paid tithes was certainly common, but it was by no means obligatory in the late eighth and ninth centuries.[65]

That situation changed considerably over the next two hundred years, however. Some historians have argued that it was the reforming churchmen of the late eleventh and early twelfth centuries who imposed the obligation to be buried in the parish cemetery on the faithful, as part of their efforts to regulate and improve the care of

61. *Regesta pontificum Romanorum ab condita ecclesia ad annum post Christum natum MCX-CVIII*, ed. Philipp Jaffé, 2d ed. by S. Löwenfeld, F. Kaltenbrunner, and P. Ewald, 2 vols. (Leipzig, 1885–88), 1: 315–16, no. 2536. See also Bernard, *La Sépulture en droit canonique*, p. 85.

62. Bernard, *La Sépulture en droit canonique*, p. 143.

63. Hincmar of Reims, *De ecclesiis et capellis*, in "Zwei Schriften der Erzbischofs Hinkmar von Reims," ed. Wilhelm Gundlach, *Zeitschrift für Kirchengeschichte* 10 (1889), 101.

64. Jonas of Orléans, *De institutione laicali*, 3: 15 (PL 106: 263).

65. Hincmar of Reims, *Capitula synodica*, 3: 2 (PL 125: 794); Amolo of Lyon, *Epistolae*, 1, ed. Ernst Dümmler, MGH, EPP, 5: 366–67. But compare Council of Tribur (895), c. 15, in *Capitularia regum Francorum*, 2: 221–22.

souls.[66] It is certainly true that church councils first began to formulate rules about where the faithful should be buried around the year 1100 and that canon lawyers in the twelfth and thirteenth century struggled to reconcile those rules with the earlier principle of free choice.[67] However, if parochial burial rights first entered church law at the beginning of the twelfth century, it was not because they were novelties at that time.

In the late tenth century some churches already claimed the right to bury members of certain groups or the population of a particular area. Around 970, for example, the inhabitants of Mâcon were supposed to be buried in the cemetery of Saint-Pierre, just outside the walls.[68] In 977, the bishop of Girone granted the monastery of Saint-Pierre of Besalu the right to bury all the clergy and laity who lived in a nearby settlement.[69] These rights were recognized by the church hierarchy, but it is clear that they were not established as the result of some general ecclesiastical policy, related to the spiritual needs of the population or the disciplinary concerns of the church. Rather, they grew up haphazardly and without much direction from either the spiritual or temporal authorities. When disputes arose between two churches over burial rights—as they often did in the eleventh century—they were generally resolved by an appeal to local custom rather than to episcopal decree. In 1097, for example, witnesses testified that for at least fifteen years the people who lived on the site of the castle of Fréteval had buried their dead "by custom" (*ex consuetudine*) at Saint-Lubin.[70]

Although it is difficult to prove directly, it seems probable that the seigneurial class rather than the ecclesiastical hierarchy was responsible for the establishment of burial rights in the late tenth and eleventh centuries. Landlords were, in a sense, creating monopolies on burial in the same way that they established monopolies on milling or pressing grapes for wine.[71] And the purpose was much the same as with these and other *banal* rights. The powerful claimed the bodies of those

66. Lemarignier, Gaudemet, and Mollat, *Institutions ecclésiastiques*, p. 198; Georges Duby, *La Société aux XIe et XIIe siècles dans la région mâconnaise* (Paris, 1953; rpt. 1971), p. 231.

67. E.g., Council of London (1102) (Mansi 20: 1152); Bernard, *La Sépulture en droit canonique*, pp. 85–111, 166–78.

68. *Cartulaire de Saint-Vincent de Mâcon*, no. 406 (968–71).

69. Cited by Lesne, *Histoire de la propriété ecclésiastique*, 3: 134.

70. *Cartulaire de Marmoutier pour le Dunois*, ed. Émile Mabille (Châteaudun, 1874), no. 155 (1097).

71. On these monopolies, see Duby, *La Société dans la région mâconnaise*, pp. 174–79; idem, *Rural Economy and Country Life*, pp. 56–57.

subject to their control in order to increase the revenues of their own churches—or sometimes those of another church upon which they wished to confer a benefit.

It is difficult to tell from the rather infrequent references to burial rights in the tenth-century sources exactly what rights were in question in that period. In the eleventh century, however, the situation becomes somewhat clearer. Parishioners, or the people subject to a particular church in matters of burial, were to be buried in the parish cemetery and to "offer" what was increasingly a customary fee (*sepultura*) in return for the privilege. Sometimes people were allowed to choose another burial site for themselves, so long as they first paid sepultura to the church in which they were supposed to be buried.[72] However, written records were still rare in this period and "rights" were often determined by the memory of the local population. Allowing people to choose where they wished to be buried could set a dangerous precedent, which might undermine one's right to collect sepultura—and, indeed, other parochial revenues—from the same group in the future. As a result, the parish, or the church which held burial rights, might demand possession of a corpse regardless of whether sepultura had already been paid.[73] The parishioners of these churches thus lost all opportunity to determine where they would be buried and commemorated after death.

Ugly situations could arise when two churches both tried to assert their right to bury a particular person. Sometime around 1075, for example, a man named Isenbard was buried by the monks of Cunault, over the protests of the monks of Saint-Aubin of Angers, who held the parish of Trèves. Saint-Aubin complained to the episcopal court in Angers, claiming that Isenbard was a "native parishioner" (*naturalis parrochianus*) of Trèves and should be buried in their cemetery. The court granted Saint-Aubin the right to have the body exhumed, carried back to Isenbard's house and then reburied at Trèves, and ordered Cunault to pay a fine. The monks of Cunault then asked the count of Anjou, Fulk le Réchin, to intercede on their behalf. Through his intervention a settlement was finally reached. The monks of Cunault recognized their fault and agreed never to do such a thing again, but they were allowed to keep the body, in part because moving it would be "difficult for them because of its decomposition

72. E.g., *Cartulaire de l'abbaye cardinale de la Trinité de Vendôme*, no. 301 (1081).
73. Jean-Marc Bienvenu, "Les Conflits de sépulture en Anjou aux XIe et XIIe siècles," *Bulletin philologique et historique* (1966), especially pp. 679–85.

and intolerable because of the smell." However, Saint-Aubin claimed the burial fee of twenty solidi.[74] It should be noted that Isenbard's own wishes and those of his family are never mentioned in the records of the case.

The principle of free choice of burial site was never denied by the canonists of the tenth and eleventh centuries, but it was certainly not very well observed by the proprietors of churches. At the very beginning of the twelfth century, in fact, the nuns of Le Ronceray of Angers explicitly denied that their parishioners had any right to "be buried here and there, wherever they wanted."[75] This discrepancy between legal principle and practice suggests that burial rights had their origin in seigneurial initiative rather than ecclesiastical policy. Such an hypothesis may also help to explain the peculiar distribution of such rights over the population. In most cases, the right to bury someone seems to have been derived from that person's status as the parishioner of a particular church. If burial rights belonged to a monastery, it was generally because the proprietor of the parish had granted them to that monastery, as he might grant the right to collect tithes or a share in the profits from baptisms, or because the monastery was itself the proprietor of the parish.

Sometimes, however, burial rights seem to have been derived directly from the seigneurial relationship itself; that is, a church obtained the right to bury someone because of that person's status within the local political structure. At the end of the eleventh century, for example, a dispute arose over burial rights between the monks of Marmoutier, who served the chapel of the castle of Le Puiset, and the monks of Saint-Martin-des-Champs, who were the proprietors of the parish of Janville within which the castle was located. After many difficulties, a compromise was finally reached at the beginning of the twelfth century: the free inhabitants of Le Puiset could be buried where they liked, but royal serfs had to be buried at the cemetery of Janville "as had been the custom before."[76] Here the question was not

74. "Le Droit de sépulture: Charte de l'an 1075," ed. Paul Marchegay, *Bibliothèque de l'École des Chartes*, 3d series, 5 (1854), 528–31; Bienvenu, "Les Conflits de sépulture." Twenty solidi is a remarkably large sum for a burial fee; it may have represented some sort of penalty as well.

75. *Cartularium monasterii beatae Mariae caritatis Andegavensis vulgo dicti Le Ronceray*, ed. Paul Marchegay (Angers, 1854), no. 58 (1110).

76. Adolphe de Dion, *Le Puiset au XIe et au XIIe siècle: Châtellenie et prieuré* (Chartres, 1886), pièces justificatives, no. 3 (ca. 1095), 6 (1100–1104). On the special parochial status of castle-dwellers, see Gabriel Fournier, *Le Château dans la France médiévale: Essai de sociologie monumentale* (Paris, 1978), pp. 191–96.

who was a parishioner of Janville, but rather who was most firmly subjected to seigneurial control. Such interlockings of parochial and *banal* obligations were common in this period.

While lack of resources had limited the liturgical options available to the poorest members of society in the ninth century, by the late tenth and eleventh centuries most of the laity had little choice about where they would be buried and commemorated after death. The ordinary Christian's association with the parish church was enforced by obligations imposed from above, and it is not clear whether he or she acquiesced willingly. Those who had money to spare did sometimes pay sepultura to their parish church and then seek burial and prayer elsewhere. Other methods might also be tried. Sometime around 1075, for example, a young man who lived in the parish of La Trinité, in the suburbs of Angers, helped to found a confraternity in honor of St. Nicholas. The parish of La Trinité belonged to the nuns of Le Ronceray, but the confraternity was associated with the nearby monastery of Saint-Nicholas. When the young man died, his friends wished to bury him in the cemetery of Saint-Nicholas, even though he was a parishioner of La Trinité and should have been buried in its cemetery. They tried to sneak his body out to Saint-Nicholas, but were caught by the abbess and her nuns as they passed the gates of Le Ronceray.[77] Incidents such as this would seem to indicate that not everyone was satisfied with the parish church and its liturgy.

At the same time, it would be a mistake to assume that the relationship between the humiles and the parish church was always coerced. The faithful seem to have made some spontaneous efforts to fraternize with their parish clergy. The priest often joined his parishioners at meetings of the local gild or confraternity, which provided prayer for its members as well as opportunities to socialize.[78] These organizations, already flourishing in the ninth century, were voluntary in nature—or at least any pressure to join probably came from neighbors rather than from the authorities. The continued presence of the parish priest in the gilds thus suggests that people were willing to make the best of what was, in any case, an unavoidable association with the parish and its liturgy.

77. *Cartularium monasterii beatae Mariae caritatis*, no. 47 (no date); Bienvenu, "Les Conflits de sépulture," pp. 675–76.

78. On the relationship between parish priests and the gilds in the ninth century, see Hincmar of Reims, *Capitula synodica*, 1: 16 (PL 125: 777). See also Oexle, "*Conjuratio* et *ghilde*," pp. 3–7; Meersseman, *Ordo fraternitatis*, pp. 35–40.

But could parish priests really offer much in the way of services for their dead parishioners? It must be admitted that we know very little about the ordinary round of prayer in the parish churches of the early middle ages, and even less about any special services that may have been performed there. To judge by the reforming legislation of the late eighth and early ninth centuries, many priests were ill-prepared for their parochial duties.[79] They often had to be reminded of what was due to the dead. Capitularies and episcopal decrees urged them to be ready to administer the viaticum to the dying,[80] to know the *ordo commendationis animae*,[81] to be able to say masses for the dead using the correct grammatical forms, masculine or feminine, singular or plural.[82] They were to try to eradicate, and certainly not participate in, the "superstitious" practices that went on at funerals.[83] It is not clear whether ordinary parish priests were any better prepared in later centuries, although presumably the liturgy was properly performed in parishes served by members of monastic communities.

Despite these problems, probably many people in the early Carolingian period and most in the tenth and eleventh centuries received the last rites and a funeral service in return for their payment of *sepultura*. They would have been mentioned in the bidding prayers on the Sunday following the funeral, and the priest very likely performed a series of funerary masses as well.[84] The dead of the parish may also have been commemorated when all the priests in each rural deanery got together for their monthly meeting.[85] But beyond that it is hard to say how ordinary Christians were commemorated. No

79. Guy Devailly, "La Pastorale en Gaule au IXe siècle," *Revue d'histoire de l'église de France* 59 (1973), 23–54; McKitterick, *The Frankish Church and the Carolingian Reforms*, pp. 45–79.

80. *Karoli magni capitulare primum* (769), c. 10, in *Capitularia regum Francorum*, 1: 45; *Capitula a sacerdotibus proposita* (802), c. 21, ibid., p. 107; *Capitula ecclesiastica* (810–13), c. 16, ibid., p. 179.

81. *Quae a presbyteris discenda sunt*, c. 6, in *Capitularia regum Francorum*, 1: 235; Hincmar of Reims, *De ecclesiis et capellis* (p. 122).

82. *Capitula de examinandis ecclesiasticis* (802), c. 3, in *Capitularia regum Francorum*, 1: 110.

83. *Karlmanni principis capitulare* (742), c. 5, in *Capitularia regum Francorum*, 1: 25; *Karoli magni capitulare primum* (769), c. 6, ibid., p. 45; *Capitulare ecclesiasticum* (818/19), c. 28, ibid., p. 279.

84. Hincmar of Reims, *Capitula synodica*, 1: 14 and 3: 2 (PL 125: 776 and 794); Theodulf of Orléans, *Capitula ad presbyteros parochiae suae*, 45 (PL 105: 205).

85. Riculf of Soissons, *Statuta*, 20 (PL 131: 22–23). See also Gilles Gerard Meersseman, "Die Klerikervereine von Karl dem Grossen bis Innocenz III," *Zeitschrift für schweizerische Kirchengeschichte* 46 (1952), 3–9.

trace has come down to us of any parish necrologies or other name lists from this period.[86] The records of confraternities from other parts of Europe (we have none from early medieval France) suggest that the dead were remembered only as long as those who had known them survived.[87] In all probability, then, the commemoration of departed parishioners was ordinarily neither very elaborate, nor very long-lasting.

Sometimes, however, people did try to arrange for more intense or longer-lasting commemoration of their deceased relatives and friends. Offerings continued to be made "on behalf of the dead" throughout this period; these could constitute an important addition to the parish revenues.[88] At the very end of the eleventh century or the beginning of the twelfth, the monks of Montier-la-Celle agreed to divide the revenues of their church of Saint-Aigulph with the priest who served there. They specifically referred to income from offerings made in association with funerals, or with the masses for the dead performed regularly on Mondays or Wednesdays.[89] In this case, parishioners were making offerings to have their dead mentioned during regularly scheduled masses.

Sometimes the faithful also paid for special masses to be performed in the parish church, apparently in conjunction with funerals. The nuns of Le Ronceray divided the revenues from the parish of La Trinité with the canons who served in the parish church. These revenues included the income from tricennaria, septennaria, and other masses for the dead.[90] References to such masses are relatively rare, however, even in the eleventh-century sources. This need not reflect a lack of interest in prayer for the dead among the humble. It is not clear how many members of the poorest class in a generally impoverished society were capable of expending any of their limited resources on masses for the dead, even if they had wanted to. Because the options available to the humiles were so limited by parochial

86. J. B. Molin and T. Maertens, *Pour un renouveau des prières du prône* (Bruges, 1961), p. 42.

87. Herbert Westlake, *The Parish Guilds of Mediaeval England* (London, 1919), pp. 3–4; Meersseman, *Ordo fraternitatis*, pp. 55–65.

88. Hincmar of Reims, *De ecclesiis et capellis* (p. 117).

89. *Cartulaire de Montier-la-Celle*, ed. Charles Lalore (Paris-Troyes, 1882), no. 216 (1098–1122).

90. *Cartularium monasterii beatae Mariae caritatis*, no. 1 (1028). See also *Cartulaires de l'abbaye de Molesme, ancien diocèse de Langres, 916–1250*, ed. Jacques Laurent, 2 vols. (Paris, 1907–11), premier cartulaire, no. 253 (ca. 1097).

obligations and by poverty, it is, in the end, almost impossible to tell what they wanted from the clergy and their prayers.

THE FEUDAL ELITE AND THE LITURGICAL COMMUNITY

The dominant members of early medieval society, the potentes, had a very different kind of relationship with the communities that prayed from the one just described. Because they wielded greater political and economic power than the humiles, they were able to choose more freely where they would attend services in life and be commemorated after death. To begin with, the seigneurs who helped impose parochial obligations on their dependents generally managed to evade such obligations themselves. It is not at all clear whether the upper class paid tithes from the produce of their estates.[91] On the contrary, it was in many cases the landed proprietor who actually received the tithes due to the churches on his or her property. The parish priest, generally a seigneurial nominee, perhaps of servile origin, was in no position to exercise pastoral discipline over his master or mistress.[92] Indeed, even bishops were hard pressed to control the behavior of the nobles and their unruly retainers. The great magnates were, thus, never identified as "parishioners" of a particular local church and even the lesser members of the military class often managed to avoid the obligations that went along with such a designation.

In the eleventh century castellans and knights were sometimes specifically exempted from the obligation to be buried in the parish cemetery. In 1061 Bishop Heddo of Soissons consecrated the church of Saint-Adrien, recently constructed by the castellan Richard at his castle of Béthisy. Heddo announced that a knight (*miles*) or peasant (*rusticus*) could be buried at the new church, so long as he first fulfilled his obligation (i.e., paid sepultura) to the old parish church. How-

91. Viard, *Histoire de la dîme ecclésiastique*, pp. 149–60.
92. Amann and Dumas, *L'Église au pouvoir des laïques*, pp. 281–83. The freedom of the upper class from parish discipline can be seen in the fact that lords sometimes made their confessions to bishops rather than parish priests: e.g., Ademar of Chabannes, *Chronicon*, 3: 66, ed. Jules Chavanon (Paris, 1897), p. 192. Confessions were also made to monks: e.g., *Cartulaire de l'abbaye de Saint-Vincent du Mans (ordre de Saint Benoît)*, ed. R. Charles and S. Menjot d'Elbenne (Mamers-Le Mans, 1886–1913), nos. 480 (1068–78) and 484 (1067–78).

ever, the castellan and his household were "not to be bound by this
law"; they had the absolute right to be buried at Saint-Adrien.[93] In
this document, a knight was subject to parochial obligations, though
the castellan of Béthisy was not. Elsewhere, however, *milites* were
also exempted from sepultura. In 1081 the canons of Beaugency
reached an agreement with the monks of La Trinité of Vendôme
concerning burial rights in a parish under the canons' control. The
canons agreed:

> . . . that the bodies of any *milites*, along with their wives and chil-
> dren, who want to be buried in the monks' cemetery may be re-
> ceived by the monks without any contradiction by [the canons]. As
> to other men: whoever wants to be carried in the same way to the
> monks for burial, if sepultura has first been given to the appropriate
> parish church, and if none [of the canons] object, they can all, in
> general, have the free right.[94]

Even when *milites*—those on the social boundary between nobles
and peasants—were subject to parochial obligations in this matter,
they generally had the resources to pay the customary fees and go
elsewhere for burial and commemoration after death.[95] Thus, their
relationship with the liturgical community, like that of their superi-
ors, was essentially determined by their own choice.

In fact, the powerful often chose to be associated with more than
one church in this period. Many of the more important members of
the feudal elite had their own chaplains, who offered them the same
services they would have found in a parish church.[96] The whole
household, including both family members and retainers, could attend mass, make confessions, and even be buried in the castle chapel
—as in the case of Saint-Adrien of Béthisy. However, most of the
potentes who had their own chaplains also established relationships
with one or more other churches, where they might also attend
services, confess, take vows, marry, and be buried. The elite did

93. *Recueil des actes de Philippe Ier, roi de France (1059–1108)*, ed. Maurice Prou (Paris,
1908), no. 11 (1061).
94. *Cartulaire de l'abbaye cardinale de la Trinité de Vendôme*, no. 301 (1081).
95. For example, *Cartulaire de l'abbaye cardinale de la Trinité de Vendôme*, no. 78 (1040–
49): in this case, the monks forgave the payment of a double sepultura—to the monastery
and to its parish church—in return for a large gift to the house.
96. Henri Leclercq, "Chapelle," *DACL* 3: 1, cols. 414–21. By the eleventh century
chapels were being constructed within castles: see Fournier, *Le Château dans la France
médiévale*, pp. 126–28.

not generally turn to the parish for these purposes, however. By and large, they were interested in forging ties to more prestigious churches: the cathedrals, the larger rural churches served by communities of canons, and above all the monasteries.

Their choice of liturgical community might be affected by any of a number of factors. One of the most important was family tradition. Family members often supported and protected the same church for generations, sometimes one that their ancestors had founded or restored to the regular life. In 980, for example, Count Milo I and Countess Ingeltrude of Tonnerre reformed the monastery of Saint-Michel, which stood across the valley from their castle. Their descendants continued to make gifts to the house until the late eleventh century, when the direct line died out.[97] Child oblation created a further link between the noble family and the important churches it patronized. Nobles did not install their children as priests in the parish churches under their jurisdiction: by and large, such churches were staffed by clerics drawn from the lower classes. The children of the powerful were offered instead to cathedral churches and monasteries, and most often to those with which their family was already connected.[98] Their presence there encouraged further support for the religious community.[99] Finally, as one might expect, relatives often expressed a wish to be buried near one another, in the cemetery of the church associated with their family.[100] The institution of the "family" church, which had its roots in the Merovingian period, remained important throughout the early middle ages.

Sometimes, however, individuals broke with family tradition, switching their allegiance to a different liturgical community or even founding a new one. Both political and religious considerations might lie behind such a change. As Jean-François Lemarignier has pointed out, the patronage of a monastic community conferred special prestige on a political figure in the tenth and eleventh centuries. This was because the role of "protector of the monasteries" had been a royal

---

97. See especially *Cartulaire général de l'Yonne: Recueil des documents authentiques pour servir à l'histoire des pays qui forment ce Département*, ed. Maximilien Quantin, 2 vols. (Auxerre, 1854–60), no. 94 (1046); Bouchard, *Sword, Miter, and Cloister*, pp. 239, 369–72.

98. Magnou-Nortier, *La Société laïque et l'église*, pp. 387–89, 432–33; Bouchard, *Sword, Miter, and Cloister*, pp. 46–51.

99. E.g., *Cartulaire de Marmoutier pour le Dunois*, no. 149 (1095); *Cartulaire de l'abbaye de Saint-Vincent du Mans*, no. 502 (ca. 1097).

100. E.g., *Cartulaire de l'abbaye de Beaulieu (en Limousin)*, ed. J. E. M. Deloche (Paris, 1859), no. 57 (882).

prerogative in the Merovingian and Carolingian periods, and continued to be associated with public authority. As royal authority declined
from the late ninth century on, first the great territorial princes, then
lesser nobles took over what had formerly been royal functions, including that of monastic patronage. The powerful wanted sanctuaries
of their own, served by regular communities, which would serve as
symbols of their authority and as gathering places for their supporters
and allies. From the late tenth century on, many new monasteries
were founded, usually in carefully selected sites near the founder's
castle or in the most important population centers under his or her
control. Those who could not afford to found a monastery often
established collegiate churches, which required a smaller endowment.[101] Moreover, those who wished to be associated politically
with an important noble might cement the alliance by establishing
their own relationships with the religious community he or she had
founded or patronized.[102]

To recognize such political motives is not, however, to deny the
importance of religious concerns in determining the nobility's choice
of liturgical community. Many members of the elite went to considerable lengths to obtain for themselves the most effective intercessors
possible. They sometimes abandoned their allegiance to their "family" church or alienated important pieces of property over the protests
of their relatives, in order to be associated with the holiest community
they could find. The tremendous success of the reformed monasteries
in the late tenth and eleventh centuries, in particular, must be attributed to such concerns.[103]

It has long been recognized that many of the most powerful members of society were plagued by religious insecurities in this period.
Both the language of the documents recording the elite's interaction
with clerical communities and much of noble behavior itself reflect a

---

101. Jean-François Lemarignier, "Aspects politiques des fondations de collégiales dans
le royaume de France au XIe siècle," in *La vita comune del clero nei secoli XI e XII*, 1: 18–49;
idem, "Structures monastiques et structures politiques dans la France de la fin du Xe et des
débuts du XIe siècle," in *Il monachesimo nell'alto medioevo e la formazione della civiltà occidentale*, pp. 357–400; Bouchard, *Sword, Miter, and Cloister*, pp. 102–10. Jean Hubert has argued
that the huge Benedictine churches of this period were actually built to accommodate the
laity who attended services in them: "La Place faite aux laïques dans les églises monastiques
et dans les cathédrales," in *I laici nella "societas christiana" dei secoli XI e XII*, pp. 471–74.
102. Southern, *The Making of the Middle Ages*, pp. 156–57; and see the works listed
above, in n. 20 to the Introduction.
103. I agree with Bouchard *(Sword, Miter, and Cloister,* pp. 225–46) on this point;
however, I believe she rejects too readily other, "secular" motivations.

keen awareness of sin, fear of divine judgment, and uncertainty about the prospects for salvation.[104] While these insecurities are no longer thought to be the products of the "terrors of the year 1000," there is still some disagreement about how to account for them. H.E.J. Cowdrey has suggested that a change in penitential practice around the turn of the eleventh century made the more spiritually sophisticated members of society uneasy about the sins for which they had not yet done penance. He believes that noble donors saw the reformed monasteries, with their elaborate liturgies, as sources of almsgiving and prayer which could serve as "vicarious penance" for those sins.[105]

Barbara Rosenwein, on the other hand, has argued that the instability of social and political institutions in this period created a sense of anomie, especially in those members of the elite whose own status was shifting up or down. In the face of disorder and uncertainty, those who could afford to do so strove to associate themselves with religious communities whose holiness was both evident and reliable; their choice fell on the reformed monasteries.[106] Rosenwein is not directly concerned with the monastic community as a source of prayer, but her argument would help to explain why these houses were perceived as the most desirable intercessors. While cathedrals and other secular churches might provide prayer, they were not very reliable, for with the breakdown of episcopal authority and the usurpation by the laity of control over these churches, both the mores and the liturgical standards of the secular clergy tended to decline. Even those churches whose clergy still maintained their zeal and upheld their liturgical obligations could not be depended on to remain in that state when the political situation shifted again.[107] In contrast, the reformed monasteries, and especially those exempt from local control, appeared as islands of stability and purity in a sinful world— havens of prayer. This view of the monastic life as the *vita angelica* was vigorously promoted by the leaders of reformed monasticism, and it seems to have been very influential with the feudal elite.[108]

104. Magnou-Nortier, *La Société laïque et l'église*, pp. 436–44; and see below, Chapter 5.

105. Herbert Edward John Cowdrey, *The Cluniacs and the Gregorian Reform* (Oxford, 1970), pp. 121–29.

106. Barbara Rosenwein, *Rhinoceros Bound: Cluny in the Tenth Century* (Philadelphia, 1982), pp. 31–56, 101–6.

107. Amann and Dumas, *L'Église au pouvoir des laïques*, pp. 476–82; H. Maisonneuve, "La Morale d'après les conciles des Xe et XIe siècles," *Mélanges de science religieuse* 18 (1961), especially pp. 5–9.

108. Rosenwein, *Rhinoceros Bound*, pp. 84–100, 106–12. And see below, Chapter 5.

These two interpretations are by no means mutually exclusive. It is quite possible that changes in penitential practice contributed to the insecurities induced by an unstable social situation, making the nobles turn all the more eagerly to monasteries such as Cluny for intercession. It would be a mistake, however, to regard these communities, as some historians have in the past, simply as sources of prayer and almsgiving, which could serve as "vicarious penance" for the sins of the powerful. As I shall argue in the next chapter, nobles in this period were much more interested in forming close ties with the religious community and its way of life than in simply acquiring more and more prayer for themselves.

Regardless of whether their motives were political, religious or, as seems likely, a combination of the two, the fact remains that members of the upper class were turning with increasing urgency to the monasteries —and above all to the *reformed* monasteries—in the tenth and eleventh centuries. If we use the choice of burial site as an indicator of liturgical allegiance, this development becomes particularly clear. In earlier centuries, some powerful men and women had been buried in monastic cemeteries, but many others were interred elsewhere, in cathedrals, rural churches, or private chapels. Among the early Carolingian kings, for example, Pepin was laid to rest at the monastery of Saint-Denis, but Charlemagne was buried at the palace chapel at Aix, Louis the Pious at the cathedral of Metz—the old "family diocese" of the Arnulfing house—and Charles the Bald and Louis the Stammerer at the royal chapel at Compiègne.[109] On the other hand, all the Capetian kings of the eleventh century were buried in Benedictine houses: Robert the Pious and Henry I at Saint-Denis, Philip I at Fleury.[110] Whereas the first dukes of the Normans in the early tenth century had chosen the cathedral of Rouen as their burial church, by the eleventh century they too had switched their allegiance to monasteries: Fécamp, Caen, Faversham, and Bec.[111] The same is true of the other great princes of the time.[112] Monastic burial was not reserved

109. Erlande-Brandenburg, *Le Roi est mort*, pp. 60–73. On the strange fate of Charles the Bald's body, see *Cartulaire de l'abbaye de Saint-Bertin*, p. 126; Elizabeth A. R. Brown, "Death and the Human Body in the Later Middle Ages: The Legislation of Boniface VIII on the Division of the Corpse," *Viator* 12 (1981), 226.

110. Erlande-Brandenburg, *Le Roi est mort*, pp. 73–75.

111. Lucien Musset, "Les Sépultures des souverains normands: Un aspect de l'idéologie du pouvoir," *Annales de Normandie* 27 (1977), 350.

112. On the burial sites of the counts of Anjou, see Louis Halphen, *Le Comté d'Anjou au XIe siècle* (Paris, 1906), pp. 234–36 (Fulk Nerra at Beaulieu), 126–27, 325 (Geoffrey Martel at Saint-Nicholas), 202, n. 1 (Fulk le Réchin at l'Evière).

for the greatest magnates. Many lesser members of the military elite followed them to the monastic cemeteries.[113] One result was the kind of exemption of *milites* from parochial obligations mentioned earlier.

Between the late eighth and the eleventh centuries, then, wealth and power became the determining factors in a layperson's relationship with the clerical communities that prayed. The members of the lower class had been, for the most part, tied to the parish church by obligations imposed from above. The upper class, on the other hand, had tied itself to the more prestigious churches, especially the monasteries. Obviously, the categories of parishioner and monastic benefactor should not be considered any more hard and fast than the categories of humilis and potens. Some monasteries not only held proprietary rights over parish churches, but sent some of their members to serve the churches there. Thus, the parishioners might actually benefit from the liturgy performed by a small community of monks.[114]

Occasionally, too, a monastery might bury or pray for someone of low social status who did not belong to the monastic parish—provided that he or she could make an appropriate gift to the house. In 1077, for example, a boy who lived in Vendôme was killed in the rough "pagan" games associated with St. John's Eve; he died without confessing or taking communion. His father, a cobbler, was distressed by this sudden and impious death, and asked the abbot of La Trinité to tell him how his son could be helped. The abbot suggested that the monks should say masses for the boy's soul, and so the cobbler granted various small pieces of property to the monastery in return for a tricennarium.[115] Clearly, though, this was an exceptional case. The father wanted monks to say masses for his son because of the unusual circumstances under which the boy had died. Normally a cobbler and his family would not have been commemorated in the monastic liturgy.

Exceptions might also occur at the other end of the social scale. Members of the military elite, who would normally have been associated with a more prestigious community, sometimes had to be buried in the parish cemetery. In Normandy, in the early eleventh century,

113. By the end of the eleventh century an increasing number of *milites* were seeking burial at Cluny: Poeck, "Laienbegräbnisse in Cluny," p. 156. See also Chapter 4 below.
114. Constable, "Monasteries, Rural Churches, and the *Cura Animarum*," in *Cristianizzazione ed organizzazione ecclesiastica*, 1: 366–80.
115. *Cartulaire de l'abbaye cardinale de la Trinité de Vendôme*, no. 261 (1077). See also Poeck, "Laienbegräbnisse in Cluny," p. 157.

two closely related families quarreled over the protectorship of the abbey of Saint-Étienne of Fontenay, which they had jointly founded. In the end, the Taissons continued to be buried in the abbey cemetery, while Erneis and his wife Hacinsa were reduced to burial in the cemetery of a parish under their control. The aftermath of the quarrel, however, shows how unusual these burials were. After the battle of Hastings, William the Conqueror imposed a reconciliation on the two families. As a result Erneis' son Robert, who had been killed at Hastings, was buried at Fontenay, and his parents' bodies were exhumed and transported to the abbey for reburial.[116] This, then, is the exception which proves the rule. In the end, Erneis and his family found their resting place in the monastic cemetery, leaving the parish cemetery for their lower-class dependents.

As we have seen, by the eleventh century the humiles had very little choice about where or how they would be commemorated after death. Their relationship with the liturgical community was determined largely by obligations imposed on them by the ecclesiastical hierarchy and their own lords. Under the circumstances, it is impossible to determine what they thought of the clergy and their prayers for the dead, except in such rare cases as that of the cobbler of Vendôme. In contrast, the potentes were free to establish the kind of relationship they wanted with the churches of their choice. Their dealings with monasteries and other religious communities may, if interpreted cautiously, be used as a guide to their understanding of and attitude toward the liturgy. In the following chapter, I describe more fully those dealings and the attitudes they embody.

116. Musset, "Le Cimetière dans la vie paroissiale," p. 13.

4 *FAMILIARITAS*

In December, 833 a young man named Deurhoiarn watched as his father, Riwalt, donated some property to the newly established monastery of Redon. Deurhoiarn must have been often at Redon in the years that followed, for he appears regularly as a witness to the monks' dealings with the outside world. They returned the favor, serving as witnesses (and perhaps as intermediaries) in 844, when Riwalt paid compensation to the duke of Brittany for one of his vassals, whom Deurhoiarn had killed. By 859 Riwalt was dead and Deurhoiarn had taken over his title of *machtiern* or local ruler. He and his wife, Roiantken, began making their own gifts to Redon, and he continued to witness the monks' transactions through the 860s and into the 870s. Deurhoiarn was present in 868 when Duke Salomon granted the monks the right to elect their abbot freely, and again the following year when Salomon gave them his villa at Plélan as a refuge from the Vikings. The new house at Plélan, dedicated to Saint-Maxent, was even closer to the center of Deurhoiarn's holdings than the old monastery at Redon, so he continued to visit the monks frequently. Thus, when Deurhoiarn and Roiantken came to Saint-Maxent in the summer of 875 to see where they would be buried and make their final gifts to the saint and his monks, they were actually putting the finishing touches on a relationship that had been established more than forty years earlier.[1]

1. *Cartulaire de l'abbaye de Redon*, nos. 5 (833), 6 (833), 24 (859), 79 (863), 107 (844 or

Much of our information about the early medieval nobility's dealings with the communities that prayed comes from the documents
preserved in the cartularies of elite religious houses. One problem
with this type of evidence is that it tends to fragment experience into
separate moments—a gift of land, the oblation of a child, a quarrel,
the burial of a benefactor—each of which is recorded in a single
charter. The connections between those moments are obscured, especially when the charters which record them appear in different
parts of a cartulary. The activities of Deurhoiarn and Roiantken, for
example, are recorded in some fifteen different documents scattered
throughout the huge collection of ninth-century charters from Redon. Only when they are brought together does the duration and
intensity of the family's relationship with the abbey become clear.

A number of recent studies based on the analysis of groups of
charters involving the same people and the same pieces of property
have demonstrated that what appear at first glance to be discrete and
unrelated transactions were often part of long-term, multifaceted relationships between nobles and religious communities. Constance
Bouchard used this approach to examine the "intimate" ties that bound
together the nobility and the upper clergy in eleventh- and twelfth-
century Burgundy. She concluded that the two groups were "socially
and biologically one."[2] Stephen White also notes the "ongoing social
relationship[s]" established by noble donations to monasteries in
western France between 1050 and 1150, but he emphasizes the complexity and ambiguity of these transactions more than Bouchard
does.[3] White argues that the exchange of property between a noble
kin-group and a monastic community was never simple or quickly
accomplished, for it "was supposed to set in motion a series of further
exchanges within, as well as between, each group and, if properly
performed, to implicate God, who did not automatically become a
party to the transaction."[4] He points out that these transactions often
involved considerable tension, and argues that they should be viewed
not as a means of reinforcing a stable social order, but rather as efforts

---

850), 122 (846–58), 123 (833), 173 (867), 174 (869), 175 (852 or 858), 193 (856), 204 (859),
236 (875–78), 240 (868), 241 (869). Deurhoiarn and Roiantken's visit to Saint-Maxent in
875 is discussed in the Introduction above.

2. Bouchard, *Sword, Miter, and Cloister*, p. 247.
3. White, *Custom, Kinship, and Gifts to Saints*, p. 27.
4. White, *Custom, Kinship, and Gifts to Saints*, p. 159.

"to structure, manipulate, and control a treacherous social and supernatural world."[5]

An important contribution to this growing literature is Barbara
Rosenwein's study of the social meaning of Cluny's property in the
tenth and early eleventh centuries. In analyzing the rich collection of
Cluniac charters from that period, Rosenwein observed a curious fact:
some pieces of property were being passed back and forth between
the great monastery and the noble families in its neighborhood. The
same people, or at least members of the same families, might give a
piece of land to Cluny, reclaim it, then later give it again—acting at
different times as both friends and enemies to the monks. Moreover,
when the monks received a piece of property, they did not always
keep it. Sometimes they granted it back to the donor *in precaria* or
exchanged it for another piece of property. Behind these complex
exchanges lay a concept of property which involved social as well as
economic meanings. Land continued to be identified with its former
owners long after it was transferred to new ones; it served as a point
of connection between the two parties.[6] Thus, in the region around
Cluny, noble and clerical efforts to create and affirm relationships
coexisted with efforts to increase their respective landholdings. Indeed, Rosenwein argues that in the tenth and early eleventh centuries
the social aspects of these transactions predominated over the purely
economic aspects, although both were important. Donations, claims,
redonations, precarial grants, and exchanges were not discrete events,
but different moments in a complex process of social bonding. Nobles saw their transactions with Cluny primarily as a way to become
and remain the neighbors of St. Peter and his monks.[7]

Within the last few years, then, increasing attention has been devoted to the nobility's dealings with religious communities in the
tenth and eleventh centuries. The current consensus seems to be that
the various activities recorded in the charters of this period formed
part of long-term, complex, but ultimately close relationships. But
what part did prayer for the dead play in those relationships? And
what part did it play in the less well studied dealings of late eighth-

---

5. White, *Custom, Kinship, and Gifts to Saints*, p. 173. Bouchard also notes the ambiguity and tension in these relationships (*Sword, Miter, and Cloister*, p. 43), but devotes less
attention to them than White does.

6. Rosenwein, *To Be the Neighbor of St. Peter*, pp. 49–143.

7. Rosenwein, *To Be the Neighbor of St. Peter*, especially pp. 202–5.

and ninth-century nobles with religious communities? Since the early 1900s, scholars have emphasized the importance of prayer for the dead as a motive for noble gift-giving. In particular, they have explained the explosion of gifts to reformed monasteries in the late tenth and eleventh centuries as an effort to obtain a share in the large quantity of prayer for the dead performed in those houses.[8] These views have been played down in the most recent literature on the nobility and the church in the early middle ages, but they have not yet been seriously challenged.

Bouchard asserts that many of the gifts made to Burgundian monasteries in the eleventh and twelfth centuries were made "when the donor felt he was dying or when one of his relatives or close friends had just died."[9] She also discusses some of the liturgical privileges that resulted from those gifts.[10] However, she does not devote much space to this subject, or analyze the phenomena she describes very closely. White, like Bouchard, associates gifts to saints with moments of crisis such as illness or death, even arguing that people who made donations at other times "must have had such moments in mind."[11] He also discusses some of the liturgical privileges that resulted from those transactions, although again, not in much detail.[12] Rosenwein, on the other hand, does question the traditional association of donation with the desire for prayer.[13] She argues that before the middle of the eleventh century other motives lay behind noble dealings with the monks of Cluny.[14] However, her work is concerned with property transactions rather than with the liturgy, and as a result she devotes relatively little attention to the problem of prayer for the dead.

In this chapter I look more closely at how nobles came to be buried and commemorated after death, and assess the importance such liturgical privileges had in their relationships with elite religious houses. My conclusions are based on the evidence of charters, and

8. The first to suggest a connection between prayer for the dead and the donation of private churches to reformed monasteries in this period was Schreiber, "Kirchliches Abgabenwesen an französischen Eigenkirchen," in his *Gemeinschaften des Mittelalters*, pp. 171–81. Schreiber's work has inspired several generations of German scholars, including Jorden, Tellenbach, Schmid, Wollasch, and Oexle, among others, and has influenced other scholars such as Cowdrey and Southern.
9. Bouchard, *Sword, Miter, and Cloister*, p. 190.
10. Bouchard, *Sword, Miter, and Cloister*, pp. 192–97.
11. White, *Custom, Kinship, and Gifts to Saints*, p. 33.
12. White, *Custom, Kinship, and Gifts to Saints*, pp. 26–27.
13. Rosenwein, *To Be the Neighbor of St. Peter*, pp. 38–43.
14. Rosenwein, *To Be the Neighbor of St. Peter*, pp. 202–7.

especially on the analysis of two major data sets. This analysis, which is summarized in the appendices to this book, provides the basis for my general statements. However, I have also used illustrations drawn from documents outside my two main data sets.

The first data set is made up of the extant acts of four kings: Charlemagne (768–814), Charles the Bald (840–77), Lothar (954–86), and Philip I (1060–1108). Charlemagne and Philip I were chosen because their reigns corresponded with the beginning and the end of the period I focus on in this book; Charles the Bald and Lothar because their reigns fell at roughly equal intervals within that period. Their acts will be used to illustrate the laity's changing preferences in liturgical services between the mid-eighth and the end of the eleventh century. The advantage of analyzing royal diplomas is that it offers us some idea of the range of services a particular individual might enjoy. The difficulty, of course, is that kings were not "normal" nobles. (Indeed, one might argue that after they were anointed they were not even laymen.) It is not clear to what extent being a king affected the solemnity and frequency of liturgical commemoration. However, it is clear that royal dealings with religious communities were similar in many—perhaps most—respects to those of the great nobles. Furthermore, the evidence of the second data set suggests that the commemoration of kings differed more in scale than in character from the commemoration of the great magnates and lesser nobles.

This second data set consists of the extant charters of five religious houses: the cathedrals of Mâcon and Angers and the monasteries of Conques, Redon, and Saint-Bertin. These houses were chosen primarily because for each a fairly substantial number of charters survive for the entire period from 800 to 1100.[15] They were also chosen because they represent different regions of France and different forms of religious life.[16] I hope to show that the same changes occurred in patterns of intercession throughout the Frankish realm, and that the same kinds of services were performed for outsiders—although not necessarily with the same frequency—by cathedrals and by monasteries.

My approach to the charter evidence differs from that of the

15. I begin this data set at the year 800 rather than at 750 because I was unable to find five religious communities with a continous series of charters running from 750 to 1100.

16. In fact, there are relatively few charters for the cathedral of Angers, but Angers offers the most consistent series of any cathedral in the west or north of France, which it seemed important to include.

scholars discussed above, in that I have focused on transactions that involve liturgical privileges, rather than on groups of documents associated with particular families or pieces of property. However, I have tried to keep the findings of those scholars in mind when analyzing the ways in which nobles came to be commemorated after death. For it is clear that the men and women who benefited from the prayers of elite religious communities in the early medieval period were not strangers to those communities. They were the relatives, neighbors, friends or—to use a contemporary term—the familiares of the saints and their servants. And it is also clear that the liturgical privileges they received were only one aspect of much broader and more complicated relationships.

PRAYER AND PROPERTY

Liturgical privileges are associated with various kinds of transactions in early medieval charters. Nobles were sometimes granted such privileges because they had confirmed a gift made by someone else, because they had given up their claims on a disputed piece of property, or even as part of an agreement for the joint exploitation of a villa.[17] Most often, however, the grant of liturgical privileges to a layman or laywoman was associated with a donation—especially a donation of land—to the community that prayed. This fact has led some scholars to interpret such negotiations in commercial terms. They write of "pious trafficking," through which nobles attempted to "buy" salvation, or at least "buy" prayers to help win salvation for themselves. The gifts associated with liturgical privileges are described as the "price" of prayer.[18] This interpretation has a certain plausibility. As we shall see, nobles did sometimes offer their property in return for specific liturgical services. Moreover, language reminiscent of commercial transactions occasionally appears in the char-

17. *Cartulaire de Marmoutier pour le Dunois*, no. 40 (1073–84); *Cartulaire de l'abbaye de Redon*, no. 242 (869); *Les Chartes de Saint-Bertin, d'après le grand cartulaire de Dom Charles-Joseph Dewitte*, ed. Daniel Haigneré, 4 vols. (Saint-Omer, 1886–99), no. 73 (1051).

18. See, for example, Magnou-Nortier, *La Société laïque et l'église*, p. 442; van Engen, "The 'Crisis of Cenobitism' Reconsidered," p. 293; Dominique Iogna-Prat, "Les Morts dans la comptabilité céleste des Clunisiens de l'an Mil," in Iogna-Prat and Picard, *Religion et culture autour de l'an mil*, pp. 66–67.

ters that describe grants of prayer, although such language was probably intended to be understood metaphorically.[19]

To insist too strongly on a "commercial" interpretation, however, would be to distort the social and economic, as well as the religious context within which these negotiations were carried out. For while it is true that commerce never died out in the early middle ages, it is also true that it was seldom the primary means of exchange in that period. Both religious communities and lay magnates were familiar with the marketplace and dependent on trade to obtain some of the goods they wanted, but they more often used other means to supply their needs.[20] In the years between 750 and 1100 the lay and clerical elites operated within an economy dominated not by commerce, but by plundering and giving. Their dealings with one another reflect the peculiarities of that economy.[21]

There are important—though not absolute—differences between commercial and gift exchange.[22] A sale is an exchange of property for its own sake, whereas a gift is an exchange of property intended to promote social bonding between the parties involved. A purchase may take only a moment and may be concluded between virtual strangers, whereas a gift is intended to create or maintain a more enduring relationship. The acts of selling and buying carry relatively little social meaning, whereas the acts of giving or receiving gifts are freighted with such meanings. Finally, an object purchased has only its own identity, whereas a gift has a social identity as well. That is, it

19. For example, Viscount Tecelin and his wife arranged to be buried at Montiérender, and insisted that "the price by which we purchased such a privilege" (*precium quo tantum mercati sumus beneficium*) be stated in the charter: *Cartulaire de l'abbaye de la Chapelleaux-Planches*, Montiérender, no. 41 (no later than 1060–61). Presumably, clerical scribes tried not to use commercial language too often or too literally, in order to avoid the appearance of simony.

20. Renée Doehaerd, *Le Haut Moyen Age occidental: Économies et sociétés* (Paris, 1971), pp. 219–91. The archeological evidence for commercial activity in the Carolingian period is discussed by Richard Hodges and David Whitehouse, *Mohammed, Charlemagne, and the Origins of Europe: Archaeology and the Pirenne Thesis* (Ithaca, 1983), pp. 102–22, 158–76.

21. Philip Grierson, "Commerce in the Dark Ages: A Critique of the Evidence," *Transactions of the Royal Historical Society*, 5th ser., 9 (1959), especially pp. 131–40; Georges Duby, *The Early Growth of the European Economy: Warriors and Peasants from the Seventh to the Twelfth Century*, trans. Howard B. Clarke (Ithaca, 1974), pp. 48–57. Studies of the early medieval gift economy have been strongly influenced by the work of the anthropologist Marcel Mauss. See Mauss, *The Gift*.

22. Barbara Rosenwein has recently reminded us that the "gift" and "commercial" modes are actually part of a continuum of economic behavior: *To Be the Neighbor of St. Peter*, p. 80.

retains its associations with the giver after it has passed into the hands of the recipient, serving as a reminder of the relationship between the two.[23]

In the early middle ages most important social bonds, ranging from marriages to political alliances to friendships, were cemented by an exchange of gifts.[24] The nobles who made donations to religious communities were, then, acting in accustomed ways, in accordance with recognized rules, and with expectations shaped by experience with similar transactions in other contexts. Since a gift was intended to create or confirm a lasting bond between donor and recipient, one expectation was that the two parties would be—or at least appear to be—compatible with one another. Nobles chose the recipients of their gifts with care. They generally preferred to bestow them on the most prestigious religious communities accessible to them—prestige being measured in both spiritual and social terms. Donors might be attracted by the relics a particular house possessed, the purity and regularity of the life its clergy lived, the splendor of the liturgy performed there.[25] If the members of the community were of high birth or the house was under the patronage of an important political leader, so much the better.[26]

By the same token, it was expected that the clergy who received gifts would prefer to be associated with men and women who could be most helpful to them, with whom they could deal most comfortably, for whom they could pray most eagerly. These concerns were addressed through the gift itself. For unlike the prices nobles some-

23. On the social meaning of property in medieval Europe, see Aron Gurevich, *Categories of Medieval Culture*, trans. George Campbell (London, 1985), p. 255. On the social significance of gifts of property to saints and the clergy, see White, *Custom, Kinship, and Gifts to Saints*, pp. 27–28; Rosenwein, *To Be the Neighbor of St. Peter*, pp. 44–45, 125–43.

24. In addition to the works cited above, see Roman Michalowski, "Le Don d'amitié dans la société carolingienne et les 'translationes sanctorum,'" in Évelyne Patlagean and Pierre Riché, eds., *Hagiographie, cultures, et sociétés, IVe-XIIe siècles* (Paris, 1981), pp. 399–416.

25. See *Cartulaire de l'abbaye de Conques en Rouergue*, ed. Gustave Desjardins (Paris, 1879), no. 60 (1061–65); *Cartulaire de Saint-Victeur au Mans, prieuré de l'abbaye du Mont-Saint-Michel (994–1400)*, ed. Paul de Farcy (Paris, 1895), no. 2 (955–1015); *Cartulaire du chapitre de l'église cathédrale Notre-Dame de Nîmes*, ed. Eugène Germer-Durand (Nîmes, 1874), no. 157 (1080); *Marmoutier: Cartulaire blésois*, no. 68 (1095–96); *Cartulaire de l'abbaye de Saint-Père de Chartres*, ed. Benjamin Guérard, 2 vols. (Paris, 1840), 1: 161–62 (1046). (N.B.—because of the complexities of Guérard's numbering system, the charters of Saint-Père are cited by volume and page number.)

26. R. W. Southern, *Western Society and the Church in the Middle Ages* (Harmondsworth, Eng., 1970), pp. 229–30. And see above, Chapter 3.

times paid for commodities, the gifts they made to religious communities were charged with social significance. They conveyed essential information about the giver, making a link with the recipient seem plausible, setting the terms by which their relationship could exist. When noble donors made gifts, they showed their respect for the clerical recipients and at the same time demonstrated their own worthiness to be associated with the liturgical community.[27] Specifically, donations confirmed the lay donors' ritual, moral, and social standing, and thus made it desirable for the clerical recipients to accept their friendship and perhaps even pray for them.

The act of giving was particularly significant in the ritual context, for giving was, in a sense, the proper ritual function of the laity. Giving was to them what prayer had become to the clergy: it defined their position within the ritual community.[28] The clergy did, of course, make donations to their own and other churches. Monastic cartularies, in particular, contain many examples of gifts from secular priests and bishops. But the clergy also prayed and said mass, whereas when the laity were called upon to act ritually, what they usually did was give.[29] We should remember that one of the ritual functions of the laity as an order in the ecclesia had been to give, to make the offering during mass. Indeed, one of the common terms for the lay order was the "offerers" (offerentes). While the early medieval laity no longer took an active part in the mass-liturgy on a regular basis, they did bring their offerings to church on certain feasts and important occasions (notably, for masses for the dead.) It is significant, then, that the donations made to religious communities were referred to as "offerings" (oblationes) and were made by placing a token of the gift on the altar of the church.[30]

27. Oexle, "Memoria und Memorialüberlieferung," pp. 87–95.

28. Oexle, "Memoria und Memorialüberlieferung," pp. 87–90.

29. Thus, in a period of crisis, Charlemagne and his bishops directed the clergy to pray, fast, and—if possible—give alms "for the lord king, for the army of the Franks, and for the present tribulation"; counts, royal vassals, and other laymen were ordered to fast and to give alms according to their rank: *Capitulare episcoporum* (dated 780; more likely 792–93), in *Capitularia regum Francorum*, 1: 52. See also *Karoli ad Ghaerbaldum episcopum epistola* (dated 807; more likely 805), ibid., pp. 245–46. Michael McCormick discusses these texts in "The Liturgy of War in the Early Middle Ages: Crisis, Litanies, and the Carolingian Monarchy," *Viator* 15 (1984), 10–11.

30. E.g., *Cartulaire de l'abbaye de Beaulieu*, no. 3 (866); *Cartulaire de Saint-Victeur au Mans*, no. 5 (1033–40); *Recueil des chartes de l'abbaye de Cluny*, no. 3548 (1080); *Marmoutier: Cartulaire blésois*, no. 71 (1097). See also Schreiber, "Kirchliches Abgabenwesen an französischen Eigenkirche," in his *Gemeinschaften des Mittelalters*, pp. 151–93.

Such donations were often made in the course of feast-days or
other religious celebrations; they may even have been made during
the offertory of the mass itself in some cases, though the texts are
hard to interpret on this point.[31] But even if the donation was not
made in the course of the mass, the charters nevertheless refer to it as
a gift to God and to the saint on whose altar the token was placed.[32]
Sometimes the group of clerics who would actually enjoy the donation was not even mentioned; the gift was made directly to a supernatural recipient.[33] The act of donation, then, served to identify the
donor as an "offerer," as a servant of God and the saints, and hence as
a member of the ritual community grouped around the altar.

At the same time, the act of donation helped to establish the
donor's moral status, as one who gave alms, as one who helped rather
than oppressed "God's poor," as one who performed good works.
Donations were made *in eleemosyna*, as alms, to the *pauperes Christi*—
literally "paupers of Christ," the members of a religious community.[34] Donors became *benefactores*, those who "did well," in contrast
to the *oppressores*, the *raptores*, and the *calumniatores* who threatened the
property of the house, arousing complaints in the charters and chronicles.[35] Alms were "a great pledge for all who made them before the
most high God;" they would help "open the gates of justice" to the
donor.[36] Phrases such as these have sometimes been dismissed as
pious formulae, designed to obscure the fact that the gifts were being
made to what might be very wealthy religious communities, and in
expectation of favors in return. It is quite clear, however, that not
only the clergy but the donors themselves really considered their gifts
good works.

Lists of people "for whom" a gift was made were very often
included in charters of donation; "I give," announces the donor, "for

31. *Cartulaire de l'abbaye cardinale de la Trinité de Vendôme*, no. 244 (1074): "dum canta-
batur major missa"; le Vicomte de Souancé and Charles Métais, *Saint-Denis de Nogent-le-
Rotrou, 1031–1789: Histoire et cartulaire*, rev. ed. (Vannes, 1899), documents complémentaires, no. 1 (1078): "inter missarum sacrarum sollempnia." On the other hand, sometimes
donors waited until mass was over to make their gifts: e.g., *Cartulaire de l'abbaye de Redon*,
no. 236 (875).

32. E.g., *Cartulaire de Saint-Vincent de Mâcon*, no. 454 (1033–65), p. 260.

33. E.g., *Recueil des chartes de l'abbaye de Cluny*, no. 1772 (987–96).

34. E.g., *Recueil des chartes de l'abbaye de Cluny*, no. 2932 (1039); *Marmoutier: Cartulaire
blésois*, no. 68 (1095–96).

35. E.g., *Cartulaire de l'abbaye de Saint-Père de Chartres*, 1: 136–37 (before 1070).

36. *Recueil des chartes de l'abbaye de Saint-Benoît-sur-Loire*, no. 61 (975) (the reference is
from the Apocrypha, Tobit 4: 11–12); *Cartulaire du chapitre de Nîmes*, no. 120 (1020).

my soul and my wife's," "for the soul of my father," "for my brother's soul and my own." The people thus listed were said to "participate" in the act of donation; it became their good work as well as the
donor's.[37] The inclusion of such lists was not simply formulaic.
Many were so long and detailed, including the names of those who
would benefit from the gift, and their relationship with the donor,
that they must actually have been provided by the person making the
gift. The laity themselves, in other words, recognized the moral value
of what they were doing.[38] Even when some return was expected for
the gift, whether in the form of prayer or in worldly goods, lists of
people "for whom" the gift was made would be included.[39] The act
of giving, then, regardless of its fruits, seems to have underlined the
moral status of the donor in his or her own eyes, as well as in the eyes
of those who benefited from such generosity.

But the gift had a further and very concrete function in the early
middle ages. It also served to confirm the donor's social status, as a
member of the elite of feudal society. We should remember that generosity was especially the attribute of the *seigneur*: lords were judged
by their open-handedness, as well as their leadership in war. Indeed, a
leader's power in a feudal society was often determined by his (or her)
willingness and ability to maintain followers. Since a reputation for
generosity was so important in this period, it is evident that donations
to religious houses, whatever other functions they may have fulfilled,
were also public demonstrations of wealth and open-handedness.[40] It
is significant that the charters sometimes refer to the "liberality" (*lib-
eralitas*) and "largesse" (*largitio*) of donors.[41]

In point of fact, the donations were liberal. Without belaboring
the obvious, we must remind ourselves that the donations we are now
considering, those that resulted in (or resulted from) liturgical commemoration in an important church, were indeed substantial. In 842
Charles the Bald gave an estate (*villa*) at Remilly, along with its cha-

37. E.g., *Recueil des chartes de l'abbaye de Cluny*, no. 2111 (993–1048); *Cartulaire général
de l'Yonne*, no. 94 (1046).

38. E.g., *Recueil des chartes de l'abbaye de Saint-Benoît-sur-Loire*, no. 61 (975). On this
point, see also Bouchard, *Sword, Miter, and Cloister*, pp. 241–43.

39. *Cartulaire de Saint-Victeur au Mans*, no. 13 (1087); *Cartulaire de l'abbaye de Beaulieu*,
no. 14 (1062–72).

40. John Howe, "The Nobility's Reform of the Medieval Church," *The American
Historical Review* 93 (1988), 334.

41. *Cartulaire de l'abbaye de Saint-Père de Chartres*, 1: 62–64 (978); *Cartulaires de l'abbaye
de Molesme*, premier cartulaire, no. 12 (1080–83); *Cartulaire de l'abbaye de Saint-Vincent du
Mans*, no. 16 (1099–1110).

pel, to the cathedral of Saint-Arnoul of Metz, so the clergy would
celebrate a *memoria* each year for Louis the Pious.[42] Sometime around
970, Idren and his wife, Ava, gave a demesne (*curtilus indominicatus*)
with a vineyard and other appurtenances to Saint-Vincent of Mâcon,
so that they might be buried in the cemetery of Saint-Pierre.[43] In the
late eleventh century, Gerbod and his wife, Ada, gave a third of the
whole estate (*villa*) of Ostreseld to Saint-Bertin, so that the brothers
of the house could enjoy a special meal on their anniversaries, and
would more willingly pray for them.[44] Many smaller donations were,
of course, made to religious houses, sometimes by people of very
limited means. As far as the people who came to be commemorated
in the liturgy of these houses were concerned, though, it is not out of
place to speak of "liberality."

The clergy were not reluctant to mention the social standing of
the men and women who made donations to them. Often they employed titles of worldly rank (*comitissa*, *vicedominus*), other, vaguer
social designations (*dominus*, *miles*) and even descriptive terms (*hon-
orabilis vir, vir multe nobilitatis et sagacitatis*). Social distinctions were
not forgotten at the church door.[45] Under these circumstances, donations made publicly and often before a crowd of followers could
indeed serve to confirm one's social standing in a dramatic fashion.[46]
The act of donation, then, emphasized the ritual, moral, and social
status of the donor. It helped to identify the layperson with the community of those who prayed, with the community of holy men or
women, with the community of highborn clerics. By confirming the
donor's status, donation made it easier to establish close relations with
a religious community. The relationship, in turn, might result in
prayer for the donor.

This was because of the expectation of reciprocity in these interactions. An essential aspect of early medieval gift-giving was the institution of the return-gift. When a gift passed between social equals, it

42. *Recueil des actes de Charles II, le Chauve, roi de France*, ed. Georges Tessier, following
Arthur Giry and Maurice Prou, 3 vols. (Paris, 1943–55), no. 9 (842).
43. *Cartulaire de Saint-Vincent de Mâcon*, no. 123 (968–71).
44. *Cartulaire de l'abbaye de Saint-Bertin*, pp. 201–2 (ca. 1084).
45. The descriptive terms come from *Cartulaire de l'abbaye de la Chapelle-aux-Planches*,
Montiérender, no. 36 (1050–82) and *Cartulaire de l'abbaye de Redon*, no. 292 (1008–26). See
also *Cartulaire de Saint-Vincent de Mâcon*, no. 103 (950–58).
46. Crowds were often present when donations were made: see, for example, *Cartulaire de Saint-Victeur au Mans*, no. 4 (1014); de Souancé and Métais, *Saint-Denis de Nogent-
le-Rotrou*, documents complémentaires, no. 1 (1078); *Cartulaire de l'abbaye de Saint-Bertin*,
pp. 220–21 (1102).

generally had to be answered with another gift, on pain of losing prestige or even breaking the bond between giver and recipient.[47] This rule of reciprocity helped maintain the equilibrium of the gift-economy, ensuring the circulation of goods and services even when commercial exchanges were limited. As a number of scholars have noted, it regulated a wide variety of transactions, including those between noble donors and elite religious houses.[48]

The men and women who made gifts to religious communities did not throw away valuable property heedlessly, without regard to its worth. They fully expected to receive something in exchange—whether in the form of small favors, property, prayer or "reward in heaven." The return-gift might not be offered at the same time as the initial donation, but sooner or later it would be forthcoming. Nobles were unabashed in expressing their hopes for some such return, and even in specifying what it might be. "We ask not for gold, nor for silver, but for the prayers of these and the other monks . . . in return for this donation," noted one donor.[49]

By the same token, the clergy expected to receive something in exchange for their acts of "liturgical generosity." It is worth noting here that prayer was not always performed in response to a gift in the early middle ages. Sometimes religious houses granted liturgical privileges on their own initiative. A monastery might, for example, bury someone as an act of good will, only later receiving a gift from the dead person's family: " . . . on the day when he died and was buried, before they ate that evening, his parents decided what they would give to God and his servants in the place where their dear son rested in Christ."[50]

47. Grierson, "Commerce in the Dark Ages," p. 137; see also Mauss, *The Gift*, p. 5. In some parts of Europe this was not only social custom, but law. Among the Lombards, for example, some gifts only legally became the property of the recipient when a return-gift (*launegildum*) had been made to the donor: Dormeier, *Montecassino und die Laien*, p. 148. On the implications of this rule for relations between the living and the dead, see Geary, "Échanges et relations entre les vivants et les morts."

48. Stephen White offers an illuminating discussion of the process and implications of these transactions within the context of the gift-economy: *Custom, Kinship, and Gifts to Saints*, pp. 27–39.

49. *Recueil des chartes de l'abbaye de Cluny*, no. 1715 (985). On prayer as a return-gift, see Schreiber, "Kirchliches Abgabenwesen an französischen Eigenkirchen," in his *Gemeinschaften des Mittelalters*, pp. 171–85; Jorden, *Das cluniazensische Totengedächtniswesen*, p. 94; Oexle, "Memoria und Memorialüberlieferung," pp. 87–95.

50. *Cartulaire de l'abbaye cardinale de la Trinité de Vendôme*, no. 326 (1085). See also *Cartulaire de l'abbaye de Redon*, no. 330 (before 1037); *Recueil des chartes de l'abbaye de Cluny*, no. 2009 (993–1048).

Churches could act in this way without a great deal of risk, for powerful members of the laity apparently felt obligated to make a gift in return for the prayers they enjoyed. To do otherwise would be to invite a charge of ingratitude and perhaps to break the ties that had resulted in prayer.[51] Concerns about social status may also have played a role. Early in the eleventh century, for example, a knight named Robert was buried at Marmoutier. He was an old friend of the house, so the monks asked no gift for his burial, but Robert's sons insisted on making one anyway—"lest his burial seem to have been conceded *gratis*, for nothing."[52] The text is somewhat ambiguous, but it suggests that the sons were trying to avoid the appearance of being unable to give something for their father's burial. The gift was in this case a public demonstration of affluence, as well as a response to the generosity of the monks.

But if religious communities expected to receive donations in return for their liturgical efforts, those efforts should not be seen as an attempt to "buy" property. Neither should the gifts nobles gave to the religious community be seen as the "price" of prayer. Whereas in a commercial transaction the objects are the focus of attention, and their respective values are carefully (if not always accurately) weighed, in a gift-exchange it is enough that the objects be appropriately large and splendid for the circumstances of the parties involved.[53] What is calculated in such an exchange is not their exact value but the details of the social bond they establish. This focus on the relationship of donor and recipient made it possible for notions of generosity, largesse, and the goodness of the act to remain attached to gifts in early medieval charters, even when the donor received—and indeed expected—some material or liturgical return-gift. It also meant that the connection between gift and prayer was far more flexible than that between price and commodity.

Sometimes, of course, the two were very closely linked. It might

51. A priest made a gift to one church, as he said, "lest I seem ungrateful" for the prayers performed for him there: *Cartulaire de l'abbaye de Saint-Vincent du Mans*, no. 508 (1080–1109).

52. *Marmoutier: Cartulaire blésois*, no. 14 (1032–64). This transaction seems to reflect assumptions about property and status similar to those of people who paid higher wergelds than they had to in compensation for a death: see Gurevich, *Categories of Medieval Culture*, p. 220.

53. Lester K. Little, *Religious Poverty and the Profit Economy in Medieval Europe* (Ithaca, 1978), p. 4; Mauss, *The Gift*, pp. 17–45. The monks of Saint-Vincent of Le Mans promised Drogo burial in return for a *congruam caritatem*: *Cartulaire de l'abbaye de Saint-Vincent du Mans*, no. 599 (1067–78).

happen that the religious community wanted a particular piece of property in the possession of one of their noble neighbors, and would offer some desirable liturgical service in return for that property. In 1014, for example, the abbot of Mont-Saint-Michel came to Hugh, count of Le Mans, asking him either to give or to sell the abbey some "useful" land, near the monks' other possessions in the area. He added, modestly, that they would prefer to get something big enough so that the monks they sent to collect the revenues would be able to feed themselves and their horses out of it, and would not lose the whole profit in traveling back and forth. Hugh made the donation, on the condition that the monks pray for him.[54]

It also sometimes happened that a wealthy person wanted a particular type of liturgical privilege, and made a gift in order to acquire it. Charles the Bald granted numerous privileges and pieces of property to Saint-Denis over a period of years. While some of these acts were not associated with the performance of prayers, others were made specifically to ensure that lamps would burn on the altar, paupers would be fed, and special meals (refectiones) would be provided for the monks in the king's memory.[55] Similarly, in the eleventh century Guy of Chaumont made a number of donations to the nuns of Le Ronceray; he then added another gift specifically "so that after his death he would be inscribed in the martyrology and the church's benefits would be granted to him in perpetuity."[56]

Some liturgical privileges were especially popular with early medieval donors. The privilege of monastic burial was frequently requested and frequently granted. One result was that a "customary" gift "for burial" developed in some areas. Dietrich Poeck has shown that in the tenth and eleventh centuries the grant of burial privileges at Cluny was very often associated with the donation of a mansus or homestead to the monastery.[57] It would be going too far, however, to see these "customary" gifts as the "price" of burial. The monks of Cluny did not insist on a donation of this size—or, indeed, of any specific size—in return for burial. Sometimes they accepted a much smaller gift (especially if it were in a desirable location); sometimes they seem to have expected more. Early in the eleventh century, for

54. *Cartulaire de l'abbaye de Saint-Victeur au Mans*, no. 4 (1014). This type of negotiation became more common in the late eleventh century: see below.

55. Those acts which resulted in prayer were: *Recueil des actes de Charles II*, nos. 135 (851), 220 (860), 238 (862), 246 (862), 247 (862), 263 (864), 379 (875), 439 (877).

56. *Cartularium monasterii beatae Mariae caritatis*, no. 165 (eleventh century).

57. Poeck, "Laienbegräbnisse in Cluny," especially pp. 177–78.

example, they entered into an agreement with Adalgis, who gave a *mansus* to the house. The monks promised to bury him in return for this gift, but they asked him to give a further ten solidi at the time of death, or—if that were impossible—five solidi.[58] Clearly the monks of Cluny were very much interested in the property they would receive in return for their liturgical efforts. However, they were willing to take more or less, depending on the donor's situation as well as the value they attributed to burial in their cemetery.

Often, too, the relationship between prayer and property was less direct than in the case of Adalgis. A single act might result in a number of liturgical privileges for the donor. Count Raoul of Bar abandoned his claim on a wood to Montiérender, in return for a weekly mass, and so that the monks would feed a pauper perpetually on his behalf.[59] Many charters could be cited in which a donation was rewarded with the privilege of entry into the societas orationum of the monastery, the right to be accepted as a monk at any time (usually it was stipulated that no further entry-gift was required) and the right to be buried in the monastic cemetery.[60]

These donations brought multiple privileges to the donor alone. In other charters, a single gift might result in services for several people. Sulpice, for example, vowed to become a monk at Saint-Père of Chartres and to grant the house some property, but he died before the vow could be fulfilled. Before his death, he made his wife and his *fideles* promise to carry his body to the monastery for burial and to make the gift, which they did. Sulpice's son gave his assent to the gift, and when he died, he was buried next to his father for its sake. Sulpice's brother also gave his assent, and was received into the societas of the house as a result. In this case, a single donation resulted in burial for two people and formal association for a third.[61]

A donation might result not only in liturgical privileges, but also in some sort of material return-gift for the donor.[62] Sometimes this

58. *Recueil des chartes de l'abbaye de Cluny*, no. 926 (ca. 1006–1008). See also no. 2957 (1042).
59. *Cartulaire de l'abbaye de la Chapelle-aux-Planches*, Montiérender, no. 33 (ca. 1050).
60. E.g., *Recueil des chartes de l'abbaye de Cluny*, no. 3806 (ca. 1100); *Cartulaire de Marmoutier pour le Dunois*, no. 134 (1071); de Souancé and Métais, *Saint-Denis de Nogent-le-Rotrou*, no. 86 (no date).
61. *Cartulaire de l'abbaye de Saint-Père de Chartres*, 2: 549 (1081). See also *Marmoutier: Cartulaire blésois*, no. 14 (1032–64); *Cartulaire de Gellone*, ed. Paul Alaus, Léon Cassan, and Edmond Meynial (Montpellier, 1898), no. 388 (1097); de Souancé and Métais, *Saint-Denis de Nogent-le-Rotrou*, no. 67 (ca. 1100).
62. E.g., *Cartulaire de l'abbaye de la Sainte-Trinité du Mont de Rouen*, ed. Achille Deville (Paris, 1840), no. 52 (eleventh century?).

return-gift took the form of a prestige-item, reflecting the esteem in which the clergy held their benefactor. Thus, William gave up his claims to certain customary rights to the priory of Saint-Victeur of Le Mans in return for formal association and a "good" horse.[63] Sometimes, however, prayer was combined with some material return because the donor could not decide whether the transaction was actually a sale or a gift. When Robert Michael and his brother Almar offered some land to Marmoutier, they both went to the abbey, "and in our chapter-meeting [noted the monastic scribe] they received the benefit of our societas . . . and in the presence of the whole chapter they confirmed and authorized the aforesaid *gift* and *sale*, and then they placed the gift of all the aforesaid things on the altar of the Lord in the church, and thus received the nine aforementioned silver marks from the hand of Lord Bernard, the *panetarius* . . ."[64] Here the gift seems to have been rewarded with formal association in the prayers of the house, while the sale was made for nine silver marks.

In the cases just cited, a single donation resulted in liturgical privileges, perhaps of several kinds, for the donor and his family. On the other hand, it often happened that a single person made a number of donations to the religious house in which he or she would later be commemorated, making it difficult to connect a particular gift with the grant of a particular liturgical privilege. Hugh Bardoul was accepted into the societas of Molesme both because of a particular gift and because of "innumerable others" he had conferred on the house.[65] Hademar offered half of a piece of property he held to Marmoutier, with the understanding that he would be buried there. Many years later, on his deathbed, he added the other half of the property, and even agreed to acknowledge a gift made by his father, which he had refused for many years to concede. Having done this, he died and was buried by the monks.[66] It is not clear, however, what role the deathbed donations had in ensuring his burial. In all these examples, the lay donor's gift and the community's prayers were closely related, but the correspondence between the gift and the liturgical privilege

63. *Cartulaire de Saint-Victeur au Mans*, no. 5 (1033–40). See also *Cartulaire de l'abbaye de Saint-Père de Chartres*, 1: 191–92 (before 1061); *Cartulaire de l'abbaye de Redon*, no. 303 (after 1050).

64. *Cartulaire de Marmoutier pour le Dunois*, no. 151 (1096). Emphasis mine. See also *Cartulaire de Saint-Vincent de Mâcon*, no. 527 (1060–1118); *Cartulaire d'Aniane*, ed. Léon Cassan and Edmond Meynial (Montpellier, 1900), no. 230 (1036–60).

65. *Cartulaires de l'abbaye de Molesme*, premier cartulaire, no. 24 (1089–1104).

66. *Marmoutier: Cartulaire blésois*, no. 14 (1032–64).

was not direct. The liturgical return-gift seems to be an outgrowth of the donor's relationship of familiaritas with the community that prayed, rather than a response to a particular gift.

In some charters of donation, the gift was treated as a way of providing for the physical needs of the community, a means of ensuring that its liturgical life could continue. A donation might be made "for the use of the brothers continually pleading for the clemency of the heavenly king,"[67] or so that "the monks serving God . . . may have it for their use and possess it . . . "[68] It was in the interests of the laity to help maintain the monks, nuns or canons in their vocation, for they could benefit from whatever prayers the clergy performed. Some hoped to be remunerated for their gifts in heaven "through the prayers of those whom we sustain by supplying temporal goods."[69] Such gifts were associated not with a particular service, but with the whole liturgy, the customary prayers of the community. Ingezo of Laon gave a church to the monks of Cluny, "so that they may live well, insofar as the faculties of this church permit, and may celebrate the divine office according to the rule, and order it as do the other monks who live under this holy regimen; and this we humbly beg, that they may pray for us and the souls of our relatives in their daily and nightly prayers, as they do for all the faithful, living and dead."[70] Here the donor offered his gift not "for prayers," but in support of the monastic life of prayer.

One form of gift-giving reflects this viewpoint with particular clarity. Wealthy individuals sometimes chose to express their generosity by endowing a festive meal, to be served—usually once a year—to the members of the religious community. In 885, for example, Ermenric made a large donation to the abbey of Beaulieu (near Limoges), so that the monks might have a refectio, a special meal, once a year.[71] Arrangements could be made for the meal to be served on any day the donor chose: Charles the Simple had meals served in several churches on the anniversary of his anointing as king.[72] Normally,

67. *Cartulaire de Marmoutier pour le Dunois*, no. 12 (1050–60).

68. de Souancé and Métais, *Saint-Denis de Nogent-le-Rotrou*, no. 21 (ca. 1080).

69. *Recueil des chartes de l'abbaye de Cluny*, no. 2812 (1029). See also *Cartulaire de Saint-Vincent de Mâcon*, no. 103 (950–58).

70. *Recueil des chartes de l'abbaye de Cluny*, no. 3415 (1068).

71. *Cartulaire de l'abbaye de Beaulieu*, no. 55 (885). See also *Cartulaire de l'abbaye de Saint-Bertin*, pp. 109–10 (861–64?).

72. *Recueil des actes de Charles III, le Simple, roi de France (893–923)*, ed. Philippe Lauer (Paris, 1949), nos. 70 (912), 88 (917), 89 (917), 92 (918).

however, after the donor died the feast would be transferred to the anniversary of his or her death.[73]

In a society constantly threatened by hunger, such endowments had not only a practical value, but also a deeper significance, as a sign of friendship. They were substantial gifts, for it must have been expensive to feed one of the larger religious communities, even for one day a year. (In the late eleventh century, the count of Mâcon offered Cluny a large gift, which included a fishpond, so that the monks could enjoy a generous fish dinner on his anniversary.[74]) But they also served as a means of reminding the community at least once a year, and in a very concrete way, of the debt of gratitude it owed to its benefactor. In fact, the charters of donation often stipulate that the meal is to be served "in [the donor's] memory."[75]

Because the anniversary meal helped to remind the community of the donor, it also offered an opportunity to pray for him or her. Charles the Bald endowed several refectiones at the cathedral of Lyon, so that the brothers of the church might "more devoutly celebrate the divine office on these days, praying God's clemency for the salvation" of the king and his relatives.[76] In the eleventh century, a certain Geoffrey stipulated that on his father's anniversary "this refectio should be prepared in a most praiseworthy manner for the lords of Cluny, so that the brothers may keep his memory more willingly in all their divine services."[77] In establishing refectiones at religious houses, then, donors did hope to be commemorated in the liturgy. However, most of the charters that describe these meals do not mention the service to be held on the anniversary, while others refer to them only as "prayers" or the "usual prayers."[78] It is generally unclear whether we are dealing with what would later be called a "solemn" anniversary, involving special masses and prayers for the dead person, or with the simpler anniversary, in which the dead were commemorated through the use of their names during the ordinary round of prayer. The emphasis in the charters is on the relationship of

73. E.g., *Cartulaire de l'abbaye de Beaulieu*, no. 11 (887).
74. *Recueil des chartes de l'abbaye de Cluny*, no. 3610 (1085–87).
75. *Cartulaire de l'abbaye de Beaulieu*, no. 11 (887); *Recueil des actes de Charles III*, no. 88 (917). As noted in Chapter 2, a vita of the person being commemorated was sometimes read during the anniversary meal. On the place of memorial meals (and the related act of memorial almsgiving) in the care of the dead, see Oexle, "Die Gegenwart der Toten," in Braet and Verbeke, *Death in the Middle Ages*, pp. 50–53; idem, "Mahl und Spende im mittelalterlichen Totenkult."
76. *Recueil des actes de Charles II*, no. 355 (871).
77. *Recueil des chartes de l'abbaye de Cluny*, no. 2940 (ca. 1040).
78. E.g., *Cartulaire de l'abbaye de Saint-Père de Chartres*, 1: 65 (978).

donor and beneficiary, the bonds of generosity and gratitude, the "remembrance" of the giver, rather than on the details of liturgical services.

The clergy were not the only ones thought to benefit from this type of endowment. Most gifts made to religious houses in the early middle ages were actually given to the saints. Indeed, as I have already noted, the clergy who stood to benefit most directly from these donations are sometimes not even mentioned. Under the circumstances, it is hardly surprising that so many charters express a desire for assistance from the saints. Indeed, a scribe working at the monastery of Conques in the late eleventh century assumed that this was the primary motive behind donations to his house. He began one document with a description of how charters of donation should be drawn up: first the current holders of the property should be listed, then the property that was to be given, and finally "the saints by whose intercession the donors wish to be helped."[79]

In some charters the prayers of the clergy are linked to the intercession of the saints. Thus, Acard gave to Saint-Vincent of Mâcon for his own soul and for those of his father and ancestors, "so that the Lord may grant me and them remission of sins and eternal life through the intercession of St. Vincent and through the prayers of his canons."[80] In others, only the prayers of the saints are mentioned. Hubert gave to St. Peter of Cluny "so that he may pray to the Lord for me and open the gates of paradise to me."[81] It might be thought that these were simply pious formulae, used in documents drawn up by clerical scribes, which did not necessarily express the interests of lay donors. However, there is some evidence that lay donors did give to religious communities specifically to gain the goodwill of the saints. In 937, a certain Adrald gave an allod to the patron saints of Conques—Peter, Vincent, and Foy—"so that they will give me rem-

79. *Cartulaire de l'abbaye de Conques*, no. 56 (1061–1108): "In conscribendis donationibus primitus intromittendi sunt heredes nominatim, deinde hereditas quae donatur, postremo sancti quorum intercessionibus datores cupiunt se adjuvari." The use of the words *heredes* and *hereditas* suggests the exchange of earthly for heavenly inheritances.

80. *Cartulaire de Saint-Vincent de Mâcon*, no. 24 (1060–1108): "ut mihi et eis Dominus per intercessionem Sancti Vincentii et per orationes canonicorum ejus tribuat remissionem peccatorum et vitam eternam." Compare *Cartulaire de l'abbaye de Saint-Victor de Marseille*, ed. Benjamin Guérard, 2 vols. (Paris, 1857), no. 269 (994–1032); *Cartulaire de la Chapelle-aux-Planches*, Montiérender, no. 16 (980).

81. *Recueil des chartes de l'abbaye de Cluny*, no. 1772 (987–96): "ut ipse Dominum roget pro me et aperiat mihi januam paradysi."

edy on the day of my departure from this world."[82] He ordered that the revenue from the property be used to purchase wax, presumably for candles, to "illuminate" those saints. Just as some noble donors arranged for the clergy to enjoy special meals on their anniversaries, Adrald arranged to provide light at the altars of the saints in order to encourage more assiduous prayer. The many gifts associated with lamps for the altars of saints in this period can probably be understood as similar efforts to gain the goodwill and prayers of saintly intercessors.[83] In return for a gift made to the saints, relics might also be deployed during the donor's funeral procession, as in the case of the Breton noble Deurhoiarn discussed earlier.[84]

If gifts of property were often associated with grants of prayer in the early middle ages, then, the connection beween the two was seldom simple and direct. Gifts should not be seen as the "price" of prayer, nor even as the "means of obtaining" prayer. Indeed, I would argue that early medieval nobles did not generally perceive "prayers" as distinct objects in their own right, to be bargained and paid for. Rather, they saw prayer as the distinguishing activity of the community with which they hoped to associate themselves. The pattern of noble interaction with religious communities suggests that members of the elite were trying not so much to obtain specific kinds of prayer as to establish relations with the community that prayed. This is not to say that the resulting prayers were unimportant. But it was the relationship itself which seems to have had priority.

THE PREDOMINANCE OF ASSOCIATIVE PRAYER

Missae speciales, that is, votive masses performed for the benefit of specific individuals or groups, have received a great deal of attention in recent studies of early medieval prayer for the dead.[85] Arnold

---

82. *Cartulaire de l'abbaye de Conques*, no. 182 (937): "ut rimedium donent michi in die exitus mei de isto saeculo."

83. Abbot Adalard of Saint-Bertin leased some land to Odwin in return for an annual rent of lights for the altar of the saint, before which Adalard's father, Count Hunroc, was buried: *Cartulaire de l'abbaye de Saint-Bertin*, pp. 93–94 (853). See also *Recueil des chartes de l'abbaye de Saint-Germain-des-Prés, des origines au début du XIIIe siècle*, ed. René Poupardin, 2 vols. (Paris, 1909–30), nos. 37 (872–75), 47 (954–95).

84. *Cartulaire de l'abbaye de Redon*, no. 236 (875–78).

85. E.g., Schmid and Oexle, "Voraussetzungen und Wirkung des Gebetsbundes von

Angenendt has argued that the development of these masses, which first appeared in the early middle ages, was associated with the development of "tariffed" penance. By the eighth century it had become possible to commute one's penitential obligations into a certain number of masses, and from that time on missae speciales assumed a more important role in the liturgical obligations of the clergy.[86] As we have seen, special masses for the dead were frequently celebrated in monasteries and other important churches. Whole series of masses were offered during the first year after a death as part of the ritual of monastic burial. They were offered for the members of the same or associated houses on a monthly or annual basis. They may also have been performed more often by individual priests as part of their personal devotions.[87]

The scholars who study the relationship of the laity to elite religious communities have tended to assume that the men and women who made gifts to those communities wanted to acquire as many of these special masses as possible for themselves. In particular, concern about incomplete penances and anxiety to have masses offered to atone for sins has been seen as the major factor behind the growth in donations to reformed monasteries such as Cluny in the late tenth and eleventh centuries. These monasteries were attractive to donors, it is argued, because they were known to be inhabited by many priest-monks, who collectively performed vast numbers of masses for the dead.[88]

The charter evidence, however, presents a rather different picture of the liturgical results of donations. Some charters do refer rather vaguely to "masses," and in most of these cases what was probably meant were special masses of some sort. In 826, for example, a wealthy landowner named Goibert confided all of his property to caretakers, just before he and his family set out on a pilgrimage to Rome. If he died on the trip, the caretakers were to dispose of the property as he directed. His holdings in one area were to be reserved for the use of his son, if he (the son) returned from the pilgrimage.

Attigny," pp. 72–73; Angenendt, "Theologie und Liturgie," in Schmid and Wollasch, *Memoria*, especially pp. 174–79.

86. See below, Chapter 5.

87. I am referring here not to masses for the dead in general, but rather to masses specifically devoted to the needs of dead individuals or distinct groups.

88. Southern, *Western Society and the Church*, pp. 225–28; Cowdrey, *The Cluniacs and the Gregorian Reform*, pp. 121–29. See below, Chapter 5.

But if he did not return, they were to be given to the monks of Saint-Bertin "in order that they may make offerings for me and my son and my father and mother, and celebrate masses or psalms."[89] Clearly what Goibert had in mind was the performance of special masses (or psalms, which could be substituted for masses in the commutation of penances) for himself and his family. In other charters, however, what seems to have been meant was the Mass—that is, the eucharistic celebration understood as part of the community's public liturgy. Thus, in 948 Asquald gave a tithe to the monastery of Conques "for the offering of the sacrifice or the maintenance of lamps."[90] I take this to be a gift for the support of the liturgical life as a whole, rather than for the performance of special masses for Asquald.

In general, however, the charter evidence suggests that missae speciales were not as important to noble donors as has often been claimed. References to specific numbers of special masses are quite rare in the charters. And even vague references to masses like the ones just cited appear less frequently than references to other kinds of liturgical privileges.[91] Some of those other privileges, of course, also included the performance of special masses. When a lay benefactor was buried in a monastic cemetery, for example, he or she probably enjoyed a full monastic burial, including a septennarium or tricennarium. The nobles who were granted the privilege of burial at an important monastery were certainly aware of what would be done for them when they died. But the way in which liturgical privileges were defined in early medieval charters suggests that what religious communities understood themselves to be granting and what noble donors understood themselves to be receiving was something rather different from the "many" masses, psalms, or prayers so often mentioned in modern studies.

It is significant, in the first place, that many of the charters that mention prayer for donors offer no concrete definition of the services to be performed. Count Robert of Rouergue and his mother, Philippa, granted a church to Conques "so that prayer shall be made there for our salvation while we remain in the body, and that we shall

89. *Cartulaire de l'abbaye de Saint-Bertin*, pp. 158–59 (826). On the dealings between Goibert, his son, and Saint-Bertin, see Nicholas Huyghebaert, "Le Comte Baudouin II de Flandre et le 'custos' de Steneland: A propos d'un faux précepte de Charles le Chauve pour Saint-Bertin (866)," *Revue Bénédictine* 69 (1959), 49–52.
90. *Cartulaire de l'abbaye de Conques*, no. 413 (948): "ad sacrificium offerendo vel ad luminaria concinanda."
91. Appendix B, Table 11.

be remembered in perpetuity after we die."[92] Two brothers, Gurdier-
nus and Glast, asked the monks of Redon to "receive them in their
prayers," granting them part of an estate in return.[93] Erchembald and
his nephew allowed some property to be transferred to Saint-Père of
Chartres in return for twenty librae and the "assistance of the monks'
prayers" (orationum suffragium).[94]

One might argue that descriptions of the liturgical services due to
donors were purposely left a little vague in the charters drawn up by
religious houses, since the clergy would not be very eager to define in
full detail the obligations their communities undertook. But the diplomas of kings and great princes, drawn up at their command and
sometimes by their own chanceries, are often just as unclear. In 845
Charles the Bald confirmed a donation made to Saint-Denis "so that
our reward before God may be more amply increased through the
intercession of [St. Denis] and the prayers of the servants of God."[95]
Stephen of Blois gave to Marmoutier in 1096 "so that both in this life
and after death, we may deserve to be helped in the sight of God by
[the community's] prayers."[96]

Even when the scribes were more precise about what was due to
lay donors for their gifts, they tended to define services in terms of the
parties involved, rather than in and of themselves. Often it was the
donor's relationship with the community that determined what
prayers were due. His or her name was to be mentioned every day
"along with the others by whose gifts our life is sustained."[97] In other
words, the donor would be included in prayers for benefactors of the
house. If the layperson entered the monastic societas, the prayers due
to him or her were defined accordingly. Thus, the monks of Cluny
promised Petronilla that she would be buried by them "as one to
whom [the abbot] had conceded the societas of the place . . ."[98]
Sometimes, indeed, prayer was not mentioned at all, and negotiations
focused on the donor's status, which was established by the gift.
Richer made a donation to Saint-Père of Chartres because he had
recently been made a familiaris of the abbey.[99] Philip I gave to the

---

92. *Cartulaire de l'abbaye de Conques*, no. 523 (1059). See also *Cartulaire de la Chapelle-
aux-Planches*, Montiérender, no. 35 (1050).
93. *Cartulaire de l'abbaye de Redon*, no. 357 (990–92).
94. *Cartulaire de l'abbaye de Saint-Père de Chartres*, 2: 416–17 (1094–95).
95. *Recueil des actes de Charles II*, no. 65 (845).
96. *Cartulaire de Marmoutier pour le Dunois*, no. 92 (1096).
97. *Cartulaire de l'abbaye de Saint-Père de Chartres*, 1: 152–53 (1060).
98. *Recueil des chartes de l'abbaye de Cluny*, no. 3233 (1049–1109).
99. *Cartulaire de l'abbaye de Saint-Père de Chartres*, 2: 490–91 (no date).

canons of Notre Dame of Poissy "so that he might be forever a *concanonicus.*"[100] Such designations of status implied liturgical privileges, to be sure, but the details of the services were not the center of attention.

Often, too, the prayer granted to a donor was defined in terms of the community's liturgical customs. One donor hoped that the monks of Cluny would "always deign to be mindful of me in their sacred daily prayers"—in other words, he sought commemoration within the ordinary round of services.[101] Ricinde and her son gave a gift to Fleury so that the monks would "associate" (*sociarent*) them in their prayers.[102] For Gunher's concessions to Saint-Père, the monks "made him a colleague" (*collegimus*) in their "prayers and in all [their] good works."[103] A donor might also obtain the right to "participate in all the good works that are done inside and outside the monastery."[104] Through their gifts, then, the laity could hope to become "associates," "colleagues," "participants" in the liturgical life of the house.

The most complete identification with the community meant that the donor would be treated "as a sister," "as a brother": *sicut soror, quasi frater.* Charles the Bald, who was lay abbot of Saint-Denis, asked the monks to pray for him "like a brother," as well as like an abbot and king.[105] Count Roger of Saint-Pol divided the proceeds of an estate with the monks of Saint-Bertin, "so that we would perform the same office of prayer for him . . . as for our brother."[106] Hugh of Vendenesse gave up all claims on a church to Saint-Vincent of Mâcon, asking in return that the canons absolve his ancestors and lords of the sin of holding the church. The canons did so, and also "associated him, like a brother and a friend, in their good deeds and prayers."[107]

References to "prayer" (unspecified) or to "prayer like that performed for a brother" are more common in early medieval charters

---

100. *Recueil des actes de Philippe Ier*, no. 12 (1061).
101. *Recueil des chartes de l'abbaye de Cluny*, no. 2006 (993–1048).
102. *Recueil des chartes de l'abbaye de Saint-Benoît-sur-Loire*, no. 37 (923–30).
103. *Cartulaire de l'abbaye de Saint-Père de Chartres*, 1: 239 (before 1102). Walter and Goslein were "joined" (*conjungi*) to the prayers of the monks of Redon: *Cartulaire de l'abbaye de Redon*, no. 310 (before 1060).
104. *Cartulaire de l'abbaye de Saint-Vincent du Mans*, no. 599 (1067–78).
105. *Recueil des actes de Charles II*, no. 379 (875).
106. *Les Chartes de Saint-Bertin*, no. 73 (1051). Material as well as liturgical benefits could be defined in this way: see *Libri confraternitatum sancti Galli*, p. 141.
107. *Cartulaire de Saint-Vincent de Mâcon*, no. 34 (1063–72). See also *Cartulaire de l'abbaye de Redon*, no. 373 (1037); *Cartulaires de l'abbaye de Molesme*, premier cartulaire, no. 246 (1076–1100); *Recueil des chartes de l'abbaye de Cluny*, no. 3765 (ca. 1100).

than are detailed accounts of the liturgical services to be performed.
Nor was this simply a matter of diplomatic convention. Some documents in which the prayers to be offered for the donor were carefully
detailed will be discussed below. But the fact that such detailed descriptions, though perfectly permissible in terms of diplomatic form,
appear relatively infrequently is, I think, significant. It seems to indicate that liturgical benefits were defined by the relationship of donor
and beneficiary, and not vice versa.

   In general, the charter evidence suggests that early medieval donors wanted to be treated as members of the community that received
their gifts. The privileges most often granted in return for those gifts
were burial in the community's cemetery, inscription in the community's liber memorialis or necrology, and commemoration every year
(occasionally more often) by the community within its regular round
of prayer. A charter from the mid-eleventh century illustrates how
desirable such associative services were thought to be. Fulk of *Rel-
liana*, brother of the archbishop of Arles and an important lord in his
own right, had offered a castle and vill, with all their appurtenances,
to the abbey of Saint-Victor of Marseille. In return, the monks offered Fulk

> our fraternity and society, praying God almighty to grant you a
> share in all our good works, so that if we do anything good and
> pleasing to him, you shall have a share in it both here and in the
> celestial paradise, according to his good will. Moreover, we ordain
> and, by ordaining, command to those who witness your death, that
> for all time, from year to year, they celebrate your anniversary like
> that of an abbot, as is proper for a man of your stature, namely by
> offering bread and wine for you *during the general mass* for the reme-
> dy of your soul . . . [108]

Clearly commemoration in the general mass—that is, within the ordinary round of prayer—was considered eminently suitable for a man
(or woman) of high status in this period.[109] This is not to say that
early medieval nobles were uninterested in the special masses, psalms,
and prayers that might be performed for them by individual priests.

   108. *Cartulaire de l'abbaye de Saint-Victor de Marseille*, no. 62 (1053). Emphasis mine.
   109. The evidence of this charter and of the other texts cited in this section suggests
that the case of Abbess Theophanu of Essen (d. 1054), who arranged to have a great many
missae speciales performed during her funeral, may have been less typical than Angenendt
assumes: "Missa specialis," p. 208.

Probably they expected to benefit from such services when they sought association with a clerical community. But special masses or psalms were seldom mentioned separately in the charters from this period. The focus was on association, rather than on the acquisition of specific numbers of prayers.

If the liturgical results of noble donations to religious communities were predominantly associative throughout the period from the mid-eighth to the end of the eleventh century, the relative popularity of particular liturgical privileges seems to have fluctuated over time. It is impossible, of course, to calculate the incidence of any given service very accurately, both because so many early medieval documents have disappeared, and because their idiosyncratic language makes them difficult to categorize. What follow are some rough estimates of the relative frequency with which various privileges are mentioned in the charters over the course of the period. They are based on my analysis of the two data sets described above.[110]

It is particularly difficult to determine what kind of services were granted to nobles in the second half of the eighth century. Among the surviving charters from that period, only a very small number mention prayer for nonclerics, and then mostly for the king and members of the royal family. We cannot be sure whether the services they enjoyed would also have been performed for lesser members of the elite as well. For example, a great many royal diplomas include formulae of this sort: "[the king acts] . . . so that these servants of God . . . may delight more and more in continually entreating the Lord's mercy for ourselves, for our children, and for the stability of our realm." Probably these phrases referred to the prayers Charlemagne is known to have required from the churches of his realm as a public duty.[111] The clergy were to pray for the king anyway, but they would pray more zealously as a result of the benefits he offered them. If this was the case, however, the kind of prayer described in these charters would only have been performed for Charlemagne and his family, not for other members of the lay elite.

Only three of Charlemagne's acts refer to prayer in less formulaic terms, and even then it is difficult to know precisely what is meant. In 769, Charlemagne gave the cell of Saint-Dié to the monastery of

110. See Appendix A and Appendix B, Table 11.
111. Ludwig Biehl, *Das liturgische Gebet für Kaiser und Reich: Ein Beitrag zur Geschichte des Verhältnisses von Kirche und Staat* (Paderborn, 1937), especially pp. 93–102. See also McCormick, "The Liturgy of War in the Early Middle Ages," pp. 1–23.

Saint-Denis, where his father was buried and where he himself then wished to be buried. He asked Saint-Denis to maintain ten or fifteen monks at the cell, who would "not fail to pray to God assiduously day and night in psalms and masses and other prayers of obsecration, and in their private prayers" for himself and Pepin.[112] Presumably the king was seeking commemoration within the monks' regular round of prayer, but it is not clear from the text what form that commemoration was to take. Perhaps he simply wanted his name and his father's name to be used in their services. This was certainly what the monks at Saint-Denis promised him in another act, drawn up in 775: "our name should be mentioned every day both in their masses and in their private prayers at the tomb of St. Denis."[113]

Finally, in 783 Charles gave an estate to Saint-Arnoul of Metz on behalf of his dead wife Hildegard. The revenue from the estate was to be used to keep a lamp burning continually at the tomb of the saint for Hildegard's benefit. Any extra revenue was to go to specially delegated clerics, who would "continually perform masses or pour out psalmody and prayers before the Lord every day for [her] soul."[114] This document is unusual, in that it describes special masses, psalms, and prayers to be performed specifically for Hildegard by a few delegated clerics; these services did not form part of the regular cursus of prayer at Saint-Arnoul. However, it is worth noting that these special services were secondary to the upkeep of the lamp, which served to link the queen with St. Arnoul and his servants on a continuing basis.

It is possible—even probable—that the liturgical privileges described in these three acts were similar to those granted to other potentes in the late eighth century. However, it is difficult to generalize from such a small number of cases even as to Charlemagne's liturgical preferences, let alone those of other members of the lay elite. The picture becomes a little clearer, though, in the ninth century, as the number of surviving documents, and hence the number of references to prayer, increases. Most of these references still occur in royal acts and deal with prayer for the king or members of the royal family, but some also appear in ordinary charters and deal with services performed for counts and even a few lesser nobles.

---

112. *Pippini, Carlomanni, Caroli Magni diplomata*, ed. Engelbert Mühlbacher, with Alfons Dopsch, Johann Lechner, and Michael Tangl, MGH, Diplomata karolinorum, 1 (Hanover, 1906), no. 55 (769).
113. *Pippini, Carlomanni, Caroli Magni diplomata*, no. 101 (775).
114. *Pippini, Carlomanni, Caroli Magni diplomata*, no. 149 (783).

The Carolingians continued to benefit from prayers described in the formulaic terms mentioned earlier—presumably performed for the king as a public duty. However, this kind of formula also occurs (albeit rarely) in the acts of great territorial princes in the late ninth century. Does this represent an effort on their part to usurp the liturgical, as well as the political, privileges of the king? In the absence of more concrete evidence as to the meaning of these formulae, it is impossible to say.[115] Leaving aside such formulae, the liturgical privileges most often mentioned in ninth-century charters are burial, vestment with the monastic habit in the last moments of life, the upkeep of lamps, and the various forms of annual commemoration. The latter merit our special attention, for they first seem to have become popular with the lay elite in this period.

Most of the anniversary services mentioned in ninth-century charters were for kings and for other members of the royal family. In most cases they involved refectiones and prayers to be offered during the king's lifetime on the anniversary of his anointing, and thereafter on the anniversary of his death. Alain Stoclet has argued, from the fact that an unusually large number of Charlemagne's charters were issued over the years on the anniversary of his and Carloman's anointing by Pope Stephen, that the royal chapel already performed some kind of anniversary ceremony on that date in the late eighth century. He attributes the introduction of such services to the efforts of Fulrad of Saint-Denis, head of the royal chapel in that period.[116] There is no evidence, however, that either Charlemagne or Louis the Pious took much interest in this ceremony. Certainly they never attempted to establish anniversaries for themselves at other churches. It is only during the reign of Charles the Bald that royal interest in annual refectiones and prayer services becomes apparent.[117] At about the same time, bishops and some of the more important nobles also began to found anniversaries for themselves. By the late ninth century, references to annual refectiones and prayers are relatively common in both royal diplomas and ordinary charters.

Stoclet suggests that the establishment of royal anniversaries in the

---

115. E.g., *Cartulaire de l'abbaye de Redon*, no. 241 (869)—for Salomon, prince of the Bretons. The fact that similar formulae sometimes appear in the acts of eleventh-century counts lends some support to this thesis. (See, for example, Hariulf, *Chronicon Centulense*, 4: 22 [p. 240].)

116. Alain J. Stoclet, "Dies Unctionis: A Note on the Anniversaries of Royal Inauguration in the Carolingian Period," *FS* 20 (1986), 542–44.

117. Whereas the acts of Charlemagne make no mention of such services, they appear in at least thirteen of the acts of Charles the Bald.

late eighth century represents an imitation of the Roman/Byzantine tradition of imperial anniversary celebrations.[118] I would suggest, however, that the growth of royal and noble interest in anniversaries in the ninth century reflects more clearly the changing liturgical practices described in Chapter 2 above. Some religious communities institutionalized the anniversaries of a few important people in the eighth century. Monastic reformers first ordered the performance of perpetual annual services for all abbots in the early ninth century. Religious communities began celebrating the anniversaries of their ordinary members somewhat later in the same century, giving rise to the first necrologies. The kings and great nobles followed this pattern when they arranged to be commemorated annually by a community grateful for their gifts.

Individualized services were sometimes performed more often than just once a year for kings and the greatest magnates. In 867, for example, Charles the Bald arranged to have the clerics of Saint-Martin of Tours perform one of the seven penitential psalms after each of the seven canonical hours for him on a daily basis.[119] Such prayers, incorporated into the ordinary daily cursus of prayer, demonstrated with particular clarity the ties of gratitude and obligation that bound the religious community to its benefactor. However, they also added to the already heavy liturgical burden carried by the clergy in this period. Religious houses did not grant such privileges readily, even to kings. Out of the 165 acts of Charles the Bald that mention prayer, only 3 refer to services of this sort. Finally, there are occasional references in the ninth-century charters to "prayers" and "masses"—presumably, as noted earlier, missae speciales.

Kings appear much less frequently as benefactors of religious houses in the tenth-century charters, and as a result the formulaic prayers for the ruler and the welfare of the realm which had been so common in the late eighth- and ninth-century documents virtually disappear. However, the great magnates continued to establish anniversaries and to endow lamps to burn perpetually in their memory. Sometimes the clergy added individualized daily or weekly services for powerful figures to their regular cursus of prayer. Minor nobles figure more prominently in tenth-century charters than in those from the preceding century, but there is relatively little change in the privileges they demanded and received. They seem to have hoped for

118. Stoclet, "Dies Unctionis," pp. 546–48.
119. *Recueil des actes de Charles II*, no. 307 (867).

burial, for vestment in the monastic habit, or for a "share" in the clergy's ordinary prayers. A few references are made to "masses" (or perhaps to "the Mass"), but when tenth-century charters mention prayer, generally they refer to association rather than to prayer performed for its own sake.

Around the year 1000, both the total number of transactions between the five religious communities and outside benefactors, and the percentage of those transactions that resulted in the establishment of liturgical services began to increase—a trend similar to that which has been observed in the charters of Cluny.[120] At the same time, a somewhat different distribution of liturgical privileges began to emerge. Burial now shared pride of place in the charters with formal association. While kings and great nobles continued to benefit from anniversaries and—much more rarely—daily or weekly services, they also began to seek admission to monastic and clerical societates with increasing urgency. Formal association was even more popular among lesser nobles and *milites*, who seldom arranged to have anniversaries performed for themselves. At the same time, a growing number of people sought vestment in monastic garb, or arranged to be admitted to the religious community at some future date.[121] This pattern of intense identification with the community that prayed became even more pronounced in the late eleventh century.

There is evidence in the cartularies of some religious houses, although not in the two data sets analyzed for this study, of a growing interest in prayer per se during the late eleventh century. A few charters from this period refer to series of missae speciales to be performed specifically for a particular person or group. One man, for example, made a gift to Beaulieu so that after his death the monks would perform a thousand masses for his soul and the souls of his father and mother.[122] Although the circumstances under which these masses would be performed are not always clear, they seem to have fallen outside the regular liturgy. The presumption is that they were to be performed privately by a delegated priest. As a result, they provided prayer without emphasizing association with the community that prayed. It is curious, then, that they should have increased in

120. Poeck ("Laienbegräbnisse in Cluny," p. 122) noted a sharp rise in the early eleventh century both in the absolute number of donations for burial and in donations for burial as a percentage of all donations.
121. Again, this echoes Poeck's findings for Cluny: "Laienbegräbnisse in Cluny," especially p. 152.
122. *Cartulaire de l'abbaye de Beaulieu*, no. 84 (late eleventh century).

popularity in the late eleventh century, when members of the lay elite were tying themselves so closely to religious communities in other ways.

Perhaps some nobles were becoming more interested in accumulating as much prayer as possible for themselves—foreshadowing trends in later medieval piety. However, it is also possible that the increase in mass series in the late eleventh century reflects the concerns of the religious community. In a number of documents from this period, masses were granted to people who had shown themselves to be troublesome, or had at least demonstrated that they were not the pious souls with whom the clergy would want to associate themselves closely. Such grants were sometimes connected with cases of murder, for example, or with the resolution of conflict.[123] They may, then, represent a response to a particular kind of situation rather than a changing attitude toward prayer. In any case, one should not overestimate the popularity of the mass series in this period. Even in the cartularies where they are mentioned, mass series appear much less often than burial, association, vestment in monastic garb, or anniversary services. As noted earlier, they do not appear at all in the two data sets under consideration here.

In general, then, early medieval nobles enjoyed liturgical privileges which emphasized their ties with the religious community. They were buried in the cemetery of the house. They "participated" in its prayers and good works. They might even be remembered in more individualized annual or daily services which became part of its regular round of prayer. Only a few charters, however, refer specifically to grants of special masses or psalms, performed outside the ordinary cursus of prayer. Nor is there evidence that noble donors wanted such services but were unable to obtain them. The men and women of the secular elite were apparently content with associative prayer.

And this is really what we might expect from people operating within a social system in which gift-giving, rather than commercial exchange, predominated. The objects exchanged as gifts have their own value, but in a process intended to promote social bonding they also have a social identity. Recent scholars have often noted the important social meanings carried by land given to religious commu-

123. *Cartulaire de l'abbaye de Saint-Vincent du Mans*, nos. 350 (1097), 434 (1080–1102). Compare *Cartulaire de l'abbaye cardinale de la Trinité de Vendôme*, no. 433 (1119).

nities in this period. A piece of property which retained its association with the donating family was intended to serve and did serve as a reminder of their relationship with the clerical community that received it. Noble donors gave property and clerical communities received it, with the understanding that this would be the case. Should we be surprised, then, that the liturgical return-gifts most readily granted by the clergy and most eagerly accepted by the nobility were those that carried the strongest social meanings? The predominance of what I have called associative prayer in charters from this period was not accidental. It was, rather, a reflection of the peculiar social, economic, and cultural structures of early medieval society.

CHANGE AND CONTINUITY

Throughout the early middle ages close relationships with elite clerical communities were central to the religious life of the nobility. For while friendship with an important community might cost a noble family possession of some valuable property, it promised them a whole range of advantages in return. In a loosely organized—indeed generally fragmented—society, it offered valuable alliances with wealthy and powerful institutions and with the other patrons of those institutions. In a universe threatened by demonic forces, it offered the most powerful supernatural protection possible. The relationships between the clerical and secular elites were not always untroubled. The same individuals and families who made gifts to the saints sometimes took them away again. Under certain circumstances *benefactores* might turn into *oppressores* of the communities that prayed. But however they may have acted at any given time, early medieval nobles were seldom indifferent to the local saints and their servants.

The general pattern of familiaritas described in this chapter prevailed throughout the period under consideration here. However, some aspects of this pattern changed significantly over the centuries. The powerful members of Carolingian society were already establishing close ties with monasteries and cathedral chapters in the late eighth and ninth century, but those ties became even closer in the tenth and eleventh centuries, as more and more nobles founded new religious houses, made gifts to existing ones, and acquired more liturgical privileges as a result.

The growth in foundations is particularly striking. It had been relatively uncommon for a lay magnate who had no immediate intention of entering the religious life to found a monastery or house of canons before the Carolingian period.[124] However, such foundations began to increase in the ninth century.[125] By the late tenth and early eleventh centuries, not only great princes but also lesser nobles and even castellans were establishing abbeys, priories, and collegiate churches in the territories under their control.[126] Often what was involved was not the establishment of a new body of clerics on a new site, but rather the reclamation of an abandoned church or the reform of a secular one.[127] But whatever the circumstances, the foundation of a religious house involved considerable expenditures of wealth and effort over a long period of time. The noble patron found someone to recruit members and direct the fledgling community, granted it an initial endowment, and often continued to act as its protector and benefactor for years to come.[128] As a result, the identification of founder and community was very close.

Noble donations to existing religious houses also increased in this period. It is hard to assess the extent of lay generosity toward religious houses before the Carolingian period, although offerings from the laity obviously played an important role in the ecclesiastical economy from a very early date.[129] What is clear, however, is that the steady stream of wealth pouring from the hands of the laity in the late eighth and ninth centuries broadened into a flood in the tenth and eleventh centuries.[130] Not only were there many new foundations

124. Most early foundations were the work of, or at least initiated by, bishops or monks: Philibert Schmitz, *Histoire de l'ordre de Saint-Benoît*, 6 vols. (Maredsous, 1942–49; 2d ed. of vols. 1 and 2, Maredsous, 1948–56), 1: 58–75. On the role of the clergy in some early "lay" foundations, see Alain Dierkens, *Abbayes et chapitres entre Sambre et Meuse (VIIe–XIe siècles): Contribution à l'histoire religieuse des campagnes du haut moyen âge* (Sigmaringen, 1985), pp. 320–27.

125. On lay foundations in the Midi under the early Carolingians, see Magnou-Nortier, *La Société laïque et l'église*, pp. 98–102.

126. Lemarignier, "Aspects politiques des fondations de collégiales," in *La vita comune del clero nei secoli XI e XII*, 1: 18–49; idem, "Structures monastiques et structures politiques," in *Il monachesimo nell'alto medioevo*, pp. 357–400.

127. Bouchard, *Sword, Miter, and Cloister*, pp. 102–3.

128. See, for example, Penelope Johnson, *Prayer, Patronage, and Power: The Abbey of La Trinité, Vendôme, 1032–1187* (New York, 1981), pp. 8–23, 69–76.

129. Wallace-Hadrill, *The Frankish Church*, pp. 123–42. But see Janet Nelson, "Making Ends Meet: Wealth and Poverty in the Carolingian Church," in W. J. Sheils and Diana Wood, eds., *The Church and Wealth* (Oxford, 1987), pp. 25–35, on the uneven distribution of clerical wealth.

130. Duby, *The Early Growth of the European Economy*, p. 165.

being sustained by gifts, but the number of donations made to each individual house seems to have grown considerably. A high proportion of those who had property at their disposal were giving it away to the monasteries and, to a lesser extent, to the great secular churches —sometimes impoverishing themselves in the process.[131]

As founders of new religious houses and as patrons of existing ones, nobles played an important role in monastic reform movements and, to a lesser extent, in the reform of the secular clergy in the eleventh century. This was not a role many laymen or laywomen had played in the Carolingian period. However, the change seems to lie in the type of house patronized and the intensity of the efforts made on its behalf. Otherwise, the tenor of noble interaction with important religious communities remained remarkably consistent throughout the period covered in this book. Nobles engaged in the same kinds of behavior in the ninth as in the eleventh century—the only significant difference being the gradual assumption by some important lords of the protective role once played by the king. More importantly, nobles distributed their efforts in much the same way in both periods. As Janet Nelson has noted, Carolingian kings and nobles exercised their personal generosity "with discrimination," showing gratitude to only a few special patrons.[132] The same was true in the eleventh century. Constance Bouchard has shown that many noble families in Burgundy maintained close ties with only one or two churches in the eleventh century.[133]

The prominence of prayer for the dead in the relationships between nobles and religious communities also changed over time. Beginning in the first half of the eleventh century, but more noticeably in the second half, there is an increase in the number of what may be called quid pro quo transactions, in which each side asks explicitly for what it wants from the other. In her study of the property of Cluny, Barbara Rosenwein has linked this development to economic and political developments. By the late eleventh century, both the monks of Cluny and their noble neighbors were becoming increasingly conscious of ways in which they could improve their economic and thereby their political status. In particular, they were beginning to consolidate their estates into compact *seigneuries*, in order to ensure ease of management and maximum political and economic profits.

131. Duby, *La Société aux XIe et XIIe siècles dans la région mâconnaise*, pp. 68–69.
132. Nelson, "Making Ends Meet," in Sheils and Wood, *The Church and Wealth*, p. 26.
133. Bouchard, *Sword, Miter, and Cloister*, p. 138. But see below, Epilogue.

The monks became anxious to acquire not just any property, but properties adjacent to ones they already held. From about 1040 on, Rosenwein has noted, Cluny began to offer desirable liturgical benefits in return for the lands it wanted.[134]

The same trend is evident in the records of other religious communities, from other regions of France. In the year 1095, for example, Haimo Guiscard, his wife Bota with her children, and Renaud *Grossa Barba* came into the chapter of the cathedral of Angers to ask a favor. They wanted to have Geoffrey *Festucam*, who had recently been killed in battle, buried above the cathedral steps; they also wanted the canons to grant Geoffrey the benefit of their alms and prayers and to inscribe his name in their martyrology. Significantly, they offered in return a piece of land which had belonged to Geoffrey, and which was located next to a property that the cathedral chapter already held.[135] Efforts to provide Geoffrey *Festucam* with a proper burial and appropriate prayers provided the canons of Angers with an opportunity to add to their possessions in a particular area.

The increase in such quid pro quo arrangements explains the higher percentage of all transactions, and of donations in particular, which mention liturgical privileges in the second half of the eleventh century.[136] Noble donors were using religious communities' desire for particular properties to acquire more privileges for themselves. One of the most important of these privileges was the right to become a member of the community in the final moments of life. The earliest explicit references to individuals who entered a religious house in anticipation of death date from the ninth century.[137] But as we have seen, such references increased in the early to mid-eleventh century.[138] By the late eleventh century, the continued growth in "deathbed" conversions had led some houses to create a special ritual for the reception of the sick *ad succurrendum* (i.e., in order to help them in their greatest need).[139] Another liturgical privilege which appears more frequently in the charters of the late eleventh century was that of association in all the prayers and good works of the community. I have already described the societas orationum, the extended circle of people associated with a particular community and its

134. Rosenwein, *To Be the Neighbor of St. Peter*, pp. 205–6.
135. *Cartulaire noir de la cathédrale d'Angers*, no. 58 (1095).
136. Appendix B, Tables 6 and 7.
137. E.g., *Cartulaire de l'abbaye de Redon*, no. 270 (878).
138. Schmitz, *Histoire de l'ordre de Saint-Benoît*, 4: 203–4; J. Valvekens, "Fratres et sorores 'ad succurrendum'," *Analecta Praemonstratensia* 37 (1961), 323–28.
139. Bernard of Cluny, *Ordo Cluniacensis*, 20, in *Vetus disciplina monastica*, p. 180.

prayers. Some monastic societates already included laymen and lay-women in the ninth century.[140] By the second half of the eleventh century, though, so many members of the feudal elite were seeking admission that special ceremonies for the formal association of layfolk began to appear in monastic customaries.[141]

The growth of quid pro quo transactions and the related expansion of certain liturgical privileges is a significant development. It does not, however, represent a revolution in the relationship between noble donors and religious houses. For strangers were not suddenly arriving at the monastery door to demand special privileges from the monks. These transactions remained part of long-term, complex relationships between religious communities and their familiares. Moreover the privileges that resulted were still associative in character; they served to express the growing intensity of the bonds between noble donors and clerical communities in the eleventh century. More and more of those donors were becoming honorary members of the community through association, and perhaps even real members through vestment ad succurrendum. The personal identification of nobles with the communities that prayed had never been so strong as it was in the late eleventh century.

Just as the humiles were being tied more tightly to the parish between 750 and 1100, so the potentes were associating themselves more closely with the important secular churches and with the increasingly prestigious regular communities. But what was the point of all this effort? Many modern scholars have seen the acquisition of prayer as the goal of noble dealings with religious houses, and the increasingly anxious desire for prayer as the factor behind increased noble generosity in the late tenth and eleventh centuries. The fact is, however, that only a fraction of the transactions recorded in the cartularies from this period mention prayer. The same is true even if we focus specifically on donations. Before the late eleventh century less than 20 percent of all donations in my sample mentioned liturgical privileges. The percentage was higher at monasteries than at cathedrals, and higher at some monasteries than at others, but it was still quite low overall.[142]

As we might expect, the percentage of donations that involved

---

140. A number of lay names appear, for example, in the ninth-century necrological materials from Fulda: Franz-Josef Jakobi, "Die geistlichen und weltlichen Magnaten in den Fuldaer Totenannalen," in Schmid, *Die Klostergemeinschaft von Fulda*, 2: 798 and passim.

141. E.g., Lanfranc, *Decreta*, 108 (pp. 93–94).

142. Appendix B, Table 7.

such privileges rose in the late eleventh century, as quid pro quo transactions became more common. At Cluny and at some other monasteries such as Redon, the percentage seems to have been very high indeed.[143] But in my sample only 28 percent of the donations made to cathedrals and 22 percent of those made to monasteries between 1050 and 1099 resulted in grants of prayer.[144] Some of the donations that did not result in prayer were made by the same people. However, it seems clear that a substantial number of donors, even in the late eleventh century, made their gifts without expecting any specific liturgical privileges in return.

Contrary to what is often assumed, they also decided to make their donations under a wide variety of circumstances. While the process of making a gift generally took a long time to complete, the initial impulse behind the gift sometimes arose suddenly, almost accidentally.[145] A wealthy individual stopped by a monastery to pray, to visit the shrines of the saints, to ask advice, or simply to pass the night on a long journey, and was moved to make a gift.[146] The motives are no longer apparent to us. It may have been respect for the religious life thus briefly revealed or gratitude for hospitality received.[147] Sometimes people became donors because their traveling companions gave gifts.[148] In most cases, unfortunately, we know nothing at all about the circumstances under which donations were made. What is clear, however, is that noble donors did not give to religious communities only—or even primarily—when threatened by illness or death. In fact, "crisis" donations made up a rather small percentage of all the gifts received by religious houses in my sample during the period from the mid-eighth to the mid-eleventh century. The percentage seems to have risen slightly in the late eleventh century, but it was still not very high.[149]

143. Appendix B, Table 7.
144. On Redon, see Appendix B, Table 7. On Cluny, see Cowdrey, "Union and Confraternity with Cluny," p. 160; Poeck, "Laienbegräbnisse in Cluny," pp. 152–74; Rosenwein, *To Be the Neighbor of St. Peter*, p. 206.
145. On the lengthy process of gift-giving, see White, *Custom, Kinship, and Gifts to Saints*, pp. 31–33.
146. E.g., *Cartulaire de l'abbaye de Redon*, nos. 385 (before 1050), 292 (1008–26); Orderic Vitalis, *Historia aecclesiastica*, 6: 5 (3: 240); *Libri confraternitatum sancti Galli*, p. 141.
147. E.g., *Cartulaires de l'abbaye de Molesme*, premier cartulaire, no. 34 (1104). See also Magnou-Nortier, *La Société laïque et l'église*, pp. 441–44.
148. E.g., *Cartulaire de l'abbaye de Saint-Vincent du Mans*, no. 436 (1080–1102). Sometimes people were pressured to give: *Cartulaire de l'abbaye de Redon*, no. 373 (1037).
149. Appendix B, Table 9. The exception here was the abbey of Redon, where a substantial number of donations were associated with crises in the eleventh century.

Moreover, when noble donors did experience moments of crisis their primary concern was not to arrange for the performance of large quantities of prayer. Indeed, some gifts made at the approach of death do not mention prayer at all. They were simple expressions of generosity, for which no liturgical "return-gift" was requested. Among the wealthier members of lay society, it was customary for the dying or the executors of their last wishes to make donations to one or more churches as a final act of Christian charity.[150] According to Einhard, Charlemagne had his property assessed, then divided into parts three years before his death. In this way he meant to prevent disputes among his heirs, and also "to ensure that the distribution of alms, which is made solemnly by Christians from their possessions, should be made methodically and sensibly from his own fortune too." Much of the emperor's treasure was to be divided up, after his death, among the metropolitan churches of his realm.[151] The other powerful members of early medieval society also arranged for such distributions after they died, although usually on a much smaller scale.[152] Deathbed acts were not always new donations. Sometimes someone on the verge of death would confirm an earlier gift by publicly repeating the act of donation and thus reaffirming his or her loyalty to the community.[153] Other people might give up their claims on a piece of property, in order to be reconciled with the saints and their servants.[154]

Nevertheless, a higher percentage of "crisis" donations than of all donations did mention liturgical privileges. These generally took one of two forms. A substantial number of deathbed gifts were intended to ensure a proper burial service for the donor. This is hardly surprising since, as we have already seen, burial was one of the privileges most often mentioned in all charters. Many people, of course, arranged in advance for the last rites, but others neglected this duty until their old age.[155] If illness or a wound brought death suddenly close, the negotiations sometimes had to be carried on at the very last minute. Thus Geoffrey of *Fluriaco*, seized by the illness of which he

150. E.g., *Recueil des chartes de l'abbaye de Cluny*, no. 3130 (1049–1109).
151. Einhard, *Vita Karoli Magni*, ed. G. Pertz and G. Waitz, 5th ed. (Hanover, 1905), p. 33.
152. E.g., *Cartulaire de l'abbaye de Conques*, no. 571 (1051).
153. E.g., *Recueil des chartes de l'abbaye de Cluny*, no. 2957 (1042); *Marmoutier: Cartulaire blésois*, no. 83 (eleventh century).
154. See, for example, the case of Wigo of Berzé, cited by Bouchard, *Sword, Miter, and Cloister*, p. 213.
155. *Recueil des chartes de l'abbaye de Cluny*, no. 3177 (1049–1109). See also *Cartulaire de l'abbaye de Conques*, no. 462 (1061–1108).

later died, had to send his wife and son to Saint-Père of Chartres to place the token of his gift on the altar of St. Peter; he was later buried in the cemetery there.[156]

The other privilege that commonly resulted from deathbed generosity, especially in the eleventh century, was vestment ad succurrendum. Sometimes donors exhibited a strikingly fervent desire to enter the religious community before they died. Lonus of Loches, for example, in his last illness believed "that there was no way he could be saved unless he were made a monk." He granted his share in the revenues of a church to the abbey of Noyers for the privilege.[157] Under the circumstances, the dying were often willing to give up possessions they valued highly. Sometimes, though, the patient waited too long to make the necessary arrangements and died without having received the habit.[158] Hence the practice of arranging in advance for reception into the community on short notice, without the necessity of making a further gift.

Although burial and vestment ad succurrendum were by far the most common liturgical results of deathbed donation, it also might happen that someone who feared an imminent death would be admitted to the societas of the house. Geoffrey the Tall, for example, came to Marmoutier just before a major battle, commended himself to the prayers of the brothers, and was granted formal association. In return, he gave the monks a church and some land, with the consent of his brother and nephew.[159] Significantly, however, I have not found a single instance in which someone on the verge of death requested a series of special masses or some other nonassociative form of prayer. Those who benefited from such services did so as the result of arrangements made during their lifetime or—in a few cases—after death, as the result of other people's efforts. One cannot prove, of course, from the silence of the sources that deathbed donations never resulted in nonassociative services, but such a result must have been rare, to have left so little trace in the records. It would seem, then, that

156. *Cartulaire de l'abbaye de Saint-Père de Chartres*, 1: 237–38 (before 1102).
157. Cited by Bernard Chevalier, "Les Restitutions d'églises dans le diocèse de Tours du Xe au XIIe siècles," in *Études de civilisation médiévale (IXe-XIIe siècles): Mélanges offerts à Edmond-René Labande* (Poitiers, 1974), p. 136, n. 23.
158. *Cartulaire de l'abbaye de Saint-Père de Chartres*, 1: 222 (1069–79).
159. Angers, Arch. Dép. Maine-et-Loire, G. 785, no. 4 (1030–60). See also *Recueil des chartes de l'abbaye de Cluny*, no. 3209 (1049–1109); *Cartulaire de l'abbaye de Saint-Vincent du Mans*, no. 480 (1068–78); *Cartulaire de l'abbaye de Saint-Père de Chartres*, 1: 136–37 (before 1070).

the nobility's chief concern at the approach of death was the same as it had been in life: to be associated as closely as possible with the religious community and its liturgy, to be buried in its cemetery—if possible even to become a full-fledged member through formal association or vestment in the monastic habit. More individualized forms of prayer—never granted very often anyway—became, if anything, even less important during the last moments of life.

There remains one final set of negotiations to consider, if we are to understand how members of the lay elite dealt with death in the early middle ages. These are the negotiations undertaken by the survivors, especially the family of the dead person, after a death had occurred. It is clear, first of all, that like the dying themselves the survivors were most concerned with a proper burial. If the deceased had not arranged for this while he or she still could, the family would take care of it later. As noted earlier, some religious houses would bury the dead in anticipation of a return-gift, which usually came in the form of a donation from the grateful family. Guy of Montigny was cared for by a monk of Marmoutier during his last illness. Brother Theobald brought him medicine, and then, when he found that he was unable to cure his patient, had him carried to Marmoutier, vested as a monk, and finally buried in the abbey's cemetery. "In recompense" for the fact that the monastery had cared for him in illness and in death, Guy's brother Peter granted the abbey a tithe.[160]

The family's interest centered on the burial of their dead, but they sometimes tried to obtain other privileges for them as well. Hermengard and her children made a donation to the abbey of Gellone in 1100, so that the monks would "pray" for Raymond Berenger, struck down by his enemies while he slept.[161] It is not clear what kind of prayer was involved in this case. Often, however, the aim of these negotiations was some form of association. The sons of Joscelin Bodelle, for example, wanted their father's name inscribed in the martyrology of La Trinité of Vendôme for commemoration.[162] The families of kings and important nobles sometimes arranged to have anniversaries celebrated for the departed. However, these were not yet the norm and the survivors might have to be pushed a little to make such a foundation. Evrard of Le Puiset founded an anniversary for his father, but only when his uncle—who was a Marmoutier

---

160. *Cartulaire de Marmoutier pour le Dunois*, no. 118 (1050–60).
161. *Cartulaire de Gellone*, no. 428 (1100).
162. *Cartulaire de l'abbaye cardinale de la Trinité de Vendôme*, no. 123 (1059).

monk, and probably anxious to acquire some property for his abbey
—suggested it.[163]

Survivors were far less interested in nonassociative forms of
prayer. Only toward the end of the eleventh century do the charters
mention relatives arranging to have a series of masses performed for
their dead. These might, however, be quite extensive. On the day of
his wife's burial, William of Doucelles gave a church to Saint-Vincent
of Le Mans, asking the monks to say a thousand masses for her, [her?]
ancestors, and all the departed faithful, within forty days.[164] The
nonassociative services that the dying neglected were, then, occasionally provided for them by their relatives in the late eleventh century.
In most cases, however, no such effort was made.

In the period just after a death, when they gathered at the church
for the funeral, the family and friends might try to arrange services
for the dead person, but they also tended to look more closely at their
own relations with the liturgical community. The death and the resulting ceremonies served as both an opportunity and an encouragement for the living to establish bonds with the community that
prayed. Some people began to make donations at such times, as a
result of the clergy's care for the dead. Sometimes, too, gratitude or
grief led the survivors to resolve their disputes with a religious house.
A knight named Hugh had given a church and land to Saint-Père of
Chartres and was granted prayers in return. However, the monks
gained no profit from the gift, because the donor's family refused to
give up their claims to the property. It was only years later, at Hugh's
funeral, that his wife and sons finally renounced their rights and
conceded the gift.[165]

Under the circumstances, it is not surprising to find that these
transactions resulted in prayer for the survivors as well as the dead.
Parents might request formal association not only for their dead son
but also for themselves.[166] People might also include themselves in
the anniversaries they established for their kin.[167] But while the living
looked to their own needs and their own relationship with the liturgical community, sometimes the dead met with rather perfunc-

163. *Cartulaire de Marmoutier pour le Dunois*, no. 149 (1095). See also *Cartulaire de l'abbaye de Saint-Martin de Pontoise*, no. 56 (no date), concerning the establishment of an anniversary for Hildeburge of Gallardon in the early twelfth century.

164. *Cartulaire de l'abbaye de Saint-Vincent du Mans*, no. 823 (1080–1102).

165. *Cartulaire de l'abbaye de Saint-Père de Chartres*, 1: 218 (before 1080).

166. Orderic Vitalis, *Historia aecclesiastica*, 3 (2: 82–83).

167. E.g., *Cartulaire général de l'Yonne*, no. 90 (1036).

tory treatment. Instead of simply seeking inclusion in services established for their dead relatives, the survivors might make themselves the center of attention. Thus, Gosbert of Joué made a gift to Saint-Vincent of Le Mans in return for certain privileges, five solidi in cash, and reception in the societas of the house; he promised to remain a friend to the monks in the future. At the end of all this, the charter mentions that twenty-four masses would be performed for Gosbert's dead wife.[168] At times, then, the survivor's desire to establish a relationship with the religious community took precedence over the desire to ensure liturgical commemoration for the dead.

Sometimes, in fact, the donations occasioned by a death resulted in prayer for the survivors but no further prayer for the dead. In 1067 two brothers made a donation to Cluny for their souls and the soul of their half-brother (*uterinus*) who had been murdered; in return for their gift the two donors were to be granted the privilege of burial at Cluny and the benefit of the house's prayers, but no further mention was made of the dead man.[169] In another case, two parents decided, on the day of their son's burial at the abbey of La Trinité of Vendôme, that they would make a gift to the house. When they came to the abbey and made the donation, however, it was the mother who obtained the benefit of prayers for herself.[170] William of Doucelles had made a gift to Saint-Vincent of Le Mans in his last illness; in return he had been granted the monastic habit and was buried "honorably" as a monk. His son confirmed the gift at the grave-side and immediately asked to be admitted "like his father" to the monastic societas. The abbot invested him with the privilege, using the pastoral staff he had carried during the funeral. Nothing further, apparently, was done for the father.[171]

What are we to make of such behavior? If we assume that the laity considered it desirable to obtain as much prayer as possible for their dead, incidents such as this, when families neglected their chance to have more services performed for departed relatives in favor of getting prayer for themselves, seem to demonstrate almost unbearable

168. *Cartulaire de l'abbaye de Saint-Vincent du Mans*, no. 423 (late eleventh/early twelfth century).

169. *Recueil des chartes de l'abbaye de Cluny*, no. 3412 (1067).

170. *Cartulaire de l'abbaye cardinale de la Trinité de Vendôme*, no. 326 (1085). See also *Marmoutier: Cartulaire blésois*, no. 14 (1032–64); *Cartulaire de l'abbaye de la Sainte-Trinité du Mont*, no. 32 (1060).

171. *Cartulaire de l'abbaye de Saint-Vincent du Mans*, no. 540 (1076–80). See also *Cartulaire de Gellone*, no. 28 (1060–74).

callousness. On the other hand, if we assume that what the laity wanted was not "more" prayer, but rather a close relationship with the community that prayed, this behavior becomes perfectly explicable. It is difficult for those not immediately involved in such a relationship to make it more intimate. If someone's ties to a religious community were not well established by the time he or she died, then the survivors could do little about it. It was the duty of the surviving relatives to ensure that everything was as the dead person had wanted. In particular, they were expected to make sure that the gifts he or she had made—or wanted to make—were safe.[172] But having protected the material basis of the dead person's position, they could then lay the groundwork for their own association with the saints and their servants.

Prayer for the dead clearly played a less prominent role in noble dealings with religious communities than has usually been assumed. Most donations did not lead to the establishment of services for the donors. Even donations made under the immediate threat of death did not always have liturgical results. This had been true in the ninth and tenth centuries, and it continued to be true in the eleventh, despite the rise in quid pro quo donations. But what conclusions can we draw from these facts? We cannot conclude that burial, association, anniversaries, masses, psalms, and so forth were unimportant to the early medieval nobility. On the contrary, they appear to have valued such privileges highly. But it seems that specific liturgical privileges were only part of what nobles hoped to gain from their generosity to the communities that prayed.

The women and men who made gifts to elite religious houses between 750 and 1100 lived in a perilous and unpredictable world, in which reliable social connections with the right people were essential to survival. They were willing to part with valuable property in order to create and maintain such connections, but in return they expected gratitude and loyalty—within reason, but without set limits. Early medieval nobles did not want vassals who would dutifully appear for military service for forty days a year. They wanted *fideles* who would fight for them no matter what emergency arose.[173] By the same

---

172. E.g., *Cartulaire de l'abbaye de Beaulieu*, no. 14 (1062–72).

173. David Herlihy, ed., *The History of Feudalism* (Atlantic Highlands, N.J., 1970), p. 71. On the lack of defined obligations for vassals in the early middle ages, see François L. Ganshof, *Feudalism*, trans. Philip Grierson, 3d English ed. (New York, 1964), pp. 84–85, 89.

token, I would argue, early medieval nobles did not want intercessors who would say one hundred special masses for them. For suppose that when those masses had all been said there were still some sins left for which atonement had not been made? They wanted intercessors who would treat them "like a brother" or "sister," intercessors who could be counted on—if worse came to worst—to snatch their souls from the very jaws of hell. The specific liturgical privileges mentioned in the charters were not the goal of noble dealings with religious communities in the early middle ages. They were, rather, their first fruits and pledges of further assistance to come.

5 THE IDEOLOGY OF
PRAYER FOR THE DEAD

$\bigcup$ ntil quite recently historians interested in the meaning of prayer for the dead in the middle ages were content to trace the development of theological teachings on the subject.[1] As I noted earlier, that situation has changed somewhat in the last few decades. Now a growing number of scholars search for the meanings of religious rituals in saints' lives, poetry, inscriptions, even charters, as well as in theological texts per se.[2] Nevertheless, theology continues to exert a powerful influence, and most historians studying prayer for the dead still select and read their texts within a framework of assumptions derived from the doctrinal tradition, even when they do not confine themselves to studying that tradition.[3]

1. Michel, "Purgatoire"; C. V. Héris, "Théologie des suffrages pour les morts," *La Maison-Dieu* 44 (1955), 58–67; Yves Congar, "Le Purgatoire," in *Le Mystère de la mort et sa célébration* (Paris, 1956), pp. 279–336; Pierre Jay, "Le Purgatoire dans la prédication de saint Césaire d'Arles," *Recherches de théologie ancienne et médiévale* 24 (1957), 5–14; idem, "Saint Cyprien et la doctrine du Purgatoire," *Recherches de théologie ancienne et médiévale* 27 (1960), 133–36; Joseph Ntedika, *L'Évolution de la doctrine du Purgatoire chez saint Augustin* (Paris, 1966); Pierre Jay, "Saint Augustin et la doctrine du Purgatoire," *Recherches de théologie ancienne et médiévale* 36 (1969), 17–30.

2. This change is most apparent in studies of early Christian rituals for the dead, such as Ntedika, *L'Évocation de l'au-delà*, and Duval, *Auprès des saints*. But studies of the early medieval period have also begun to change. See, for example, Neiske, "Vision und Totengedenken;" Oexle, "Memoria und Memorialüberlieferung;" Geary, "Échanges et relations entre les vivants et les morts dans la société du haut moyen âge."

3. See, for example, Angenendt, "Theologie und Liturgie," in Schmid and Wollasch, *Memoria*; Chélini, *L'Aube du moyen âge*, pp. 450–94. See also the controversy aroused by the publication of Le Goff's *La Naissance du Purgatoire* discussed in the Introduction above.

This approach has its advantages, in that it serves to link early medieval ideas on the subject with the Christian tradition as a whole. However, I believe that it has, in the end, distorted our understanding of prayer for the dead as it was actually practiced and interpreted by Christians between the mid-eighth century and the end of the eleventh century. Modern scholars have tended to emphasize those images and ideas and those models of intercession for the dead which fit most neatly into the theological framework—at the expense of others which were of equal, if not greater importance in the early middle ages.

In this chapter I propose to examine as many of the meanings attributed to prayer for the dead by early medieval Christians as possible. That is not to say that what follows is a history of "popular beliefs" on the subject. Given the limitations of the available sources it is clearly impossible to determine what ordinary people thought about the various practices we have been considering. Rather, this chapter explores the range of ideas associated with prayer for the dead by the literate members of early medieval society, those who have left behind records, however opaque, of their views. This is a small group, of course, but not nearly so small as the tiny group of church fathers and theologians to whose work historians have usually turned for information on this subject. And it is an important group for our purposes, for these were the people who performed or sponsored most rituals for the dead, and who explained those rituals to the rest of the population.

Their views on this subject are reflected, though often only through glancing references, in a wide variety of sources, including chronicles, saints' lives, and collections of visions and miracle stories. Of particular interest in this regard, however, are the preambles (*arengae*) to charters of donation.[4] These texts often purport to express the feelings of the women and men who gave gifts to religious houses. Perhaps they really do reflect those feelings to some extent, for donors generally had, as we have seen, close ties to the communities that prayed. Presumably they discussed their prospects for salvation, as well as their political and social interests, with the recipients of their gifts. However, the language of the charters more directly

4. See Heinrich Fichtenau, *Arenga: Spätantike und Mittelalter im Spiegel von Urkundenformeln* (Graz-Cologne, 1957), especially pp. 122–56; Joseph Avril, "Observance monastique et spiritualité dans les préambules des actes (Xe–XIIIe s.)," *Revue d'histoire ecclésiastique* 85 (1990), 5–29.

reflects the views of the clerical scribes who composed them. Analysis of that language can provide a great deal of information on the meanings which these people attributed to the spiritual benefits they promised their patrons.

It is evident that the theological tradition described in the first section of this chapter influenced the way educated men and women thought about prayer for the dead. However, as I argue in the second section, theology shaped rather than controlled their thinking on this subject. The literate members of early medieval society associated a wide range of images and ideas, some not entirely orthodox, with rituals for the dead. Theological teachings form, then, only a part—albeit an important one—of the early medieval ideology of prayer for the dead, which is the true subject of this chapter.

My use of the term "ideology" in this context has two purposes. In the first place, it is intended to stand in contrast to "theology," and so to underline the distinction between my approach to this subject and more traditional ones. It is also, however, meant to suggest something else. The men and women who wrote about prayer for the dead in the early middle ages had available to them a whole repertoire of images and ideas, from which they chose those most appropriate to the situation they were describing. But, as I intend to demonstrate in the third section of this chapter, the choices they made were based not only on theological concerns, but also on their views on religious power and authority, which reflected, in turn, their own situations within the church. In short, early medieval interpretations of prayer for the dead were, to some extent, socially determined and hence "ideological."

The limited and uneven diffusion of theological teachings contributed to this situation. However, the early medieval ideology of prayer for the dead was not primarily the product of ignorance and confusion. Its peculiarities arose, rather, out of the contextual habit of thought prevalent during the early middle ages, but largely lost in later centuries. For early medieval men and women, the significance of an important act such as homage, gift-giving, or prayer was always colored by the context within which it occurred. They automatically interpreted such acts in terms of their knowledge of the actors involved and the situation within which they acted. Not surprisingly, the modern model of intercession, which tends to abstract prayer from its context, to reify and quantify it, cannot accommodate many early medieval interpretations of prayer for the dead. In the final section of this chapter I propose a different model of intercession, one which, I believe, accounts more fully for both the ideology and the practice of prayer for the dead in the period from the mid-eighth to the eleventh century.

THE FIRST EIGHT CENTURIES

Before we turn to the early middle ages, however, something must be said about the meaning of rituals for the dead in the early Christian era, for, as we have seen, many later practices and ideas had their roots in this period. A great deal has already been written about this subject and new evidence, especially in the form of inscriptions, is still coming to light. To review even the most important early Christian sources, the ways in which they have been interpreted, and the arguments to which those interpretations have given rise would take many books. What follows is intended only as a very brief summary of recent research on prayer for the dead in the early church.

While there is a great deal of evidence from the second, third, and fourth centuries to show that Christians remembered their dead in various ways, that evidence is fragmentary and often obscure. There has been considerable debate over the interpretation of individual texts and the ways in which those texts fit together. Most scholars are now agreed, however, that rituals for the dead had more than one meaning for the earliest Christians. Some were apparently performed in accordance with beliefs which Christians shared with many of their Jewish and pagan neighbors, while others carried meanings which were more specific to the Christian message.

It is clear, to begin with, that after they entered the church many converts to the new faith retained some of their old ideas about the condition of the dead and their need for assistance in the next world.[5] Like their neighbors throughout the Mediterranean region, many ordinary Christians envisioned a dark and dusty underworld, in which the dead could suffer considerable discomfort unless the living provided them with refreshment.[6] As a result, some of the faithful

---

5. Ntedika, *L'Évocation de l'au-delà*, pp. 263–64; Gauthier, "Les images de l'au-delà," especially pp. 8–14.

6. On this point see especially Alfred Stuiber, *Refrigerium Interim: Die Vorstellungen vom Zwischenzustand und die frühchristliche Grabeskunst* (Bonn, 1957); compare L. de Bruyne,

continued to bury grave-goods with the dead and to bring offerings of food and drink to their tombs.[7] Over time, some of these traditional practices were christianized. Eucharistic celebrations replaced the sacrifices once performed at the grave; "love feasts" and ritualized almsgiving took the place of funerary banquets.[8] These rituals were eventually reinterpreted so as to make them appear distinctively Christian, while practices less amenable to reinterpretation were forbidden.[9] Nevertheless, the desired outcome of these efforts was still expressed in very old-fashioned terms. Like their neighbors, Christians hoped that the dead would enjoy "refreshment, light, and peace" in the next world.[10]

Such continuity of belief was possible because ideas about the period just after death were only peripheral to the Christian message in the first few centuries.[11] The early churches lived in constant expectation of the end of the world, eagerly anticipating the resurrection and the last judgment. The faithful were told that they could look forward to these events with joy, for they would sit with Christ in judgment on their enemies, then reap their collective reward in paradise.[12] It is true that by the late second or third century doubts were beginning to arise about the imminence of Christ's Second Coming, now so long delayed.[13] However, so long as Christians remained a relatively small, close-knit, and persecuted sect, church leaders con-

---

"Refrigerium interim," *Rivista di archeologia christiana* 34 (1958), 87–118. On the pre-Christian echoes in the famous Dinocrates episode in the *Passion of Perpetua and Felicity*, see Dölger, "Antike Parallelen zum leidenden Dinocrates in der *Passio Perpetuae*"; Gauthier, "Les images de l'au-delà," pp. 12–13.

7. Gauthier, "Les images de l'au-delà," p. 13 and n. 36. Victor Saxer has argued that in Africa those who made offerings for the dead were considered, ipso facto, not Christian: *Morts, martyrs, reliques*, pp. 47–49. However, he offers no evidence that this strict view was widely held among ordinary Christians.

8. Freistedt, *Altchristliche Totengedächtnistage*, p. 114; Johannes Quasten, "*Vetus Superstitio et Nova Religio*: The Problem of *Refrigerium* in the Ancient Church of North Africa," *Harvard Theological Review* 33 (1940), especially pp. 256–57; Saxer, *Morts, martyrs, reliques*, pp. 133–49, 311–12.

9. See, for example, Augustine, *Quaestiones in Heptateuchum*, 1: 172, ed. I. Fraipont, in Augustine, *Aurelii Augustini Opera, pars 5* (Turnhout, 1958), pp. 67–68.

10. Ntedika, *L'Évocation de l'au-delà*, pp. 174–220.

11. H.-M. Féret, "La Mort dans la tradition biblique," in *Le Mystère de la mort et sa célébration*, pp. 94–97.

12. S. J. Duffy, "Parousia: In Theology," *NCE* 10: 1037–39; see also Willy Rordorf, "Liturgie et eschatologie," *Augustinianum* 18 (1978), 153–61.

13. Duffy, "Parousia," cols. 1037–38. See also Norman Cohn, *The Pursuit of the Millennium: Revolutionary Millenarians and Mystical Anarchists of the Middle Ages*, rev. ed. (New York, 1970), pp. 23–29, on the early millenarian sects.

tinued to concentrate in their writings on themes related to the final triumph of the elect. They gave little consideration to the period between death and the end of the world.[14] It was thus possible for ordinary Christians to associate traditional images and ideas about the immediate afterlife with the rituals they performed for the dead.[15]

Rituals for the dead were also linked, however, with images of the resurrection and the anticipated joys of heaven. Indeed, this seems to have been their primary meaning within a specifically Christian context. Apologists for the church in the first few centuries generally ignored or discounted the many similarities between Christian and non-Christian treatments of the dead. Instead, they set up a dichotomy between the supposed joy of Christian rituals and the sadness of non-Christian ones. This dichotomy was intended to express the differences in the eschatological expectations of the two groups. Whereas unbelievers had no hope for the future, the faithful expected to be saved. And so, the argument ran, while the pagans lamented for their dead and offered sacrifices to alleviate their sufferings, Christians rejoiced at funerals and celebrated the anniversary of death as a "birthday" into the new life.[16] The early apologists, in concentrating on the ultimate reward of the elect, largely ignored the possibility that the Christian dead might need assistance from the living immediately after death. They therefore presented the rituals the church performed for the dead as primarily affirmatory in nature, rather than instrumental.[17]

This view of prayer for the dead was possible because Christian apologists in the first few centuries generally thought of salvation as a function of membership in the church. In being baptized, the faithful renounced the world and joined the community that saved. They participated in its liturgy and proclaimed its faith. Obviously, then, they could expect to have a share in its collective reward.[18] Indeed, it was not unusual in the first few centuries for the living to turn to the

14. Stuiber, *Refrigerium Interim*, p. 43.

15. Gauthier, "Les images de l'au-delà," especially p. 7.

16. Rush, *Death and Burial in Christian Antiquity*, pp. 72–76, 193, 231–35; Ntedika, *L'Évocation de l'au-delà*, pp. 232–45; Saxer, *Morts, martyrs, reliques*, pp. 65, 69–70, 89–91, 172–73.

17. Ntedika, *L'Évocation de l'au-delà*, pp. 21–30; but see Saxer, *Morts, martyrs, reliques*, p. 113.

18. Michel, "Purgatoire," col. 1219; Joyce E. Salisbury, "'The Bond of a Common Mind': A Study of Collective Salvation from Cyprian to Augustine," *The Journal of Religious History* 13 (1985), 235–47.

departed faithful for help, on the assumption that their salvation was assured. While the martyrs were already considered the preeminent intercessors by the third century, they were by no means the only ones. The ordinary dead might also be invoked in much the same way after death, as inscriptions such as this indicate:

> Gentianus, the believer, who lived twenty-one years, eight months and sixteen days, . . . is now in peace. May you, whom we know to be with Christ, intercede for us in your prayers.[19]

Under the circumstances, it is easy to see why the cult of the martyrs and the cult of the ordinary Christian dead were so similar in the first few centuries of the church.

Even in the third and fourth centuries, when questions increasingly arose about the worthiness of individual members of the church, many people apparently continued to believe that all Christians who were not actually separated from communion through heresy or schism must eventually be saved. The "merciful" fathers used the concept of a purging fire of judgment—which might continue after judgment day—to explain how sinners who remained within the church might be saved.[20] But if one assumes that all those who die in the faith are assured of salvation, then funerals and commemorative services can be seen as primarily affirmations of the dead person's religious status; they can be performed to celebrate, rather than to bring about, a desired end.

This tendency in early Christian eschatology also meant that prayer for the dead was not yet associated with the purgation of sins after death.[21] This is not to say that the problem of sinful Christians, who might need to be purged of their sins before they could enter heaven, was ignored in the early Christian era. The early fathers did sometimes discuss the purifying fire mentioned in 1 Corinthians 3:12–15, which would test the "structure" that each person had built on the "foundation" of Christ. However, in the first few centuries this

19. *Inscriptiones latinae christianae veteres*, 1: 456, no. 2350. See also the texts cited by N. Boulet, "Les Cimetières chrétiens primitifs," in *Le Mystère de la mort et sa célébration*, p. 179, and Rush, *Death and Burial in Christian Antiquity*, p. 257.

20. For a discussion of the "merciful" position and its relation to the teachings of Origen, see Henri de Lavalette, "L'Interprétation du psaume I, 5 chez les pères 'miséricordieux' latins," *Recherches de science religieuse* 48 (1960), 544–63. On their use of the purging fire, see Le Goff, *La Naissance du Purgatoire*, pp. 88–91.

21. The earliest texts associating the two ideas date from the sixth century (see below).

fire was not always understood in eschatological terms, and when it was, it was normally associated with the end of time and the collective destiny of the church. Several of the early fathers suggested that on the "Day of the Lord" all the faithful—including the martyrs and perhaps even Christ himself—would pass through the fire. For the perfect, the passage would hold no terrors. For the imperfect, it would be painful but salvific; it would burn away their faults, allowing them to be saved "as through fire."[22] As noted earlier, this concept of a purifying fire of judgment was especially important to the "merciful" fathers, who believed that all Christians would eventually be saved. Before the end of the fourth century the fire mentioned in 1 Corinthians was apparently never associated with the suffering to which individual Christians might be subjected between death and the end of the world.[23] Neither is there any evidence that the rituals performed for the dead were thought to affect the process of purgation.[24]

The prevailing tone of most early Christian writings on the afterlife and prayer for the dead was, then, highly optimistic.[25] From the late fourth century on, however, such writings took on a more somber tone. Late patristic works reflect a growing awareness of the sin to be found within the church and a weakened confidence in the ultimate salvation of all—or even most—Christians. This new pessimism is clearly related to the changing situation of the churches in the post-persecution era.[26] In a period when baptism was becoming politically expedient, when to be a Christian required no great courage or commitment, church leaders felt graver doubts about the moral status of their flocks. As the number of converts grew, discipline seemed—and probably was—harder to maintain. If they were to enforce their standards of correct belief and behavior, bishops could not continue to promise the same assured reward they had in the past. The later fathers continually reminded the members of their churches that each person would be judged according to his or her own works. They rejected the old assumption that church membership essentially

22. Artur Landgraf, "1 Cor. 3, 10–17 bei den lateinischen Vätern und in der Frühscholastik," *Biblica* 5 (1924), 141–48; Michel, "Purgatoire," cols. 1214–19; Le Goff, *La Naissance du Purgatoire*, pp. 66, 81–91.

23. Michel, "Purgatoire," cols. 1190–1219.

24. Ntedika, *L'Évolution de la doctrine du purgatoire chez saint Augustin*, pp. 66–67; Le Goff, *La Naissance du Purgatoire*, p. 70.

25. Gauthier, "Les images de l'au-delà," pp. 4–5.

26. Gauthier, "Les images de l'au-delà," pp. 17–20.

ensured salvation, and in its place, they began to formulate distinctions between different categories of Christians, based on the gravity of their sins, and to posit a different fate for each category in the next world.

The image of the last judgment continued to dominate Christian eschatology in late antiquity. Now, however, the eager anticipation and glowing confidence of the first few centuries began to give way to fear and uncertainty. For the later fathers emphatically rejected the "merciful" position which some had accepted in the third century, whereby all members of the church would be saved. They emphasized that only the good would share in the collective rewards of the faithful; Christians guilty of grave sins would have to suffer eternal torments. As Isidore of Seville wrote in the seventh century:

> There are two divisions or orders of men at the judgment, namely, the elect and the reprobate; these, however, are divided into four. Among the perfect there is one order which will judge with God and another which will be judged. Both will reign with Christ, however. Similarly, the order of the reprobate is divided in two, for those within the church who are evil will be judged and condemned. Those outside the church will not be judged, but simply damned.[27]

The possibility of being "judged and condemned" at the last judgment on the basis of one's sins was constantly represented in sermons and treatises during the period from the fourth to the eighth century. It affected liturgical texts as well.

If the events at the end of time continued to loom large in the Christian imagination in late antiquity, the expectation that Christ would soon return to earth to judge the living and the dead had long since diminished. By the third century Christian writers were already beginning to take a greater interest in the moment of death, and the condition of the dead between death and the resurrection. The landscape of the afterlife slowly became christianized, as the discomfort or refreshment the dead experienced in the next world came to be understood as their deserved punishment or reward. Between the fourth and the eighth centuries, a body of authoritative teachings on these subjects developed.

In particular, the immediate aftermath of death came in for grow-

27. Isidore of Seville, *Sententiae*, 1: 27 (PL 83: 596–97).

ing attention. Like many of their pagan and Jewish neighbors, the Christians of the first three centuries believed that the good were somehow divided from the wicked immediately after death, and sent to a different place in the next world.[28] They also thought that the soul's journey to its assigned place might be fraught with dangers.[29] Like their neighbors, Christians performed rituals for the dead—at least in part—to ward off those dangers.

As time passed, the church fathers began to redefine the division of the just from the unjust after death in their own terms. By the late third or fourth century the word "judgment" was coming into use to describe this division; over the next few centuries, a set of teachings concerning the "individual judgment" began to take shape.[30] At first there was some resistance to the idea from those who thought that the only true judgment would come at the end of time.[31] However, most of the later fathers welcomed the idea of an individual judgment (even if they did not always call it that) immediately after death. It allowed them to refute the notion that souls simply "slept" or "rested" between death and the resurrection, an idea which threatened to undermine discipline by weakening the prospect of immediate torment for those who died in sin.[32]

The nature of the individual judgment and its relation to the great judgment at the end of time were depicted in several different ways in this period. Some of the later fathers presented the individual judgment as a foretaste of the last one. "For it is necessary to believe that just as blessedness rejoices the elect, so fire burns the reprobate from the day of their death," noted Gregory the Great.[33] Others divided

28. Jean Rivière, "Jugement," *DTC* 8: 1749–51, 1767; J. H. Wright, "Judgment, Divine (in Theology)," *NCE* 8: 30–31; Ntedika, *L'Évocation de l'au-delà*, pp. 136–40; Angenendt, "Theologie und Liturgie," in Schmid and Wollasch, *Memoria*, pp. 81–83.

29. Jean Rivière, "Rôle du démon au jugement particulier chez les pères," *Revue des sciences religieuses* 4 (1924), 43–64; Ntedika, *L'Évocation de l'au-delà*, pp. 46–59.

30. In Book 1 of his *De Trinitate*, Novatian wrote of the souls *praejudicia sentientes* (cited by Stuiber, *Refrigerium Interim*, p. 67); Augustine described how souls are judged immediately after death in *De natura et origine animae*, 2: 8, ed. Carl Urba and Joseph Zycha, in Augustine, *Opera, sectio 8, pars 1* (Vienna-Leipzig, 1913), p. 341.

31. Thus Lactantius, in his *Divinae institutiones*, 7: 7 and 21 (cited by Stuiber, *Refrigerium Interim*, p. 73), insisted that there was no judgment immediately after death. In the same treatise, however, he had already stated that the good and the wicked wait for the last judgment in different places.

32. In his *De anima*, 12 (PL 70: 1301), Cassiodorus did suggest that the period between death and resurrection was like a period of sleep. Generally his contemporaries and early medieval theologians argued against this view: see Rivière, "Jugement," cols. 1801–2.

33. Gregory the Great, *Dialogi*, 4: 29 (p. 272); cited by the anonymous eighth-century

the departed faithful into several categories, according to the gravity of their sins, and argued that the very good and the very bad would be judged immediately after death, and receive their reward or punishment, although not yet in full measure. The middle category or categories, on the other hand, would be judged only at the end of time. In the interim, they were relegated to various places in the underworld, some more pleasant than others.[34] A few of the western fathers seem to have toyed with the idea of a "provisional damnation" for some of those who fell into this middle category. Because of their sins, these people were condemned to suffer torments in the next world, which might become permanent unless they were aided by the intercession of the saints or the prayers of the living. They could only benefit from these prayers because they had done some good deeds in life.[35] This view did not gain wide acceptance among the theologians of the period, presumably because it seemed to undermine the argument that the dead would be judged solely by their own merits.

The possibility of purgation after death also received increasing attention in this period, as the leaders of the churches tried to reconcile that possibility with the principle of judgment by merit. Rejecting the "merciful" position, which had allowed for the salvation of all Christians through the purifying fire of judgment, the fathers of the late fourth and fifth centuries reminded the faithful that those guilty of serious crimes could not hope to be saved in this way. Salvation "as through fire," they argued, was reserved for those who had committed only "light" sins.[36] By the sixth century, purgation had begun to seem like a privilege reserved for only a few, rather than the common fate of most Christians. If his listeners were not careful, warned Cae-

---

author of the treatise *Utrum animae de humanis corporibus exeuntes mox deducantur ad gloriam vel ad poenam* (PL 96: 1385).

34. See, for example, Gregory the Great, *Dialogi*, 4: 26 (pp. 263–64); Isidore of Seville, *De origine creaturarum*, 13: 3–5 (PL 83: 945).

35. Joseph Ntedika argued that Augustine held this view in *L'Évolution de la doctrine du Purgatoire chez saint Augustin*, p. 45. The key text here is Augustine, *De civitate Dei*, 21: 27 (2: 804). Ntedika's views were criticized by Pierre Jay: "Saint Augustin et la doctrine du Purgatoire," p. 22. However, Ntedika has continued to defend them, convincingly in my opinion: *L'Évocation de l'au-delà*, pp. 99–105. The fifth-century bishop Peter Chrysologus also seems to have accepted the idea of a provisional damnation, which could only be lifted through the intercession of others: *Sermones*, 123 (PL 52: 539).

36. Ntedika, *L'Évolution de la doctrine du Purgatoire chez saint Augustin*, p. 24; Le Goff, *La Naissance du Purgatoire*, pp. 92–118.

sarius of Arles in one of his sermons, they were bound not for the fire of judgment but for the eternal fire of hell.[37] This attitude would find echoes in many early medieval texts.

The purifying fire was, then, increasingly associated with individual eschatology—that is, with the fate of only some of the faithful in the next world—in late antiquity. It also gradually came to be situated in the period before the end of the world. In the early fifth century, Augustine still identified the fire of 1 Corinthians primarily with the fire of judgment, although he also conceded that it might be understood as a metaphor for the "purifying fire" of tribulations suffered in this life. He treated the prospect of purgation between death and the last judgment as a mere hypothesis.[38] Only in the late sixth century did this hypothesis become a "given" in the western church, when Gregory the Great stated categorically in his *Dialogues* that "one should believe in a purging fire before the judgment for certain light faults [*levibus culpis*]."[39] From this time on in the West, the fire of 1 Corinthians was associated primarily with the period before the end of the world, although the earlier identification with the fire of judgment day persisted as well.[40]

As ideas about the afterlife changed, and as anxiety about the fate of the departed faithful grew in late antiquity, increased effort was devoted to the care of the dying and the dead. As we have seen, the whole passage from life to death was christianized during the period from the fourth to the ninth century. Prayers came to be performed around the deathbed, to ward off demonic attacks and commend the soul to God.[41] Intense prayer was also offered in the period just after

37. Jay, "Le Purgatoire dans la prédication de Césaire d'Arles," p. 7.

38. Ntedika, *L'Évolution de la doctrine du Purgatoire chez saint Augustin*, especially pp. 45–46, 52–53, 62–68. Robert Atwell has challenged Ntedika's thesis that Augustine's views on the location of purgation changed in the last years of his life: "Aspects in St. Augustine of Hippo's Thought and Spirituality Concerning the State of the Faithful Departed, 354–430," in David Loades, ed., *The End of Strife: Papers Selected from the Proceedings of the Colloquium of the Commission Internationale d'Histoire Ecclésiastique Comparée* (Edinburgh, 1984), pp. 8–9.

39. Gregory the Great, *Dialogi,* 4: 41 (p. 296). On the relationship between Augustine's and Gregory's thought on this subject, see R. R. Atwell, "From Augustine to Gregory the Great: An Evaluation of the Emergence of the Doctrine of Purgatory," *Journal of Ecclesiastical History* 38 (1987), 173–86.

40. Le Goff, *La Naissance du Purgatoire,* pp. 138–40, 142, 145.

41. On the importance of prayer around the deathbed, see Julian of Toledo, *Prognosticon,* 1: 18, in *Opera, pars 1,* ed. J. N. Hillgarth (Turnhout, 1976), p. 36. Compare Gregory the Great, *Dialogi,* 4: 40 (pp. 292–93).

death, to help the soul on its journey to the next world.[42] The practice
of burying the dead near the tombs of the saints developed in the
same period and in response to some of the same concerns. As Yvette
Duval has shown, burial ad sanctos was intended to protect the
corpse, ensuring that it would be able to rise again at the resurrection.[43] It also served to "associate" the dead with the saints, who
would act as advocates for them at the last judgment.[44] And of course
prayer was offered on a continuing basis for all the departed faithful,
as well as for individuals made "present" in the liturgy through the
ritual use of their names, in the hope that they would come in the end
to the company of saints.

It was in the context of these developments in liturgy and doctrine
that a coherent set of teachings about prayer for the dead first began to
emerge. And it is this context that explains their ambivalent tone. On
the one hand, the later fathers wanted to confirm the usefulness of
traditional liturgical practices; on the other hand, they were anxious
to remind the faithful that in the end each person would be judged by
his or her own merits. Augustine, for example, found it necessary to
assert that suffrages performed for the dead "do not contradict the
apostle's statement that 'We shall all stand before the tribunal of
Christ, so that it may be rendered to each according to what he
has done while in the body, whether good or evil [Rom. 14:10 and
2 Cor. 5:10].' For each person, while living in the body, acquired
the merit which allows him to benefit from these things."[45] He
argued elsewhere that prayer does not provide the dead with new
merits, but merely gives back to them the consequences of their old
ones.[46]

The later fathers tended to praise prayer for the dead even as they
carefully circumscribed its effects. In another passage (which would
become one of the most important authoritative bases for the medieval church's understanding of prayer for the dead), Augustine wrote:

42. Ntedika, *L'Évocation de l'au-delà*, pp. 46–83. In the seventh-century *Visio Baronti*,
prayers bring the dying monk an angelic protector, who helps to ward off demons as the
soul travels to heaven to be judged: *Visio Baronti*, MGH, SRM, 5: 377–94.
43. Duval, *Auprès des saints*, pp. 179–82, 194–201.
44. Duval, *Auprès des saints*, pp. 182–85.
45. Augustine, *Enchiridion ad Laurentium de fide et spe et caritate*, 110, ed. E. Evans, in
Augustine, *Aurelii Augustini Opera, pars 13* (Turnhout, 1969), p. 108. See also, on this point,
Augustine, *Sermones*, 172 (PL 38: 935–37): another popular text in the early middle ages.
46. Augustine, *Sermones*, 172 (PL 38: 937).

It cannot be denied that the souls of the dead are helped by the piety of the living who are close to them, when the sacrifice of the Mediator is offered or alms are given in church for them. But these things benefit those who earned while living the privilege of being helped by them afterwards. For there is a certain way of living which is not so good that the person does not require these things after death, nor so bad that these things do not benefit him after death. Indeed, there are those so good that they do not require these things, and again, there are those so bad that they cannot be helped by them after they have passed from this life. . . . So when the sacrifice of the altar or alms are offered for all the dead who have been baptized, they serve as thanksgiving for the very good; for those who were not very good they serve as propitiations; in the case of the very bad they serve as a kind of consolation for the living, even though they are of no help to the dead. For those whom they do help, however, they serve either to bring about a full remission, or certainly, to make their condemnation [*damnatio*] more tolerable.[47]

There are traces in this passage of the ancient affirmatory function of prayer: it will serve as "thanksgiving" for the very good. However, because of Augustine's concerns about the status of sinful Christians, the focus has shifted to instrumentality, to what prayer can and cannot do for the dead. From this point on western theologians would be increasingly—though never exclusively—preoccupied with defining and delimiting the practical effects of prayer.

In Augustine's day, however, those effects were still not very clear. It should be noted that he does not discuss the condition of the "not very bad" in the passage just cited. It is not clear whether *damnatio* refers to eternal damnation or to some temporary condemnation to suffering. Neither can we tell whether the remission (of sins) he mentions can take place without the assistance of the living. The obscurities of this passage are not entirely due to the distance that separates us from the early fifth century. Ideas about the afterlife were still in flux in late antiquity, and cautious thinkers like Augustine were unwilling to take too definite a stand on these matters when no clear guidance was available from their predecessors or from scripture.[48]

47. Augustine, *Enchiridion*, 110 (pp. 108–9).
48. Attwell, "Aspects in St. Augustine of Hippo's Thought and Spirituality Concerning the State of the Faithful Departed," in Loades, *The End of Strife*, pp. 5–6.

As a result, a clear set of ideas about the condition of the "deserving" dead in the afterlife, and what prayer might do for them, emerged very slowly. Gradually, however, a solution was found which would explain how prayer could help the dead, even though they were to be judged according to their own merits. It turned on the idea of purgation after death, which was itself undergoing important changes in late antiquity.

The two sets of ideas were not so readily linked as, in retrospect, we might expect. In the early fifth century Augustine described a middle category of Christians ("not very bad") who could be helped by prayer for the dead and a middle category of Christians ("not guilty of serious crimes") who could benefit from purgation after death, but he never drew the—to us—obvious connection between the two groups.[49] In fact, the first text to make an explicit link between purgation and prayer for the dead comes from the "Dialogue on the Nature of the Soul" of the early sixth-century grammarian, Julian Pomerius:

> Those spirits which neither go forth from here in such perfect holiness that they can enter immediately into paradise once their bodies are put aside, nor have lived so criminally and damnably, persevering in their crimes, that they deserve to be damned with the devil and his angels, will—with the church in this world supplicating effectively for them, and once they have been purged by remedial sufferings—receive their bodies back in blessed immortality, and, once made participants in the kingdom of heaven, will remain there with no detriment to their joy. . . .[50]

In this passage the church's prayers clearly affect the middle category of Christians who must undergo purgation before they are "made participants in the kingdom of heaven." It is hard to tell, though, what such prayer was actually thought to do for the members of this group.

The tenuous connection between suffrages for the dead and the process of purgation suggested by Julian Pomerius became stronger as ideas about purgation became more concrete from the sixth centu-

---

49. Ntedika, *L'Évolution de la doctrine du Purgatoire chez saint Augustin,* p. 66.

50. Cited by Julian of Toledo, *Prognosticon,* 2: 10 (p. 49); and by later writers perhaps from Julian—e.g., Haimo, *De varietate librorum,* 3: 7 (PL 118: 939). The "Dialogue" of Julian Pomerius itself is lost.

ry on. Once again, the *Dialogues* of Gregory the Great played an important role in this development. Like Augustine, Gregory set up a category of Christians who could benefit from prayer and a category who could benefit from purgation; in the theoretical passages of his *Dialogues* he never identified these groups with one another.[51] However, he did suggest a connection between prayer and purgation in the anecdotes he used to illustrate his theoretical points.

In one such anecdote, the soul of a deacon of the Roman church named Paschasius appeared to the bishop of Capua while the latter was taking a cure amid the vapors of a thermal bath. Paschasius was renowned in life for his virtues, and especially for his generosity to the poor, so the bishop was amazed to see him in such a place after his death. The apparition explained that he was sent to this "place of punishment" (*poenali loco*) because he had taken the part of the antipope, by mistake, in a schism. The bishop remembered Paschasius in his prayers for a few days, and when next he returned to the bath he could no longer find the spirit.[52] In another vision (again set in a thermal bath) the soul undergoing purgation asked a priest to make an offering at mass for him, "that you may intervene for my sins. And you will know that you have been heard when you come here again to bathe and do not find me here."[53] Gregory offered these cases as proof that prayer did help some of the dead. The implication was that prayer liberated them from the torments of purgation. However, Gregory was content to present the stories as they were told to him, and to let his readers draw their own conclusions. He made no clear theoretical statement about the way in which prayer might help the dead.

The theologian who finally explained, in explicit terms, the nature of the link between prayer and purgation was the Venerable Bede. In an Advent homily, Bede described how the perfect saw God immediately after death, and how the just enjoyed repose in paradise, awaiting the day when they would see God. He continued:

> But there are some, preordained for election because of their good works, who, because of some evil with which they are polluted when they die, are exposed after death to severe punishment in the

---

51. Compare Gregory the Great, *Dialogi*, 4: 52 and 59 (pp. 311 and 322), with *Dialogi*, 4: 41 (pp. 296–97).
52. Gregory the Great, *Dialogi*, 4: 42 (pp. 297–300).
53. Gregory the Great, *Dialogi*, 4: 57 (pp. 315–17).

flames of the purifying fire; they will either be cleansed from the stain of vice by this long trial until the day of judgment, or else, absolved earlier from their torments by their Christian friends' prayers, alms, fasting, weeping, and offerings of the sacrifice, they will enter into the repose of the blessed.[54]

Bede, then, identified a category of Christians who were already assured of salvation because of their works, but who needed to be purified of their sins before they could enter heaven. He believed that suffrages could serve to shorten their period of purgation, which would otherwise last until judgment day.

By the eighth century a basic framework of accepted teachings on prayer for the dead was in place in the West. Theologians had reconciled traditional liturgical practices with the principle that the ultimate fate of each Christian would depend on what he or she had done in life, by carefully delimiting the role of prayer for the dead. They continued to acknowledge the ancient affirmatory function of liturgical commemoration: it could serve as "thanksgiving" for the "very good." However, their attention had shifted from affirmation to instrumentality. Now their chief concern was with the effects of prayer, with its ability to help those of the dead who both deserved and needed to be helped. That group was identified with the good but imperfect Christians, who had to be purged of their sins before they could enter heaven. Most theologians assumed that the ultimate fate of these Christians was already assured at the moment of death,[55] but that their sufferings could be alleviated or their liberation from torment hastened through the help of others. Thus, in theological texts, prayer for the dead had come to be associated primarily with the process of purgation after death.

The Limits of Theology

From the time of Bede to the twelfth century this doctrinal framework underwent virtually no development. Theologians, concerned

54. Bede, *Homiliae*, 1:4 (PL 94: 30).
55. On this point, see Hrabanus Maurus, *Homiliae*, 1: 68 (PL 110: 128–30): "And therefore everyone who dies can only have in the next life what he or she earned in this one." See also Peter Damian, *Epistolae*, 121 (3: 396).

with other matters, did not speculate on the meaning of prayer for the dead; they were content to cite the authoritative comments of Augustine, Gregory, and Bede. But if the theology of prayer for the dead stagnated after the eighth century, at least the Carolingian Renaissance ensured that patristic and insular writings on the subject were widely diffused throughout the Frankish realm. The passages cited earlier in this chapter appear not only in theological works, but also in liturgical commentaries, canon law texts, sermons, and spiritual guidebooks. In short, they shaped all learned discussion of prayer for the dead in the early middle ages.

Images and ideas derived from this learned tradition influenced less scholarly works as well, including the rich body of vision literature which provides our most concrete information on the early medieval understanding of the afterlife and prayer for the dead.[56] Most modern historians have focused on images of purgation in these visions and the association of those images with the development of penitential and commemorative practices. However, for the sake of completeness, it should be noted that prayer for the dead was still occasionally seen as a form of "thanksgiving" for the "very good" in these texts. In Walahfrid Strabo's *Life of St. Gall*, for example, the saint feels obliged to offer mass for the repose of his master Columban, even though he has already witnessed Columban's passage into heaven.[57] Here the celebration of mass serves to affirm the status of a saint; it is not a means of helping the dead man, but a recognition of his right to be remembered in the liturgy of his community.[58]

However, in the early middle ages, few men and even fewer women were thought to be so holy that their funerals could be treated as triumphal processions. More often, in the vision literature as in theology, the dead were assumed to stand in need of assistance in the afterlife. Thus a great many visions from this period depict the good but imperfect dead undergoing purgation for their sins. It should be noted that the localization of that process varies greatly from case to case. Purgation might take place in the underworld—

56. Among recent studies of the early medieval vision literature, see Michel Aubrun, "Caractères et portée religieuse et sociale des '*visiones*' en Occident du VIe au XIe siècle," *Cahiers de civilisation médiévale* 23 (1980), 109–30; Peter Dinzelbacher, *Vision und Visionsliteratur im Mittelalter* (Stuttgart, 1981); Claude Carozzi, "La Géographie de l'au-delà et sa signification pendant le haut moyen âge," in *Popoli e paesi nella cultura altomedievale*, 2 vols. (Spoleto, 1983), 2: 423–81; Neiske, "Vision und Totengedenken."
57. Walahfrid Strabo, *Vita sancti Galli abbatis*, 1: 26 (PL 114: 999).
58. Compare Donatus, *Vita Trudonis*, 21, MGH, SRM, 6: 291.

often in an "infernalized" place of punishment[59]—or in a variety of settings on earth. Indeed, in one eleventh-century vision, those undergoing purgation form a procession which travels through the countryside.[60] As Jacques Le Goff has pointed out, there was no shared notion of a single "purgatory" in the early middle ages.[61]

In many visions recorded between the mid-eighth century and the eleventh century prayer and almsgiving serve to help the dead undergoing purgation.[62] Often the suffrages performed by the living help to liberate the dead from their torments, as they did in the writings of Gregory the Great and Bede. Peter Damian, for example, tells of a cleric who unexpectedly encounters the soul of Severinus, former bishop of Cologne. Severinus is suffering because he postponed his liturgical obligations while engaged in secular business at the emperor's court. He asks that prayers be said and alms distributed for his sake, noting that, "when these things have been done, I will undoubtedly be freed from the bonds of this punishment and joined, rejoicing, to the choirs of blessed citizens who are expecting me."[63]

Sometimes, on the other hand, prayer merely mitigates the sufferings of the dead. Thus, in Heito of Basel's version of the *Vision of Wetti*, an abbot, undergoing purgation in a wretched hut on a mountain in the next world, sends a message to a bishop, asking him to have prayers said for him. The prayers will serve to close off the gaps in the hut, keeping out the intolerable smell of two counts who are "bathing" in a hot spring nearby.[64] Nothing is said about the final liberation of the soul from its torments in visions like these, but this does not mean that the need for prayer seemed any less urgent. Given the "infernalized" character of purgation in most visions, the absence of aid from the living could become a positive torment for the dead. Thus, in the *Vision of Bernold,* the souls of those for whom no one intercedes are in a deeper pit, suffering more than all the others.[65]

Sometimes, and especially in the visions recorded by the great

---

59. An eighth-century Anglo-Saxon monk described the torments inflicted on sinners submerged in flaming pits. He noted, however, that all of the souls he was describing would be liberated on judgment day or before: Boniface and Lull, *Epistolae*, 115, ed. E. Dümmler, MGH, EPP, 3: 404.

60. Orderic Vitalis, *Historia aecclesiastica*, 8: 17 (4: 237–51).

61. Le Goff, *La Naissance du Purgatoire.*

62. See especially Neiske, "Vision und Totengedenken."

63. Peter Damian, *De variis miraculosis narrationibus*, 5 (PL 145: 578–79).

64. Heito of Basel, *Visio Wettini*, 10, ed. Ernst Dümmler, MGH, PP, 2: 270–71.

65. Hincmar of Reims, *De visione Bernoldi presbyteri* (PL 125: 1117).

scholars of the Carolingian era, the effects of prayer for the dead are carefully circumscribed, in keeping with late patristic teachings on this subject. A case in point is Walahfrid Strabo's poetic account of the *Vision of Wetti*. Walahfrid's verses were based on Heito's prose *Vision of Wetti*, but the poet added a great deal of extra material, including the following comment on the episode, described above, in which an abbot undergoing purgation asks for prayers:

> This episode indicates that much is won by pious prayers. But do not be confident that when your life is over, the fires which you build by your own evil deeds will be dispersed by the pleas of another. Though there are many whose sins can be purged by intercession, no one can confidently rely on this, since no one knows how heavily his deeds will weigh. Hence for my own part I maintain that it is practical to atone for my acts beforehand. Every man will be dogged by his own deeds.[66]

Walahfrid was only eighteen when he composed this, his first major poem, but he was a learned young man. His comment neatly encapsulates established teaching on prayer for the dead—including a warning not to rely too much on it.

There can be no doubt, then, that the theological tradition described above influenced many people's ideas about prayer for the dead between 750 and 1100. That influence is apparent in a wide variety of texts. What is doubtful, however, is the assumption, still to be found at work in many recent studies, that theology actually determined the meanings attributed to funerals and commemorative services in the early middle ages. That this was the case is unlikely on the face of it, both because of the serious limitations of the early medieval educational system and because little effort was devoted at the time to teaching about prayer for the dead.

It is important to remember that very few people—even within the tiny educated elite of early medieval society—had more than a passing acquaintance with works of doctrine and fewer still had the training which would have allowed them to follow the reasoning behind those works. Most monks and nuns, most bishops and cathedral canons, let alone ordinary priests and the small number of edu-

---

66. Walahfrid Strabo, *Visio Wettini*, lines 438–45, ed. Ernst Dümmler, MGH, PP, 2: 318; the translation is that of David A. Traill, *Walahfrid Strabo's Visio Wettini: Text, Translation, and Commentary* (Bern-Frankfurt, 1974), p. 55.

cated layfolk, never received any formal training in theology at all.[67] Thus, while the writings of Augustine, Gregory, and Bede on suffrages for the dead were available in early medieval libraries, there is no reason to suppose that modestly educated men and women had much direct contact with them. Even those who had read these works sometimes understood them in idiosyncratic ways.[68]

It should also be noted that while the leaders of the church might have monitored clerical and (less often) popular views on controversial matters such as the eucharist or the nature of Christ's divinity, prayer for the dead was not yet one of those matters. More effort was devoted in this period to encouraging the performance of suffrages than to disseminating correct teaching about them. As a result, even literate men and women often held theologically unsophisticated ideas on the subject. They did not, for example, invariably assume that the dead would be judged according to their own merits. The fact that church leaders had to reassert this principle publicly from time to time shows that it had not gained full acceptance within the population as a whole. In the early ninth century "many Christians" apparently believed—rather like the "merciful" fathers in the first centuries of the church—that all those who had been baptized would eventually be saved through the purging fires of the next world, regardless of their sins. The council held at Paris in 829 had to issue a stern reminder that this was not the case.[69] The problem was not confined to the illiterate masses, however. Even members of the educated elite often seem to have been confused on this point.[70]

By the same token, some educated people seem to have thought that prayer could do more than render to the dead the "consequences of their own merits." This is evident from one of the canons of the

67. Pierre Riché, *Les Écoles et l'enseignement dans l'Occident chrétien de la fin du Ve siècle au milieu du XIe siècle* (Paris, 1979), pp. 235–36, 280–84.

68. The ninth-century noblewoman Dhuoda, for example, cites the passage from Augustine's *Enchiridion* on the uses of prayer for the dead in her *Liber manualis*, 8: 11–13 (pp. 312–18). However, Dhuoda suggests both that the pains of those in hell can be mitigated through the merits of others and that prayers can be offered for non-Christians. On the education of the laity in this period, see Riché, *Les Écoles et l'enseignement*, pp. 287–313; Rosamond McKitterick, *The Carolingians and the Written Word* (Cambridge, 1989), pp. 211–70.

69. Council of Paris (829), c. 10, in *Concilia aevi Karolini*, 1: 661–63.

70. See, for example, Hrabanus Maurus, *Enarrationes in epistolas beati Pauli*, 9: 3 (PL 112: 38–39); Haimo, *De varietate librorum*, 3: 6 (PL 118: 935–36). In the tenth century, see Ratherius of Verona, *Sermones*, 2 (PL 136: 700). But for evidence of wide familiarity with this principle, see *Recueil des actes de Philippe Ier*, no. 8 (1060).

council which met at Tribur in 895. The council dealt with a great many issues, among them the question of where the dead should be buried—a complicated problem in an area where churches and cemeteries were still few and far between. Ideally, the assembled clergy decided, a dead Christian should be buried in the cemetery associated with the bishop's seat. But if this was impossible, they added, "let him look for a place of burial where some holy congregation of canons or monks or nuns lives as a community, so that he [the dead person] may present himself to his judge commended by their prayers, and so that the remission of sins which he does not obtain by his own merit, he may receive by their intercession."[71] This group of eminent churchmen readily assumed that intercession could accomplish what the merits of the dead person could not. Similar notions lie behind a number of other texts from this period.[72]

My point is not that non-theologians (including some church leaders) completely ignored the question of merit, so important to the theologians. I am merely suggesting that modestly educated men and women held more flexible views on prayer for the dead than the great scholars of their day. Their ideas on the subject were not dictated by the doctrinal tradition, since they were not very familiar with that tradition. As a result, they were able to associate prayer for the dead with a much wider range of images and ideas, drawn from a variety of authoritative sources. Among the most important of these sources were the prayers themselves. Indeed, it seems obvious that more people were familiar with liturgical texts, which they performed or heard performed on a regular basis, than with the writings of the church fathers and the theologians. Presumably what they said shaped their understanding of what they were doing when they prayed for the dead.[73] Other authoritative texts, including visions and saints' lives, and probably popular folklore, contributed to the stock of images and ideas associated with this practice. Some of these images and

71. Council of Tribur (895), c. 15, in *Capitularia regum Francorum*, 2: 221–22: "remissionem delictorum, quam meritis non obtinet, illorum intercessionibus percipiat." Compare *Vita sancti Amati confessoris*, 13, ed. Bruno Krusch, MGH, SRM, 4: 220.

72. In the late eleventh century four brothers made a donation to Saint-Vincent of Mâcon. According to the scribe, they asked that the gift be used to rebuild the church of St. Martin and his companions, "so that through their merits we may acquire the joys of heaven": *Cartulaire de Saint-Vincent de Mâcon*, no. 544 (1074–96). See also the charter from Narbonne dated 988 cited by Magnou-Nortier, *La Société laïque et l'église*, p. 443.

73. Hence the aphorism *lex orandi, lex credendi*, attributed to Prosper of Aquitaine and often evoked by modern liturgical historians.

ideas cannot easily be reconciled with the doctrinal tradition described above, but this presented no difficulty for those who were only imperfectly familiar with that tradition. The early medieval ideology of prayer for the dead, in other words, was not circumscribed by theological teachings on the subject. Indeed, it often reached well beyond the limits of theology.

Consider, for example, the association of prayer with the individual judgment. From late antiquity on, the orthodox view had been that the outcome of the individual judgment depended on the personal merits of the dead person. Indeed, in order to underline that point, some church leaders had depicted the judgment in allegorical terms. A sort of *psychomachia*, or contention between the virtues and the vices for control of the soul, appears in the visions related by Gregory the Great in his *Dialogues* and by Boniface, in a letter to an Anglo-Saxon abbess.[74] Others treated the individual judgment as a real event, involving real (if supernatural) actors. Bede, in his *Ecclesiastical History*, recounts the tale of a dying man who saw two handsome young men enter his room with a tiny book, which turned out to contain all his good deeds. They were followed by a horde of evil spirits, who produced an immense volume in which all his sins had been recorded. The chief demon asked the two young men why they were there, since the dying man clearly belonged to him. They agreed, telling the demons to "take him and enroll him in the company of the damned."[75]

This vision reflects the ancient belief that the devil and his forces had certain rights over sinful souls, and that they might therefore serve as accusers of the dead at the individual judgment.[76] It should be noted, however, that Bede's demons assert and prove their rights in an orderly manner, with the concurrence of the two "handsome young men," who presumably represent angels. The fate of the dying man is determined by his good and bad deeds; there is no real disagreement over the outcome.

In many early medieval texts, however, composed by less learned writers, the demons act in a much more unruly way. Sometimes they continue to press their claims despite proof of the dead person's vir-

74. Gregory the Great, *Dialogi*, 4: 37 (especially pp. 288–89), and 4: 38 (pp. 290–91); Boniface and Lull, *Epistolae*, 10, MGH, EPP, 3: 252–57.
75. Bede, *Historia ecclesiastica*, 5: 13 (p. 500). I have modified Colgrave and Mynors's translation slightly.
76. On this point, see Rivière, "Rôle du démon au jugement particulier."

tue. Sometimes they are not represented as accusers at all, but as a lurking threat to souls departing the body.[77] In such a situation, the intercession of the living, the saints, and the angels on behalf of the dead becomes of critical importance.[78] As we have seen, some of the early medieval funeral ordines, and most of the monastic customaries, emphasized that the whole community should be present at the moment of death, and urged those present to keep up a continual flow of prayers until the body was buried. Other texts also emphasize the importance of intercession at this time.[79]

Much of the prayer performed at the moment of death invoked the assistance of the angels and the saints on behalf of the dying person. The response *Subvenite*, which was performed as soon as the soul left the body, began: "Come help, saints of God; hasten, angels of the Lord, receiving his soul, offering it before the highest one . . . ." The help of powerful saints might be necessary to defeat the demons lying in wait for the soul. In the ninth-century *Deeds of Dagobert*, a hermit, praying for the soul of the Frankish king, sees it being carried off toward a volcano by black spirits. Dagobert calls upon Denis, Maurice, and Martin to free him and, with thunder and lightning, the saints appear, snatch the king's soul from the hands of the demons and prepare to carry it to the bosom of Abraham.[80] Outright battles between the forces of good and evil for possession of a soul leaving its body are not uncommon in early medieval visions.[81]

77. See Boniface and Lull, *Epistolae*, 115, MGH, EPP, 3: 404.

78. Michel Aubrun recognized this, without noting the discrepancy between it and the orthodox view of the judgment. See his "Caractères et portée religieuse et sociale des '*Visiones*'," pp. 114–15.

79. In 978, for example, Archbishop Hugh of Bourges made certain concessions to the canons of Sainte-Croix of Orléans; in return, the archbishop asked the canons to chant the *De profundis* for him after he died "for our repose . . . so that with Christ's help, through the intervention of their prayers, we may deserve to be delivered from the profound danger of [eternal?] death": *Cartulaire de Sainte-Croix d'Orléans (814–1300)*, ed. Joseph Thillier and Eugène Jarry (Orléans, 1906), no. 62 (978). See also Peter Damian, *Epistolae*, 106 (3: 171–72).

80. *Gesta Dagoberti I. regis francorum*, 44, ed. Bruno Krusch, MGH, SRM, 2: 421–22. See also *Recueil des chartes de l'abbaye de Cluny*, no. 1784 (988), in which a donor invokes the assistance of St. Andrew: "so that he may obtain forgiveness of sins for me from God through his prayers, and deliver me from the dark power of Satan on the day of my departure from this wretched world." Compare *Recueil des actes de Philippe Ier*, no. 75 (1075): "so that when the day of our death arrives, the deadly enemy may not rejoice over us, but rather Christ's mercy deliver us, through the intercession of Blessed Mary, from the hands of the devil and the punishments of hell and transfer us to the joys of paradise."

81. Flodoard, *Historia Remensis ecclesiae*, 1: 25, ed. M. Lejeune, 2 vols. (Reims, 1854), 1: 216; Ademar of Chabannes, *Chronicon* 3: 19 (p. 136); Boniface and Lull, *Epistolae*, 10, MGH, EPP, 3: 252–57; see also Rivière, "Rôle du démon."

The angels and saints intervened not only in the moments before death and during the journey to heaven, but also at the individual judgment itself. That intervention was not always helpful to great sinners. A ninth-century text recounts the vision of an eighth-century bishop, Eucher of Orléans. While the bishop was praying one day, he fell into an ecstasy in which he saw Charles Martel suffering in hell. Eucher's angelic guide informed him that Charles was "condemned body and soul to eternal torment before the last judgment, by the judgment of the saints who will sit with the Lord at the last judgment." When he awoke from his vision, Eucher called on Abbots Fulrad of Saint-Denis and Boniface of Fulda to go with him to the tomb of Charles Martel. When the tomb was opened, a dragon escaped and the interior was found to be blackened as though by fire.[82] Here the saints condemn the king who had despoiled their churches. In other visions, however, the saints intervene at the individual judgment to save souls from hell.[83]

In early medieval visions of the individual judgment the dead person is usually presented as good, but imperfect. There is hope for the salvation of the soul, but because it is sullied by sin the demons can also lay claim to it. In many of these texts, however, the soul is depicted as remarkably helpless before the powers of evil at the moment of death. While the dead person clearly cannot be saved without merit, there often seems to be no assurance that he or she will be saved by merit alone. Frequently it is assumed that unless the dead are protected by prayer, unless the angels or the saints intervene, the demons' claims will prevail. Thus intercession is represented as not just helpful, but of crucial importance if the dead are to evade the clutches of demons just after death.

But even if the forces of darkness did gain possession of the soul all was not lost. Prayer could be effective even on behalf of those in hell, if only to lessen their sufferings. The belief that the torments of hell were not necessarily continuous, or always of the same intensity, goes back to antiquity. The early Christians may have adopted it from a Jewish tradition which held that the souls in gehenna enjoy a respite from their sufferings on the Sabbath.[84] The association of prayer with

82. *Epistola synodi Carisiacensis* (858), in *Capitularia regum Francorum*, 2: 432–33.

83. E.g., Peter Damian, *De variis miraculosis narrationibus*, 5 (PL 145: 589–90).

84. Israel Lévi, "Le Repos sabbatique des âmes damnées," *Revue des études juives* 25 (1892), 1–13; Cabassut, ""La Mitigation des peines de l'enfer," pp. 65–66. See also *Visio Baronti*, 17, MGH, SRM, 5: 390–92.

such a respite is also very old. In the *Vision of Paul*, an early apocalypse, probably written in Egypt in the third century, Christ grants
the souls of the damned refreshment on Sundays because of Paul's
intervention on their behalf.[85]

Despite the popularity of the *Vision of Paul*, the possibility that
prayer might alleviate the sufferings of those in hell never received the
sanction of the church fathers. Augustine did suggest, in the passage
cited earlier from his *Enchiridion*, that prayer for the dead might make
their *damnatio* more tolerable, but it is not clear whether he used this
word to mean condemnation to purgation or to eternal torment.[86]
Some of the scholastic theologians of the high middle ages understood Augustine to refer to eternal damnation in this passage, but I
have found no early medieval theologian who interpreted the text in
this way.[87] The great scholars of the period from the eighth to the
eleventh century generally rejected the possibility that prayer could
help the damned.[88]

More modestly educated men and women often took a broader
view, however. These people may have been acquainted with Augustine's assertion that prayer could make the dead's *damnatio* more
tolerable (the passage was very widely cited in early medieval flo-
rilegia), without understanding it in the same way as the theologians
did. Or perhaps they were influenced by the liturgical texts they
heard or performed. Included in the late eighth-century Sacramentary
of Gellone, for example, is a mass for those "whose soul is in doubt."
The second prayer of this mass runs as follows:

> Omnipotent and merciful God, incline, we pray, your venerable
> ears to our poor prayers, which we humbly pray before your majes-
> ty for the soul of your servant, brother N., so that while we despair
> of the quality of his life, we may be consoled from the abundance of
> your kindness. And if we cannot obtain full forgiveness for his soul,

---

85. Theodore Silverstein, ed., *Visio sancti Pauli: The History of the Apocalypse in Latin,
Together with Nine Texts* (London, 1935), pp. 3, 12; Martha Himmelfarb, *Tours of Hell: An
Apocalyptic Form in Jewish and Christian Literature* (Philadelphia, 1983), pp. 16–19; Claude
Kappler, "L'Apocalypse latine de Paul," in Claude Kappler et al., eds., *Apocalypses et voyages
dans l'au-delà* (Paris, 1987), pp. 237–66.
86. Augustine, *Enchiridion*, 110 (p. 109); on Augustine's reaction to the argument that
the sufferings of the damned were mitigated on Sundays, see Cabassut, "La Mitigation des
peines de l'enfer," p. 66.
87. Landgraf, *Dogmengeschichte der Frühscholastik*, 4: 2, pp. 256–320.
88. Gregory the Great, *Dialogi*, 4: 46 (pp. 304–5). See also Haimo, *De varietate librorum*, 3: 39 and 46 (PL 118: 949–50, 958).

let him at least, among the torments which he perhaps suffers, feel some refreshment from the abundance of your mercy.[89]

These prayers were omitted from the revised Gregorian sacramentary, which became the "official" prayer book of the Carolingian church—perhaps because they seemed too unorthodox. Nevertheless, the older books remained in use in some places into the eleventh century, and may well have suggested to the clerics who used them the possibility that prayer could alleviate the sufferings of those in hell.[90]

In any case, some educated people in the period from the mid-eighth century to the end of the eleventh century clearly believed that the suffrages of the living could mitigate the sufferings of the damned. Early in the ninth century, for example, the monks of Fleury decided to pray for some men who had died in an unjust feud, so that "even if they did not deserve to be freed from their perpetual torments, at least the strict judge might change their punishments for lighter ones."[91] The literate noblewoman Dhuoda likewise informed her son that alms were to be given even "for the very bad and the unworthy," because if this did not provide any (lasting?) gain for their souls, at least, "thanks to the merits of others, namely the poor, they would receive a little bit of respite which would refresh them."[92]

If some early medieval texts suggest that suffrages could alleviate the torments of the damned, an even larger number associate intercession with the liberation of souls from hell. A number of prayer texts refer to this goal. Probably the best-known is the famous offertory of the mass for the dead, the *Domine Jesu Christe*, composed in the tenth century, which begins: "Lord Jesus Christ, king of glory, free the souls of all the departed faithful from the torments of hell, and from the deep pit; deliver them from the lion's mouth, lest Tartarus swallow them, lest they fall into darkness. . . ." Some modern scholars have attempted to explain away texts like these, by suggesting that they were not meant to be taken literally or that phrases like "the

89. *Liber sacramentorum Gellonensis*, ed. Antoine Dumas, 2 vols. (Turnhout, 1981), 2: 468, no. 2924.

90. Cabassut, "La Mitigation des peines de l'enfer," pp. 67–70.

91. Adrevald, et al., *Miracula sancti Benedicti*, 1: 21, ed. E. de Certain (Paris, 1858), p. 51. On Adrevald and his work, see Alexandre Vidier, *L'Historiographie à Saint-Benoît-sur-Loire et les miracles de Saint-Benoît*, rev. by the monks of Fleury (Paris, 1965), pp. 153–58.

92. Dhuoda, *Liber manualis*, 8: 13 (pp. 312–14).

torments of hell" actually referred to the torments of purgation carried out in the underworld.[93] In the end, though, such explanations only twist the meanings of the texts they purport to explain, in an effort to make them conform to the doctrinal framework described above. For it is clear that some people did associate prayer for the dead with the salvation of souls who were otherwise destined for eternal torment.

A number of early medieval narrative texts describe the salvation through intercession, of pagans or of people so wicked that they are unequivocally damned. By far the most famous incident of this sort occurs in the early biographies of Gregory the Great. According to the eighth-century English monk who wrote the very first vita of the saint, Gregory was passing through the forum of Trajan in Rome one day when he was reminded by the monuments around him of the pagan emperor's virtue, and especially his willingness to do justice to the poor. Gregory was so moved that he went to the basilica of St. Peter and "wept floods of tears" for Trajan. Soon thereafter he had a vision in which it was revealed that "he had been heard"—but only because he did not make a habit of praying for pagans.[94]

The legend of Trajan became a standard feature of both insular and continental lives of Gregory.[95] However, the story was clearly troubling to the more theologically sophisticated hagiographers, who were familiar with Gregory's own condemnation of prayer for infidels and the damned. Thus, John the Deacon, in his ninth-century version of the life, specified that Gregory had not really prayed for Trajan, but only wept. He went on to argue that Trajan could not have been admitted to heaven, since he had never been baptized; Gregory's tears could only have brought about a liberation from tor-

93. See Hilferty, *The Domine Jesu Christe, Libera Me, and Dies Irae*, pp. 61–111, especially pp. 93–111.
94. *The Earliest Life of Gregory the Great by an Anonymous Monk of Whitby*, 29, ed. and trans. Bertram Colgrave (Lawrence, 1968), pp. 126–28.
95. Gaston Paris, "La Légende de Trajan," *Bibliothèque de l'Ecole des hautes études, sciences philologiques, et historiques*, fasc. 35 (1878), 261–98; this study has been largely superseded by that of Gordon Whatley, "The Uses of Hagiography: The Legend of Pope Gregory and the Emperor Trajan in the Middle Ages," *Viator* 15 (1984), 25–63. In addition to the texts they cite, see the letter sent by Empress Agnes of Poitou to the monks of Fruttuaria in 1062: Tilman Struve, ed., "Zwei Briefe der Kaiserin Agnes," *Historisches Jahrbuch* 104 (1984), 424. Agnes asked the monks "ut Gregoriana pietate in Traianum petatis mihi veniam a Domino: quia namque ille unus homo ab inferni claustris exoravit paganum, multi vos facile salvabitis christianam unam."

ment, not salvation.[96] The theologians of the high middle ages continued to wrestle with the problems presented by this story.[97]

Theologically outrageous episodes, in which pagans or very wicked people escape from hell, recur with some regularity in early medieval writings, and especially in hagiographical works. More often, however, early medieval texts associate prayer with the liberation from hell of moderately sinful Christians, who may have accomplished some good during their lives but who are nevertheless doomed to eternal torment unless someone intercedes on their behalf. This seems akin to the notion of "provisional damnation," which was, as we have seen, proposed by some of the church fathers. This notion was never accepted by the great scholars of the early middle ages, who generally agreed that the fate of the dead would be determined by their own merits.[98] However, less learned writers do sometimes describe sinners who can only hope to escape from hell with the help of others.

Early in the ninth century, for example, the anonymous author of the *Acts of the Bishops of Le Mans* described the crimes of bishop Goslein, who had died several decades earlier. He then added: "But all the bishops and priests who hear these things should pray all the more for this Goslein, that he may be freed from all the aforesaid evils and misdeeds, and, God willing, evade the pains of hell."[99] A similar belief is reflected in a passage from the *Annals of Fulda*. One night in 874, Louis the German dreamt he saw his long-dead father, Louis the Pious. The emperor begged his son to deliver him from the torments in which he was detained, "so that at last sometime I may have eternal life." Terrified by this vision, Louis the German sent letters to all the monasteries of his realm, urging them to pray for his father. The author of this entry in the *Annals* explained that while Louis the Pious had done many praiseworthy things in his life, he nevertheless permitted many things to be done in his kingdom which were contrary to the law of God. "Not only those who do them, but also those who consent to their doing them, are worthy of death [Rom. 1:32]," he

96. John the Deacon, *Sancti Gregorii Magni vita*, 44 (PL 75: 105).
97. Paris, "La Légende de Trajan," pp. 285–86; Whatley, "The Uses of Hagiography," pp. 36–40.
98. Haimo, *De varietate librorum*, 3: 46 (PL 118: especially col. 958).
99. *Actus pontificum Cenomannis in urbe degentium*, 17, ed. G. Busson and A. Ledru (Le Mans, 1901), p. 262.

noted.[100] The implication is that Louis the Pious was worthy of death and would remain in hell unless his son intervened on his behalf.

In the eleventh century, the German monk Othlo of St. Emmeram told of a nun who saw a spirit appear before her, dressed in "miserable garments" and begging for her prayers. It turned out to be the former empress, Theophano. She was suffering severe torments because of her immoderate love of fine clothes and ornaments. Not having considered this love a sin, she never did penance for it and so was condemned to suffer after death. But as she told the nun: "I know that, however great the suffering I may deserve to endure, yet because I persevered in the Catholic faith, if any of the servants of God are willing to pray constantly for me, they can free me from perpetual damnation."[101] In this, as in a number of other eleventh-century visions, "provisional damnation" is associated with an incomplete penance, or with a wrong left unrighted at the time of death. Only if the irregular situation is corrected can the dead person hope to evade eternal torment.[102]

As H. E. J. Cowdrey has suggested, fear of damnation if an assigned penance remained incomplete at the time of death may explain the laity's support for reformed monasteries such as Cluny in the eleventh century.[103] Lay donors seem to have hoped that the prayers and alms of the monks, or the intervention of a patron saint, would make up any deficits in their moral accounts, and allow them to evade the eternal torments of hell. Certainly many more charters of donation invoke the assistance of the saints or the clergy for this purpose, than for help in simply speeding up an entry into heaven that was already assured. Isembran and his wife, Teisa, for example, made a gift to Saint-Vincent of Mâcon so that "this same illustrious witness to the Lord, by his intercession, will deign to liberate the soul [of their dead son] from the pains of hell."[104] Likewise, a number of donors gave to Cluny for the souls of Magengod and his wife Jotselt, " . . . so that through the intercession of the blessed Peter and Paul

100. *Annales Fuldenses*, a. 874, ed. George H. Pertz, rev. Friedrich Kurze (Hanover, 1891), p. 82.
101. Othlo of St. Emmeram, *Liber visionum*, 17 (PL 146: 373).
102. Othlo of St. Emmeram, *Liber visionum*, 12 (PL 146: 366–68); compare the situation of William of Glos, in Orderic Vitalis, *Historia aecclesiastica*, 8: 17 (4: 244).
103. Cowdrey, *The Cluniacs and the Gregorian Reform*, pp. 121–29.
104. *Cartulaire de Saint-Vincent de Mâcon*, no. 137 (no date).

and the other saints, the Lord Almighty may deign to deliver their souls from the snares of death and to liberate them from the pains of hell."[105] This prospect of "provisional damnation" was still present in some twelfth-century texts.[106]

The influence of the notion of "provisional damnation" may help to explain another peculiarity of the early medieval ideology of prayer for the dead—its association with a favorable outcome for the soul at the last judgment. This association may be somewhat difficult for modern historians to understand, but it is hardly surprising, given the continued prominence of judgment day in early medieval eschatology.[107] Ideas about the individual judgment and the fate of souls immediately after death were becoming more and more concrete in the early middle ages, but they never ousted the image of the last judgment from its central place in the Christian imagination.

Representations of the second coming and the resurrection played a prominent role in early medieval literature and art, and pastors used images of the strict judge and the threat of eternal damnation to try to frighten their flocks into abandoning their sins.[108] Jonas of Orléans, in the moral guide he composed for Count Matfrid, painted the terrors of the approaching judgment and the torments awaiting those who failed to repent in lurid colors: "Who is of such a stolid mind, who has such an iron heart that these things do not terrify him?"[109]

105. *Recueil des chartes de l'abbaye de Cluny*, no. 253 (925). The aid of St. Peter, who had been granted the power to "bind and loose," was particularly sought after. Donors apparently hoped that Peter would simply "loosen the bonds" of their sins, freeing them to enter heaven. See *Cartulaire de l'abbaye de Saint-Père de Chartres*, 1: 154 (before 1061); 1: 183–84 (1062), 1: 156–58 (ca. 1078); *Recueil des chartes de l'abbaye de Cluny*, no. 2777 (1023).

106. King Henry I of England was reported to have appeared after his death to reveal that "I would have been doomed to an eternal death, if the Lord Abbot Peter of Cluny, with all his [monks], had not come to my aid" ("morti aeternae deputatus fuissem, nisi dominus Petrus abbas Cluniacensis cum omnis suis subvenisset"): Rudolf, *Vita Petri Venerabilis*, 13 (PL 189: 25). See also *Cartulaire de Notre-Dame de Josaphat*, ed. Charles Métais, 2 vols. (Chartres, 1911–12), no. 132 (1138–44); "Since many of the dead would be given over to unending torment in eternal fires unless they were assisted by the pious care of the living, Christian devotion customarily offers many gifts by which the paupers of Christ, who are bound to pray for the dead, may be sustained" ("Quia plerique defunctorum nisi pia vivorum cura juvarentur, perpetuis incendiis sine fine cruciandi traderentur, consuevit christiana religio plurima largiri beneficia quibus Christi pauperes pro defunctis oraturi sustentarentur").

107. E.g., Hrabanus Maurus, *Enarrationes in epistolas beati Pauli*, 9: 3 (PL 112: 36–39). Isidore of Seville's description of the last judgment (see above) was cited in the ninth century by Jonas of Orléans, *De institutione laicali*, 3: 18 (PL 106: 272) and Haimo, *De varietate librorum*, 3: 18 (PL 118: 943).

108. Eligius of Noyon, *Homiliae*, 8 (PL 87: especially col. 619).

109. Jonas of Orléans, *De institutione laicali*, 3: 19 (PL 106: 274–75).

Not everyone took these messages to heart. In the ninth century, as we have seen, "many" people continued to believe that all those who had been baptized would ultimately be saved. However, there is reason to believe that fear of the coming judgment became more widespread and more intense in the tenth and eleventh centuries, leading a growing number of people to look for intercessors to help them evade the torments of hell.[110]

But what role had intercession to play in the outcome of the judgment? There are really two kinds of prayer at issue here. The first is prayer performed at the very moment of judgment, by those in a position to intercede before Christ, such as the martyrs. According to the theologians such intercession would be of no avail, for each person would be judged according to his or her own merits. "Each one shall be presented at the judgment just as he goes forth from here."[111] Those who failed to repent in time could expect no help on the last day: "To what apostles, to what other saints, shall we then flee, since we have despised both their example and their teachings?"[112]

However, if we turn to other kinds of sources, it becomes clear that not everyone shared this point of view. The preambles to charters often depict donors who are uncertain of their worthiness to join the company of saints, who fear that they cannot be saved by their own merits at the last judgment, and who long for help at that critical moment: "Considering the enormity of our sins, and thinking over the examination—greatly to be feared—in the coming judgment, when everything that is hidden in our hearts shall be made plain to all, and knowing that in such an examination we cannot be safe without intercessors, we give . . ."[113] According to the scribes, a sense of helplessness in the face of the last judgment encouraged donors to make gifts to religious houses, not only because such good deeds would be credited to their account on the last day, but also because they hoped in this way to gain the help of the saints or the clergy to

110. Certainly references to judgment day are much more frequent than references to purgation in charters from this period. Among many other examples, see *Cartulaire de l'abbaye de Conques*, no. 395 (1004); *Cartulaire de Saint-Vincent de Mâcon*, nos. 430 (1031–62) and 431 (1031–62); *Cartulaire de Gellone*, no. 168 (1077–99); *Recueil des chartes de l'abbaye de Saint-Benoît-sur-Loire*, no. 61 (975).

111. Gregory the Great, *Dialogi*, 4: 41 (p. 296). Cited in Haimo, *De varietate librorum*, 3: 20 (PL 118: 943).

112. Julian Pomerius, *De vita contemplativa*, 3: 12 (PL 59: 491). Cited in the ninth century by Jonas of Orléans, *De institutione laicali*, 3: 17 (PL 106: 271) and Haimo, *De varietate librorum*, 3: 14 (PL 118: 941).

113. *Recueil des chartes de l'abbaye de Cluny*, no. 1831 (990).

whom the gifts were made as "intercessors" and "advocates."[114]
Clearly clerical scribes, and probably many lay donors as well,
thought that it would be possible to look to others for help on judgment day—even though they might also recognize that each person
was supposed to be judged according to his or her own merits: "Since
we shall all stand before the tribunal of Christ, in order that each may
be recompensed according to what he did while in the body, whether
good or evil, let each person take care to acquire the patronage of the
saints and the faithful of God, whom he may have as advocates in that
terrible hour, and who can receive him into the eternal tabernacles."[115]
It is not at all clear how the scribe responsible for this eleventh-
century charter reconciled the idea of judgment according to what
each one did in life with the role of the saints as advocates at that
"terrible hour." Nevertheless, like the authors of many other charters, he represented donation to religious communities as a means to
ensure effective intercession at the end of time.

Prayers performed before the end of the world were also directed
toward judgment day. Indeed, this is suggested by the language of the
liturgy itself. The clauses which express the purpose of a prayer or
chant are generally introduced by *ut*, "so that," as in the phrase "may
this sacrifice profit your servants, so that . . . " In the liturgy of the
dead these *ut* clauses often point to the events at the end of time rather
than to the period just after death. The desired end is not liberation
from purgation, but rather the ultimate salvation of the dead person.
Thus, these texts express the hope that the dead may "breathe again"
with the saints at the time of the resurrection,[116] that when the day of
judgment arrives God may command them to be revived with his
saints and with the elect.[117]

The language of the liturgy tends to be dualistic, reflecting the
dualism of the last judgment. Then a final division will be made, the
elect will pass to the right and eternal joy, the damned to the left and
eternal torment. Sometimes the prayer texts refer explicitly to this
division:

114. E.g., *Pippini, Carlomanni, Caroli Magni diplomata*, no. 90 (775), p. 130; *Recueil des actes de Lothaire et de Louis V, rois de France (954–987)*, ed. Louis Halphen and Ferdinand Lot (Paris, 1908), no. 4 (955), pp. 8–10. Around the year 1079, Gilbert of Heugleville established a priory of monks at Auffray, "by whose prayers and merit he would be assisted at the last judgment": Orderic Vitalis, *Historia aecclesiastica*, 6 (3: 247).
115. "Chartes mancelles de l'abbaye de Saint-Florent près Saumur, 848–1200," ed.
Paul Marchegay, *Revue historique et archéologique du Maine* 3 (1878), no. 3 (ca. 1020).
116. *Le Sacramentaire grégorien*, 1: 459, no. 1404.
117. *Le Sacramentaire grégorien*, 1: 461, no. 1409.

Lord, we ask that this communion may purge us of our sins, and bestow upon the soul of your servant N. a part in the joys of heaven, and that, separated before the throne of glory of your Christ with those on the right, it may have nothing in common with those on the left.[118]

In other texts there is no direct mention of the judgment or the events at the end of time, but the duality associated with that time, the dichotomy between heaven and hell, the society of saints and that of demons, remains:

God, eternal lover of human souls, make the soul of your servant N., which the true faith held while it remained in the body, a stranger to every infernal torment, so that separated from the confines of hell, it may deserve to be joined to the company of the saints.[119]

It is possible, of course, that prayers such as these were understood not as instruments but as simple evocations of a desired end. As we have seen, some of the more sophisticated members of early medieval society understood participation in the liturgy of an earthly community as a foretaste of membership in the company of saints, the monastic *liber vitae* as a reflection of the heavenly "Book of Life." Even sophisticated scholars, who probably did not believe that prayer could affect the outcome of the last judgment, sought suffrages for themselves on these terms. As Peter Damian put it, in a letter asking the monks of Cluny to record his name for commemoration in their prayers, "may the clemency of heaven, through you, deign to liberate my soul from infernal torments; and may I deserve, through your inscription, to be inscribed among the just . . ."[120]

However, we can assume that the liturgical texts were also sometimes taken at face value. Certainly some educated people believed that prayers and good works performed within historical time could affect the ultimate fate of the dead. In 848, for example, Charles the Bald made a gift to Saint-Florent-le-Vieil, hoping, according to the scribe, that his action would benefit not only his own soul but also that of his deceased father "on the fearful day of the great judg-

118. Paris, BN, Latin 818, fol. 191v. This seems to be a variant form of a prayer from the Gelasian Sacramentary: see *Liber sacramentorum Augustodunensis*, p. 250, no. 1971.

119. *Le Sacramentaire grégorien*, 1: 460, no. 1408.

120. Cited by Jorden, *Das cluniazensische Totengedächtniswesen*, p. 115.

ment."[121] Perhaps what he had in mind was something like the "provisional damnation" mentioned earlier. Those who died with an important sin unconfessed or with an assigned penance incomplete could not hope to be saved through the fires of purgation in the next world. Unless the saints or the living intervened on their behalf, they would be "judged and condemned." But if their faults were somehow made good, they could still hope to be saved on the last day.[122]

Prayer for the dead, then, fulfilled a variety of functions in early medieval texts. The theologians agreed that it might help to speed up or mitigate the process of purgation after death, or simply celebrate the passage of a saint to heaven. But other members of early medieval society attributed powers to prayer for the dead which were not recognized by the theologians: the power to mitigate the sufferings of the damned or liberate souls from hell, the power to affect the outcome of the individual judgment or even the last judgment. In many cases, intercession was seen not just as helpful but as necessary to the salvation of a sinful soul.

IDEOLOGY AND INTERCESSION

Anxiety about the fate of the dead gave rise to a search for effective intercessors, for only someone with special standing in the spiritual realm could hope to intervene effectively for imperiled souls. We have already seen how the clergy and the saints emerged as intercessors for the rest of the faithful in late antiquity. In the early middle ages, however, the figure of the intercessor took on an even greater importance. The evidence for this does not come from theological texts. Early medieval theologians actually devoted very little attention to the role of the intercessor. In discussing prayer for the dead, they invariably focused on the merits of the dead person rather than on suffrages or the people who performed them. Some scholars did argue that the mass, in which the whole church was united in prayer, was the most effective form of intercession. This view seems to have

---

121. *Recueil des actes de Charles II*, no. 109 (848); compare *Cartulaire de l'abbaye de Conques*, no. 391 (918).

122. E.g., Thietmar of Merseburg, *Chronicon*, 4: 10, ed. Robert Holtzmann, 2d ed. (Berlin, 1955), p. 142, which suggests that a soul might be "recalled" to eternal repose "on the very last day."

been widely held in the period from 750 to 1100.[123] However, other scholars, like Jonas of Orléans, maintained that private prayer, fasting, and almsgiving were equally effective, and warned the faithful not to be taken in by unscrupulous priests who, wanting to receive as many donations as possible, argued that only their prayers could benefit the departed faithful.[124]

Except for such brief discussions of sacerdotal prayer in the mass, early medieval theologians seldom considered the role of the person who prayed for the dead.[125] It is only when we turn to nontheological texts that the real importance of the intercessor in the early medieval ideology of prayer for the dead becomes apparent. There are two aspects to this "ideology of the intercessor." On the one hand, even educated people often assumed that those guilty of serious sins could not intercede for the dead. In Heito of Basel's *Vision of Wetti*, for example, worldly priests are said to be unable to serve as intercessors "either for themselves or for others."[126] On the other hand, it was commonly believed that the dead would benefit most from the prayers of especially humble or holy people, such as good priests and the poor (either real paupers or the monastic "paupers of Christ"). Thus, Dhuoda encouraged her son to intercede for the sins of his godfather Thierry "as much as you can, through the prayers of holy priests. And, by giving alms to the poor."[127]

There are also many early medieval texts in which the intercession of a particular individual or religious community is presented as essential to the well-being of the dead. A tale found in the earliest biographies of Abbot Odilo of Cluny, composed in the mid-eleventh century, illustrates this point. Some time after Odilo's dear friend Pope Benedict VIII died, several churchmen had a vision in which they saw the former pope surrounded not by light but by shadows. Benedict asked them to have the new pope send someone to Odilo, asking for his prayers. Odilo ordered the monks of Cluny to pray and offer alms for his friend, and as a result the pope was freed from his torments. It might seem that the point of this story was to demon-

---

123. Dhuoda, for example, encouraged her son to have masses said "frequently" for his godfather Thierry and for all the departed faithful—"for no prayer is better for this purpose than the offering of the sacrifice": *Liber manualis*, 8: 16 (p. 322).

124. Jonas of Orléans, *De institutione laicali* 3: 15 (PL 106: 264).

125. A rare exception to this rule occurs in a passage from John the Scot's *De divisione naturae*, 5: 36 (PL 122: 977).

126. Heito of Basel, *Visio Wettini*, 7, MGH, PP, 2: 270.

127. Dhuoda, *Liber manualis*, 8: 15 (p. 322).

strate Odilo's charity, and perhaps the effectiveness of prayer for the dead as well. However, the moral drawn from it by the two biographers was slightly different. They took it as proof of Odilo's great merit, which made his intercession (which apparently included that of his monks) especially effective. According to Peter Damian:

> In this [tale] it can clearly be apprehended what opinion one should rightly hold of the blessed Odilo's merits. For certainly he [the pope] who above all mortals held the keys of the church, according to the privilege of the apostolic dignity, he who by right possessed the preeminent power of binding and loosing, when he lay under that invisible sentence could neither be released from his sins nor liberated from penal suffering except through [Odilo's] prayers.[128]

Jotsald, the other biographer, concluded that God's whole purpose in revealing Benedict's condition was to demonstrate Odilo's merit.[129] Thus, this story was included in the vitae as proof of Odilo's special effectiveness as an intercessor.

Intercessors did not differ only in the degree to which they were able to perform the same task. They also differed in the kind of task they were expected to perform. Here the limits of theology as a guide to the early medieval understanding of prayer for the dead are again apparent. Whereas the theologians assigned meanings to suffrages according to their assumptions about the dead person ("thanksgiving" for the very good, "propitiations" for the not very good, and so on), many other early medieval writers assigned meanings to suffrages according to their perception of the intercessor. The particular function attributed to prayer for the dead in an early medieval text often depended on the author's ideas about the religious power and authority vested in the person who prayed. These ideas were, in turn, often affected by the author's own situation and interests. Thus, the wide variation in meanings assigned to prayer for the dead described in the preceding section should be seen not as accidental but as ideological in nature.

I am not suggesting here that early medieval writers consciously and cynically manipulated their descriptions of intercession to serve their own ends. Rather, I believe that they selected, out of the wide range of images and ideas available to them, those that seemed most

---

128. Peter Damian, *Vita sancti Odilonis* (PL 144: 938).
129. Jotsald, *De vita et virtutibus sancti Odilonis abbatis*, 2: 14 (PL 142: 928): "ad significandum beati Odilonis meritum."

appropriate to the particular situation they were describing. Thus, hagiographers engaged in promoting the cult of their community's patron saint gravitated toward certain images of saintly intercession, while those who identified themselves with the pastoral concerns of the secular clergy found other images appropriate for discussions of the church's intercession, especially in the mass. As the role of the monasteries in Frankish society changed over time, so too did the depiction of monastic intercession by monastic writers. In early medieval texts, then, the prayers of the saints, the secular clergy, and the regular clergy tended to fulfill different functions, functions which best expressed each group's claims to special dignity and power.

This is most clear in the case of the saints, who were, from at least the fourth century on, the intercessors par excellence for the dead as well as the living. There is no need at this point to retrace the rise of the cult of the martyrs, and the dramatic expansion of that cult in the early middle ages. However, one relevant fact must be emphasized here. The saints interceded for others by virtue of a direct relationship with the divine, a relationship unmediated by office or tradition. Theirs was an invisible and mysterious power, invested in an invisible person. There was no way to be sure of a saint's power unless it were manifested openly, in the form of a miracle. But the more dramatic the miracle, the more abrupt the break from the normal order of the world, the more powerful the saint was shown to be. Consequently, the promoters of the cult of the saints (the bishops, the abbots, the hagiographers—whoever was concerned to uphold the honor of the local holy man or woman) tended to emphasize in their writings the most extreme effects of prayer for the dead—interference in the process of judgment after death or the liberation of souls from hell.

Many early medieval visions depict the patron saint of the author's or visionary's community protecting newly departed souls from the threat of evil spirits.[130] Sometimes the saints bring dead sinners back to life, so that they can confess and do penance for their sins.[131] In other visions, however, such as that from the *Deeds of Dagobert* described above, the saints actually help the dead evade hell

---

130. St. Peter, for example, used his keys to drive off some persistent demons who refused to give up their claims on the soul of Barontus: *Visio Baronti*, 12, MGH, SRM, 5: 387. St. Martin was said to have rescued the souls of men killed in a battle from the *ministris tenebrarum*; he then brought them to a place of refreshment and light in the next world: Raoul Glaber, *Historiae*, 3: 15, ed. Maurice Prou (Paris, 1886), p. 64.

131. *Visio Baronti*, 13, MGH, SRM, 5: 387–88; Bernard of Angers, *Liber miraculorum sancte Fidis*, 4: 1, ed. A. Bouillet (Paris, 1897), pp. 170–76; Peter Damian, *Epistolae*, 106 (3: 171–74).

and arrive safely in the next world.[132] In both types of vision, the tension between the ordinary workings of divine justice and the mercy obtained for sinners through the intervention of saints serves to emphasize the tremendous power of the intercessor, and confirm his or her status in the spiritual realm.

This tension is evoked with special clarity by the chronicler of the Italian monastery of Monte Cassino describing the intercession of his community's patron, St. Benedict. He tells of a man who, after a life of sin, accepted the monastic habit on his deathbed. A crowd of devils gathered, ready to carry him off, but Benedict appeared suddenly in their midst, pastoral staff in hand, come to defend his monk. When the demons complained about the injustice of this, the saint replied, "lest I seem to do you any injustice, let him be yours if, when an examination of him has been made, it is found that he remained conscious of any of your works after he accepted my habit." The demons realized they had lost their prey and vanished.[133] The Benedictines began circulating stories like this one, which describe the intervention of their founder on behalf of sinners who wore his habit, in the eleventh century. These stories probably contributed to the growing popularity of vestment *ad succurrendum* in that period.

Even more dramatic are the tales in which damned souls are freed from hell through the saint's intervention. Although the best-known case of this kind occurs in the lives of Gregory the Great, discussed earlier, there is a long tradition of such incidents in the hagiographical writings of antiquity and the early middle ages. The earliest example can be found in *The Acts of Paul and Thecla*, composed in the late second century. According to the anonymous author of this work, a noblewoman adopted the Christian saint, Thecla, to replace her dead daughter, Phalconilla, a pagan. At her foster-mother's request, Thecla prayed for Phalconilla's salvation. Although it is never explicitly stated in *The Acts* that Phalconilla was saved through these prayers, this was how the episode was interpreted in later centuries,

---

132. *Gesta Dagoberti I. regis francorum*, 44, MGH, SRM, 2: 421–22. This work was composed by a monk of Saint-Denis, so it is not surprising that the saints who save the king from demons are Denis, Maurice, and Martin. See also Raoul Glaber, *Historiae*, 3: 15 (p. 64); Hugh of Tours, *Dialogus ad Fulbertum amicum suum*, in *Vetera analecta*, ed. Jean Mabillon (Paris, 1723), p. 216; on these texts, see Farmer, *Communities of Saint Martin*, pp. 226–27. Compare *Recueil des chartes de l'abbaye de Cluny*, no. 1784 (988).

133. Leo Marsicanus et al., *Chronica monasterii Casinensis*, 3: 40, ed. Hartmut Hoffmann, MGH, SS, 34: 418.

not only in Byzantium where it enjoyed great popularity, but also in the West.[134]

Thecla's fellow-missionary Paul was also credited with liberating souls from hell. In an especially long and elaborate version of the *Vision of Paul*, probably composed in the Merovingian period, the apostle discovers that his relatives have been condemned to hell for usury. He throws himself down upon hell (which is represented as a sealed pit) and cries bitterly, begging to be admitted to hell for the sake of his kin. In the end, Paul's relatives are released from the infernal regions—in fact, they are pulled out of the pit by the famous camel mentioned in Matt. 19:24.[135] This theme continues to occur in saints' lives throughout the early middle ages. A late ninth- or early tenth-century biographer credited Odilia of Hohenburg with liberating her abusive father, who had failed to do penance for his many sins, from hell.[136] Similarly, St. Dunstan of Canterbury was said to have transferred King Edwy from damnation to the "fate of penitent souls" through his prayers.[137]

As we have seen, the legend of Trajan was troubling to the theologically sophisticated in the early middle ages. Presumably the other episodes of saintly intervention on behalf of the damned would also have troubled these scholars if they had known of them. However, the slightly unorthodox character of these stories was precisely what made them so useful to hagiographers. For the tension between mercy and justice, between the generosity of the saint's impulse and the inappropriateness of his or her prayers, gave their depiction of the intercessor a special edge. Only a very great saint, they suggest, could get away with something like this.

Those who promoted the cult of the saints emphasized the astonishing powers of the saints and the remarkable results of devotion to their cult; they paid little attention to the merits of the dead person.[138] Indeed, in their writings, saints often aid their friends regardless of

134. Willy Rordorf, "La prière de Sainte Thècle pour une défunte païenne et son importance oecumenique," in A. M. Triacca and A. Pistoia, eds., *Eschatologie et liturgie: Conférences Saint-Serge: XXXIe semaine d'études liturgiques, Paris, 1984* (Rome, 1985), pp. 249–59; Neiske, "Vision und Totengedenken," pp. 138–39.

135. Silverstein, *Visio sancti Pauli*, p. 218.

136. *Vita Odiliae abbatissae Hohenburgensis*, 12, ed. Bruno Krusch and Wilhelm Levison, MGH, SRM, 6: 44.

137. Osbern, *Vita sancti Dunstani*, 30, in *Memorials of Saint Dunstan, Archbishop of Canterbury*, ed. William Stubbs (London, 1874), pp. 104–5.

138. Peter Damian, *De variis miraculosis narrationibus*, 5 (PL 145: 589–90).

whether they deserve help, regardless even of whether they belong to the Catholic church. Paul the Deacon, for example, in his *History of the Lombards*, describes how John the Baptist protected the tomb of one of the Lombard kings—an Arian—from a grave-robber. "How dare you approach the body of this man?" he demanded. "Even though he did not believe correctly, still he has commended himself to me."[139]

As Paul's use of the term "commended" indicates, the intervention of the saints on behalf of the dead often followed the pattern of earthly patronage, that essential relationship in the societies of late antiquity and the early middle ages. Those who became the clients of the saints in life—through commendation, through their liturgical efforts, through assumption of the monastic habit, through donations to the saint's community, or by some other means—could expect to be protected by their patron after death regardless of their own merits.[140] These people became identified with the saints and their place in the next world. As Maximus of Turin wrote in regard to the practice of burial ad sanctos: "So long as Tartarus cringes before them, its torments do not touch us; while Christ illuminates them, darkness flees before us; and so, while we repose beside the holy martyrs we evade the shadows of hell, and even share in sanctity, as a result of their merits."[141] The intercession of the saints, then, was often seen as the exercise of supernatural influence in the court of heaven. It turned not on the personal merits of the dead but on their relationship—as "servant" or "client"—with the saints. When a great saint claims a departed soul as his or her own, the results are swift and often dramatic: the demons disperse, the soul is freed from the flames. For in choosing to intercede for one of the dead, the saints make that person part of their clientele, a member—by extension—of the *societas sanctorum*.

If we turn from the works of the hagiographers to the writings of those responsible for the care of souls, a very different picture of prayer for the dead emerges. Early medieval pastors described and interpreted their efforts on behalf of the dead in sermons, theological

139. Paul the Deacon, *Historia Langobardorum*, 4: 47, ed. George Waitz (Hanover, 1878), p. 171.

140. On the saints as patrons of the dead, see Fredegar, *Chronicorum liber quartus cum continuationibus*, ed. J. M. Wallace-Hadrill (London, 1960), p. 66; Hariulf, *Chronicon Centulense*, 3: 21 (p. 147). See also Atwell, "From Augustine to Gregory the Great," pp. 178–79.

141. Maximus of Turin, *Homiliae*, 81 (PL 57: 428–29).

treatises, liturgical commentaries, and spiritual guidebooks, intended for their own use and for the enlightenment of the faithful. These works reflect the special concerns of men responsible for the spiritual leadership of an imperfectly christianized society. The ambivalent attitude toward prayer for the dead which we observed in late patristic and early medieval theological writings is evident in these texts, which, of course, draw directly on the theological tradition.

On the one hand, pastors sought to justify traditional liturgical practices and encourage the exercise of charity toward the departed faithful. They argued that the intercession of the church could help the deserving dead, and so prayers for the departed faithful were to be included in every mass and in the regular offices. Masses were to be performed for the dead as a pious duty. As we saw in earlier chapters, the result of this attitude among those responsible for the organization of the liturgy was a remarkable expansion of prayer for the dead in the early middle ages. On the other hand, early medieval pastors were anxious to ensure the good behavior of their flocks by asserting the principle that the faithful would be judged by their own merits. And so they admonished the faithful not to rely too heavily on prayer to help them in the next world.[142] They thus emphasized the limited usefulness of prayer for the dead rather than its most dramatic effects. Whereas hagiographers often represented the intercession of the saints as a sudden eruption of mercy into the cosmos at a moment of crisis, those reponsible for the care of souls viewed the intercession of the church as part of the regular administration of God's justice. They tended to associate it not with liberation from hell, but with the process of purgation after death, which had become linked by this time with the penitential system.

Between the middle of the eighth and the end of the. eleventh centuries two systems of penance were in operation in France. The reforming councils of the early ninth century attempted to reestablish something like the ancient system of public penance. Under this system, the sinner confessed publicly before the bishop and the whole Christian community and was formally excluded from the church,

---

142. See Gregory the Great, *Dialogi*, 4: 60 (pp. 322–23): "it is a safer way for each person to do himself, during his life, the good that he hopes will be done by others after his death. For truly it is more blessed to go forth in freedom than to seek liberty after bondage." This text was cited by a number of ninth-century authors, including Florus of Lyons, *De expositione missae*, 70 (PL 119: 62), and Haimo, *De varietate librorum*, 3: 9 (PL 118: 938). See also Hincmar of Reims, *De visione Bernoldi* (PL 125: 1120).

entering upon a special status as a penitent, which entailed certain disabilities (excommunication, exclusion from church office, etc.) as well as obligations of an expiatory nature such as fasting. The penitent retained this status until he or she was publicly absolved and reconciled with the Christian community.[143]

This system of public penance coexisted with another system—that of private or "tariffed" penance—which had been introduced to the Continent by Irish and Anglo-Saxon monks in the seventh and eighth centuries. Under this system, the sinner confessed privately to a priest, who assigned him or her a penance appropriate to the sin involved (the penitential "tariff"). The penitent was never formally excluded from the church under this system and had no special disabilities to distinguish him or her from other Christians, but only when the penance was completed (or commuted) was the sin considered forgiven. The priest was expected to pray for the sinner's absolution, immediately after confession or certainly before he or she received communion.[144] Private confession and penitential "tariffs" were well established in France by the middle of the eighth century and the Carolingian reforming councils were unable to replace them entirely with public penance. In the end, both systems were retained and the principle was established that public penance should be performed for especially grave or public faults, while private penance was sufficient for most sins.[145]

Early medieval pastors wanted the faithful committed to their care to do penance, either public or private, for their faults. Consequently, they threatened the impenitent with terrible retribution after death. Nevertheless, they also cautiously held out the prospect that some sins could be expiated in the purging fires of the next world. Many church leaders saw the process of purgation after death as an extension of the penitential system into the next world. They emphasized that only the contrite, who had wanted to atone for their sins through ordinary penance before they died, could hope to be purged in this way after death. And they often associated the duration of sufferings in the next world with assigned periods of penance in this one.

In this model, however, suffrages for the dead serve some of the

143. Cyrille Vogel, *Les Libri paenitentiales* (Turnhout, 1978), pp. 34–35.

144. Vogel, *Les Libri paenitentiales*, pp. 35–36.

145. Rosamond Pierce [McKitterick], "The 'Frankish' Penitentials," in Derek Baker, ed., *The Materials, Sources and Methods of Ecclesiastical History* (Oxford, 1975), pp. 31–39.

same functions as suffrages offered for living penitents. Christians could intervene on behalf of sinners undergoing penance in two ways—through vicarious penance or through absolution. By the eighth century, the idea that penance could be performed vicariously was well established in western Europe. Any of the faithful could, as an act of charity, pray, fast, or give alms on behalf of penitents. Such assistance was thought to speed up the process of atonement. In the same way, early medieval pastoral writings often treated suffrages for the dead as vicarious reparation for sins not atoned for in life.[146] Pastors frequently urged the faithful to fast, offer alms, or have masses performed on behalf of those who died with their penance incomplete.[147]

Even ordinary Christians could do penance vicariously for their departed friends and relatives. However, just as clerical prayer in the form of the mass or recitations of the psalter was considered the most effective form of vicarious penance for living penitents,[148] so clerical prayer in the form of masses or psalters for the dead soon came to be viewed as the most effective form of intercession for those who died before penance was complete.[149] Early medieval pastors were certainly anxious to have such services performed for themselves. As we have seen, they often entered into prayer associations, which linked together several clerical communities. The purpose of these associations was to have masses or psalters recited for the members' souls after they died.[150] It seems likely, as Arnold Angenendt has recently suggested, that these services were understood as the equivalent of commonly assigned periods of penance.[151] Thus, the prayer associations of the early middle ages can be seen as agreements to perform

146. E.g., pseudo-Alcuin, *De divinis officiis*, 50 (PL 101: 1279); Gerard of Cambrai, *Acta synodi Atrebatensis in Manichaeos*, 9 (PL 142: 1298). Compare Othlo of St. Emmeram, *Liber visionum*, 13 (PL 146: 366–68). On this point, see Angenendt, "Theologie und Liturgie," in Schmid and Wollasch, *Memoria*, pp. 135, 165–68, 171–73, 174–79.

147. Halitgar of Cambrai, *Liber poenitentialis* (PL 105: 702). This idea was adopted by members of the laity, who saw prayer for the dead as vicarious penance: see Dhuoda, *Liber manualis*, 8: 15 (p. 322). The clergy also followed such practices themselves: e.g., *Vita Remberti*, 3, AA.SS., Feb. 1, p. 561.

148. Cyrille Vogel, *Le Pécheur et la pénitence au moyen âge* (Paris, 1969), pp. 28–30; idem, *Les Libri paenitentiales*, pp. 51–52.

149. Angenendt, "Theologie und Liturgie," in Schmid and Wollasch, *Memoria*, p. 177.

150. E.g., Synod of Attigny (ca. 760), in *Capitularia regum Francorum*, 1: 221–22; Bavarian Council (805), in *Concilia aevi Karolini*, 1: 233; Council of Le Mans (840), ibid. 2: 784–85.

151. Angenendt, "Theologie und Liturgie," in Schmid and Wollasch, *Memoria*, pp. 174–79.

vicarious penance for the dead, although the way in which these agreements were carried out suggests other meanings as well.

A related idea often associated with prayer for the dead in the pastoral writings of the early middle ages was that of the loosing or absolution of sins. A synod held in Bavaria in the mid-eighth century, for example, encouraged the faithful to make offerings for themselves and their relatives, living and dead, for in this practice, "as is well known, there is great absolution of souls from [their] sins."[152] Similarly, in the ninth century, Bishop Rainon of Angers arranged for the canons of his cathedral to sing two psalms and a mass for him every day, "for the absolution of [his] soul from all sins."[153]

Generally suffrages were presented as an indirect means to the end of absolution, which was thought to lie in the hands of God. In other words, intercessors simply asked God to free the dead from their sins. Thus, in the mass (found in the eighth-century Gelasian Sacramentary) for those who sought but failed to complete penance before they died, the following text occurs:

> Omnipotent and merciful God on whose power the human condition depends, we ask that you absolve the soul of your servant N. from all sins, so that he may not, prevented by mortality, lose the fruit of penance which his will desired.[154]

Presumably, though, the accumulation of vicarious penitential acts led God to absolve the dead more rapidly than would otherwise have been the case.

Sometimes, however, the intercession of those with authority over their fellow Christians was understood as absolution in a more specialized sense. Bishops, priests, and (in some texts) the heads of monastic communities were said themselves to absolve the dead, as a function of their special power to bind and loose, in heaven as on earth. In the ancient church and on into the early middle ages, absolution by the bishop brought an end to the period of public penance. Episcopal absolution was a formal act of reconcilation with the church, without which the penitent remained excluded from communion and could not hope to be saved. This is not to say that such absolution sufficed for salvation. The relationship between ecclesiastical absolution, which made salvation possible, and God's forgiveness

---

152. Bavarian Council (740–50), c. 4, in *Concilia aevi Karolini*, 1: 52.
153. *Cartulaire noir de la cathédrale d'Angers*, no. 16 (882–86).
154. *Liber sacramentorum Gellonensis*, 2: 474, no. 2964. *Liber sacramentorum Augustodunensis*, p. 250, no. 1973.

of sins, which made salvation actual, remained unclear in late patristic and early medieval theology. But if the bishop's prayer of absolution was not considered to have full sacramental force before the eleventh century, it was nevertheless more than a simple act of intercession on behalf of a penitent.[155] In some crucial sense it was thought to bring the sinner back into the society of those who could hope to be saved.

As we have seen, Christians who practiced private penance were not formally excommunicated. Absolution thus did not represent a formal act of reconciliation with the church for these penitents. Nevertheless, even under the system of private penance, the ancient idea lingered that sin brought about a separation from the church, at least in a moral, if not in a juridical sense. Most penitents abstained voluntarily from communion until they had been absolved by their pastor (an act which often took place before their assigned penance was complete).[156] Under both systems of penance, then, clerical absolution served as authorization to receive communion and as a symbol of good standing in the church. In the same way, clerical intercession for the dead was sometimes seen as an act of formal absolution, which was of crucial importance for the soul in the next world.

A passage from the eighth-century pseudo-Theodoran penitential reflects this idea.[157] The author of the penitential, which was widely circulated on the Continent in the eighth and ninth centuries, describes how masses were to be performed after the funeral according to the "tradition of the Roman church." For monks, there was to be a mass on the day of burial; for good layfolk, the first mass would be on the third day. For a penitent, however, the first mass was not to be performed until the thirtieth day, or —if his relatives and neighbors fasted for him first—on the seventh day.[158] Remarkably, the penitent sinner, whom we might suppose would "need" prayers the most, was to wait for them the longest—presumably until after a period of penitential suffering in the next world. This suggests that for the author of this penitential, masses for the dead represented not vicarious penance, but formal absolution—the clerical act of reconciliation by which the sinner was readmitted to communion.

A similar view is expressed in a tenth-century treatise on the

155. Bernhard Poschmann, *Der Ablass im Licht der Bussgeschichte* (Bonn, 1948), pp. 2–28.

156. Poschmann, *Der Ablass*, pp. 18–25.

157. On this text, see Allen J. Frantzen, *The Literature of Penance in Anglo-Saxon England* (New Brunswick, N.J., 1983), pp. 63–69.

158. *Die Canones Theodori*, pp. 318–19.

liturgy. The author discusses the series of masses following the funeral in the allegorical terms so characteristic of early medieval interpretations of the liturgy. Thus, he says, the mass "is celebrated on the third day especially for the absolution of the soul, because it has a triple nature, irascible, concupiscent, and rational, and because it thrives with intelligence, understanding, and memory. And so, because of this, the sacrifice is performed on the third day, so that if the soul has contracted any weakness from its residence in the flesh, this may be obliterated, and [the soul's] likeness to the Trinity may be restored."[159] In this text, the mass of the third day "loosens" the bonds of a threefold sin, restoring the soul's likeness to the Trinity and reconciling the dead person with the church at the same time. It should be remembered that the masses held on the third, seventh, and thirtieth days were public events, like the public absolution of penitents in the early Christian era. In these masses of absolution, the whole Christian community affirmed the participation of the dead person in its collective destiny.

This understanding of masses for the dead as formal absolution rather than vicarious penance may explain the rather abrupt end of the torments in some of the visions of purgation described by early medieval pastors. In these visions, as soon as the sinner was prayed for (and thus absolved), his or her period of purgation was over. Thus, they stand in contrast to many other visions in which the performance of a certain number of prayers (viewed as vicarious penance) leads to the liberation of the soul.

Archbishop Hincmar of Reims recorded the *Vision of Bernold* (a layman of his diocese) shortly after the death of King Charles the Bald in 877. In this text, Bernold sees Charles suffering horribly in the next world "because of [his] sins." In particular, the king has paid no attention to the good counsel of Hincmar and his other *fideles*. Charles asks the visionary to go to Hincmar, and tell him that he has great faith in his ability to help liberate him from his torments. Bernold finds Hincmar in a church (located, significantly, on the visionary's road to paradise), accompanied by his clergy, all vested for mass. He gives him the message, returns to Charles, and finds him already in a much better situation than before. The suggestion is that the archbishop prayed formally for Charles at mass and thus liberated him

159. Pseudo-Alcuin, *De divinis officiis*, 51 (PL 101: 1280). On the date of this work, see J. Joseph Ryan, "Pseudo-Alcuin's *Liber de divinis officiis* and the *Liber 'Dominus vobiscum'* of St. Peter Damiani," *Mediaeval Studies* 14 (1952), 160.

from his sufferings.[160] As Jean Devisse has pointed out, Hincmar has certainly reworked the vision as it was told to him by Bernold's confessor in order to support his own views on church discipline and the role of the *ordo sacerdotum*, the priestly order, in the salvation of the laity.[161] In the *Vision of Bernold*, the intercession of the archbishop is both essential and sufficient for the soul's liberation from torment.

Early medieval pastors, then, generally fit intercession for the dead into the context of their penitential concerns. Eager to encourage repentance in life, they did not encourage the faithful committed to their care to rely on prayer after death. Whereas the hagiographers touted the remarkable effects of saintly intercession, pastors emphasized the limits of prayer for the dead. At the same time, the leaders of the early medieval church attempted to enforce ecclesiastical discipline even beyond the grave. Those Christians who refused to repent of their sins and were excommunicated in life remained excommunicate after death; the church did not pray for them.[162] On the other hand, church leaders made every effort to ensure that those who wanted to repent should be allowed to confess and receive absolution before they died.[163] Sinners who had confessed and undertaken penance before death could and should be prayed for, even if they had not been absolved.[164] Thus, early medieval pastors understood their efforts on behalf of the dead as an extension of their role in the earthly church into the hereafter. They interpreted prayer for the dead as vicarious penance or as absolution for the dead. In this, they differed greatly from the hagiographers. Whereas the intercession of the saints was a manifestation of power, the intercession of the clergy was essentially an exercise of authority.

Members of monastic communities generally seem to have felt less ambivalent about prayer for the dead than did the bishops and

160. Hincmar of Reims, *De visione Bernoldi* (PL 125: 1116–17).

161. Devisse, *Hincmar: Archevêque de Reims 845–882*, 2: 821–23, and especially n. 699.

162. Leo I, *Epistolae*, 167 (PL 54: 1205–6). See also Synod of Rispach (798), c. 17, in *Concilia aevi Karolini*, 1: 201; Synod of Pavia (850), c. 12, in *Capitularia regum Francorum*, 2: 120; *Capitulare Carisiacense* (857), ibid., 2: 289.

163. Ghaerbald of Liege, *Capitula* (802–10), c. 244, in *Capitularia regum Francorum*, 1: 244; Council of Aix (836), c. 29, in *Concilia aevi Karolini*, 1: 711–12; Council of Mainz (847), c. 26, in *Capitularia regum Francorum*, 2: 182.

164. Halitgar of Cambrai, *Liber poenitentialis*, 83 (PL 105: 702); Council of Mainz (847), c. 27, in *Capitularia regum Francorum*, 2: 182–83. In fact, the sacramentaries in use during the early middle ages contained masses for the dead who had wanted to undertake penance but were unable to confess because they could not speak when the priest arrived: *Le Sacramentaire grégorien*, 1: 465–66.

priests who were responsible for the care of souls. Monastic writers devoted much less space in their works to the dangers of reliance on prayer than to the obligations of charity toward the departed. It is evident that early medieval monastic communities took great pride in their efforts on behalf of the dead.[165] "Blessed, indeed, are the riches of charity which [the hermits of Fonte Avellana] not only freely offer for the living, but which they also expend for the dead," wrote Peter Damian.[166] Monks and nuns could afford to take a more positive attitude on this subject, since they normally wrote for an audience (the monastic community) which was already committed to leading a religious life and which was not likely to allow the promise of prayers after death to undermine their struggle for virtue in this world.

Monastic writers, like those responsible for pastoral care, tended to see the suffrages they performed for the dead in terms of the penitential system and the process of purgation in the next world. Indeed, in this regard, the monasteries, with their emphasis on continuous repentance and their special penitential practices, exerted a strong influence on the secular clergy and on the church's teachings on prayer for the dead. It was in the monasteries of Ireland and the Anglo-Saxon kingdoms that the institution of private or "tariffed" penance developed, and in monasteries influenced by that insular tradition that private penance first appeared on the Continent. The monasteries provided the impetus for the formation of prayer associations, each of whose members agreed to perform a set number of psalms and masses—apparently the equivalent of commonly assigned penances—for one another after death. And, as we have seen, monastic writers such as Bede played an important role in the formulation of teachings on prayer for the dead. It is hardly surprising, then, that in monastic writings suffrages for the dead were often seen as vicarious penance. Nor is it surprising that descriptions of monastic customs mention the performance of penance for former members of the community.[167]

It should be noted, however, that monastic writers also understood prayer for the dead as a form of absolution, through which the soul of a dead monk or nun was reconciled with the monastic com-

165. E.g., Angilbert, *Institutio*, 16, in *Initia consuetudinis Benedictinae*, pp. 301–2.

166. Peter Damian, *Epistolae*, 18 (1: 175); trans. Owen J. Blum in Peter Damian, *The Letters of Peter Damian, 1–30* (Washington, D.C., 1989), pp. 166–67.

167. E.g., Peter Damian, *Epistolae*, 18 (1: 175); trans. in idem, *The Letters of Peter Damian, 1–30*, p. 166. See also a twelfth-century text, which purports to describe eleventh-century events: *De rebus gestis in Majori-monasterio saeculo 11*, in *Acta sanctorum ordinis sancti Benedicti*, Saec. 6, pt. 2, p. 395.

munity and liberated from torment. This view lies behind what is beyond a doubt the most famous late patristic story of intercession for the dead, related by Gregory the Great in his *Dialogues*, and cited by many writers throughout the early middle ages. Justus, a member of Gregory's monastery in Rome, had, contrary to the community's rule, secretly kept some money to himself. When this came to Gregory's attention, he decreed that Justus should not receive any assistance from the other monks on his deathbed and that when he died his body would not be buried with the other members of the community, but tossed onto a dungheap along with the money. It was hoped that the bitterness of his death would purge him of his sin. At first no prayers were offered by the community for the dead man's soul. Thirty days after Justus's death, however, Gregory decided to do something to rescue the sinner from the fire in which he had been tormented "for so long." He arranged to have thirty masses performed for Justus on thirty consecutive days, "so that no day shall pass on which the salutary sacrifice is not offered for his absolution." On the thirtieth day, the dead man appeared in a vision to his brother. Asked how he was, Justus replied: "Until now I did badly, but now I am well, for today I received communion."[168] In this text, suffrages represent more than simple intercession or vicarious penance, which leads God to absolve the dead more rapidly than might otherwise have been the case. The prayers of the monks, ordered by their abbot, are actually essential to the salvation of the sinner. They show that he has been reconciled with the community and absolved on earth, and so is ready to be absolved in heaven.

The monastic understanding of prayer for the dead paralleled in many ways that of the secular clergy. However, other themes are also apparent in early medieval monastic writings, themes which seem much more closely related to those found in the works of the hagiographers. These themes become especially prominent in the monastic writings of the eleventh century, undoubtedly as a result of the special position of the monasteries in that period, when the reputation of the secular clergy was at its lowest point, and the prestige of the monasteries—or at least the reformed houses such as Cluny—at its height.

The "golden age of monasticism" in western Europe corresponds with the dislocation of Carolingian structures and the gradual emergence of new ones. The condition of society and of the church at the

---

168. Gregory the Great, *Dialogi*, 4: 57 (pp. 317–20).

approach of the year 1000 did not encourage confident belief in a neatly ordered universe, in which recognized leaders administered the justice of God in an effective manner. As we have seen, early medieval pastors understood their efforts on behalf of the dead as an expression of their authority as the designated leaders of the church, the successors of the apostles. By the late tenth century, however, that authority was increasingly coming into question. The troubles of the period had led to a failure of discipline, which left the lower ranks of the clergy in disarray, their morality and even their competence to perform the sacraments in doubt. Moreover, abrupt transitions from one position in the hierarchy to another, nepotism, and the practice of simony raised doubts about some bishops' authority, and even about their ability to perform the office entrusted to them.[169] It should be noted that much of our evidence for concern about the authority of the secular clergy comes from monastic texts. This is hardly surprising, since the late tenth and the eleventh century was a period of considerable tension between the secular and regular clergy. It was at this time that the reformed monasteries began strongly to assert their independence from episcopal control. What justified such claims to exemption, however, were claims of episcopal unworthiness, combined with assertions of monastic superiority.[170]

For even when no specific conflict with episcopal power was at hand, the monastic writers of the eleventh century extolled the virtues of their order to an unprecedented extent. In particular, they developed the theme of monastic life as the *vita angelica*. The monastery became the heavenly Jerusalem "in anticipation," while the community of monks or nuns foreshadowed the community of saints in heaven.[171] The principal link between the monastery and the angels above was their common activity, the praise of God. Through their masses, their offices of psalmody, their prayers, the monks joined in

169. The classic picture of the decline of the secular church in this period is presented by Amann and Dumas, *L'Église au pouvoir des laïques*; that picture has been modified in a variety of ways in recent years.

170. E.g., Abbo of Fleury, *Apologeticus ad Hugonem et Rodbertum reges Francorum* (PL 139: 464). On this theme, see also Georges Duby, *Les Trois Ordres, ou l'imaginaire du féodalisme* (Paris, 1978), pp. 112–18, 174–79; Dominique Iogna-Prat, *Agni immaculati: Recherches sur les sources hagiographiques relatives à saint Maieul de Cluny (954–994)* (Paris, 1988), pp. 345–57.

171. Jean Leclercq, *The Love of Learning and the Desire for God*, trans. Catharine Misrahi, 2d ed. (New York, 1974), pp. 66–73; Kassius Hallinger, "The Spiritual Life of Cluny in the Early Days," trans. F. Sandeman and M. Boulding, in Noreen Hunt, ed., *Cluniac Monasticism in the Central Middle Ages* (Hamden, Conn., 1971), pp. 40–41; Iogna-Prat, *Agni immaculati*, especially pp. 319–39.

the joyous chanting of the celestial hosts; a door was opened between this world and the next. Indeed, in many monastic texts, the monks and the angels join in the same prayer. The saints were said actually to be present during a monastic vigil; angels descended to participate in the conventual mass.[172]

Such texts justify not only monastic independence from episcopal control, but also lay reliance on monastic intercessors. Monks and nuns intercede for the living and the dead not as a function of office and authority, but by virtue of their own charity and holiness. And the monastic texts of the eleventh century suggest that this monastic holiness is easily observable and therefore certain. They suggest that lay donors, however doubtful they may feel about their local bishop's authority to "bind and loose," can witness for themselves the awesome splendor of the monastic liturgy and the spectacular asceticism of the monastic life. The charters of the period stress the obvious virtues of the monastic community. Often praise is placed in the mouths of lay donors, in order to underline this point. According to the preamble of an Italian charter, for example, one noblewoman chose to be associated with the abbey of Monte Cassino because it was "*known to herself and to all Christians*" that there was a "holy and religious congregation there."[173] Similar ideas are expressed (although often in less blatantly boastful terms) in French charters of the eleventh century. It is not at all clear whether these documents accurately represent the views of the lay elite, but they certainly show how monastic scribes understood their relationship with the laity at this time.

Monks and nuns, these holy men and women who joined already in the praises of the heavenly host, surely had a secure place among the elect. Many charters—and other monastic writings of the eleventh century—take this for granted as well. They go on to suggest that monastic intercession could therefore be especially effective, helping to ensure the salvation of others. Thus Gilo, a Breton lord, was said to have made a gift to the monks of Marmoutier, to those "poor men of Christ," to whom the kingdom of heaven belonged. By making them his friends, he hoped to be "received by them into the eternal tabernacle of heaven."[174]

---

172. See, for example, Raoul Glaber, *Historiae*, 2: 9 (p. 45); Hariulf, *Chronicon Centulense*, 4: 30 and 31 (pp. 256–58, 259–60).

173. Cited by Dormeier, *Montecassino und die Laien*, p. 188. Emphasis mine.

174. *Marmoutier: Cartulaire blésois*, no. 68 (1095/96).

In texts such as these what is emphasized is not the nature or quantity of prayer performed for the dead in the monasteries; nor is the goal simply a rapid release from purgation. In the eleventh century, monastic intercession, like the intercession of the saints, was often seen as an expression of holiness and power, which could have more immediate and dramatic effects. Many charters suggest that donors were seeking a share in the monks' ultimate reward when they made gifts to the monasteries. Count William confirmed his mother's donation to the Cluniac nunnery at Marcigny, so that he might be a "co-heir, on earth and in heaven, with all the brothers and sisters of the monastery of Cluny, and a participant in all the good deeds they do."[175] The monks of Saint-Père of Chartres promised one of their donors that he would be associated in all their prayers and good works, so that he might be a "participant," with them in their "reward in the kingdom of heaven."[176] These themes are reminiscent of those sounded by Maximus of Turin writing on burial ad sanctos. Just as through burial near the body of a saint the faithful could expect to share its "sanctity," so through association in the prayers of the monastic community the laity could hope to share in its heavenly destiny.

The powerful intercession of holy monks could even help those whose fate in the next world was otherwise in doubt. Such an assumption lay behind the story of Pope Benedict VIII and Abbot Odilo cited earlier in this section, and also, I would suggest, behind the establishment of the feast of All Souls at Cluny in the early eleventh century. Most modern historians have seen All Souls as the fullest expression of traditional monastic charity toward the dead. It has been assumed that the founder of the feast—the same Abbot Odilo who interceded for Benedict VIII—felt pity for the sufferings of the dead in the next world and wanted to have a great deal of prayer performed as vicarious penance for them. The feast is, thus, generally associated in modern works with a keen awareness of the situation of souls undergoing purgation after death and with a benevolent desire to offer as much prayer as possible on their behalf. It has been seen, in short, as the finest expression of the "purgatorial mentality" supposedly at work in the monasteries of this period. A closer consider-

175. *Le Cartulaire de Marcigny-sur-Loire (1045–1144): Essai de reconstitution d'un manuscrit disparu*, ed. Jean Richard (Dijon, 1957), no. 102 (1095).

176. *Cartulaire de l'abbaye de Saint-Père de Chartres*, 1: 239 (before 1102, corrected to before 1088).

ation of the texts which describe the establishment of All Souls, however, throws a rather different light on the situation.

The earliest such text and the only one directly related to liturgical practice is the "Statute of St. Odilo Concerning the Dead." This is actually a decree of the chapter of Cluny, dating to around 1025, which confirms the foundation of an annual feast at Cluny for all the departed faithful and describes how it is to be celebrated. The "Statute" does not explain why the feast was established, beyond suggesting that the Cluniacs found it appropriate to celebrate a feast for all the departed faithful on November 2, just as they celebrated for all the saints on November 1.[177] For more information about the rationale behind All Souls, we must turn to three slightly later works. These are the *Histories* of Raoul Glaber, completed at Cluny shortly before the death of Abbot Odilo in 1049, and the two early vitae of Odilo— the first composed by Jotsald, a monk of Cluny, around 1050, the second by Peter Damian about a decade later.

Raoul Glaber never actually mentions the feast of All Souls in his chronicle. However, he is the first to recount the tale, later associated with the establishment of All Souls, of a traveler's encounter with a hermit in a remote region of the world. In Glaber's account, the meeting takes place in Africa, where the hermit has lived for twenty years without human contact. Nevertheless, he knows (by supernatural means?) of Cluny and its continuous celebration of masses, which are performed so reverently that they seem "more angelic than human." Despite (or perhaps because of) his isolation from the world, the hermit is able to inform the traveler that "more than all other [monasteries] in the Roman church, [Cluny] is effective in the liberation of souls from the domination of demons. So much does the frequent offering of the life-giving sacrifice flourish there, that scarcely any day passes in which this activity does not snatch souls from the power of evil demons."[178] Here, in the characteristic style of eleventh-century monastic writings, we find a community whose liturgy is so angelic that demons quail before it, whose holiness is so palpable that even hermits in Africa come to know of it. The dead, in this account, are completely eclipsed by the brilliance of Cluny. Their sufferings are not described. Even their status in the next world— whether they are simply being purged or are forever damned unless

177. *Statutum "S. Odilonis" de defunctis* (PL 142: 1037–38); on the date of this text, see Leclercq, "Mort," *DACL* 12: 37.
178. Raoul Glaber, *Historiae*, 5: 1 (pp. 124–25).

the monks intervene—remains unclear. The whole focus here is on
the intercessor, not on those interceded for.

A similar tale occurs in the two lives of Odilo composed shortly
after his death in 1049. However, in these texts the hermit learns
about Cluny in a vision, which he tells to the traveler and which is
then reported at Cluny, leading Abbot Odilo to establish a feast there
for the dead. In Jotsald's biography, the visionary hermit lives on an
island near Sicily and has visited places where—in the volcanic geog-
raphy of that area—flames burst from the ground. In the flames he
has seen the souls of sinners suffering various torments, "for the
designated length of time" (*ad tempus statutum*). He tells the traveler
that

> a multitude of demons are always deputed there to renew their
> torments. . . . However, I have frequently heard [the demons] la-
> menting and making great complaint because the souls of the
> damned [*damnatorum*] are liberated from their sufferings by the
> prayers of pious men and the alms which are given to the poor at
> various places devoted to the saints, and mostly through the mercy
> of God. Among all the others they mentioned and made complaint
> especially of the convent of Cluny and its abbot . . . [179]

The use of the phrase "for the designated length of time" and of the
word "sinners" to designate those being punished suggest that these
torments were only the temporary ones of purgation (although it is
striking that later in the passage Jotsald uses the word "damned" to
refer to those being tormented by the demons). However, what is
described here is not the orderly and predictable fulfillment of divine
justice, for the demons have some claim on these souls, and so complain bitterly about the effects of monastic suffrages for the dead and
above all about the liturgical efforts of Cluny. The story is reminiscent of those stories of saintly intercession described earlier, in which
the tension between justice and mercy underlines the tremendous
power of the saint.

A very similar passage occurs in Peter Damian's *Life of Saint Odilo*,
although in his account the hermit does not see the souls of "sinners,"
suffering for a "designated length of time," but rather those of "the
reprobate" (*reproborum*) suffering "according to the quality of their

179. Jotsald, *De vita sancti Odilonis*, 2: 13 (PL 142: 926–27).

merits" (*pro qualitate meritorum*). The visionary again hears the demons complain:

> I have frequently heard them bewailing with querulous lamentations and bemoaning with tearful cries the fact that the souls of the damned [*damnatorum*] are often ripped from their hands by the prayers and alms of certain men striving implacably against them. They made complaint, among others, especially of the convent of Cluny and its abbot, because through them they often lost those enslaved to their law.[180]

Damian's language further serves to emphasize the dramatic effect of monastic suffrages for the dead. The souls mentioned here are "enslaved" to demonic law and so must be "ripped" from the hands of the demons through the heroic efforts of Cluny. In another of Damian's works the bishop of Ostia, alluding to this story, describes the souls snatched from hell as Cluny's "booty" [*praedam*].[181]

What is remarkable about all of these texts is their concentration not on the sufferings of the dead, but on the power of Cluny's intercession. The dead are faceless entities in all three passages; in Glaber's account it is not even clear why they are in the power of demons. We do not really know what their status is, nor how long they will suffer without help. Our attention is drawn, instead, to the contest between the demons and the holy men who pray for the dead. More specifically, our attention is drawn to the monks of Cluny, who surpass all other monasteries—indeed all the faithful—in the liberation of souls. These accounts may encourage concern for the dead, but their main effect is to exalt the reputation of Cluny and its heroic liturgy.

The feast of All Souls reflects Cluny's sense of power as much as its sense of charity toward the dead. This power was demonstrated by the dramatic results of the monastery's intercession. As the demons bewail their losses, we are reminded of how great Cluny's victory has been. The liberation of souls from the power of demons who have some claim to them is a theme borrowed from the miracle-stories of the saints, rather than the more sober accounts found in pastoral writings of clerical intervention on behalf of souls undergoing purga-

---

180. Peter Damian, *Vita sancti Odilonis* (PL 144: 936).

181. Peter Damian, *Epistolae*, 110 (3: 243). King Edwy's soul is similarly described as "booty" captured by demons before it is rescued by Dunstan and transferred to the "fate of penitent souls": see Osbern, *Vita Sancti Dunstani*, 30 (p. 104).

tion. It is perhaps not surprising that this theme is found in hagiographical texts such as the two lives of Odilo. However, it is worth remembering that in these works holiness and power are attributed not just to the individual saint but to his community as well. This sanctification of the monastic community is apparent not only in hagiographical texts, but in a variety of eleventh-century writings.

Thus, as the position of the monasteries changed from the late tenth into the eleventh century, we find a shift in the monastic ideology of prayer for the dead. Without completely abandoning the traditional association of suffrages with vicarious penance and the process of purgation after death, monastic writers now began to paint monastic intercession in more brilliant colors, using images drawn from the hagiographical tradition to suggest the great holiness and power of their communities. There is no reason to suppose, moreover, that these ideas remained confined to the monasteries. In all probability they came to influence many members of the lay elite as well, through their close dealings with religious houses. Certainly this would help to explain why the nobility, who had the power to choose their intercessors, turned away from the secular clergy in the late tenth and early eleventh centuries, directing their generosity instead toward monastic houses.

PRAYER AS OBJECT AND AS SYMBOL

I suggested in the introduction to this book that the model of intercession which prevails in most modern studies of prayer for the dead is based on late medieval and early modern practices and beliefs. By the later middle ages, the doctrinal tradition which began to take shape in late antiquity had been elaborated and refined by the scholastic theologians and disseminated throughout Christian society. Prayer for the dead had become inextricably linked with the process of purgation after death; most of the other images and ideas associated with the practice in the early middle ages had long since been discarded. But because the theological tradition completely dominated the apologetic debates over prayer for the dead in the sixteenth century, it has continued to dominate modern discussions of the subject. Most scholars writing on early medieval prayer for the dead still focus on the role of prayer in expiating sins and liberating the soul from its purgatorial sufferings in the next world, ignoring the other meanings associated with prayer in the early middle ages.

The currently prevailing model of intercession also reflects late medieval and early modern mental habits. By the end of the middle ages, intercession, like many other human activities, had been abstracted from its social context and reified. The act of intercession had been transformed into a series of intercessory "units" (masses, offices, absolutions, psalters, etc.), each with a value virtually independent of the person or persons who performed it. As a result, the effects of intercession had come to be described in essentially mechanical terms. Each mass, each psalter or absolution performed for the dead tended to be seen as a unit of force which could push against the weight of sin until the soul was finally released from its sufferings in the next world. This reification of prayer was associated with its quantification. In fourteenth- and fifteenth-century wills and charters of donation, and in the apologetic debates of the sixteenth century, the amount of prayer performed—the number of "units" accumulated—determined how quickly the soul would be freed from purgatorial torment.

Recent historians have sought the roots of these late medieval practices and beliefs in late antiquity, when a complex set of factors transformed the meaning and practice of the liturgy. The rapid growth in conversions, the increasingly complex structure of the Christian community, and the clericalization of the liturgy were only some of the most important of these factors. Between the fourth and the eighth century the prayers of the eucharistic celebration and the hours were gradually abstracted from their original context in the collective activity of the ecclesia, until they came to be perceived as objects in their own right—as "masses" or "offices." A growing emphasis on instrumentality led to the creation of special services, which could be used for a variety of special purposes, including the needs of the dead. In late antiquity, then, we see the beginnings of the reification of prayer.

What most recent scholars have not recognized, however, is that these are only the beginnings of a complex process of change, which would take many centuries to complete. In fact, that process came to a virtual halt between the eighth and eleventh centuries, for the conditions of life in the early middle ages encouraged the interpretation of important activities such as prayer in contextual rather than in abstract terms.[182] In the first place, society was extremely fragmented in this period. While there were significant variations over time and among different social groups, it is generally true that early medieval men and women lived in a more regionalized and particularized world than their descendants in the later middle ages. Much of what happened in their lives occurred within the same small and relatively isolated communities. Under such circumstances every action carried with it the weight of what had gone before and what was expected in the future among the members of those communities; it had to be interpreted within the dense web of meanings laid down by ongoing relationships rather than simply measured by some externally imposed rule.

Limited literacy contributed both to the isolation of particular communities from one another, and to the relative flexibility of interpretive practices in the early middle ages. There were always a certain number of people who could read and write, of course. These people played the central role in preserving and transmitting the Christian religious tradition in their own time; we depend on their writings for our knowledge of the meaning and practice of prayer for the dead in the early middle ages. However, it is important to remember that these texts were composed and used within a society dominated not by literacy but by orality.[183] The evidence suggests that many—perhaps most—members of the literate elite shared the mental habits of the illiterate majority.

182. On the symbolic interpretation of conduct and appearance in the tenth century, see Heinrich Fichtenau, *Living in the Tenth Century: Mentalities and Social Orders*, trans. Patrick J. Geary (Chicago, 1991), pp. 30–35. As a number of scholars have recently suggested, the tendency to abstract human interactions from their context and reify them became increasingly pronounced from the twelfth century on. After 1100 there is a growing interest in fixed rules, in the measurement of human behavior in quantitative terms, using external standards: Brian Stock, *The Implications of Literacy: Written Language and Models of Interpretation in the Eleventh and Twelfth Centuries* (Princeton, 1983), p. 86 and passim. In the religious sphere, see especially Peter Brown, "Society and the Supernatural: A Medieval Change," *Daedalus* 104: 2 (Spring, 1975), 146–51; Benedicta Ward, *Miracles and the Medieval Mind: Theory, Record, and Event, 1000–1215* (Philadelphia, 1982), p. 22.

183. Rosamond McKitterick has recently reviewed the evidence for literacy and reliance on written texts in the eighth and ninth centuries: *The Carolingians and the Written Word*. She has convincingly demonstrated that the "Carolingian Renaissance" was much more than a minor countertrend in an otherwise continuous decline in literacy from the fifth to the eleventh century. She has also shown that literacy was by no means confined to the clergy in the Carolingian period. I think she goes too far, however, when she asserts that the written word was "central" to Carolingian society (p. 273).

Brian Stock has argued that in oral societies meaning is a compromise between a standard set of rhetorical figures and the individual interchange to which they are adapted.[184] While early medieval France cannot be called an oral society, the limited diffusion of texts there created a situation comparable to that found in oral societies. As we have seen, even members of the literate elite often had only limited access to theological writings on prayer for the dead. There was no well-known and fully integrated textual tradition to impose a fixed meaning on the practice. Rather, individuals absorbed a whole range of meanings, from a variety of texts—probably as often by ear, during the hours of prayer and during mealtimes, as by eye. They then drew upon that set of meanings to interpret prayer for the dead within the particular situation with which they were concerned.

Social fragmentation and limited literacy obviously did not make abstract thought impossible, but they did encourage interpretations of behavior that took context into account. As a result, important activities were never completely reified in the early middle ages; they always retained a social as well as an intrinsic identity. The homage of one great lord to another, performed *en marche*, had a very different significance and carried very different expectations from the homage performed by a poor knight to his lord in the latter's hall.[185] A king's gift to a famous monastery had a very different significance and carried very different expectations from a lesser noble's donation to a neighboring house.[186] It is not surprising, then, that a monastic community's commemorative services for a pious abbot and the intercession of a great saint for a sinner were also interpreted in very different ways.

A number of signs indicate that the reification of prayer was far from complete in the early middle ages: the prominence of ecclesiological symbolism in services for the dead, the focus on associative rather than special services in the negotiations between lay donors and religious communities, the importance attributed to intercessors in texts from this period. Most telling of all is the emphasis on appropriateness found in early medieval prescriptions for and descriptions

184. Brian Stock, *The Implications of Literacy*, p. 15.
185. Jean-François Lemarignier, *Recherches sur l'hommage en marche et les frontières féodales* (Lille, 1945), pp. 82–83; Duby, *La Société dans la région mâconnaise*, pp. 158–65.
186. Compare the relationship between Cluny and Alfonso VI of Castile (see Bouchard, *Sword, Miter, and Cloister*, pp. 143–45) with that between Cluny and the Burgundian nobles.

of prayer for the dead. In late antiquity Augustine had encouraged prayer for anyone who might be helped by it, arguing that "it is better that these things be superfluous to those whom they can neither harm nor help, than that they be lacking to those whom they might benefit."[187] This approach seems reasonable if prayer is simply a mechanism that would fail to work for the really wicked. But if prayer has a social identity, if its ecclesiological symbolism is thought to express the intercessor's acceptance of the person interceded for, then the situation is not so simple. A more common attitude in the early middle ages was expressed in a tenth-century collection of lessons for the office of the dead: "Let us pray for those who are to be prayed for, and let us be silent concerning those who are not to be prayed for."[188]

As we have seen, early medieval liturgical communities felt a strong obligation to offer the "usual" prayers and alms for their departed members and associates. Those who were responsible for the organization of the liturgy between the middle of the eighth and the end of the eleventh century often used the language of entitlement in discussing services for the dead: the former members of the community had a *right* to commemoration in its liturgy. By the same token, those who were not members of the community were not entitled to a share in its prayers. Early medieval hagiographers presented Pope Gregory's intercession for the pagan emperor Trajan as an expression of his charity and love for justice, but they were still troubled by his action. Indeed, in two versions of the legend, Gregory was explicitly rebuked for his audacity in daring to intercede for someone outside the church.[189] How are we to explain these texts if we assume that prayer had no social identity in this period?

Most early medieval church leaders generally agreed that one should not pray for pagans or heretics. As Pope Leo the Great had pointed out, "We cannot communicate with the dead with whom we did not communicate in life."[190] But what was to be done about those who, while not actually excommunicate, were obviously wicked? The prospect of praying for such people was very troubling to early

187. Augustine, *De cura pro mortuis gerenda*, 18 (p. 658); cited by Amalar of Metz, *Liber officialis*, 3, 44: 15 (2: 385).

188. "Un Ancien Recueil de leçons," p. 29.

189. *The Earliest Life of Gregory the Great*, 29 (p. 129); Paul the Deacon, *Sancti Gregorii magni vita*, 27 (PL 75: 57). This passage does not occur in Paul's original text; it is an interpolation of the late ninth or early tenth century: see Whatley, "The Uses of Hagiography," p. 30, n. 19.

190. Leo I, *Epistolae*, 167 (PL 54: 1205–6).

medieval clerics, precisely because prayer retained its social identity in this period. The pseudo-Dionysius had stated that "he who offers masses for a bad man commits blasphemy against God," and this point was reiterated in a number of penitentials and collections of canon law.[191] Early medieval clerics constantly struggled with the question of appropriate and inappropriate prayer, without ever reaching a resolution of all the complex issues involved. But the fact that this issue was so important indicates that prayer retained a strong social as well as instrinsic value in this period.

A number of recent scholars have associated the reification of prayer in late antiquity with its quantification in the early middle ages. Arnold Angenendt has pointed out that the shift toward instrumentality that became evident in interpretations of intercession in late antiquity gave rise by the Carolingian period to a whole range of special services tailored to special needs, and then to calculations of the numbers of services to be performed under specific circumstances.[192] The spread of the system of "tariffed" penance played a crucial role in this development, for it led to a "quantification" of the spiritual works due for sins.[193] The system of "tariffed" penance affected not only penance in life, but also prayer for the dead. Indeed, Angenendt asserts that prayer for the dead, even more than penance, shows a tendency toward number and abundance in the Carolingian period.[194] He suggests that this reflects the desire for many masses, the importance of accumulating suffrages, in order to expiate sins and speed the liberation of the dead from their sufferings in the next world.[195] Other recent scholars have drawn on Angenendt's formulation of the traditional "accumulation" model in their studies of early medieval prayer for the dead.[196]

It is certainly true that numbers were increasingly associated with services for the dead from the eighth century on, and in a variety of documents. Numbers almost invariably appear in confraternity

---

191. *Die Canones Theodori*, p. 246; Burchard of Worms, *Decretum*, 3: 65 (PL 140: 687).
192. Angenendt, "Missa Specialis," pp. 154–81.
193. Angenendt, "Missa Specialis," p. 163.
194. Angenendt, "Missa Specialis," p. 208.
195. Angenendt, "Theologie und Liturgie," in Schmid and Wollasch, *Memoria*, p. 174.
196. Neiske, "Vision und Totengedenken," p. 156. A French scholar, Dominique Iogna-Prat, has borrowed a phrase from Jacques Chiffoleau's work on the later middle ages *(La Comptabilité de l'au-delà)* to describe Cluny's care for the dead: "Les Morts dans la comptabilité céleste des Clunisiens de l'an Mil," in Iogna-Prat and Picard, *Religion et culture autour de l'an mil*, especially p. 67.

agreements dating from the Carolingian period.[197] Numbers also appear, although less consistently, in the Carolingian vision literature. A frequently cited example occurs in Walahfrid Strabo's version of the *Vision of Wetti*. After his terrifying journey through the other world, Wetti prepares for his own impending death. He sends notes to ten of his friends, each couched in the same terms:

> To the most venerable father in Christ, your devoted friend Wetti wishes eternal salvation in the Lord. I am writing to you on the brink of death though still in the flourishing years of my prime. In my life to come, please comfort my infirmity so that once the hulk of this corrupt existence has been laid aside, I will not be oppressed there, too, with a heavy weight of punishments. If your intercession amounts to a hundred masses and a hundred psalms, there will be a sure reward. Farewell. I am to see you no more.[198]

A similar use of numbers is found in the *Vision of a Poor Woman*, which, like the *Vision of Wetti*, dates to the ninth century. In the *Vision of a Poor Woman*, the visionary sees Charlemagne suffering torments in the next world. She asks her guide whether the former ruler is destined for eternal life, and he replies that Charlemagne will be freed if the Emperor Louis, his son, "fully distributes seven *agapes* on his behalf."[199] (Presumably what was meant by *agape* was some form of funerary banquet or formal distribution of food to the poor.)

Not only were numbers frequently associated with suffrages for the dead in Carolingian texts, but there is also evidence that the number of prayers performed was thought to affect their results. As Angenendt has shown, the numbers that appear in Carolingian confraternity agreements often correspond with those found in contemporary penitentials.[200] In other words, there is reason to think that the organizers of confraternities viewed their efforts on behalf of the dead as equivalent to specific periods of penance. When a priest-monk

197. See, for example, the texts cited in Chapter 2 concerning the agreements established at the Synod of Attigny around 762, and between Saint-Denis and Saint-Remi in 840.

198. Walahfrid Strabo, *Visio Wettini*, MGH, PP, 2: 332; trans. in idem, *Walahfrid Strabo's Visio Wettini*, pp. 72–73.

199. *Visio cuiusdam pauperculae mulieris*, ed. Heinz Löwe, in his *Deutschlands Geschichtsquellen im Mittelalter: Vorzeit und Karolinger*, vol. 3: *Die Karolinger vom Tode Karls des Grossen bis zum Vertrag von Verdun* (Weimar, 1957), pp. 317–18, n. 85.

200. Angenendt, "Theologie und Liturgie," in Schmid and Wollasch, *Memoria*, pp. 174–79.

celebrated thirty masses for one of his confratres, for example, he may
have thought that he was performing the equivalent of one year of
earthly penance.[201] Presumably Carolingian clerics believed that just
as living penitents would be absolved and readmitted to communion
when their assigned penances were complete, so the dead would be
liberated from their torments when the appropriate amount of expia-
tion had been made for their sins. In both the *Vision of Wetti* and the
Vision of a Poor Woman, it is explicitly stated that the performance of a
specific number of prayers by designated individuals will lead to the
liberation of the soul from its sufferings in the next world.

Clearly, then, prayers were associated with numbers in early medieval texts. However, this does not necessarily represent an interest
in the accumulation of suffrages per se. The Carolingian confraternity
agreements, for all their numerical language, were not really designed
to provide a specific number of prayers for the dead. Indeed, it is often
impossible to determine how many prayers were actually performed
for the members of these confraternities when they died. The total
number of suffrages would depend on who was available to perform
them, and it would fluctuate over time according to the size of the
clerical communities involved. The numbers found in Carolingian
confraternity agreements serve rather to delineate the obligations of
each individual cleric within a framework of collective effort.[202] The
intention was not to provide a certain number of prayers, but to have
every member of a designated community contribute to the commemoration of the dead in an appropriate way, according to his or her
abilities. The same intention seems to lie behind the passage from
Walahfrid Strabo's *Vision of Wetti* cited earlier. Significantly, Wetti
does not simply ask to have one thousand masses and one thousand
psalters performed for him; he asks each of his ten friends to offer one
hundred masses and one hundred psalters on his behalf. In this text, as
in the confraternity agreements, numbers are not the goal of commemoration, but its structuring principle.[203]

201. According to the commutation system found in a late ninth-century version of
the Double Penitential of Bede-Egbert: cited by Angenendt, "Theologie und Liturgie," in
Schmid and Wollasch, *Memoria*, p. 174.

202. For example, the agreement reached between Saint-Remi and Saint-Denis in 840
called for each member of the community to perform a complete psalter or (in the case of
monk-priests) "masses equivalent to that psalter" within thirty days after the death of a
monk of the associated house: Molinier and Longnon, *Obituaires de la province de Sens*, 1: 2,
p. 1023.

203. The *Vision of a Poor Woman* is more difficult to interpret, because the author has
imposed the obligation of helping the dead not on a group but on an individual. Still, it is

Neither does the association of numbers with services for the dead necessarily reflect "quantification" in the modern sense. Some scholars have assumed that the belief that every mass has its own expiatory value must have as its correlate the belief that two masses have twice the effect of one, three masses three times the effect, and so forth.[204] In other words, they assume that the organization of commemorative services in the early middle ages was based on arithmetic. In fact, however, most early medieval texts that count acts of intercession do not use a full range of numbers, as one might expect in a system predicated on simple arithmetic. On the contrary, in both penitentials and works dealing with prayer for the dead certain numbers constantly recur, while others are never used. The most common numbers associated with masses for the dead are three, seven, ten (less often, twelve), thirty (less often, forty) and one hundred. The same numbers might be associated with the recitation of psalters, although one also finds the one hundred fifty psalms divided up into sets of five or fifty, which might then be multiplied in various ways.[205]

The point is that these are all "sacred" numbers, numbers which held a mystical meaning within the well-developed tradition of Christian numerology.[206] In some cases there is reason to think that the numbers associated with services for the dead were actually selected on the basis of their numerological significance.[207] In other cases, early medieval clerics continued to use numbers that had been associated with the care of the dead since antiquity, but interpreted them in numerological terms.[208] Amalar of Metz, for example, writing in the first half of the ninth century, accounted for the well-established practice of offering thirty masses for the dead over the course of thirty days in this way:

---

worth noting that in this text too the liberation of the dead depends not simply on the offering of seven *agapes*, but on their offering *by Louis the Pious*. The number seven does designate the goal in this text, but it structures the obligation of a designated intercessor at the same time.

204. Angenendt, "Missa Specialis," p. 213.

205. See the texts cited by Angenendt, "Missa Specialis," pp. 172–74, 203–8; idem, "Theologie und Liturgie," in Schmid and Wollasch, *Memoria*, pp. 171–79; and in Chapter 2 above.

206. Vincent Foster Hopper, *Medieval Number Symbolism: Its Sources, Meaning, and Influence on Thought and Expression* (New York, 1938); Ursula Grossman, "Studien zur Zahlensymbolik des Frühmittelalters," *Zeitschrift für katholische Theologie* 76 (1954), 19–54.

207. See the discussion below of Walahfrid Strabo's use of the number ten in his version of the *Vision of Wetti*.

208. On the association of three, seven and thirty with prayer for the dead, see above, Chapters 1 and 2.

Thirty days make a month. A month represents the course of this present life, as may easily be discerned from the state of the moon. Whence Gregory, in his *Moralia on Job* (Book VIII): "By the name of 'month' is signified the collection and sum of days. Therefore every act can be expressed through 'day,' but the end of action through 'month.'" When we desire that the works of our friends may be fulfilled before God, we sacrifice for them for thirty days.[209]

The pseudo-Alcuin, writing in the first half of the tenth century, also explained the traditional practice of offering mass on the thirtieth day after death in numerological terms:

> There are those who say that this is done because of the perfection of the number thirty: for the Lord was baptized at the age of thirty years, and David became the ruler of a kingdom at the age of thirty years. The learned assert that the first man was created thirty years old, and we believe and hope that our bodies will rise again in the measure of Christ's maturity. Many other mysteries are also evident in this matter.[210]

For these authors, the number thirty represented the full course or the perfection of human life on earth; by offering mass for the dead thirty times—or even once, on the thirtieth day—the church helped to bring about the fulfillment of that life in heaven.

The explosion of sacred numbers in Carolingian texts describing intercession for the dead reflects something much more interesting than a simple desire to accumulate prayer. It reflects the efforts of Carolingian clerics to enclose the dead in perfectly integrated structures of prayer which would symbolize their membership in the community that prayed. These liturgical structures were based on clearly articulated units (masses, psalters, vigils, etc.) arranged in combinations based on sacred numbers (three, ten, one hundred, etc.). The principle at work here, I would suggest, was more qualitative than quantitative, and was closely related to what has been called the "Carolingian modular aesthetic."

This phrase was first used by the architectural historian Walter Horn.[211] In his study of the Plan of Saint-Gall, Horn showed how

209. Amalar of Metz, *Liber officialis*, 3, 44: 7 (2: 383).
210. Pseudo-Alcuin, *De divinis officiis*, 51 (PL 101: 1280).
211. Walter Horn, with Ernest Born, "On the Selective Use of Sacred Numbers and

Carolingian planners and architects dealt with large spaces in ways very different from those of their predecessors in late antiquity. Whereas the architects of the fourth and fifth centuries had constructed basilicas whose interiors consisted of essentially undivided space, the architects of the eighth and ninth centuries created interior spaces in which clearly articulated spatial modules such as bays, aisles, and steps were arranged in combinations based on sacred numbers.[212] That similar aesthetic principles were at work in the Carolingian literary revival has long been recognized.[213] Unlike the more convoluted and varied Latin poetry of the first few centuries of our era, much of Carolingian poetry consists of a few poetic modules (notably, the "locked" stanza of the Ambrosian hymn) combined, again through the use of sacred numbers, into larger structures which were apparently highly satisfying to their creators and much admired by their audience.[214] "Numerical composition" was also a feature of Carolingian prose works.[215] Finally, Richard Crocker has noted a similar "modular aesthetic" at work in the most innovative musical form of the ninth century—the sequence.[216]

The learned clerics, trained in the tradition of Christian numerology, who planned the great churches, wrote the elegant poetry, and composed the new music of the Carolingian Renaissance using sacred numbers as an organizational principle, were also the organizers of prayer associations and the recorders/authors of a rich vision literature, in which the purpose of prayer for the dead was made concrete. It is not unreasonable to assume that they applied the same aesthetic principles to their liturgical as to their architectural, poetic, and musical endeavors—for all these activities were closely related to one another.[217]

---

the Creation in Carolingian Architecture of a New Aesthetic Based on Modular Concepts," *Viator* 6 (1975), 351–90.

212. Horn, "On the Selective Use of Sacred Numbers," pp. 368–69; Heitz, "Symbolisme et architecture," in *Simboli e simbologia*, 1: 387–420. On the continuation of this tradition in the tenth century, see Fichtenau, *Living in the Tenth Century*, p. 72.

213. Ernst Robert Curtius, *European Literature and the Latin Middle Ages*, trans. Willard R. Trask (London, 1953), pp. 501–9.

214. Charles W. Jones, "Carolingian Aesthetics: Why Modular Verse?" *Viator* 6 (1975), 309–40.

215. Horn, "On the Selective Use of Sacred Numbers," pp. 384–85.

216. Richard L. Crocker, "The Early Frankish Sequence: A New Musical Form," *Viator* 6 (1975), 341–49.

217. Heitz has discussed the role of sacred numbers in the organization of liturgical processions at Saint-Riquier: "Symbolisme et architecture," in *Simboli e simbologia*, 1: 394–97. See also Häussling, *Mönchskonvent und Eucharistiefeier*, pp. 111–12, 274–75.

Walahfrid Strabo, for example, was one of the major poets of the ninth century and an ardent devotee of "numerical composition." Is it any accident, then, that in his poetic version of the *Vision of Wetti* he described an elaborate liturgical structure based on sacred numbers—a structure, incidentally, never mentioned in Walahfrid's model, Heito of Basel's prose *Vision of Wetti*? Walahfrid seems to have found special satisfaction in poetry structured by tens. A number of his poems contain ten lines, "ten times ten" lines, or ten stanzas. [218] But in the Christian numerology of the Carolingian period, ten was often interpreted as the number of perfection and of reward. [219] This is why Walahfrid's Wetti is able to assure his ten friends that if each of them performs one hundred (ten times ten) masses and one hundred psalters for him, his "reward" will be "sure."[220]

Early medieval clerics were numerate, but they were not accountants, and they certainly did not share the "arithmetical mentality" that emerged in the high middle ages. [221] They probably did use some of the same numbers in confraternity agreements as in the penitentials, in the hope that their prayers would help the dead atone for their sins. However, those numbers do not correspond to the actual sins committed by the members of their *societas orationum*, which would obviously be different in each case. In some instances, the numbers correspond to the periods marked off by those days on which prayers had traditionally been said for the dead (the third, seventh, and thirtieth days after death)—periods which were now interpreted as periods of penance in the next world. [222] In other texts, such as Walahfrid's *Vision of Wetti,* the numbers of prayers simply represent "perfection" or "reward."

Some early medieval clerics seem to have been acutely aware of the need to atone for every sin actually committed. In the mid-eleventh century, for example, Abbot Thierry of Saint-Evroul used to tell his monks a cautionary tale about "a certain brother in a certain monastery"—a diligent worker in the scriptorium, but otherwise reprehensible. When the brother died, his soul was brought before the

---

218. Curtius, *European Literature and the Latin Middle Ages*, p. 506.

219. Curtius, *European Literature and the Latin Middle Ages*, p. 503.

220. This interpretation was suggested by Häussling, *Mönchskonvent und Eucharistiefeier*, p. 274, n. 468; however, Häussling never notes Walahfrid's predilection for the number ten.

221. On the "arithmetical mentality" see Alexander Murray, *Reason and Society in the Middle Ages*, rev. ed. (Oxford, 1985), especially pp. 162–210.

222. Angenendt, "Missa Specialis," pp. 200–201; idem, "Theologie und Liturgie," in Schmid and Wollasch, *Memoria*, pp. 172–73.

tribunal of the Just Judge. Evil spirits acted as his accusers, pointing out his "innumerable" sins. The angels, in his defense, brought out a huge book which he had copied, and tallied up the individual letters, one by one, against his sins. In the end, a single letter remained against which the demons could offer no sin. The Judge then mercifully ordered the brother's soul returned to his body, so that he could do penance for all those sins.[223] In this story the inadequacy of eleventh-century accounting methods, as well as the characteristic eleventh-century anxiety about sins too numerous to be counted accurately, is evident.[224] In the face of such anxiety, reliance could hardly be placed on some set number of prayers, however large. In this case the monk was actually returned to life to perform his own penance. In other texts, the sinner seeks a powerful intercessor (a saint) or community of intercessors (a monastery), whose outstanding (but unnumbered) "prayers and merits" could make up for innumerable sins.[225]

For early medieval clerics, the most significant number of all was one: the number of the Creator and of the unity from which all other numbers sprang.[226] It is not surprising, then, that in a number of early medieval texts those in need are helped not by the accumulation of many suffrages, but rather by a single act of intercession. In his *Dialogues*, Gregory the Great briefly related the story of a man who was captured in battle and held in chains; meanwhile his wife had masses offered for him. From time to time the captive's chains were loosed, and when he was finally freed, he discovered that this had happened on the days when his wife had had masses offered.[227] The point here is not accumulation, for each mass performed is fully effective—it looses the prisoner's chains. The repeated performance of masses serves to verify their effects; it does not increase them.

The Venerable Bede, writing in the early eighth century, offered an updated version of Gregory's story, in which the wife of the earlier version is replaced by an Anglo-Saxon priest. Bede's priest celebrated masses for his imprisoned brother, thinking he was dead. However,

---

223. Orderic Vitalis, *Historia aecclesiastica*, 3 (2: 50).

224. Other texts from this period reflect concern about sins that were overlooked and hence not atoned for. See Othlo of St. Emmeram, *Liber visionum*, 12 and 17 (PL 146: 366–68, 372–73); Hariulf, *Chronicon Centulense*, 4: 34 (p. 270).

225. E.g., *Recueil des chartes de l'abbaye de Cluny*, no. 1831 (990).

226. Hopper, *Medieval Number Symbolism*, p. 100; and see Jones, "Carolingian Aesthetics," p. 318.

227. Gregory the Great, *Dialogi*, 4: 59 (p. 320).

the brother was really in prison and every time a mass was celebrated for him his chains fell off. When his captor asked why he could not be kept bound, the prisoner replied: "I have a brother who is a priest in my own province, and I am sure that, thinking me killed, he is saying many masses for me; and were I now in another life, my soul would be freed of its pains by his prayers."[228] In Bede's version, the masses in question are clearly masses for the dead; the story suggests that just as the prisoner's chains were loosed, so the bondage of the dead will be loosed with *each* celebration of the mass. In the ninth century, the Frankish liturgist Amalar of Metz used this version of the story in his exposition of the mass for the dead.[229] It also appears in Abbo of Fleury's tenth-century canon law collection.[230]

The effectiveness of a single mass in liberating the dead from their torments appears most clearly in a story recounted by Orderic Vitalis. He reports that at the end of the eleventh century a priest in northern France saw a strange and frightening purgatorial procession passing through the countryside. The priest spoke to a number of the dead and learned why they were suffering as they were. One of them turned out to be his own brother, a former knight, who was condemned to travel with the procession weighted down by his earthly arms and armor. He told the priest, ". . . when you were ordained in England and sang your first mass for the departed faithful, your father Ralph was delivered from his torments, and my shield, which caused me great pain, fell off. As you see, I still carry this sword, but I look in faith for release from this burden within a year."[231] The last sentence suggests that the passage of time will bring further benefits— perhaps the assumption is that further suffrages will be performed for the dead within the next year. However, in this text, as in the others just cited, the crucial factor is not the accumulation of suffrages, but the fact that intercession has occurred. One soul is liberated and another's burdens are lightened when the very first mass is performed.

It is clear, then, that the association of numbers with intercessory

228. Bede, *Historia ecclesiastica*, 4: 22 (pp. 400–404). The translation is my own.

229. Amalar of Metz, *Liber officialis*, 3, 44: 10 (2: 384). Compare the stories related by Gregory of Tours, *De gloria confessorum*, 65 (PL 71: 875–76) and Peter Damian, *Epistolae*, 106 (3: 179–80), in which each celebration of the mass relieves suffering, rather than producing liberation.

230. Abbo of Fleury, *Collectio canonum*, 49 (PL 139: 505–6).

231. Orderic Vitalis, *Historia aecclesiastica*, 8: 17 (4: 248). I have modified Chibnall's translation slightly. On this text see also McGuire, "Purgatory, the Communion of Saints, and Medieval Change," pp. 78–79.

acts in early medieval texts must be treated with great caution. For numbers did not mean the same thing to the educated men and women of the early middle ages as they did to later medieval merchants or modern historians. Numbers were more closely associated in this period with measure and proportion, seen as aspects of divine harmony, than with accumulation. As Alexander Murray has pointed out, the educated elite of the early middle ages used numbers only infrequently and then generally with less regard to accuracy than to artistic effect.[232] A model of prayer for the dead based on modern notions of number and quantity may account for some early medieval texts, but it may also create serious problems when used to interpret texts in which numbers do not appear at all, or in which they are used in ways to which we are not accustomed today.

It may be useful, then, to replace the mechanical model with a new one, which takes early medieval habits of thought more fully into account. I would suggest that prayer might better be seen as a symbol of identity than as an object. We can envision it as a boundary, as part of the symbolic barrier dividing the cosmos in two—for prayer, fasting, and almsgiving were among the things which separated the church from the world, communicants from excommunicates, the *societas sanctorum* from the *societas diaboli*. Understood in this way, it was the fact of commemoration in the liturgy, the fact of being remembered as a *familiaris*, the fact of being accepted as a client of a saint that mattered. The exact number of intercessory acts performed might be important as a measure of the relationship between intercessor and interceded-for, as an indication of devotion to the dead, but it is not as inherently significant as the fact that intercession has occurred. Hence the importance of even a single intercessory act in the texts from this period.

To say that prayer served as a symbol is not to say that it had no effects. It is clear that prayer was expected to help the dead in the early middle ages. But I would suggest that prayer "worked" in a more magical than mechanical way in this period. It served to draw a liturgical line around the person prayed for, making them "present" within the community delineated by prayer. When religious communities prayed for their former members, they identified them as "brothers" or "sisters" of the house and kept them within reach of fraternal assistance, while they underwent purgation in the next

232. Murray, *Reason and Society*, pp. 175–80.

world. When a great saint interceded for a pagan or someone guilty of serious sin, he or she might actually move that person across the symbolic boundary, out of the community of the damned and into the company of the elect—but only at the risk of being reprimanded for inappropriate behavior.

If prayer is understood as a symbol of religious community, it can be associated not only with the process of purgation after death, but also with thanksgiving, with protection on the journey to heaven, and with dramatic intervention at the moment of judgment. Thus a symbolic model of intercession helps to account for the wide variety of functions attributed to prayer for the dead in early medieval texts. It also helps to account for many of the other peculiarities of the early medieval pattern of prayer for the dead, including, most obviously, the predominance of associative services with their elaborate ecclesiological symbolism, but also the pattern of familiaritas which characterized noble relationships with religious communities, and the importance attributed to intercessors in this period. The mechanical model of prayer, with its emphasis on numbers and accumulation, cannot explain the urgent concern with the horizontal relationships between the dead and those who pray for them evident in all of these areas. But that concern becomes entirely explicable if we assume that early medieval prayer for the dead worked precisely through the symbolic assertion of such relationships.

EPILOGUE

The abbey of Conques stands on a hill above a green valley, through which runs the little river called the Dourdou. The present abbey church, built at the time of Conques's greatest prosperity in the eleventh and early twelfth century, is an unusually fine example of Romanesque architecture; the remarkable tympanum above the west portal is one of the triumphs of Romanesque sculpture.[1] At the center of the tympanum a stern-faced Christ sits enthroned, while above him two angels sound trumpets to announce the last judgment. The Savior welcomes the procession of saints approaching on his right and rejects the sinners on his left. Beneath Christ's feet, the souls of the dead are weighed in a balance held by an angel and a demon. The demon is cheating by pushing down on one side of the scales with his finger; however, his interference may be counterbalanced by that of St. Foy, the patron of Conques, who appears beneath the saints on Christ's right hand interceding for the departed faithful. In the lowest register, the souls of the condemned are fed through the mouth of hell into a chaotic space filled with demons inflicting ingenious torments on the damned. The saved pass through a doorway to join the gracefully ordered ranks of the saints.

In many ways, the tympanum of Conques epitomizes early medieval hopes and fears for the afterlife—the dominance of the last judg-

---

1. On the difficulties of dating the construction of the church and tympanum more precisely see Jean-Claude Bonne, *L'Art roman de face et de profil: Le tympan de Conques* (Paris, 1984), pp. 313–17.

ment, the dangers of the passage to salvation, the dualistic structure of the cosmos. It also reflects early medieval assumptions about the ways in which the dead could and should be helped, in particular the importance of horizontal relationships in ensuring one's well-being in the next world. On the far left side of the composition, behind the figure of St. Foy, hang the shackles of former prisoners who have been freed by her intercession and who have dedicated their chains to her in gratitude: their presence suggests that while the saint may be interceding for all the departed faithful, she is most directly concerned with her own devotees, with those who had allied themselves with her in life.[2]

It has been the thesis of this book that a particular pattern of prayer for the dead, very different from that of earlier and later times, prevailed in France between the mid-eighth and the end of the eleventh century. Among the distinctive features of this pattern was the prominence accorded to ecclesiological symbolism in rituals for the dead. The association of the dead with a specific liturgical community on earth—through the choice of burial site, the ritual use of names, and the integration of prayers for the departed faithful into the liturgy as a whole—was intended to link them as well to the community of the saints. Elaborate ecclesiological symbolism had not been present in rituals for the dead during the first few centuries of the church, because death rituals were not yet fully christianized in that period and also, perhaps, because the status of the departed faithful was not yet a cause for anxiety. The prominence of ecclesiological symbolism declined in the later middle ages, as concerns about the quantity and effectiveness of prayer replaced concerns about its quality and appropriateness. In the early middle ages, however, ecclesiological symbolism was so central that the death rituals of that period can properly be characterized as "associative."

The relationship of the laity to the clericalized liturgy of death was another distinctive feature of the early middle ages. By the eighth century layfolk no longer participated directly in most rituals for the dead. Rather, they attempted to associate themselves in various ways with clerical efforts on behalf of the departed faithful. But unlike the later medieval laity, these men and women seldom focused their attention on the acquisition of prayers per se. In the period from the mid-eighth to the end of the eleventh century, the negotiations that

---

2. On St. Foy as intercessor for the dead, see Bonne, *L'Art roman*, pp. 243–45.

resulted in commemoration after death formed part of long-term, complex relationships between religious communities and the laity who lived nearby. It is difficult to identify the motives of the laity in these negotiations. However, they seem to have been much more interested in creating and maintaining close bonds with potentially powerful intercessors—the local saints and their servants—than in specifying the kinds and quantities of prayers to be performed for them after death.

Finally, early medieval Christians had distinctive ways of interpreting the rituals they performed for the dead. On the one hand, their interpretations were influenced by the coherent if somewhat sketchy theological tradition concerning prayer for the dead which had developed in late antiquity. On the other hand, their ideas on the subject were determined by that theological tradition to a much more limited extent than would be the case in the later middle ages. In the early middle ages, interpretations of prayer for the dead were based on a variety of authoritative texts—liturgical and hagiographical, as well as theological—selected and interpreted according to the social and cultural context within which they were used. Which of the many potential functions was attributed to prayer for the dead depended on the interpreter's beliefs about the status of the dead person, the status of the intercessor, and the relationship between the two. In any case, the primary function of such prayer was to identify the dead as members of the Christian community, as friends of the clergy and as clients of the saints on earth and therefore in heaven. The model of prayer for the dead was qualitative and symbolic, rather than quantitative and mechanical. Hence the many parallels between descriptions of intercession in written texts and depictions of intercession in works of art such as the tympanum of Conques.

The early medieval pattern of prayer reflects certain fairly consistent features of early medieval society and culture. The general fragmentation of society in this period promoted intense bonding at the local level and the metonymic identification of the immediate community with society as a whole. The economy of the early middle ages, based more on plundering and gift-giving than on commerce, placed long-term bonding rather than commodity exchange at the center of social transactions. Limited literacy and poor communications hindered the diffusion of standardized meanings and encouraged contextual habits of thought. As a result, prayer remained largely unreified in the early middle ages. Intercession was always freighted with social, political, spiritual, moral, and emotional meanings, which shifted constantly according to the circumstances within which it was carried out.

The assertion that the overall pattern of prayer was consistent throughout the early middle ages does not mean that no development took place in the practice and understanding of prayer for the dead. On the contrary, both funerary and nonfunerary prayer for the dead evolved considerably during this period. The eighth and ninth centuries witnessed the development of a complete Christian ritual covering the passage from sickness through death and burial. Funerary ritual was further elaborated in the monasteries during the tenth and eleventh centuries. The general expansion of the liturgy produced an expansion of prayer for the dead outside of funerals as well, with the addition to the regular round of prayer of masses, psalms, and feasts for the dead. The spread of confraternities from the eighth century on represented an effort to integrate the liturgy of death carried out by separate liturgical communities into larger structures of prayer. The introduction of necrologies in the ninth century provided for the continuing commemoration of individuals after death in ways very different from those provided by the earlier libri memoriales. Yet despite all these changes, the desire to integrate prayer for the dead into the liturgy as a whole, the desire to commemorate individuals through association in the regular prayers of the liturgical community, and a keen awareness of ecclesiological symbolism remained consistent features of liturgical practice throughout the early middle ages.

The relationship of the laity to the clerical community that prayed also underwent significant changes over the course of the early middle ages. The loose affiliations of late antiquity gradually were replaced by closer bonds. The poor were tied more tightly to the parish church; the powerful chose to associate themselves with elite religious houses—from the late tenth century on, primarily with the reformed monasteries. We see noble affiliation with those monasteries reach its greatest intensity in the late eleventh century, as an increasing number of powerful men and women chose not only burial, but also formal association and even vestment with the monastic habit in their last days of life. Yet throughout this period, for both the poor and the powerful, prayer for the dead remained only one aspect of their complex relationship with a local religious community—liturgical reflections of a much deeper identification.

Changes over time in the ideology of prayer for the dead are more difficult to pinpoint, because of the wide range of images and ideas associated with such prayer in the early middle ages. Nevertheless, important changes can be discerned in this realm as well. Because of the preeminent role in the Carolingian church of clerics well-versed in theology and concerned with pastoral care, images of orderly intercession through carefully integrated structures of prayer, gradually leading to the liberation of souls from purgation after death, predominated in the writings of the eighth and ninth centuries. In the eleventh century, these images were displaced by more dramatic ones, presented by the monastic communities which had become the most important intercessors of the period. These images, drawing on hagiographical tradition, depicted the sudden and unexpected liberation of souls from demonic powers through the force of the monastic liturgy and the power of monastic patron saints. Here too, though, we find change overlying essential consistency. Throughout this period an essentially symbolic model of intercession, very unlike the mechanical model of the later middle ages, prevailed, allowing early medieval Christians to interpret the rituals they performed for the dead according to the particular circumstances under which they were carried out.

I have argued that the existence of this associative pattern of prayer was predicated on the existence of certain distinctive and enduring structures in early medieval society and culture. But as the pace of social and cultural change quickened in the late eleventh century, those structures began to give way to new ones. The fragmented world of early medieval France became somewhat more closely integrated, as the population grew, the economy expanded, and the great princes and bishops of the realm began to consolidate their power. Settlements, castles, parish churches, and religious houses multiplied, bringing formerly isolated communities into closer contact with one another, and as this happened, the intense bonding with the local community characteristic of the early middle ages began to give way to more complex social relationships. The expansion of commercial activities, the increased circulation of money and growing concern for profit began to transform the meaning of property transactions in this period, lessening their social implications and conferring increased importance on the commodities exchanged. Finally, the appearance of new schools, the spread of literacy, and the improved communications associated with political consolidation, religious reform, and commercial revival transformed the cultural world.

Accelerated change in the structures of society and culture after 1050 had important implications for the practice and understanding of the liturgy, including the liturgy of death. While old practices remained in full vigor in the second half of the eleventh century, subtle signs indicate that the configurations within which those practices had existed were beginning to dissolve and re-form. By the first decades of the twelfth century those signs were becoming more numerous and more obvious; by 1150 or so a new pattern of prayer for the dead had largely replaced the old one. This is not the place to describe the shape of that new pattern or to trace all the steps by which it emerged.[3] However, it may be worthwhile to take note of some of the signs of change in the practice and understanding of prayer for the dead that became visible around the turn of the twelfth century.

To begin with, the new directions taken by monastic reform in this period were beginning to displace collective prayer from the center of religious life. As is well known, in the final decades of the eleventh century a small but growing number of clerics began to question the value of traditional monasticism, with its emphasis on the ceremonious public service of God and the saints.[4] Some even abandoned the older Benedictine monasteries to pursue what they saw as the more rigorous life of a hermit. As John van Engen has shown, the appearance of such criticism in the late eleventh century does not constitute a true "crisis of cenobitism." The black monks retained their dominant role in spiritual life well into the twelfth century.[5] But by 1100 the rise of eremiticism had already complicated the religious landscape in important ways, providing new options for those in search of salvation. Moreover, those new options inevitably entailed new approaches to the opus Dei, for even if they had wanted to, hermits were incapable of maintaining the elaborate round of prayer for the living and for the dead that had been the raison d'être of the older Benedictine houses. The full impact of monastic reform on

3. For a discussion of these developments, see McLaughlin, "Consorting with Saints," pp. 282–465.
4. See, for example, G. Morin, "Rainaud l'ermite et Ives de Chartres: Un épisode de la crise du cénobitisme au XIe -XIIe siècle," *Revue Bénédictine* 40 (1928), 99–115, especially 106–7.
5. van Engen, "The 'Crisis of Cenobitism' Reconsidered."

the liturgy of death becomes clear only when one examines the early liturgical customs of the Carthusians, Cistercians, Premonstratensians, and so forth, which survive in twelfth-century manuscripts.[6] However, the institutional groundwork for the changes apparent in those documents was already being laid in the late eleventh century.

Signs of a transformation in the laity's relationship to the liturgical community also begin to appear in this period. References to spiritual association, burial, the inscription of names in necrologies, and other liturgical privileges appear much more frequently in the charters of the late eleventh century than in the records of earlier times. As noted earlier, this change was probably related to the economic and social changes occurring in this period, which encouraged religious communities and lay donors to bargain more explicitly for what they wanted. The growth in quid pro quo transactions does not in itself represent a revolution in the relationship between noble donors and religious houses. However, it does indicate that the focus of lay attention was beginning to shift from the relationship itself to the liturgical benefits it offered. Moreover, this was happening in the same period when the number of religious communities which might provide liturgical benefits to lay donors was growing. By the early twelfth century, we begin to see signs of a breakdown in the traditional pattern of *familiaritas* between lay donors and religious houses. Men and women were not only requesting liturgical benefits more often, but now they were actually shopping around for them, forming associations with a larger number and wider variety of religious communities. One noblewoman from western France, for example, spent the early years of her widowhood giving gifts to, and obtaining formal association from, the houses of Saint-Père of Chartres, Coulombs, Bec, Saint-Taurin, Sainte-Marie of Ivry, and Pontoise.[7]

6. On the Carthusian liturgy, see Archdale A. King, *The Liturgies of the Religious Orders* (London, 1956), pp. 16–65; on the Cistercians, see Chrysogonus Waddell, "The Early Cistercian Experience of Liturgy," in *Rule and Life: An Interdisciplinary Symposium*, ed. M. Basil Pennington (Spencer, Mass., 1971), pp. 79–86; on the Premonstratensians, see François Petit, *La Spiritualité des Prémontrés aux XIIe et XIIIe siècles* (Paris, 1947), pp. 220–33. On the practice of prayer for the dead in the new religious orders during the twelfth century, see J. Laurent, "La Prière pour les défunts et les obituaires dans l'ordre de Cîteaux," in *Mélanges Saint Bernard* (Dijon, 1954), pp. 383–96; McLaughlin, "Consorting with Saints," pp. 282–328. The full implications of this shift in the focus of religious life become apparent only in the later middle ages: see François Vandenbroucke, "Liturgie et piété personnelle: Les prodromes de leur tension à la fin du moyen âge," *La Maison-Dieu* 69 (1962), 56–66.

7. Hildeburge of Gallardon was active in the first two decades of the twelfth century;

Finally, subtle changes in the interpretation of prayer for the dead begin to appear in texts from the late eleventh and early twelfth century, especially in texts emanating from the intellectual centers of the period. In a collection of *sententiae* from the school of Laon, for example, we find a discussion of prayers and offerings made for the damned. The author of this collection juxtaposes two passages from Augustine's *Enchiridion*, one of which clearly states that prayer cannot help the damned, while the other is more ambiguous on the question. Highlighting the apparent contradiction, the author then resolves it by reinterpreting the language of the second passage. The result is an unequivocal rejection of the possibility that prayer might help the damned—a possibility that had long been accepted by at least some members of the literate elite, probably on the basis of the very text reinterpreted here.[8] As these and other related questions were debated in the schools, and as authoritative texts came to be read more critically, more and more of the meanings which had been associated with prayer for the dead in earlier centuries were discarded, laying the groundwork for the eventual triumph of Purgatory in the later middle ages.[9]

The changes that were beginning to transform early medieval society and, with it, the early medieval pattern of prayer for the dead are perhaps most visible around the year 1100 in population centers such as the courts of great princes and the bustling towns with their new schools. More isolated communities show fewer obvious signs of change. The Benedictine monks who served God and St. Foy at Conques, for example, continued to perform the elaborate liturgy that had developed over the course of the early middle ages, for that liturgy formed the center of their collective life and provided much of their prestige. Their new abbey church was designed to provide a suitable setting for the solemn round of collective prayer and for the jewel-encrusted reliquaries of the community's patron saints. Much of the wealth that made the building project possible was provided by

---

on her ties to religious communities see *Cartulaire de l'abbaye de Saint Martin de Pontoise*, no. 56 (no date).

    8. *Sententie Anselmi*, 3, ed. Franz P. Bliemetzrieder, in his *Anselms von Laon systematische Sentenzen* (Münster, 1919), pp. 85–86. On the school of Laon and its contributions to the development of twelfth-century theology, see Marcia Colish, "Another Look at the School of Laon," *Archives d'histoire doctrinale et littéraire du moyen âge* 53 (1986), 7–22.

    9. On the later development of theological views concerning prayer for the damned see Landgraf, *Dogmengeschichte der Frühscholastik*, 4: 2, pp. 265–320. On the triumph of Purgatory, see Le Goff, *La Naissance du Purgatoire*, pp. 319–479.

local benefactors, who hoped through close association with St. Foy
and her servants on earth to come safely through the last judgment
depicted so vividly above the western portal. Their gifts took traditional forms, were made in traditional ways, and were associated with
traditional liturgical return-gifts such as burial and formal association
into the early decades of the twelfth century.

Yet currents of social and cultural change were beginning to touch
even this isolated region around the year 1100. Certainly the rebirth
of the money economy and improved communications played a role
in the rebuilding of the abbey church, for if a large part of the necessary funds came from local donors, another important source was the
offerings of pilgrims, who flocked in ever larger numbers to the
shrine of St. Foy, bringing with them small coins and bits of news
from far away. Conques had become a station on the route to San-
tiago de Compostela, and the monks realized that their new church
would have to accommodate a constant stream of visitors as well as
provide a setting for the community's liturgy. Wisely, they brought
in architects who had worked on other churches along the road to
Compostela and the result was a building with its own distinctive
character, but very much in the "pilgrimage route" style.

Social and cultural change had given the servants of St. Foy the
resources they needed to create an appropriately sumptuous setting
for their elaborate round of liturgical prayer. Yet by the early twelfth
century those same developments were beginning to pose a threat to
the monks and their traditional occupations. For others besides pilgrims and itinerant craftsmen were traveling the roads of southern
France. Sometime in the 1120s word must have come to Conques of
two barefoot and bearded preachers who were proclaiming extremely
radical ideas to audiences of peasants and townspeople in the region.[10]
Just at the time when the new church at Conques was reaching com-
pletion, Henry of Lausanne and Peter of Bruys were calling for the
demolition of all churches—claiming that God could be worshiped
just as well in a stable as in a fine stone building. Just at the time when
the great tympanum with its depiction of St. Foy interceding for the
departed faithful was being erected, the two heresiarchs had already
announced that prayer was of no use to the dead. Their message had,

10. On the careers and teachings of Henry and Peter see Malcolm Lambert, *Medieval
Heresy: Popular Movements from Bogomil to Hus* (New York, 1976), pp. 49–54, and Robert
Ian Moore, *The Origins of European Dissent* (London, 1977), pp. 82–114. Conques had
property and dependent houses throughout the area where these two preachers were active.

admittedly, only limited effects. Certainly the monks of Conques continued to intercede for the dead as well as for the living, and those of the local laity who could afford it continued—for a time at least—to seek association in all their prayers and good works. Yet in this region as elsewhere, accelerated social and cultural change inevitably engendered new attitudes toward the ancient practice of prayer for the dead. Slowly the inhabitants of the narrow Dourdou valley, like the inhabitants of other, hitherto isolated communities throughout France, were being drawn into a new and wider world. And as that happened, their expectations for this present life and for the next could not fail to be transformed.

Liturgical Privileges
in Royal Acts, 768–1108

The figures that follow are based on an analysis of the extant acts of four kings: Charlemagne (768–814), Charles the Bald (840–77), Lothar (954–84), and Philip I (1060–1108).

Table 1 shows the percentage of royal acts that mention liturgical privileges of any kind. Most of the references to "prayer" in these acts have to do with prayers for ruler and realm, performed as a public service by the churches of the kingdom. I have distinguished between this kind of prayer and other services which a king chose to establish for himself and the members of his family. The number of churches at which each king sought these other privileges is indicated on the last line of this table.

The figures in Table 2 represent the percentage of transactions involving liturgical privileges which mention particular types of

Table 1. Percentage of royal acts mentioning liturgical privileges

	Charlemagne (N = 164)	Charles the Bald (N = 427)	Lothar (N = 56)	Philip I (N = 165)
All liturgical privileges	41	39	30	11
Prayers for ruler and realm	40	31	27	4
Other liturgical privileges	2	8	4	7
# Churches at which other liturgical privileges sought	2	20	2	9

Table 2. Preferred liturgical privileges, in percent

	Charlemagne (N = 68)	Charles the Bald (N = 165)	Lothar (N = 17)	Philip I (N = 19)
Prayer for ruler	96	80	88	39
Use of name/commem. in usual prayers	3	0	0	0
Lights	1	4	0	0
Daily/weekly special masses	1	1	0	6
Daily conventual psalmody	0	1	0	0
Annual service/refectio	0	15	0	17
Feed paupers	0	2	0	6
Association in prayers	0	1	0	11
"Special prayers"*	0	0	6	0
Unspecified "prayers"	0	1	0	22
Unspecified "memoria"	0	1	6	0

*"orationes speciales"

prayer. For example, 96 percent of the acts of Charlemagne that mention prayer at all mention prayer for ruler and realm. Since some acts mention more than one liturgical privilege, the totals are higher than 100 percent.

Grants of Liturgical Privileges by Five Religious Communities, 800–1099

The figures that follow are based on an analysis of the charters of five religious communities: the cathedral chapters of Angers (Maine-et-Loire) and Mâcon (Saône-et-Loire), and the monasteries of Conques (Aveyron), Redon (Ille-et-Vilaine), and Saint-Bertin (Pas-de-Calais). They were chosen because they were important communities, representing different forms of religious life and different regions of France, and because for each a more or less continuous series of records running from the early ninth to the end of the eleventh century has survived. The tables begin at the year 800 rather than 750 because I was unable to find five religious communities with a continuous series of records running from 750 to 1100.

The transactions counted here are those involving both the religious community and the outside world. I have excluded those transactions concerning only the community itself (e.g., a redistribution of property among members of a cathedral chapter), and those in which only outsiders and no members of the community itself were involved (e.g., the record of a sale of land, included in a monastic cartulary because the purchaser later gave the land to the community). Proven forgeries and charters which could not be dated even approximately have also been excluded.

Tables 3 through 10 include subtotals for cathedral chapters and for monasteries as well as totals for all five houses. I found that the same types of liturgical privileges were granted at cathedrals as at monasteries, so Table 11 provides a composite picture of practices at all five houses.

Tables 8, 9, and 10 represent the percentage of different kinds of transactions associated with crises such as an actual death or the threat of death.

The figures in Table 11 represent the percentage of transactions involving liturgical privileges (see Table 5) which mention particular types of prayer. For example, in the early ninth century, 72 percent of all transactions involving liturgical privileges mention prayer for ruler and realm. Since some acts mention more than one liturgical privilege, the totals for each period are higher than 100 percent.

All figures have been rounded off to the nearest hundredth.

Table 3. Total transactions

Date	800–49	850–99	900–49	950–99	1000–49	1050–99
Cathedral chapters	**19**	**30**	**84**	**106**	**124**	**76**
Angers	7	9	1	5	11	29
Mâcon	12	21	83	101	113	47
Monasteries	**95**	**190**	**57**	**73**	**196**	**221**
Conques	4	5	43	63	173	144
Redon	79	165	11	1	17	54
St-Bertin	12	20	3	9	6	23
TOTAL	114	220	141	179	320	297

Table 4. Total donations

Date	800–49	850–99	900–49	950–99	1000–49	1050–99
Cathedral chapters	**4**	**14**	**43**	**68**	**77**	**39**
Angers	0	2	1	1	6	13
Mâcon	4	12	42	67	71	26
Monasteries	**70**	**120**	**44**	**54**	**114**	**152**
Conques	2	5	33	47	98	114
Redon	62	107	8	1	14	30
St-Bertin	6	8	3	6	2	8
TOTAL	74	134	87	122	191	191

Table 5. Transactions involving liturgical privileges

Date	800–49	850–99	900–49	950–99	1000–49	1050–99
Cathedral chapters	**6**	**4**	**4**	**4**	**11**	**14**
Angers	4	0	0	0	4	6
Mâcon	2	4	4	4	7	8
Monasteries	**12**	**23**	**11**	**6**	**22**	**43**
Conques	2	0	8	2	12	20
Redon	6	13	1	1	9	19
St-Bertin	4	10	2	3	1	4
TOTAL	18	27	15	10	33	57

Table 6. Percentage of transactions involving liturgical privileges (N = see Table 3)

Date	800–49	850–99	900–49	950–99	1000–49	1050–99
Cathedral chapters	**32**	**13**	**5**	**4**	**9**	**18**
Angers	57	0	0	0	36	21
Mâcon	17	19	5	4	6	17
Monasteries	**13**	**12**	**19**	**8**	**11**	**19**
Conques	50	0	19	3	7	14
Redon	8	8	9	100	53	35
St-Bertin	33	50	67	33	17	17
TOTAL	16	12	11	6	10	19

Table 7. Percentage of donations involving liturgical privileges (N = see Table 4)

Date	800–49	850–99	900–49	950–99	1000–49	1050–99
Cathedral chapters	**0**	**21**	**9**	**3**	**9**	**28**
Angers	—	0	0	0	33	38
Mâcon	0	25	10	3	7	23
Monasteries	**11**	**13**	**25**	**9**	**17**	**22**
Conques	50	0	24	4	11	16
Redon	8	9	12	100	50	43
St-Bertin	33	75	67	33	50	25
TOTAL	11	14	17	6	14	23

Table 8. Percentage of transactions associated with crises (N = see Table 3)

Date	800–49	850–99	900–49	950–99	1000–49	1050–99
Cathedral chapters	**0**	**0**	**0**	**3**	**2**	**7**
Angers	0	0	0	20	0	10
Mâcon	0	0	0	2	2	4
Monasteries	**8**	**8**	**11**	**7**	**4**	**12**
Conques	0	20	7	6	2	7
Redon	8	8	9	0	24	31
St-Bertin	17	10	67	11	0	0
TOTAL	7	7	4	4	3	11

Table 9. Percentage of donations associated with crises (N = see Table 4)

Date	800–49	850–99	900–49	950–99	1000–49	1050–99
Cathedral chapters	**0**	**0**	**0**	**4**	**3**	**8**
Angers	—	0	0	100	0	8
Mâcon	0	0	0	3	3	8
Monasteries	**11**	**10**	**14**	**9**	**6**	**13**
Conques	0	20	9	9	3	7
Redon	10	9	12	0	29	40
St-Bertin	33	12	67	17	0	0
TOTAL	11	9	7	7	5	12

Table 10. Percentage of transactions involving liturgical privileges associated with crises (N = see Table 5)

Date	800–49	850–99	900–49	950–99	1000–49	1050–99
Cathedral chapters	**0**	**0**	—	**0**	**9**	**14**
Angers	0	—	—	—	0	17
Mâcon	0	0	—	0	14	12
Monasteries	**33**	**42**	**25**	**17**	**18**	**29**
Conques	0	—	0	0	25	14
Redon	50	57	100	0	11	53
St-Bertin	25	20	50	33	0	0
TOTAL	22	38	25	12	15	25

Table 11. Preferred liturgical privileges, in percent

Type	800–49	850–99	900–49	950–99	1000–49	1050–99
Prayer for ruler	72	15	0	10	0	0
Burial	17	33	20	40	48	39
Vestment ad suc.	11	11	7	0	9	19
Lights	6	15	73	10	0	0
Annual service/ refectio	0	26	33	20	6	4
Daily service	0	4	0	0	3	0
Unspecified "masses" or "psalms"	6	0	20	10	9	2
Unspecified "prayers"	0	11	0	0	21	11
Unspecified "memoria"	0	0	0	0	0	4
Unspecified re- fectiones	0	0	0	10	0	0
Confraternity between houses	0	4	0	0	9	2
Association in prayers	0	0	0	10	18	44
Prayers for health	0	19	0	0	0	0

WORKS CITED

Abbreviations for frequently cited sources and depositories are listed at the end of the acknowledgments section.

MANUSCRIPT SOURCES

Angers, Arch. Dép. de Maine-et-Loire, G. 785 (charters of Marmoutier)
   G. 562 (charters of Saint-Maurice)
Boulogne–sur–Mer, BM, Ms. 144 (Charters of Saint-Bertin)
   Ms. 146A (Cartulary of Saint-Bertin)
   Ms. 146B (Cartulary of Saint-Bertin)
Mâcon, Arch. Dép. de Saône-et-Loire, G. 198 (Cartulary of Saint-Vincent)
Paris, BN, Latin 818 (Sacramentary of Troyes)
   Latin 823 (Missal/Sacramentary of Remiremont)
   Latin 991 (Necrology of Saint-Jean-en-Vallée)
   Latin 2290 (Sacramentary of Saint-Denis)
   Latin 2291 (Sacramentary of Saint-Amand)
   Latin 2294 (Sacramentary of Paris)
   Latin 2298 (Missal of Saint-Gervais-de-Fos)
   Latin 5439 (Cartulary of Saint-Bertin)
   Latin 9434 (Missal/Sacramentary of Saint-Martin of Tours)
   Latin 17086 (Cartulary of Saint-Vincent of Mâcon)
   Latin 17306 (Missal/Sacramentary of Amiens)
   Français 22450 (Charters of Saint-Maurice of Angers)
   Collection de Bourgogne, 108, fols. 111–61 (Charters of Saint-Vincent of Mâcon)
   Collection Doat, 143 (Charters of Conques)

Rennes, Bibliothèque de l'Archevêché, Cartulary of Redon
Rodez, Arch. Dép. de l'Aveyron, 4. H.1 (Charters of Conques)
Rodez, Bibliothèque de la Société des Lettres, Sciences, et Arts de l'Aveyron, Cartulary of Conques

Printed Sources

Works in this section are listed under author's name, if there is one, or else by title. Chapter, page, or column numbers given parenthetically after a title in the notes refer to the edition cited here.

Abbo of Fleury. *Apologeticus ad Hugonem et Rodbertum reges Francorum.* PL 139: 461–72.
——. *Collectio canonum.* PL 139: 473–508.
Abbo of Saint-Germain. *Sermones.* PL 132: 763–778.
Acta sanctorum ordinis sancti Benedicti. Edited by Jean Mabillon and Luc d'Archery. 9 vols. Venice: Coletti and J. Bettinelli, 1733–38.
The Acts of the Christian Martyrs. Edited by Herbert Musurillo. Oxford Early Christian Texts. Oxford: Clarendon, 1972.
Actus pontificum Cenomannis in urbe degentium. Edited by G. Busson and A. Ledru. Archives historiques du Maine, vol. 2. Le Mans: Société Historique du Maine, 1901.
Ademar of Chabannes. *Chronicon.* Edited by Jules Chavanon. Collection de textes pour servir à l'étude et à l'enseignement de l'histoire. Paris: A. Picard, 1897.
Adrevald et al. *Miracula sancti Benedicti.* Edited by E. de Certain. La Société de l'histoire de France. Publications in 8°, vol. 96. Paris: J. Renouard, 1858.
Alcuin. *Epistolae.* PL 100: 139–512.
——. *De fide sanctae et individuae trinitatis libri tres.* PL 101: 11–58.
Pseudo-Alcuin. *De divinis officiis.* PL 101: 1173–1286.
Die Altarplatte von Reichenau-Niederzell. Edited by Dieter Geuenich, Renate Neumullers-Klauser, and Karl Schmid. MGH, LMN, n.s., vol. 1: Supplementum. Hanover: Hahn, 1983.
Amalar of Metz. *Opera liturgica omnia.* Edited by I. M. Hanssens. Studi e testi, vols. 138–40. 3 vols. Vatican City: Biblioteca Apostolica Vaticana, 1948–50.
Ambrose. *De excessu fratris sui Satyri.* PL 16: 1289–1354.
——. *De obitu Valentiniani consolatio.* PL 16: 1357–84.
Amolo of Lyon. *Epistolae.* Edited by Ernst Dümmler. MGH, EPP, 5: 363–78.
"Un Ancien Recueil de leçons pour les vigiles des défunts." Edited by Jean Leclercq. *Revue Bénédictine* 54 (1942), 16–40.
Annales Fuldenses. Edited by Georg H. Pertz; revised by Friedrich Kurze. SRG. Hanover: Hahn, 1891.
Augustine. *De civitate Dei.* Edited by Bernard Dombart and Alphonse Kalb.

Aurelii Augustini Opera, pars 14. CC, SL, vols. 47–48. 2 vols. Turnhout: Brepols, 1955.

———. *De cura pro mortuis gerenda.* Edited by Joseph Zycha. In *Opera, sectio 5, pars 3.* CSEL, vol. 41. Vienna: F. Tempsky, 1900.

———. *De natura et origine animae.* Edited by Carl Urba and Joseph Zycha. In *Opera, sectio 8, pars 1.* CSEL, vol. 60. Vienna: F. Tempsky; Leipzig: G. Freytag, 1913.

———. *Enchiridion ad Laurentium de fide et spe et caritate.* Edited by E. Evans. In *Aurelii Augustini Opera, pars 13.* CC, SL, vol. 46. Turnhout: Brepols, 1969.

———. *Quaestiones in Heptateuchum.* Edited by I. Fraipont. *Aurelii Augustini Opera, pars 5.* CC, SL, vol. 33. Turnhout: Brepols, 1958.

———. *Sermones.* PL 38–39.

Bede. *Historia ecclesiastica gentis anglorum.* Edited and translated by Bertram Colgrave and R. A. B. Mynors. Oxford Medieval Texts. Oxford: Clarendon, 1969.

———. *Homiliae.* PL 94: 9–268.

Benedict of Nursia. *Regula monachorum.* Edited by Adalbert de Vogüé. Translated (into French) by J. Neufville. Sources chrétiennes, vols. 181–86. 7 vols. Paris: Cerf, 1971–77.

Bernard of Angers. *Liber miraculorum sancte Fidis.* Edited by A. Bouillet. Collection de textes pour servir à l'étude et à l'enseignement de l'histoire. Paris: A. Picard, 1897.

Boniface and Lull. *Epistolae.* Edited by E. Dümmler. MGH, EPP, 3: 231–433.

Burchard of Worms. *Decretum.* PL 140: 537–1058.

Caesarius of Arles. *Sermones.* PL 67: 1041–90.

Candidus of Fulda. *Vita Eigilis Abbatis Fuldensis.* Edited by Georg Waitz. MGH, SS, 15: 222–33.

Die Canones Theodori Cantuariensis und ihre Uberlieferungsformen. Edited by Paul Finsterwalder. Untersuchungen zu den Bussbüchern des 7., 8., und 9. Jahrhunderts, vol. 1. Weimar: H. Böhlaus, 1929.

Capitularia regum Francorum. MGH, Leges, sect. 2, pts. 1–2. Vol. 1 edited by Alfred Boretius; vol. 2 edited by Alfred Boretius and Victor Kraus. Hanover: Hahn, 1883–97.

Cartulaire d'Aniane. Edited by Léon Cassan and Edmond Meynial. Vol. 2 of *Cartulaires des abbayes d'Aniane et de Gellone.* Société archéologique de Montpellier. Montpellier: Jean Martel Aîné, 1900.

Cartulaire de Gellone. Edited by Paul Alaus, Léon Cassan, and Edmond Meynial. Vol. 1 of *Cartulaires des abbayes d'Aniane et de Gellone.* Société archéologique de Montpellier. Montpellier: Jean Martel Aîné, 1898.

Cartulaire de l'abbaye cardinale de la Trinité de Vendôme. Edited by Charles Métais. Société archéologique du Vendômois. 5 vols. Paris: A. Picard, 1893–1904.

Cartulaire de l'abbaye de Beaulieu (en Limousin). Edited by J. E. M. Deloche. Collection de documents inédits sur l'histoire de France. Paris: Imprimerie Impériale, 1859.

Cartulaire de l'abbaye de la Chapelle-aux-Planches, chartes de Montiérender, de Saint-Étienne et de Toussaints de Châlons, d'Andecy, de Beaulieu, et de Rethel. Edited by Charles Lalore. Collection des principaux cartulaires du diocèse de Troyes, vol. 4. Paris: Thorin; Troyes: Léopold Lacroix, 1878.

Cartulaire de l'abbaye de Conques en Rouergue. Edited by Gustave Desjardins. Documents historiques publiés par la Société de l'École des Chartes. Paris: A. Picard, 1879.

Cartulaire de l'abbaye de Redon en Bretagne. Edited by Aurélien de Courson. Collection des documents inédits sur l'histoire de France. Paris: Imprimerie Impériale, 1863.

Cartulaire de l'abbaye de Saint-Bertin. Edited by Benjamin Guérard. Collection de documents inédits sur l'histoire de France. Paris: Crapelet, 1840.

Cartulaire de l'abbaye de Saint-Martin de Pontoise. Edited by Joseph Depoin. Pontoise: Société Historique du Vexin, 1895–1909.

Cartulaire de l'abbaye de Saint-Père de Chartres. Edited by Benjamin Guérard. Collection de documents inédits sur l'histoire de France. 2 vols. Paris: Crapelet, 1840.

Cartulaire de l'abbaye de la Sainte-Trinité du Mont de Rouen. Edited by Achille Deville. Collection de documents inédits sur l'histoire de France. Paris: Crapelet, 1840.

Cartulaire de l'abbaye de Saint-Victor de Marseille. Edited by Benjamin Guérard. Collection de documents inédits sur l'histoire de France. 2 vols. Paris: C. Lahure, 1857.

Cartulaire de l'abbaye de Saint-Vincent du Mans (ordre de Saint Benoît). Edited by R. Charles and S. Menjot d'Elbenne. Publications de la Société historique et archéologique du Maine. Mamers: Imprimerie Fleury; Le Mans: A. de Saint-Denis, 1886–1913.

Le Cartulaire de Marcigny-sur-Loire (1045–1144): Essai de reconstitution d'un manuscrit disparu. Edited by Jean Richard. Analecta Burgundica. Dijon: Bernigaud et Privat, 1957.

Cartulaire de Marmoutier pour le Dunois. Edited by Émile Mabille. Publications de la Société Dunois, vol. 22. Châteaudun: H. Lecesne, 1874.

Cartulaire de Montier-la-Celle. Edited by Charles Lalore. Collection des principaux cartulaires du diocèse de Troyes, vol. 6. Paris: Thorin; Troyes: Léopold Lacroix, 1882.

Cartulaire de Notre-Dame de Josaphat. Edited by Charles Métais. 2 vols. Chartres: Société Archéologique d'Eure-et-Loir, 1911–12.

Cartulaire de Saint-Victeur au Mans, prieuré de l'abbaye du Mont-Saint-Michel (994–1400). Edited by Paul de Farcy. Publications de la Société d'agriculture, sciences, et arts de la Sarthe. Paris: A. Picard, 1895.

Cartulaire de Saint-Vincent de Mâcon: Connu sous le nom de Livre Enchaîné. Edited by M.-C. Ragut. Collection des documents inédits sur l'histoire de France. Mâcon: Emile Protat, 1864.

Cartulaire de Sainte-Croix d'Orléans (814–1300). Edited by Joseph Thillier and Eugène Jarry. Orléans: Paul Pigelet, 1906.

Cartulaire du chapitre de l'église cathédrale Notre-Dame de Nîmes. Edited by Eugène Germer-Durand. Nîmes: A. Catélan, 1874.

Cartulaire général de l'Yonne: Recueil de documents authentiques pour servir à l'histoire des pays qui forment ce département. Edited by Maximilien Quantin. Publications de la Société des sciences historiques et naturelles de l'Yonne. 2 vols. Auxerre: Perriquet et Rouillé, 1854–60.

Cartulaire noir de la cathédrale d'Angers. Edited by Charles Urseau. Documents historiques sur l'Anjou publiés par la Société d'agriculture, sciences, et arts d'Angers, vol. 5. Angers: Germain & G. Grassin, 1908.

Cartulaires de l'abbaye de Molesme, ancien diocèse de Langres, 916–1250. Edited by Jacques Laurent. 2 vols. Paris: A. Picard, 1907–11.

Cartularium monasterii beatae Mariae caritatis Andegavensis vulgo dicti Le Ronceray. Edited by Paul Marchegay. Archives d'Anjou, vol. 2. Angers: Cosnier et Lachèse, 1854.

Cassiodorus. *De anima.* PL 70: 1279–1308.

Les Chartes de Saint-Bertin, d'après le grand cartulaire de Dom Charles-Joseph Dewitte. Edited by Daniel Haigneré. Société des antiquaires de la Morinie. 4 vols. Saint-Omer: H. D'Homont, 1886–99.

"Chartes mancelles de l'abbaye de Saint-Florent près Saumur, 848–1200." Edited by Paul Marchegay. *Revue historique et archéologique du Maine* 3 (1878), 347–70.

Chronicon Morigniacensis. Edited by Léon Mirot. Collection de textes pour servir à l'étude et à l'enseignement de l'histoire. Paris: A. Picard, 1912.

Collectio canonum in V libris. Edited by M. Fornasari. CC, CM, 6. Turnhout: Brepols, 1970.

Concilia aevi Karolini. Edited by Albert Werminghoff. MGH, Leges, sect. 3, pt. 2. 2 vols. Hanover: Hahn, 1906–08.

Concilia Africae, A. 345-A. 525. Edited by C. Munier. CC, SL, 149. Turnhout: Brepols, 1974.

Concilia Galliae, A. 314-A. 506. Edited by C. Munier. CC, SL, 148. Turnhout: Brepols, 1963.

Concilia Galliae, A. 511-A. 695. Edited by Carlo de Clercq. CC, SL, 148A. Turnhout: Brepols, 1963.

Consuetudinum saeculi X/XI/XII: Monumenta non-cluniacensia. Edited by Kassius Hallinger. Corpus consuetudinum monasticarum, vol. 7. 4 vols. Siegburg: F. Schmitt, 1984–86.

Cyprian. *Epistulae.* In *S. Thasci Caecili Cypriani opera omnia.* Edited by Wilhelm Hartel. CSEL, 3. 3 vols. Vienna: C. Gerold, 1868–71.

Cyril of Jerusalem. *Catéchèses mystagogiques.* Edited by Auguste Piédagnel. Translated into French by Pierre Paris. Sources chrétiennes, vol. 126. Paris: Cerf, 1966.

Dhuoda. *Liber manualis.* Edited by Pierre Riché. Translated into French by B. de Vregille and C. Mondésert. Sources chrétiennes, vol. 225. Paris: Cerf, 1975.

"Documents sur la mort des moines." Edited by Jean Leclercq. *Revue Mabillon* 45 (1955), 165–80; 46 (1956), 65–81.

Donatus. *Vita Trudonis confessoris Hasbaniensis.* Edited by Bruno Krusch and Wilhelm Levison. MGH, SRM, 6: 273–98.

"Le Droit de sépulture: Charte de l'an 1075." Edited by Paul Marchegay. *Bibliothèque de l'École de Chartes.* 3d ser., 5 (1854), 528–31.

The Earliest Life of Gregory the Great by an Anonymous Monk of Whitby. Edited and translated by Bertram Colgrave. Lawrence: University of Kansas Press, 1968.

Einhard. *Vita Karoli Magni.* Edited by G. Pertz and G. Waitz. SRG. 5th ed. Hanover: Hahn, 1905.

Eligius of Noyon. *Homiliae.* PL 87: 593–654.

Flodoard. *Historia Remensis ecclesiae.* Edited by M. Lejeune. *Oeuvres de Flodoard,* vols. 1–2. Publications de l'Académie impériale de Reims. 2 vols. Reims: P. Regnier, 1854.

Florus of Lyons. *De expositione missae.* PL 119: 15–72.

Fredegar. *Chronicorum liber quartus cum continuationibus.* Edited by J. M. Wallace-Hadrill. London: Thomas Nelson and Sons, 1960.

Gerard of Cambrai. *Acta synodi Atrebatensis in Manichaeos.* PL 142: 1269–1312.

Gerbert (Sylvester II). *Epistolae.* Edited by Jules Havet. Collection de textes pour servir à l'étude et à l'enseignement de l'histoire. Paris: A. Picard, 1889.

Gesta Dagoberti I. regis Francorum. Edited by Bruno Krusch. MGH, SRM, 2: 401–25.

Gregory of Tours. *De gloria confessorum.* PL 71: 827–910.

———. *Historia Francorum.* PL 71: 159–572.

———. *Vitae patrum.* PL 71: 1009–1096.

Gregory the Great (Pope). *Dialogi.* Edited by Umberto Moricca. Fonti per la storia d'Italia, pubblicate dall'Istituto Storico Italiano, vol. 57. Rome: Tipografia del Senato, 1924.

Guibert of Nogent. *Monodiae de vita sua.* Edited by Georges Bourgin. Collection de textes pour servir à l'étude et à l'enseignement de l'histoire. Paris: A. Picard, 1907.

Haimo. *De varietate librorum.* PL 118: 875–958.

Haimo of Halberstadt. *Homiliae.* PL 118: 11–816.

Halitgar of Cambrai. *Liber poenitentialis (De vitiis et virtutibus et de ordine poenitentium).* PL 105: 651–710.

Hariulf. *Chronicon Centulense.* Edited by Ferdinand Lot. Collection de textes pour servir à l'étude et à l'enseignement de l'histoire. Paris: A. Picard, 1894.

Heito of Basel. *Visio Wettini.* Edited by Ernst Dümmler. MGH, PP, 2: 267–75.

Helgaud of Fleury. *Epitoma vitae regis Roberti pii.* Edited by Robert-Henri Bautier and Gillette Labory. Sources d'histoire médiévale, vol. 1. Paris: Centre National de la Recherche Scientifique, 1965.

Hildefonse of Toledo. *Liber de cognitione baptismi.* PL 96: 111–72.

Hincmar of Reims. *Capitula synodica.* PL 125: 773–804.

———. *De cavendis vitiis et virtutibus exercendis.* PL 125: 857–930.

———. *De ecclesiis et capellis.* In "Zwei Schriften der Erzbischofs Hinkmar von Reims." Edited by Wilhelm Gundlach. *Zeitschrift für Kirchengeschichte* 10 (1889), 92–145, 258–310.

——. *De visione Bernoldi presbyteri.* PL 125: 1115–1120.

Hrabanus Maurus. *Enarrationes in epistolas beati Pauli.* PL 111: 1273–1616 and PL 112: 9–834.

——. *Homiliae.* PL 110: 9–468.

Initia consuetudinis benedictinae: Consuetudines saeculi octavi et noni. Edited by Kassius Hallinger. Corpus consuetudinum monasticarum, vol. 1. Siegburg: F. Schmitt, 1963.

Inscriptiones latinae christianae veteres. Edited by Ernst Diehl. 3 vols. Berlin: Weidmann, 1924–31.

Isidore of Seville. *De ecclesiasticis officiis.* PL 83: 737–826.

——. *De ordine creaturarum.* PL 83: 913–54.

——. *Sententiae.* PL 83: 537–738.

Pseudo-Isidore. *Regula monachorum.* PL 103: 555–72.

Ivo of Chartres. *Decretum.* PL 161: 47–1022.

John. *Vita sancti Odonis abbatis Cluniacensis.* PL 133: 43–86.

John VIII (Pope). *Epistolae et decreta.* PL 126: 651–966.

John Chrysostom. *In Epistola ad Philippenses, I: Homiliae.* PG 62: 181–212.

John of Avranches. *De officiis ecclesiasticis.* PL 147: 27–62.

John the Deacon. *Sancti Gregorii Magni vita.* PL 75: 59–242.

John the Scot. *De divisione naturae.* PL 122: 441–1022.

Jonas of Orléans. *De institutione laicali.* PL 106: 121–278.

Jotsald. *De vita et virtutibus sancti Odilonis abbatis.* PL 142: 897–940.

Julian of Toledo. *Opera, pars 1.* Edited by J. N. Hillgarth. CC, SL, 115. Turnhout: Brepols, 1976.

Julian Pomerius. *De vita contemplativa.* PL 59: 415–520.

Lanfranc. *Decreta monachis Cantuariensibus transmissa.* Edited by David Knowles. Corpus consuetudinum monasticarum, vol. 3. Siegburg: F. Schmitt, 1967.

——. *In omnes Pauli epistolas commentarii cum glossula interjecta.* PL 150: 101–406.

Leo I (Pope). *Epistolae.* PL 54: 593–1218.

Leo Marsicanus et al. *Chronica monasterii Casinensis.* Edited by Hartmut Hoffman. MGH, SS, 34.

Liber Memorialis von Remiremont. Edited by Eduard Hlawitschka, Karl Schmid, and Gerd Tellenbach. MGH, LM, vol. 1. Zurich: Weidmann, 1970.

Liber sacramentorum Augustodunensis. Edited by O. Heiming. CC, SL, 159B. Turnhout: Brepols, 1984.

Liber sacramentorum Gellonensis. Edited by Antoine Dumas. CC, SL, 159. Turnhout: Brepols, 1981.

Liber tramitis aevi Odilonis abbatis. Edited by Peter Dinter. Corpus consuetudinum monasticarum, 10. Siegburg: F. Schmitt, 1980.

Der Liber vitae der Abtei Corvey. Edited by Karl Schmid and Joachim Wollasch. Veröffentlichungen der historischen Kommission für Westfalen, vol. 40, part 2. 2 vols. Wiesbaden: Dr. Ludwig Reichert, 1983–89.

Libri confraternitatum sancti Galli, Augiensis, Fabariensis. Edited by Paul Piper. MGH, LC, vol. 1. Berlin: Weidmann, 1884.

Mansi, Giovanni Domenico, ed. *Sacrorum conciliorum nova et amplissima collectio.* 31 vols. Florence: A. Zatta, 1759–98.

Un Manuscrit chartrain du XIe siècle. Edited by René Merlet and M. Clerval. Chartres: Garnier, 1893.

Marmoutier: Cartulaire blésois. Edited by Charles Métais. Blois: E. Moreau, 1889–91.

Das Martyrolog-Necrolog von St. Emmeram zu Regensburg. Edited by Eckhard Freise, Dieter Geuenich, and Joachim Wollasch. MGH, LMN, n.s., vol. 3. Hanover: Hahn, 1986.

Maximus of Turin. *Homiliae.* PL 57: 221–530.

Mémoires pour servir de preuves à l'histoire ecclésiastique et civile de Bretagne. Edited by Hyacinthe Morice. 3 vols. Paris: Charles Osmont, 1742–46.

The Monks of Redon: "Gesta Sanctorum Rotonensium" and "Vita Conuuoionis". Edited and translated by Caroline Brett. Studies in Celtic History, edited by David Dumville, vol. 10. Woodbridge, Eng.: The Boydell Press, 1989.

Les Obituaires de la province de Sens. Edited by Auguste Molinier and Auguste Longnon. Recueil des historiens de la France, Obituaires, vols. 1–2. 3 vols. Paris: Imprimerie Nationale, 1902–6.

Odorannus of Sens. *Opera omnia.* Edited and translated into French by Robert-Henri Bautier and Monique Gilles. Sources d'histoire médiévale, vol. 4. Paris: Centre National de la Recherche Scientifique, 1972.

"Un Office monastique pour le 2 novembre." Edited by André Wilmart and L. Brou. *Sacris Erudiri* 5 (1953), 247–330.

Orderic Vitalis. *Historia aecclesiastica.* Edited and translated by Marjorie Chibnall. Oxford Medieval Texts. 6 vols. Oxford: Clarendon, 1969–80.

Pseudo-Origen. *In Job commentarius.* PG 17: 371–522.

Osbern. *Vita Sancti Dunstani.* In *Memorials of Saint Dunstan, Archbishop of Canterbury.* Edited by William Stubbs. Chronicles and Memorials of Great Britain and Ireland during the Middle Ages, vol. 63. London: Longman, 1874.

Otholo of St. Emmeram. *Liber visionum.* PL 146: 341–88.

Pascal II (Pope). *Epistolae et privilegia.* PL 163: 31–444.

Paul the Deacon. *Historia Langobardorum.* Edited by Georg Waitz. SRG. Hanover: Hahn, 1878.

———. *Sancti Gregorii Magni vita.* PL 75: 41–60.

Paulinus. *Vita sancti Ambrosii.* PL 14: 27–46.

Peter Chrysologus. *Sermones.* PL 52: 183–666.

Peter Damian. *Epistolae.* In *Die Briefe des Petrus Damiani.* Edited by Kurt Reindel. MGH, Die Briefe der deutschen Kaiserzeit, vol. 4. 3 vols. to date. Munich: Monumenta Germaniae Historica, 1983–.

———. *The Letters of Peter Damian, 1–30.* Translated by Owen J. Blum. The Fathers of the Church, Mediaeval Continuation, vol. 1. Washington, D.C.: Catholic University of America Press, 1989.

———. *Sermones.* PL 144: 505–924.

———. *De variis miraculosis narrationibus (opusculum 34).* PL 145: 571–90.

———. *Vita sancti Odilonis.* PL 144: 925–44.

Pippini, Carlomanni, Caroli Magni diplomata. Edited by Engelbert Mühlbacher, with Alfons Dopsch, Johann Lechner, and Michael Tangl. MGH, Diplomata karolinorum, vol. 1. Hanover: Hahn, 1906.

Raoul Glaber. *Historiae.* Edited by Maurice Prou. Collection de textes pour servir à l'étude et à l'enseignement de l'histoire. Paris: A. Picard, 1886.

Ratherius of Verona. *Sermones.* PL 136: 689–758.

Recueil des actes de Charles II, le Chauve, roi de France. Edited by Georges Tessier, following Arthur Giry and Maurice Prou. Chartes et diplômes relatifs à l'histoire de France, vols. 8–10. 3 vols. Paris: Imprimerie Nationale, 1943–55.

Recueil des actes de Charles III, le Simple, roi de France (893–923). Edited by Philippe Lauer. Chartes et diplômes relatifs à l'histoire de France, vol. 9. Paris: Imprimerie Nationale, 1949.

Recueil des actes de Lothaire et de Louis V, rois de France (954–987). Edited by Louis Halphen and Ferdinand Lot. Chartes et diplômes relatifs à l'histoire de France, vols. 2–3. Paris: Imprimerie Nationale, 1908.

Recueil des actes de Philippe Ier, roi de France (1059–1108). Edited by Maurice Prou. Chartes et diplômes relatifs à l'histoire de France, vol. 1. Paris: Imprimerie Nationale, 1908.

Recueil des chartes de l'abbaye de Cluny. Edited by Auguste Bernard and Alexandre Bruel. Collection de documents inédits sur l'histoire de France. 6 vols. Paris: Imprimerie Nationale, 1876–1903.

Recueil des chartes de l'abbaye de Saint-Benoît-sur-Loire. Edited by Maurice Prou and Alexandre Vidier. Documents publiés par la Société historique et archéologique du Gatinais, vols. 5–6. 2 vols. Paris: A. Picard, 1907–32.

Recueil des chartes de l'abbaye de Saint-Germain-des-Prés, des origines au début du XIIIe siècle. Edited by René Poupardin. La Société de l'histoire de Paris et de l'Ile-de-France, Documents, vol. 15. 2 vols. Paris: Champion, 1909–30.

Regesta pontificum Romanorum ab condita ecclesia ad annum post Christum natum MCXCVIII. Edited by Philipp Jaffé. 2d ed. by S. Löwenfeld, F. Kaltenbrunner, and P. Ewald. 2 vols. Leipzig: Veit, 1885–86.

Regino of Prüm. *De ecclesiasticis disciplinis.* PL 132: 187–370.

"Le Règlement ecclésiastique de Berne." Edited by André Wilmart. *Revue Bénédictine* 51 (1939), 37–52.

Richer. *Historiae.* Edited by Georg Waitz. SRG. 2d ed. Hanover: Hahn, 1877.

Riculf of Soissons. *Statuta.* PL 131: 15–24.

Rouleaux des morts du IXe au XVe siècle. Edited by Léopold Delisle. Société de l'histoire de France. Publications in 8°, vol. 135. Paris: J. Renouard, 1866.

Rudolf. *Vita Petri venerabilis.* PL 189: 15–28.

Le Sacramentaire grégorien: Ses principales formes d'après les plus anciens manuscrits. Edited by Jean Deshusses. Spicilegium Friburgense, 16, 24, 28. 3 vols. Fribourg: Éditions Universitaires, 1971–82.

Sacramentarium Veronese (Cod. Bibl. Capit. Veron. LXXXV [80]). 2d ed. Edited by Leo Cunibert Mohlberg with Leo Eizenhöfer and Petrus Siffrin. Rerum ecclesiasticarum documenta, series maior: fontes, vol. 1. Rome: Herder, 1966.

Sententie Anselmi. Edited by Franz P. Bliemetzrieder, in his *Anselms von Laon systematische Sentenzen.* Beiträge zur Geschichte der Philosophie des Mittelalters, Texte und Untersuchungen, vol. 18: 2–3. Münster: Aschendorff, 1919.

Statutum "S. Odilonis" de defunctis. PL 142: 1037–38.

Suger. *Vita Ludovici grossi regis.* Edited by Henri Waquet. Les Classiques de l'histoire de France au moyen âge, vol. 11. Paris: Les Belles Lettres, 1929.

Synopse der cluniacensischen Necrologien. Edited by Joachim Wollasch, with Wolf Dieter Heim et al. Münstersche Mittelalter-Schriften, vol. 39. 2 vols. Munich: Wilhelm Fink, 1982.

Taio of Saragossa. *Sententiae.* PL 80: 727–990.

Tertullian. *Opera.* CC, SL, 1–2. 2 vols. Turnhout: Brepols, 1954.

Theodulf of Orleans. *Capitula ad presbyteros parochiae suae.* PL 105: 191–208.

Thietmar of Merseburg. *Chronicon.* Edited by Robert Holtzmann. SRG, n.s. Berlin: Weidmann, 1955.

Die Totenbücher von Merseburg, Magdeburg, und Luneburg. Edited by Gerd Althoff and Joachim Wollasch. MGH, LMN, n.s., vol. 2. Hanover: Hahn, 1983.

Ulric of Cluny. *Consuetudines Cluniacenses.* PL 149: 643–778.

Utrum animae de humanis corporibus exeuntes mox deducantur ad gloriam vel ad poenam. PL 96: 1379–1386.

Das Verbrüderungsbuch der Abtei Reichenau (Einleitung, Register, Faksimile). Edited by Johanne Autenrieth, Dieter Geuenich, and Karl Schmid. MGH, LMN, n.s., vol. 1. Hanover: Hahn, 1979.

Vetera analecta sive collectio veterum aliquot operum et opusculorum omnis generis. . . . Edited by Jean Mabillon. Paris: Montalant, 1723.

Vetus disciplina monastica. Edited by Marquard Herrgott. Paris, 1726.

Visio Baronti monachi Longoretensis. Edited by Bruno Krusch and Wilhelm Levison. MGH, SRM, 5: 377–94.

Visio cuiusdam pauperculae mulieris. Edited by Heinz Löwe, in his *Deutschlands Geschichtsquellen im Mittelalter: Vorzeit und Karolinger, Vol. 3: Die Karolinger vom Tode Karls des Grossen bis zum Vertrag von Verdun.* Weimar: Hermann Böhlaus Nachfolger, 1957.

Vita Austrebertae virginis. AA. SS., Feb. 2: 419–27.

Vita Odiliae abbatissae Hohenburgensis. Edited by Bruno Krusch and Wilhelm Levison. MGH SRM, 6: 37–50.

Vita Remberti archiepiscopi Hamburgensis. AA. SS. Feb. 1: 559–66.

Vita Sancti Amati confessoris. Edited by Bruno Krusch. MGH, SRM, 4: 215–21.

Vita Vedastis episcopi Atrebatensis. Edited by Bruno Krusch. MGH, SRM, 3: 406–25.

Walahfrid Strabo. *Visio Wettini.* Edited by Ernst Dümmler. MGH, PP, 2: 301–333.

Walahfrid Strabo's Visio Wettini: Text, Translation, and Commentary. Edited and translated into English by David A. Traill. Lateinische Sprache und Literatur des Mittelalters, edited by Alf Önnerfors, vol. 2. Bern: Herbert Lang; Frankfurt: Peter Lang, 1974.

Walahfrid Strabo. *Vita Sancti Galli abbatis.* PL 114: 975–1030.

Widukind. *Rerum gestarum saxonicarum libri tres.* Edited by Georg Waitz and Karl Kehr. SRG. 4th ed. Hanover: Hahn, 1904.

William of Hirsau. *Constitutiones Hirsaugienses.* PL 150: 927–1146.

SECONDARY WORKS

Anthologies appear in this section under the editor's name or under the title when there is no editor. There are no separate entries for articles from these anthologies. Journal articles are listed under the author's name.

Althoff, Gerd. *Adels- und Königsfamilien im Spiegel ihrer Memorialüberlieferung: Studien zum Totengedenken der Billunger und Ottonen.* Münstersche Mittelalter-Schriften, vol. 47. Munich: Wilhelm Fink, 1984.

——. *Amicitiae und Pacta: Bündnis, Einung, Politik und Gebetsgedenken im beginnenden 10. Jahrhundert.* Schriften der Monumenta Germaniae Historica, vol. 37. Hanover: Hahn, 1992.

——. *Verwandte, Freunde und Getreue: Zum politischen Stellenwert der Gruppenbindungen im früheren Mittelalter.* Darmstadt: Wissenschaftliche Buchgesellschaft, 1990.

Althoff, Gerd, et al., eds. *Person und Gemeinschaft im Mittelalter: Karl Schmid zum fünfundsechzigsten Geburtstag.* Sigmaringen: Jan Thorbecke, 1988.

Amann, Émile. *L'Époque carolingienne.* Histoire de l'Église depuis les origines jusqu'à nos jours, edited by Augustin Fliche and Victor Martin, vol. 6. Paris: Bloud & Gay, 1937.

Amann, Émile, and Auguste Dumas. *L'Église au pouvoir des laïques (888–1057).* Histoire de l'Église depuis les origines jusqu'à nos jours, edited by Augustin Fliche and Victor Martin, vol. 7. Paris: Bloud & Gay, 1940.

Andrieu, Michel. *Immixtio et consecratio: La consécration par contact dans les documents liturgiques du moyen âge.* Université de Strasbourg, Bibliothèque de l'Institut de droit canonique, vol. 2. Paris: A. Picard, 1924.

——. "L'Insertion du 'Memento' des morts au canon romain de la messe." *Revue des sciences religieuses* 1 (1921), 151–54.

Angenendt, Arnold. "Missa specialis: Zugleich ein Beitrag zur Entstehung der Privatmessen." *FS* 17 (1983), 153–221.

Ariès, Philippe. *L'Homme devant la mort.* L'Univers historique. Paris: Seuil, 1977. Translated by Helen Weaver as *The Hour of Our Death.* New York: Knopf, 1981.

——. "Le Purgatoire et la cosmologie de l'au-delà." *Annales: Économies, sociétés, civilisations* 38: 1 (1983), 151–57.

——. *Western Attitudes toward Death from the Middle Ages to the Present.* Translated by Patricia M. Ranum. The Johns Hopkins Symposia in Comparative History. Baltimore: The Johns Hopkins University Press, 1974.

Atti del IX congresso internazionale di archeologia cristiana (Roma, 21–27 settembre, 1975). Studi di antichità cristiana, vol. 32. 2 vols. Rome: Pontificio Istituto de Archeologia Cristiana, 1978.

Atwell, R. R. "From Augustine to Gregory the Great: An Evaluation of the Emergence of the Doctrine of Purgatory." *Journal of Ecclesiastical History* 38 (1987), 173–86.

Aubrun, Michel. *L'Ancien Diocèse de Limoges des origines au milieu du XIe siècle.* Publications de l'Institut d'études du Massif Central, vol. 21. Clermont-Ferrand: Institut d'Études du Massif Central, 1981.

———. "Caractères et portée religieuse et sociale des 'visiones' en Occident du VIe au XIe siècle." *Cahiers du civilisation médiévale* 23 (1980), 109–30.

———. *La Paroisse en France, des origines au XVe siècle.* Paris: Picard, 1986.

Avril, Joseph. "Observance monastique et spiritualité dans les préambules des actes (Xe–XIIIe s.)." *Revue d'histoire ecclésiastique* 85 (1990), 5–29.

Baker, Derek, ed. *The Church in Town and Countryside.* Studies in Church History, vol. 16. Oxford: Blackwell, 1979.

———, ed. *The Materials, Sources, and Methods of Ecclesiastical History.* Studies in Church History, vol. 11. Oxford: Blackwell, 1975.

Benoît, Fernand. *Les Cimetières suburbains d'Arles dans l'antiquité chrétienne et au moyen âge.* Studi di antichità cristiana, vol. 11. Rome: Pontificio Istituto di Archeologia Cristiana, 1935.

Berger, Rupert. *Die Wendung "offerre pro" in der römischen Liturgie.* Liturgiewissenschaftliche Quellen und Forschungen, vol. 41. Münster: Aschendorff, 1964.

Bernard, Antoine. *La Sépulture en droit canonique du Décret de Gratien au Concile de Trente.* Paris: Domat-Montchrestien, 1933.

Bernard, P. "Communion des saints (son aspect dogmatique et historique)." *DTC* 3: 429–54.

Bernstein, Alan E. Review of *La Naissance du Purgatoire,* by Jacques Le Goff. *Speculum* 59 (1984), 179–83.

Biehl, Ludwig. *Das liturgische Gebet für Kaiser und Reich: Ein Beitrag zur Geschichte des Verhältnisses von Kirche und Staat.* Görres-Gesellschaft zur Pflege des Wissenschaft im katholischen Deutschland: Veröffentlichungen der Sektion für Rechts- und Staatswissenschaft, vol. 75. Paderborn: Ferdinand Schöningh, 1937.

Bienvenu, Jean-Marc. "Les Conflits de sépulture en Anjou aux XIe et XIIe siècles." *Bulletin philologique et historique* (1966), 673–85.

Bishop, Edmund. *Liturgica Historica: Papers on the Liturgy and Religious Life of the Western Church.* Oxford: Clarendon, 1918.

Bloch, Marc. *Feudal Society.* Translated by L. A. Manyon. 2 vols. Chicago: University of Chicago Press, 1961.

Boase, Thomas Sherrer Ross. *Death in the Middle Ages: Mortality, Judgment, and Remembrance.* Library of Medieval Civilization. New York: McGraw-Hill, 1972.

Bonne, Jean-Claude. *L'Art roman de face et de profil: Le tympan de Conques.* Féodalisme. Paris: Le Sycomore,1984.

Borderie, Arthur de la. "La Chronologie du cartulaire de Redon." *Annales de Bretagne* 5 (1889–90), 535–630; 12 (1896–97), 473–522; 13 (1897–98), 11–42, 263–79, 430–58, 590–611.

Borgolte, Michael. "Freigelassene im Dienst der *Memoria." FS* 17 (1983), 234–50.

Borgolte, Michael, Dieter Geuenich, and Karl Schmid, eds. *Materialien und Untersuchungen zu den Verbrüderungsbüchern und zu den älteren Urkunden des Stiftsarchivs St. Gallen.* Subsidia Sangallensia, vol. 1. St. Gall: Kommissionsverlag am Rosslitor, 1986.

Bornscheur, Lothar. *Miseriae Regum: Untersuchungen zum Krisen- und Todesgedanken in den herrschaftstheologischen Vorstellungen der ottonisch-salischen Zeit.* Institut für Frühmittelalterforschung der Universität Münster, Arbeiten zur Frühmittelalterforschung, edited by Karl Hauck, vol. 4. Berlin: Walter de Gruyter, 1968.

Bosl, Karl. *Frühformen der Gesellschaft im mittelalterlichen Europa: Ausgewählte Beiträge zu einer Strukturanalyse der mittelalterlichen Welt.* Munich: R. Oldenbourg, 1964.

Bouchard, Constance Brittain. *Sword, Miter, and Cloister: Nobility and the Church in Burgundy, 980–1198.* Ithaca: Cornell University Press, 1987.

Bougerol, Jacques Guy. "Autour de *La Naissance du Purgatoire." Archives d'histoire doctrinale et littéraire du moyen âge* 50 (1983), 7–59.

Braet, Herman, and Herman Verbeke, eds. *Death in the Middle Ages.* Mediaevalia Lovaniensia, Studia, vol. 9. Louvain: Louvain University Press, 1983.

Braunfels, Wolfgang, ed. *Karl der Grosse: Lebenswerk und Nachleben.* 5 vols. Düsseldorf: L. Schwann, 1965–68.

Bredero, Adriaan H. "Le Moyen Age et le Purgatoire." *Revue d'histoire ecclésiastique* 78 (1983), 429–52.

Brown, Elizabeth A. R. "Death and the Human Body in the Later Middle Ages: The Legislation of Boniface VIII on the Division of the Corpse." *Viator* 12 (1981), 221–70.

Brown, Peter. *Augustine of Hippo: A Biography.* Berkeley and Los Angeles: University of California Press, 1967.

——. *The Cult of the Saints: Its Rise and Function in Latin Christianity.* Chicago: University of Chicago Press, 1981.

——. "Society and the Supernatural: A Medieval Change." *Daedalus* 104: 2 (Spring, 1975), 133–51.

——. *The World of Late Antiquity, A. D. 150–750.* History of European Civilization Library. New York: Harcourt Brace Jovanovich, 1971.

Bruyne, L. de. "Refrigerium Interim." *Rivista di archeologia cristiana* 34 (1958), 87–118.

Cabassut, A. "La Mitigation des peines de l'enfer d'après les livres liturgiques." *Revue d'histoire ecclésiastique* 23 (1927), 65–70.

Callewaert, Camillus. *Sacris erudiri: fragmenta liturgica collecta a monachis Sancti Petri de Aldenburgo in Steenbrugge ne pereant.* Steenbrugge: Abbey of St. Peter; The Hague: Martinus Nijhoff, 1940.

Chaume, Maurice. "La Mode de constitution et de délimitation des paroisses rurales aux temps mérovingiens et carolingiens." *Revue Mabillon* 27 (1937), 61–73; 28 (1938), 1–9.

Chavasse, Antoine. *Le Sacramentaire gélasien (Vaticanus Reginensis 316): Sacramentaire presbytéral en usage dans les titres romains au VIIe siècle.* Bibliothèque de théologie, 4th ser., Histoire de la théologie, vol. 1. Paris: Desclée, 1958.

Chélini, Jean. *L'Aube du moyen âge: Naissance de la chrétienté occidentale. La vie religieuse des laïcs dans l'Europe carolingienne (750–900).* Paris: Picard, 1991.

——. "La Pratique dominicale des laïcs dans l'église franque sous le règne de Pepin." *Revue d'histoire de l'église de France* 42 (1956), 161–74.

Chiffoleau, Jacques. *La Comptabilité de l'au-delà: Les hommes, la mort, et la religion dans la région d'Avignon à la fin du moyen âge (vers 1320–vers 1480).* Collection de l'École française de Rome, vol. 47. Rome: École Française de Rome, 1980.

Chitty, Derwas. *The Desert a City: An Introduction to the Study of Egyptian and Palestinian Monasticism under the Christian Empire.* Oxford: Blackwell, 1966.

Clanchy, Michael T. *From Memory to Written Record: England, 1066–1307.* Cambridge: Harvard University Press, 1979.

Clerck, Paul de. *La "Prière universelle" dans les liturgies latines anciennes: Témoignages patristiques et textes liturgiques.* Liturgiewissenschaftliche Quellen und Forschungen, vol. 62. Münster: Aschendorff, 1977.

Cohn, Norman. *The Pursuit of the Millennium: Revolutionary Millenarians and Mystical Anarchists of the Middle Ages.* Rev. ed. New York: Oxford University Press, 1970.

Colish, Marcia L. "Another Look at the School of Laon." *Archives d'histoire doctrinale et littéraire du moyen âge* 53 (1986), 7–22.

Collins, Mary, and David Power. *Can We Always Celebrate the Eucharist?* Concilium, vol. 152. Edinburgh: T. & T. Clark; New York: Seabury Press, 1982.

Congar, Yves. *L'Ecclésiologie du haut moyen âge, de saint Grégoire le Grand à la désunion entre Byzance et Rome.* Paris: Cerf, 1968.

Constable, Giles. *Monastic Tithes, from Their Origins to the Twelfth Century.* Cambridge Studies in Medieval Life and Thought, n.s., vol. 10. Cambridge: Cambridge University Press, 1964.

——. "Resistance to Tithes in the Middle Ages." *Journal of Ecclesiastical History* 13 (1962), 172–85.

Cowdrey, Herbert Edward John. *The Cluniacs and the Gregorian Reform.* Oxford: Clarendon, 1970.

——. "Unions and Confraternity with Cluny." *Journal of Ecclesiastical History* 16 (1965), 152–62.

Cristianizzazione ed organizzazione ecclesiastica delle campagne nell'alto medioevo: Espansione e resistenze. Settimane di Studio del Centro Italiano di Studi sull'alto Medioevo, vol. 28. 2 vols. Spoleto: Presso la Sede del Centro, 1982.

Crocker, Richard L. "The Early Frankish Sequence: A New Musical Form." *Viator* 6 (1975), 341–49.

Curtius, Ernst Robert. *European Literature and the Latin Middle Ages.* Translated by Willard R. Trask. London: Routledge & Kegan Paul, 1953.

Daniélou, Jean. *The Origins of Latin Christianity.* Edited by John A. Baker. Translated by David Smith and John A. Baker. Vol. 3 of *A History of Early Christian Doctrine before the Council of Nicea.* Philadelphia: Westminster Press, 1977.

Davies, Wendy. *Small Worlds: The Village Community in Early Medieval Brittany.* London: Gerald Duckworth, 1988.

Dekkers, Eloi. "Les Anciens Moines cultivaient-ils la liturgie?" *La Maison-Dieu* 51 (1957), 31–54.

Delaruelle, Étienne. "La Gaule chrétienne à l'époque franque." *Revue d'histoire de l'église de France* 38 (1952), 64–72.

Delisle, Léopold. "Des monuments paléographiques concernent l'usage de prier pour les morts." *Bibliothèque de l'École des Chartes,* 2d ser., 3 (1846), 361–411.

Devailly, Guy. "Les Documents antérieurs au XIIe siècle conservés aux Archives Départementales d'Ille-et-Vilaine." *Bulletin et mémoire de la Société archéologique du département d'Ille-et-Vilaine* 30 (1978), 1–15.

———. "La Pastorale en Gaule au IXe siècle." *Revue d'histoire de l'église de France* 59 (1973), 23–54.

Devisse, Jean. *Hincmar: Archevêque de Reims 845–882.* Travaux d'histoire ethico-politique, vol. 29. 3 vols. Geneva: Droz, 1975–76.

Dierkens, Alain. *Abbayes et chapitres entre Sambre et Meuse (VIIe–XIe siècles): Contribution à l'histoire religieuse des campagnes du haut moyen âge.* Beihefte der Francia, vol 14. Sigmaringen: Jan Thorbecke, 1985.

Dillay, Madelaine. "Le Régime de l'église privée du XIe au XIIIe siècle dans l'Anjou, le Maine, la Touraine: Les restitutions d'églises par les laïques." *Revue historique de droit français et étranger,* 4th ser., 4 (1925), 253–94.

Dinzelbacher, Peter. *Vision und Visionsliteratur im Mittelalter.* Monographien zur Geschichte des Mittelalters, vol. 23. Stuttgart: Anton Hiersemann, 1981.

Dion, Adolphe de. *Le Puiset au XIe et au XIIe siècle: Châtellenie et prieuré.* Chartres: Garnier, 1886.

Dix, Gregory. *The Shape of the Liturgy.* 2d ed. London: Dacre Press/ Adam & Charles Black, 1945.

Dodds, E. R. *Pagan and Christian in an Age of Anxiety: Some Aspects of Religious Experience from Marcus Aurelius to Constantine.* Cambridge: Cambridge University Press, 1965.

Doehaerd, Renée. *Le Haut Moyen Age occidental: Économies et sociétés.* Nouvelle Clio, vol. 14. Paris: Presses Universitaires de France, 1971.

Dokumentationsband zum EDV-Kolloquium, 1985. Schriftenreihe des Rechenzentrums der westfälischen Wilhelms-Universität Münster, vol. 59. Münster: Das Zentrum, 1985.

Dölger, Franz J. "Antike Parallelen zum leidenden Dinocrates in der *Passio Perpetuae.*" *Antike und Christentum: Kultur- und religiongeschichtliche Studien* 2 (1930), 1–40.

Dormeier, Heinrich. *Montecassino und die Laien im 11. und 12. Jahrhundert.* Schriften der Monumenta Germaniae Historica, vol. 27. Stuttgart: Anton Hiersemann, 1979.

Duby, Georges. *The Early Growth of the European Economy: Warriors and Peasants from the Seventh to the Twelfth Century.* Translated by Howard B. Clarke. World Economic History. Ithaca: Cornell University Press, 1974.

———. *Rural Economy and Country Life in the Medieval West.* Translated by Cynthia Postan. Columbia: University of South Carolina Press, 1968.

———. *La Société aux XIe et XIIe siècles dans la région mâconnaise.* 1953. Reprint. Bibliothèque générale de l'École pratique des hautes études, 6ᵐᵉ section. Paris: Service d'Édition et de Vente des Publications de l'Éducation Nationale, 1971.

———. *Les Trois Ordres, ou l'imaginaire du féodalisme.* Paris: Gallimard, 1978.

Duffy, S. J. "Parousia: In Theology." *NCE* 10: 1037–39.

Duval, Yvette. *Auprès des saints corps et âme: L'inhumation "ad sanctos" dans la chrétienté d'Orient et d'Occident du IIIe au VIIe siècle.* Études augustiniennes. Paris: Études Augustiniennes, 1988.

Duval, Yvette, and Jean-Charles Picard, eds. *L'Inhumation privilégiée du IVe au VIIIe siècle en Occident: Actes du colloque tenu à Creteil les 16–18 mars 1984.* Paris: de Boccard, 1986.

Ebner, Adalbert. *Die klösterlichen Gebets-Verbrüderungen bis zum Ausgang des karolingischen Zeitalters.* Regensburg: F. Pustet, 1890.

Edwards, Graham Robert. "Purgatory: 'Birth' or Evolution?" *Journal of Ecclesiastical History* 36 (1985), 634–46.

Erlande-Brandenburg, Alain. *Le Roi est mort: Étude sur les funérailles, les sépultures, et les tombeaux des rois de France jusqu'à la fin du XIIIe siècle.* Bibliothèque de la Société français d'archéologie, vol. 7. Geneva: Droz, 1975.

Études de civilisation médiévale (IXe–XIIe siècles): Mélanges offerts à Edmond-René Labande. Poitiers: Centre d'Études Supérieures de Civilisation Médiévale, 1974.

Faire croire: Modalités de la diffusion et de la réception des messages religieux du XIIe au XVe siècle. Collection de l'École française de Rome, vol. 51. Rome: École Française de Rome, 1981.

Fälschungen im Mittelalter: Internationaler Kongress der Monumenta Germaniae Historica München, 16.-19. September 1986. Schriften der Monumenta Germaniae Historica, vol. 33. 4 vols. Hanover: Hahn, 1988.

Farmer, Sharon. *Communities of Saint Martin: Legend and Ritual in Medieval Tours.* Ithaca: Cornell University Press, 1991.

Feffer, Laure-Charlotte, and Patrick Périn. *Les Francs.* Vol. 2: *A l'origine de la France.* Collection civilisations. Paris: Armand Colin, 1987.

Festgabe Friedrich von Bezold dargebracht zum 70. Geburtstag von seinen Schülern, Kollegen und Freunden. Bonn: Kurt Schroeder, 1921.

Février, Paul-Albert, et al. *La Ville antique des origines au IXe siècle.* Histoire de la France urbaine, vol. 1. Paris: Seuil, 1980.

Fichtenau, Heinrich. *Arenga: Spätantike und Mittelalter in Spiegel von Urkundenfor-*

meln. Mitteilungen des Instituts für Österreichische Geschichtsforschung, Ergänzungsband, 18. Graz-Cologne: Verlag Hermann Böhlaus, 1957.

———. *Living in the Tenth Century: Mentalities and Social Orders.* Translated by Patrick J. Geary. Chicago: University of Chicago Press, 1991.

Fournier, Gabriel. *Le Château dans la France médiévale: Essai de sociologie monumentale.* Collection historique. Paris: Aubier-Montaigne, 1978.

———. *Le Peuplement rural en basse Auvergne durant le haut moyen âge.* Publications de la Faculté des lettres et sciences humaines de Clermont-Ferrand, 2d ser., vol. 12. Paris: Presses Universitaires de France, 1962.

Fourquin, Guy. *Histoire économique de l'Occident médiéval.* Collection "U", histoire médiévale. 2d ed. Paris: A. Colin, 1971.

Frank, H. "Allerseelentag (Liturgiegeschichte)." *Lexikon für Theologie und Kirche* 1: 349.

Frantzen, Allen J. *The Literature of Penance in Anglo-Saxon England.* New Brunswick, N.J.: Rutgers University Press, 1983.

Franz, Adolph. *Die Messe im deutschen Mittelalter: Beiträge zur Geschichte der Liturgie und des religiösen Volkslebens.* Freiburg im Breisgau: Herder, 1902.

Freistedt, Emil. *Altchristliche Totengedächtnistage und ihre Beziehung zum Jenseitsglauben und Totenkultus der Antike.* Liturgiegeschichtliche Quellen und Forschungen, vol. 24. Münster: Aschendorff, 1928.

Gaiffier, B. de. "Réflexions sur les origines du culte des martyrs." *La Maison-Dieu* 52 (1957), 19–44.

Galpern, A. N. *The Religions of the People in Sixteenth-Century Champagne.* Harvard Historical Studies, vol. 92. Cambridge: Harvard University Press, 1976.

Galtier, P. "Pénitents et 'convertis': De la pénitence latine à la pénitence celtique." *Revue d'histoire ecclésiastique* 33 (1937), 1–26, 277–305.

Ganshof, François L. *Feudalism.* Translated by Philip Grierson. 3d English ed. New York: Harper & Row, 1964.

Gaudemet, Jean. "La Paroisse au moyen âge: État des questions." *Revue d'histoire de l'église de France* 59 (1973), 5–21.

Gauthier, Nancy. "Les Images de l'au-delà durant l'antiquité chrétienne." *Revue des études augustiniennes* 33 (1987), 3–22.

Gay, Claude. "Formulaires anciens pour la messe des défunts." *Études grégoriennes* 2 (1957), 83–129.

Geary, Patrick. "Échanges et relations entre les vivants et les morts dans la société du haut moyen âge." *Droit et cultures* 12 (1986), 3–17.

Geuenich, Dieter, Otto Gerhard Oexle, and Karl Schmid. *Die Listen geistlicher und monastischer Kommunitäten aus dem früheren Mittelalter.* Münstersche Mittelalter-Schriften, vol 49. Munich: Wilhelm Fink, 1989.

Giesey, Ralph E. *The Royal Funeral Ceremony in Renaissance France.* Travaux d'humanisme et renaissance, vol. 37. Geneva: Droz, 1960.

Gindele, C. "Die gallikanischen 'Laus Perennis'-Klöster und ihr 'Ordo Officii'." *Revue Bénédictine* 69 (1959), 32–48.

Godman, Peter, and Roger Collins, eds. *Charlemagne's Heir: New Perspectives on the Reign of Louis the Pious (814–840).* Oxford: Clarendon, 1990.

Gougaud, Louis. *Dévotions et pratiques ascétiques du moyen âge.* Collection "pax," vol. 21. Paris: Desclée, 1925.

——. "Étude sur les *ordines commendationis animae.*" *Ephemerides liturgicae* 49 (1935), 3–27.

Graus, Frantisek. *Volk, Herrscher, und Heiliger im Reich der Merowinger: Studien zur Hagiographie der Merowingerzeit.* Prague: Nakladatelství Ceskoslovenské akademie ved, 1965.

Grierson, Philip. "Commerce in the Dark Ages: A Critique of the Evidence." *Transactions of the Royal Historical Society,* 5th ser., 9 (1959), 123–40.

Griffe, E. "Les Paroisses rurales de la Gaule." *La Maison-Dieu* 36 (1953), 33–62.

Grossmann, Ursula. "Studien zur Zahlensymbolik des Frühmittelalters." *Zeitschrift für katholische Theologie* 76 (1954), 19–54.

Gryson, Roger. *Les Origines du célibat ecclésiastique du premier au septième siècle.* Recherches et synthèses, section d'histoire, vol. 2. Gembloux: J. Duculot, 1970.

Guillot, Olivier. *Le Comte d'Anjou et son entourage au XIe siècle.* Paris: A. & J. Picard, 1972.

Gurevich, Aron J. *Categories of Medieval Culture.* Translated by George Campbell. London: Routledge & Kegan Paul, 1985.

——. "Popular and Scholarly Medieval Cultural Traditions: Notes in the Margin of Jacques Le Goff's Book." *Journal of Medieval History* 9 (1983), 71–90.

Gy, Pierre-Maric. "La Signification pastorale des prières du prône." *La Maison-Dieu* 30 (1952), 125–36.

Halphen, Louis. *Le Comté d'Anjou au XIe siècle.* Paris: A. Picard, 1906.

Häussling, Angelus. *Mönchskonvent und Eucharistiefeier: Eine Studie über die Messe in der abendländischen Klosterliturgie des frühen Mittelalters und zur Geschichte der Messhäufigkeit.* Liturgiewissenschaftliche Quellen und Forschungen, vol. 58. Münster: Aschendorff, 1973.

Head, Thomas. *Hagiography and the Cult of Saints: The Diocese of Orléans, 800–1200.* Cambridge: Cambridge University Press, 1990.

Heath, Robert G. *Crux Imperatorum Philosophia: Imperial Horizons of the Cluniac Confraternitas, 964–1109.* Pittsburgh Theological Monograph Series, vol. 13. Pittsburgh: Pickwick Press, 1976.

Hein, Kenneth. *Eucharist and Excommunication: A Study in Early Christian Doctrine and Discipline.* European University Papers, Series 23: Theology, vol. 19. Frankfurt: Peter Lang, 1973.

Héris, C. V. "Théologie des suffrages pour les morts." *La Maison-Dieu* 44 (1955), 58–67.

Herlihy, David, ed. *The History of Feudalism.* Atlantic Highlands, N.J.: Humanities Press, 1970.

Hilferty, Mary Cecilia. *The Domine Jesu Christe, Libera Me, and Dies Irae of the Requiem: A Historical and Literary Study.* Catholic University of America, Studies in Medieval History, n.s., vol. 19. Washington, D.C.: Catholic University of America Press, 1973.

Hillebrandt, Maria. "The Cluniac Charters: Remarks on a Quantitative Approach for Prosopographical Studies." *Medieval Prosopography* 3 (1982), 3–25.

Himmelfarb, Martha. *Tours of Hell: An Apocalyptic Form in Jewish and Christian Literature*. Philadelphia: University of Pennsylvania Press, 1983.

Hlawitschka, E. "Gebetsverbrüderung." *Lexikon für Theologie und Kirche* 4: 554–55.

Hodges, Richard, and David Whitehouse. *Mohammed, Charlemagne, and the Origins of Europe: Archaeology and the Pirenne Thesis*. Ithaca: Cornell University Press, 1983.

Hopper, Vincent Foster. *Medieval Number Symbolism: Its Sources, Meaning, and Influence on Thought and Expression*. New York: Columbia University Press, 1938.

Horn, Walter, with Ernest Born. "On the Selective Use of Sacred Numbers and the Creation in Carolingian Architecture of a New Aesthetic Based on Modular Concepts." *Viator* 6 (1975), 351–90.

Hourlier, Jacques. "S. Odilon et la fête des morts." *Revue grégorienne* 28 (1949), 209–12.

Howe, John. "The Nobility's Reform of the Medieval Church." *The American Historical Review* 93 (1988), 317–39.

Hunt, Noreen, ed. *Cluniac Monasticism in the Central Middle Ages*. Hamden, Conn.: Archon, 1971.

Huyghebaert, Nicholas. "Le Comte Baudouin II de Flandre et le 'custos' de Steneland: A propos d'un faux précepte de Charles le Chauve pour Saint-Bertin (866)." *Revue Bénédictine* 69 (1959), 49–67.

——. *Les Documents nécrologiques*. Typologie des sources du moyen âge occidental, edited by Léopold Genicot, vol. 4. Turnhout: Brepols, 1972.

Imbart de la Tour, Pierre. *Les Origines religieuses de la France: Les paroisses rurales du IVe au XIe siècle*. Paris: A. Picard, 1900.

Iogna-Prat, Dominique. *Agni immaculati: Recherches sur les sources hagiographiques relatives à saint Maieul de Cluny (954–994)*. Paris: Cerf, 1988.

Iogna-Prat, Dominique, and Jean-Charles Picard, eds. *Religion et culture autour de l'an mil: Royaume capétien et Lotharingie*. Paris: Picard, 1990.

Le istituzioni ecclesiastiche della "societas christiana" dei secoli XI-XII: Diocesi, pievi, et parrocchie. Miscellanea del Centro di Studi Medioevali dell'Università Cattolica del Sacro Cuore, vol. 8. Milan: Vita e Pensiero,1977.

Jakobi, Franz-Josef. "Diptychen als frühe Form der Gedenk-Aufzeichnungen: Zum 'Herrscher-Diptychon' im Liber Memorialis von Remiremont." *FS* 20 (1986), 186–212.

Jay, Pierre. "Le Purgatoire dans la prédication de Saint Césaire d'Arles." *Recherches de théologie ancienne et médiévale* 24 (1957), 5–14.

——. "Saint Augustin et la doctrine du Purgatoire." *Recherches de théologie ancienne et médiévale* 36 (1969), 17–30.

——. "Saint Cyprien et la doctrine du Purgatoire." *Recherches de théologie ancienne et médiévale* 27 (1960), 133–36.

Jedin, Hubert, Kenneth Scott Latourette, and Jochen Martin. *Atlas zur Kirchengeschichte: Die christlichen Kirchen in Geschichte und Gegenwart.* Freiburg: Herder, 1970.

Johnson, Penelope. *Prayer, Patronage, and Power: The Abbey of La Trinité, Vendôme, 1032–1187.* New York: New York University Press, 1981.

Jones, Charles W. "Carolingian Aesthetics: Why Modular Verse?" *Viator* 6 (1975), 309–40.

Jorden, Willibald. *Das cluniazensische Totengedächtniswesen, vornehmlich unter den drei ersten Äbten Berno, Odo, und Aymard (910–954).* Münsterische Beiträge zur Theologie, vol. 15. Münster: Aschendorff, 1930.

Jungmann, Josef A. *The Early Liturgy, to the Time of Gregory the Great.* Translated by Francis A. Brunner. University of Notre Dame Liturgical Studies, vol. 6. Notre Dame, Ind.: University of Notre Dame Press, 1959.

———. *Die lateinischen Bussriten in ihrer geschichtlichen Entwicklung.* Forschungen zur Geschichte des innerkirchlichen Lebens, vols. 3–4. Innsbruck: F. Rauch, 1932.

———. *The Mass of the Roman Rite: Its Origins and Development.* Translated by Francis A. Brunner. 2 vols. New York: Benziger, 1951–55.

———. *Pastoral Liturgy.* New York: Herder and Herder, 1962.

———. "Von der 'Eucharistia' zur 'Messe'." *Zeitschrift für katholische Theologie* 89 (1967), 29–40.

Junyent, E. "Le Rouleau funéraire d'Oliba, abbé de Notre-Dame de Ripoll et de Saint-Michel de Cuixa, évêque de Vich." *Annales du Midi* 63 (1951), 249–63.

Kantorowicz, Ernst. *The King's Two Bodies: A Study in Mediaeval Political Theology.* Princeton: Princeton University Press, 1957.

Kappler, Claude, et al., eds. *Apocalypses et voyages dans l'au-delà.* Études annexes de la Bible de Jérusalem. Paris: Cerf, 1987.

Kemp, Eric Waldram. *Canonization and Authority in the Western Church.* Oxford: Oxford University Press, 1948.

Kerin, Charles A. *The Privation of Christian Burial: An Historical Synopsis and Commentary.* Catholic University of America Canon Law Studies, vol. 136. Washington, D.C.: Catholic University of America Press, 1941.

Kern, L. "Sur les rouleaux des morts." *Études suisses d'histoire générale (Schweizer Beiträge zur allgemeinen Geschichte)* 14 (1956), 139–47.

King, Archdale A. *Concelebration in the Christian Church.* London: Mowbray, 1966.

———. *The Liturgies of the Religious Orders.* Rites of Western Christendom. London: Longmans, Green and Co., 1956.

Kirk, Kenneth E., ed. *The Apostolic Ministry: Essays on the History and the Doctrine of Episcopacy.* London: Hodder & Stoughton, 1946.

Klauser, Theodor. *A Short History of the Western Liturgy: An Account and Some Reflections.* Translated by John Halliburton. 2d ed. Oxford: Oxford University Press, 1979.

Koch, Marie Pierre. *An Analysis of the Long Prayers in Old French Literature with Special Reference to the "Biblical-Creed-Narrative" Prayers.* Washington, D.C.: Catholic University of America Press, 1940.

Kottje, Raymund, and Helmut Maurer, eds. *Monastische Reformen im 9. und 10. Jahrhundert*. Konstanzer Arbeitskreis für mittelalterliche Geschichte, Vorträge und Forschungen, vol. 38. Sigmaringen: Jan Thorbecke, 1989.

Kreider, Alan. *English Chantries: The Road to Dissolution*. Harvard Historical Studies, vol. 97. Cambridge: Harvard University Press, 1979.

Krüger, Karl H. *Königsgrabkirchen der Franken, Angelsachsen, und Langobarden bis zur Mitte des 8. Jahrhunderts: Ein historischer Katalog*. Münstersche Mittelalter-Schriften, vol. 4. Munich: Wilhelm Fink, 1971.

I Laici nella "societas christiana" dei secoli XI e XII. Miscellanea del Centro di Studi Medioevali dell'Università Cattolica del Sacro Cuore, vol. 5. Milan: Vita e Pensiero, 1968.

Lambert, Malcolm. *Medieval Heresy: Popular Movements from Bogomil to Hus*. New York: Holmes & Meier, 1976.

Lamirande, Émilien. *The Communion of Saints*. Translated by A. Manson. The Twentieth Century Encyclopedia of Catholicism. New York: Hawthorn Books, 1963.

Landgraf, Artur. "1 Cor. 3, 10–17 bei den lateinischen Vätern und in der Frühscholastik." *Biblica* 5 (1924), 140–72.

———. *Dogmengeschichte der Frühscholastik*. 4 vols. Regensburg: Friedrich Pustet, 1952–56.

Lauwers, Michel. "La Mort et le corps des saints: La scène de la mort dans les *vitae* du haut moyen âge." *Le Moyen Âge* 94 (1988), 21–50.

Lavalette, Henri de. "L'Interprétation du psaume 1, 5 chez les pères 'misericordieux' latins." *Recherches de science religieuse* 48 (1960), 544–63.

Lawrence, C. H. *Medieval Monasticism: Forms of Religious Life in Western Europe in the Middle Ages*. 2d ed. London: Longman, 1989.

Leclercq, Henri. "Ad Sanctos." *DACL* 1: 479–509.

———. "Aliscamps." *DACL* 1: 1211–18.

———. "Chapelle." *DACL* 3: 406–28.

———. "Cimetière." *DACL* 3: 1625–65.

———. "Défunts (Commémoraison des)." *DACL* 4: 427–56.

———. "Mort." *DACL* 12: 15–52.

———. "Obituaire." *DACL* 12: 1834–57.

Leclercq, Jean. "Culte liturgique et prière intime dans le monachisme au moyen âge." *La Maison-Dieu* 69 (1962), 39–55.

———. *La Liturgie et les paradoxes chrétiens*. Lex orandi, vol. 36. Paris: Cerf, 1963.

———. *The Love of Learning and the Desire for God: A Study of Monastic Culture*. Translated by Catharine Misrahi. 2d ed. New York: Fordham University Press, 1974.

Le Goff, Jacques. *La Naissance du Purgatoire*. Bibliothèque des histoires. Paris: Gallimard, 1981. Translated by Arthur Goldhammer as *The Birth of Purgatory*. Chicago: University of Chicago Press, 1984.

Lemaître, Jean-Loup. "La Commémoration des défunts et les obituaires dans l'Occident chrétien." *Revue d'histoire de l'église de France* 71 (1985), 131–45.

———. "Les Obituaires français: perspectives nouvelles." *Revue d'histoire de l'église de France* 64 (1978), 69–81.

———, ed. *Répertoire des documents nécrologiques français*. Publié sous la direction de Pierre Marot. Recueil des historiens de la France, Obituaires, vol. 7. 2 vols. Paris: Imprimerie Nationale and C. Klincksieck, 1980. *Supplément*. 1987.

Lemarignier, Jean-François. *Recherches sur l'hommage en marche et les frontières féodales*. Travaux et mémoires de l'Université de Lille, n.s., Droit et lettres, vol. 24. Lille: Bibliothèque Universitaire, 1945.

Lemarignier, Jean-François, Jean Gaudemet, and Guillaume Mollat. *Institutions ecclésiastiques*. Histoire des institutions françaises au moyen âge, edited by Ferdinand Lot and Robert Fawtier, vol. 3. Paris: Presses Universitaires de France, 1962.

Leroquais, Victor. *Les Sacramentaires et les missels manuscrits des bibliothèques publiques de France*. 3 vols. Paris: N.p., 1924.

Lesne, Émile. *Histoire de la propriété ecclésiastique en France*. Mémoires et travaux publiés par les professeurs des facultés catholiques de Lille, vols. 6, 19, 30, 44, 50, 53. 6 vols. in 7. Lille: R. Giard, 1910–43.

Lévi, Israel. "Le Repos sabbatique des âmes damnées." *Revue des études juives* 25 (1892), 1–13.

Little, Lester K. "Formules monastiques de malédiction aux IXe et Xe siècles." *Revue Mabillon* 58 (1975), 377–99.

———. *Religious Poverty and the Profit Economy in Medieval Europe*. Ithaca: Cornell University Press, 1978.

Loades, David, ed. *The End of Strife: Papers Selected from the Proceedings of the Colloquium of the Commission Internationale d'Histoire Ecclésiastique Comparée Held at the University of Durham 2 to 9 September 1981*. Edinburgh: T. & T. Clark, 1984.

Lorcin, Marie-Thérèse. *Vivre et mourir en Lyonnais à la fin du moyen âge*. Paris: Centre National de la Recherche Scientifique, 1981.

Lorenz, Rudolf. "Die Anfänge des abendländischen Mönchtums im 4. Jahrhundert." *Zeitschrift für Kirchengeschichte* 77 (1966), 1–61.

Lourdaux, W. and D. Verhelst, eds. *Benedictine Culture 750–1050*. Mediaevalia Lovaniensia, ser. 1, vol 11. Louvain: Louvain University Press, 1983.

Lubac, Henri de. *Corpus mysticum: L'eucharistie et l'église au moyen âge. Étude historique*. Théologie, vol. 3. 2d ed. Paris: Aubier, 1949.

Luther, Martin. *Ein Widerruf vom Fegefeuer*. Edited by O. Clemen and O. Brenner. In *D. Martin Luthers Werke: Kritische Gesammtausgabe, sect. 1, vol. 30, pt. 2*. Weimar: Hermann Böhlaus Nachfolger, 1909.

Luykx, B. "L'Influence des moines sur l'office paroissial." *La Maison-Dieu* 51 (1957), 67–79.

Lynch, Joseph H. *Simoniacal Entry into Religious Life from 1000 to 1260: A Social, Economic, and Legal Study*. Columbus: Ohio State University Press, 1976.

McCormick, Michael. "The Liturgy of War in the Early Middle Ages: Crisis, Litanies, and the Carolingian Monarchy." *Viator* 15 (1984), 1–23.

McGuire, Brian Patrick. "Purgatory, the Communion of Saints, and Medieval Change." *Viator* 20 (1989), 61–84.

McKitterick, Rosamond. *The Carolingians and the Written Word.* Cambridge: Cambridge University Press, 1989.

———. *The Frankish Church and the Carolingian Reforms, 789–895.* Studies in History. London: Royal Historical Society, 1977.

McLaughlin, Megan. "On Communion with the Dead." *Journal of Medieval History* 17 (1991), 23–34.

———. "Consorting with Saints: Prayer for the Dead in Early Medieval French Society." Ph.D. diss., Stanford University, 1985.

Magnou-Nortier, Elisabeth. *La Société laïque et l'église dans la province ecclésiastique de Narbonne (zone cispyrénéenne) de la fin du VIIIe à la fin du XIe siècle.* Publications de l'Université de Toulouse–Le Mirail, ser. A, vol. 20. Toulouse: Association des Publications de l'Université de Toulouse–Le Mirail, 1974.

Maisonneuve, H. "La Morale d'après les conciles des Xe et XIe siècles." *Mélanges de science religieuse* 18 (1961), 1–46.

Martimort, Aimé-Georges. "Comment meurt un chrétien." *La Maison-Dieu* 44 (1955), 5–28.

———. "La Fidelité des premiers chrétiens aux usages romains en matière de sépulture." *Société toulousaine d'études classiques, mélanges* 1 (1946), 167–89.

———, ed. *L'Église en prière: Introduction à la liturgie.* Paris: Desclée, 1961.

Massaut, Jean-Pierre. "La Vision de l'au-delà au moyen âge: A propos d'un ouvrage récent." *Le Moyen Âge* 91 (1985), 75–86.

Mauss, Marcel. *The Gift: Forms and Functions of Exchange in Archaic Societies.* Translated by I. Cunnison. New York: Norton, 1967.

Meersseman, Gilles Gerard. "Die Klerikervereine von Karl dem Grossen bis Innocenz III." *Zeitschrift für schweizerische Kirchengeschichte* 46 (1952), 1–42, 81–112.

Meersseman, Gilles Gerard, with Gian Piero Pacini. *Ordo fraternitatis: Confraternite e pietà dei laici nel medioevo.* Italia sacra: studi e documenti di storia ecclesiastica, vol. 24. Rome: Herder, 1977.

Megivern, James. *Comcomitance and Communion: A Study in Eucharistic Doctrine and Practice.* Studia Friburgensia, n.s., vol. 33. Fribourg: University of Fribourg Press, 1963.

Mélanges d'histoire du moyen âge dediés à la mémoire de Louis Halphen. Paris: Presses Universitaires de France, 1951.

Mélanges Saint Bernard: XXIVe Congrès de l'Association bourguignonne des sociétés savantes, 1953. Dijon: L'Abbé Marilier, 1954.

Michel, Albert. "Purgatoire." *DTC* 13: 1163–1326.

Miscellanea liturgica in onore di Sua Eminenza il Cardinale Giacomo Lercaro. 2 vols. Rome: Desclée, 1966–67.

"Mittelalterforschung in Münster in der Nachfolge des Sonderforschungsbereichs 7." *FS* 24 (1990), 392–429.

Mohrmann, Christine. "Missa." *Vigiliae Christianae* 12 (1958), 67–92.

Molien, A. *La Prière pour les défunts.* La Prière et la vie liturgique. Avignon: Aubanel, 1928.

Molin, J. B., and T. Maertens. *Pour un renouveau des prières du prône.* Paroisse et liturgie, vol. 53. Bruges: Éditions de l'Apostolat Liturgique, 1961.

Il monachesimo nell'alto medioevo e la formazione della civiltà occidentale. Settimane di Studio del Centro Italiano di Studi sull'alto Medioevo, vol. 4. 2 vols. Spoleto: Presso la Sede del Centro, 1957.

Moore, Robert Ian. *The Origins of European Dissent.* London: Allen Lane, 1977.

Mordek, Hubert, ed. *Aus Kirche und Reich: Studien zu Theologie, Politik, und Recht im Mittelalter (Festschrift für Friedrich Kempf zu seinem fünfundsiebzigsten Geburtstag und fünfzigjährigen Doktorjubiläum).* Sigmaringen: Jan Thorbecke, 1983.

Morin, G. "Rainaud l'ermite et Ives de Chartres: Un épisode de la crise du cénobitisme au XIe-XIIe siècle." *Revue Bénédictine* 40 (1928), 99–115.

La Mort au moyen âge: Colloque de l'Association des historiens médiévistes français réunis à Strasbourg en juin, 1975 au Palais Universitaire. Publications de la Société savante d'Alsace et des régions de l'Est. Collection "recherches et documents," vol. 25. Strasbourg: Istra, 1977.

"Der Münsterer Sonderforschungsbereich 7: 'Mittelalterforschung (Bild, Bedeutung, Sachen, Wörter und Personen'." *FS* 19 (1985), 520–65.

Murray, Alexander. *Reason and Society in the Middle Ages.* Rev. ed. Oxford: Clarendon, 1985.

Musset, Lucien. "Le Cimetière dans la vie paroissiale en Basse-Normandie (XIe–XIIIe siècles)." *Cahiers Léopold Delisle* 12 (1963), 7–27.

——. "'Cimiterium ad refugium tantum vivorum non ad sepulturam mortuorum'." *Revue du moyen âge latin* 4 (1948), 56–60.

——. "Les Sépultures des souverains normands: Un aspect de l'idéologie du pouvoir." *Annales de Normandie* 27 (1977), 350–51.

Le Mystère de la mort et sa célébration. Lex orandi, vol. 12. Paris: Cerf, 1956.

Neiske, Franz. "Frömmigkeit als Leistung? Überlegungen zu grossen Zahlen im mittelalterlichen Totengedenken." *Zeitschrift für Literaturwissenschaft und Linguistik* 80 (1990), 35–48.

——. "Vision and Totengedenken." *FS* 20 (1986), 137–85.

Ntedika, Joseph. *L'Évocation de l'au-delà dans la prière pour les morts: Étude de patristique et de liturgie latines (IVe-VIIIe s.).* Recherches africains de théologie, vol. 2. Paris: Nauwelaerts, 1971.

——. *L'Évolution de la doctrine du purgatoire chez saint Augustin.* Publications de l'Université Lovanium de Léopoldville, vol. 20. Paris: Études Augustiniennes, 1966.

Nussbaum, Otto. *Kloster, Priestermönch, und Privatmesse: Ihr Verhältnis im Westen von den Anfängen bis zum hohen Mittelalter.* Theophaneia, vol. 14. Bonn: Peter Hanstein, 1961.

Oexle, Otto Gerhard. "*Conjuratio* et *ghilde* dans l'antiquité et dans le haut moyen âge: Remarques sur la continuité des formes de la vie sociale." *Francia* 10 (1982), 1–19.

———. *Forschungen zu monastischen und geistlichen Gemeinschaften im westfränkischen Bereich.* Münstersche Mittelalter-Schriften, 31. Munich: Wilhelm Fink, 1978.

———. "Mahl und Spende im mittelalterlichen Totenkult." *FS* 18 (1984), 401–420.

———. "Memoria und Memorialüberlieferung im früheren Mittelalter." *FS* 10 (1976), 87–95.

Ombres, Robert. "Latins and Greeks in Debate over Purgatory, 1230–1439." *Journal of Ecclesiastical History* 35 (1984), 1–14.

Panvinio, Onofrio. *De ritu sepeliendi mortuos apud veteres christianos.* Cologne, 1568.

Paris, Gaston. "La Légende de Trajan." *Bibliothèque de l'École des hautes études, sciences philologiques et historiques,* fasc. 35 (1878), 261–98.

Patlagean, Évelyne, and Pierre Riché, eds. *Hagiographie, cultures, et sociétés, IVe–XIIe siècles: Actes du colloque organisé à Nanterre et à Paris (2–5 mai 1979).* Paris: Études Augustiniennes, 1981.

Paxton, Frederick S. *Christianizing Death: The Creation of a Ritual Process in Early Medieval Europe.* Ithaca: Cornell University Press, 1990.

Pennington, M. Basil, ed. *Rule and Life: An Interdisciplinary Symposium.* Cistercian Studies, vol. 12. Spencer, Mass.: Cistercian Publications, 1971.

Perham, Michael. *The Communion of Saints: An Examination of the Place of the Christian Dead in the Belief, Worship, and Calendars of the Church.* Alcuin Club Collections, vol. 62. London: Alcuin Club/ S.P.C.K., 1980.

Petit, François. *La Spiritualité des Prémontrés aux XIIe et XIIIe siècles.* Études de théologie et d'histoire de la spiritualité, vol. 10. Paris: J. Vrin, 1947.

Picard, Jean-Charles. *Le Souvenir des évêques: Sépultures, listes épiscopales, et culte des évêques en Italie du Nord des origines au Xe siècle.* Bibliothèque des Écoles françaises d'Athènes et de Rome, vol. 268. Rome: École Française de Rome, 1988.

Pietri, Charles. "Remarques sur la christianisation du nord de la Gaule (IVe–VIe siècles)." *Revue du Nord* 66 (1984), 55–68.

Pietri, Luce. *La Ville de Tours du IVe au VIe siècle: Naissance d'une cité chrétienne.* Collection de l'École française de Rome, vol. 69. Rome: École Française de Rome, 1983.

Poeck, Dietrich. "Laienbegräbnisse in Cluny." *FS* 15 (1981), 68–179.

Popoli e paesi nella cultura altomedievale. Settimane di Studio del Centro Italiano di Studi sull'alto Medioevo, vol. 29. 2 vols. Spoleto: Presso la Sede del Centro, 1983.

Poschmann, Bernhard. *Der Ablass im Licht der Bussgeschichte.* Theophaneia, vol. 4. Bonn: Peter Hanstein, 1948.

Prinz, Friedrich. *Frühes Mönchtum im Frankenreich: Kultur und Gesellschaft in Gallien, den Rheinlanden, und Bayern am Beispiel der monastischen Entwicklung (4. bis 8. Jahrhundert).* Munich: Oldenbourg, 1965.

Provost, Michel. *Angers gallo-romain: Naissance d'une cité.* Angers: Les Jeunes Andecaves, 1978.

Quasten, Johannes. "*Vetus Superstitio et Nova Religio*: The Problem of *Refrigerium* in the Ancient Church of North Africa." *Harvard Theological Review* 33 (1940), 253–66.

Quéguiner, Jean. "Recherches sur les chapellenies au moyen âge." Thesis, École Nationale des Chartes, 1950.

La Religion populaire en Languedoc du XIIIe siècle à la moitié du XIVe siècle. Cahiers de Fanjeaux, vol. 11. Toulouse: Privat, 1976.

Reynolds, Susan. *Kingdoms and Communities in Western Europe, 900–1300.* Oxford: Clarendon, 1984.

Riché, Pierre. *Les Écoles et l'enseignement dans l'Occident chrétien de la fin du Ve siècle au milieu du XIe siècle.* Collection historique. Paris: Aubier-Montaigne, 1979.

Rivière, Jean. "Jugement." *DTC* 8: 1721–1828.

——. "Rôle du démon au jugement particulier chez les pères." *Revue des sciences religieuses* 4 (1924), 43–64.

Roles in the Liturgical Assembly: The Twenty-Third Liturgical Conference Saint-Serge (Paris, 1976). Translated by Matthew J. O'Connell. New York: Pueblo Publishing, 1981.

Rordorf, Willy. "Liturgie et eschatologie." *Augustinianum* 18 (1978), 153–61.

Rosenthal, Joel T. *The Purchase of Paradise: Gift Giving and the Aristocracy, 1307–1485.* Studies in Social History, edited by Harold Perkins. London: Routledge & Kegan Paul, 1972.

Rosenwein, Barbara. "Feudal War and Monastic Peace: Cluniac Liturgy as Ritual Aggression." *Viator* 2 (1971), 129–57.

——. *Rhinoceros Bound: Cluny in the Tenth Century.* The Middle Ages. Philadelphia: University of Pennsylvania Press, 1982.

——. *To Be the Neighbor of Saint Peter: The Social Meaning of Cluny's Property, 909–1049.* Ithaca: Cornell University Press, 1989.

Rush, Alfred C. *Death and Burial in Christian Antiquity.* Catholic University of America, Studies in Christian Antiquity, vol. 1. Washington, D.C.: Catholic University of America Press, 1941.

Ryan, J. Joseph. "Pseudo-Alcuin's *Liber de divinis officiis* and the *Liber 'Dominus vobiscum'* of St. Peter Damiani." *Mediaeval Studies* 14 (1952), 159–63.

Saint-Chrodegang: Communications presentées au colloque tenu à Metz à l'occasion du douzième centenaire de sa mort. Metz: de Lorrain, 1967.

Salin, Edouard. *La Civilisation mérovingienne d'apres les sépultures, les textes, et le laboratoire.* 4 vols. Paris: A. and J. Picard, 1949–59.

Salisbury, Joyce E. "'The Bond of a Common Mind': A Study of Collective Salvation from Cyprian to Augustine." *The Journal of Religious History* 13 (1985), 235–47.

Salmon, Pierre. *L'Office divin: Histoire de la formation du bréviaire.* Lex orandi, vol. 27. Paris: Cerf, 1959.

Saxer, Victor. *Morts, martyrs, reliques en Afrique chrétienne aux premiers siècles: Les témoignages de Tertullien, Cyprien, et Augustin à la lumière de l'archéologie africaine.* Théologie historique, vol. 55. Paris: Beauchesne, 1980.

Schmid, Karl. *Gebetsgedenken und adliges Selbstverständnis im Mittelalter: Aus-*

gewählte Beiträge: Festgabe zu seinem sechzigsten Geburtstag. Sigmaringen: Jan Thorbecke, 1983.

——. "Von den 'fratres conscripti' in Ekkeharts St. Galler Klostergeschichten." *FS* 25 (1991), 109–22.

——, ed. *Gedächtnis, das Gemeinschaft Stiftet.* Schriftenreihe der katholischen Akademie der Erzdiözese Freiburg. Munich: Schnell & Steiner, 1985.

——, ed. *Die Klostergemeinschaft von Fulda im früheren Mittelalter.* Münstersche Mittelalter-Schriften, vol. 8. 3 vols. Munich: Wilhelm Fink, 1978.

Schmid, Karl, and Otto Gerhard Oexle. "Voraussetzungen und Wirkung des Gebetsbundes von Attigny." *Francia* 2 (1974), 71–122.

Schmid, Karl, and Joachim Wollasch. "Die Gemeinschaft der Lebenden und Verstorbenen in Zeugnissen des Mittelalters." *FS* 1 (1967), 365–405.

——. "Societas et Fraternitas: Begründung eines kommentierten Quellenwerkes zur Erforschung der Personen und Personengruppen des Mittelalters." *FS* 9 (1975), 1–48.

——, eds. *Memoria: Der geschichtliche Zeugniswert des liturgischen Gedenkens im Mittelalter.* Münstersche Mittelalter-Schriften, vol. 48. Munich: Wilhelm Fink, 1984.

Schmidt, Herman, ed. *Liturgy: Self-Expression of the Church.* Concilium, vol. 72. New York: Herder and Herder, 1972.

Schmitz, Philibert. *Histoire de l'ordre de Saint-Benoît.* 6 vols. Maredsous: Éditions de Maredsous, 1942–49. 2d ed. of vols. 1 and 2. Maredsous: Éditions de Maredsous, 1948–49.

Schreiber, Georg. *Gemeinschaften des Mittelalters: Recht und Verfassung, Kult und Frömmigkeit.* Gesammelte Abhandlungen, vol. 1. Münster: Regensberg, 1948.

Segni e riti nella chiesa altomedievale occidentale. Settimane di Studio del Centro Italiano di Studi sull'alto Medioevo, vol. 33. 2 vols. Spoleto: Presso la Sede del Centro, 1987.

Sheehan, M. M. "Necrology." *NCE* 10: 296–97.

Sheils, W. J., and Diana Wood, eds. *The Church and Wealth.* Studies in Church History, vol. 24. Oxford: Blackwell, 1987.

Sicard, Damien. *La Liturgie de la mort dans l'église latine des origines à la réforme carolingienne.* Liturgiewissenschaftliche Quellen und Forschungen, vol. 63. Münster: Aschendorff, 1978.

Silverstein, Theodore. *Visio Sancti Pauli: The History of the Apocalypse in Latin, Together with Nine Texts.* Studies and Documents, vol. 4. London: Christophers, 1935.

Simboli e simbologia nell'alto medioevo. Settimane di Studio del Centro Italiano di Studi sull'alto Medioevo, vol 23. 2 vols. Spoleto: Presso la Sede del Centro, 1976.

Souancé, le Vicomte de, and Charles Métais. *Saint-Denis de Nogent-le-Rotrou, 1031–1789: Histoire et cartulaire.* Archives du diocèse de Chartres, vol. 1. Rev. ed. Vannes: Lafoyle, 1899.

Southern, R. W. *The Making of the Middle Ages.* New Haven: Yale University Press, 1953.

——. *Western Society and the Church in the Middle Ages.* The Pelican History of the Church, vol. 2. Harmondsworth, Eng.: Penguin Books, 1970.

Spiritualità cluniacense: Convegno del Centro di Studi sulla Spiritualità Medievale, 12–15 ottobre, 1958. Convegni del Centro di Studi sulla Spiritualità Medievale, vol. 2. Todi: Presso l'Academia Tudertina, 1960.

Stock, Brian. *The Implications of Literacy: Written Language and Models of Interpretation in the Eleventh and Twelfth Centuries.* Princeton: Princeton University Press, 1983.

Stoclet, Alain J. "Dies Unctionis: A Note on the Anniversaries of Royal Inaugurations in the Carolingian Period." *FS* 20 (1986), 541–48.

Struve, Tilman. "Zwei Briefe der Kaiserin Agnes." *Historisches Jahrbuch* 104 (1984), 411–24.

Stuiber, Alfred. *Refrigerium Interim: Die Vorstellungen vom Zwischenzustand und die frühchristliche Grabeskunst.* Theophaneia, vol. 11. Bonn: Peter Hanstein, 1957.

Taft, Robert. *The Liturgy of the Hours in East and West: The Origins of the Divine Office and Its Meaning for Today.* Collegeville, Minn.: The Liturgical Press, 1986.

Le Temps chrétien de la fin de l'antiquité au moyen âge: IIIe–XIIIe siècles. Colloques internationaux du Centre national de la recherche scientifique, no. 604. Paris: Centre National de la Recherche Scientifique, 1984.

Thomas, Heinz. "Die Namenliste des Diptychon Barberini und der Sturz des Hausmeiers Grimoald." *Deutsches Archiv für Erforschung des Mittelalters* 25 (1969), 17–63.

Trexler, Richard C., ed. *Persons in Groups: Social Behavior as Identity Formation in Medieval And Renaissance Europe: Papers of the Sixteenth Annual Conference of the Center for Medieval and Early Renaissance Studies.* Medieval & Renaissance Texts & Studies, vol. 36. Binghamton, N.Y.: Medieval & Renaissance Texts & Studies, 1985.

Triacca, A. M., and A. Pistoia, eds. *Eschatologie et liturgie: Conférences Saint-Serge: XXXIe semaine d'études liturgiques, Paris, 1984.* Bibliotheca "Ephemerides Liturgicae," Subsidia, vol. 35. Rome: Centro Liturgico Vincenziano-Edizione Liturgiche, 1985.

Ueding, Leo. *Geschichte der Klostergründungen der frühen Merowingerzeit.* Historische Studien, vol. 261. Berlin: E. Ebering, 1935.

Valvekens, J. "Fratres et sorores 'ad succurrendum.'" *Analecta Praemonstratensia* 37 (1961), 323–28.

Vandenbroucke, François. "Liturgie et piété personnelle: Les prodromes de leur tension à la fin du moyen âge." *La Maison-Dieu* 69 (1962), 56–66.

van Engen, John. "The 'Crisis of Cenobitism' Reconsidered: Benedictine Monasticism in the Years 1050–1150." *Speculum* 61 (1986), 269–304.

Vauchez, André. *La Sainteté en Occident aux derniers siècles du moyen âge d'après les procès de canonisation et les documents hagiographiques.* Bibliothèque des Écoles françaises d'Athènes et de Rome, vol. 241. Rome: École Française de Rome, 1981.

Viard, Paul. *Histoire de la dîme ecclésiastique, principalement en France jusqu'au Décret de Gratien.* Dijon: Jobard, 1909.

Vidier, Alexandre. *L'Historiographie à Saint-Benoît-sur-Loire et les miracles de Saint Benoît.* Revised by the monks of Fleury. Paris: A. & J. Picard, 1965.

La vita commune del clero nei secoli XI e XII. Miscellanea del Centro di Studi Medioevali dell'Università Cattolica del Sacro Cuore, vol. 3. 2 vols. Milan: Vita e Pensiero, 1962.

Vogel, Cyrille. "La Discipline pénitentielle en Gaule des origines au IXe siècle: Le dossier hagiographique." *Revue des sciences religieuses* 30 (1956), 1–26, 157–86.

———. *Medieval Liturgy: An Introduction to the Sources.* Translated and revised by William Storey and Niels Rasmussen, with John K. Brooks-Leonard. NPM Studies in Church Music and Liturgy. Washington, D.C.: Pastoral Press, 1986.

———. *Les Libri paenitentiales.* Typologie des sources du moyen âge occidental, edited by Léopold Genicot, vol. 27. Turnhout: Brepols, 1978.

———. "La Multiplication des messes solitaires au moyen âge: Essai de statistique." *Revue des sciences religieuses* 55 (1981), 206–13.

———. "Une Mutation cultuelle inexpliquée: Le passage de l'Eucharistie communautaire à la messe privée." *Revue des sciences religieuses* 54 (1980), 231–50.

———. *Le Pécheur et la pénitence au moyen âge.* Chrétiens de tous les temps, vol. 30. Paris: Cerf, 1969.

———. *Le Pécheur et la pénitence dans l'église ancienne.* Chrétiens de tous les temps, vol. 15. Paris: Cerf, 1966.

Vovelle, Michel. *La Mort et l'occident de 1300 à nos jours.* Bibliothèque illustrée des histoires. Paris: Gallimard, 1983.

Wagner, Johannes, ed. *Reforming the Rites of Death.* Concilium, vol. 32. New York: Paulist Press, 1968.

Wallace-Hadrill, J. M. *The Frankish Church.* Oxford History of the Church, edited by Henry Chadwick and Owen Chadwick. Oxford: Clarendon, 1983.

Ward, Benedicta. *Miracles and the Medieval Mind: Theory, Record, and Event, 1000–1215.* The Middle Ages. Philadelphia: University of Pennsylvania Press, 1982.

Wemple, Suzanne Fonay. *Women in Frankish Society: Marriage and the Cloister, 500 to 900.* The Middle Ages. Philadelphia: University of Pennsylvania Press, 1981.

Werner, Karl Ferdinand, ed. *L'Histoire médiévale et les ordinateurs/ Medieval History and Computers: Rapports d'une table ronde internationale.* Documentations et recherches publiées par l'Institut historique allemand. Munich: K. G. Saur, 1981.

Westlake, Herbert F. *The Parish Guilds of Mediaeval England.* London: Society for Promoting Christian Knowledge, 1919.

Whatley, Gordon. "The Uses of Hagiography: The Legend of Pope Gregory and the Emperor Trajan in the Middle Ages." *Viator* 15 (1984), 25–63.

White, Stephen D. *Custom, Kinship, and Gifts to Saints: The Laudatio Parentum in Western France, 1050–1150.* Studies in Legal History. Chapel Hill: University of North Carolina Press, 1988.

Wilmart, André. "Delisle (Léopold)." *DACL* 4: 515–61.

Wollasch, Joachim. "Gemeinschaftsbewusstsein und soziale Leistung im Mittelalter." *FS* 9 (1975), 268–286.

———. *Mönchtum des Mittelalters zwischen Kirche und Welt.* Münstersche Mittelalter-Schriften, vol. 7. Munich: Wilhelm Fink, 1973.

———. "Neue Methoden der Erforschung des Mönchtums im Mittelalter." *Historische Zeitschrift* 225 (1977), 529–71.

———. "Les Obituaires, témoins de la vie clunisienne." *Cahiers de civilisation médiévale* 22 (1979), 139–71.

———. "Reformmönchtum und Schriftlichkeit." *FS* 26 (1992), 274–86.

Wood-Legh, K. L. *Perpetual Chantries in Britain.* Cambridge: Cambridge University Press, 1965.

Wormald, Patrick, Donald Bullough, and Roger Collins, eds. *Ideal and Reality in Frankish and Anglo-Saxon Society: Studies Presented to J. M. Wallace-Hadrill.* Oxford: Blackwell, 1983.

Wright, J. H. "Dead, Prayers for the." *NCE* 4: 671–73.

———. "Judgment, Divine (in Theology)." *NCE* 8: 30–40.

Young, Bailey. "Exemple aristocratique et mode funéraire dans la Gaule mérovingienne." *Annales: Économies, sociétés, civilisations* 41 (1986), 379–407.

———. "Paganisme, christianisation, et rites funéraires mérovingiens." *Archéologie médiévale* 7 (1977), 5–81.

INDEX

Abbo (abbot of Fleury), 247
Absolution: of the dead, 194, 222–27; of
penitents, 220–27, 241
Adalard (abbot of Saint-Bertin), 153 n. 83
Agaune, monastery of, 60–61
Aix: Council of, 93; palace chapel at, 130
Alcuin, Pseudo-, 243
All Souls, 75–78, 230–33. *See also* Feasts
of the dead; Odilo
Almsgiving, ritualized: during anniversaries, 95–96, 182; at the approach of
death, 171; associated with meetings of
clerical society, 85; equated with mass
as effective means of helping the dead,
191, 194, 213, 232; during feasts of the
dead, 76–77, 100; during funerals, 49–
50, 53, 182; as part of the religious life,
89, 129–30, 147–48, 168, 248
Amalar of Metz, 44, 95, 242–43, 247
Amann, Émile, 228 n. 169
Angenendt, Arnold, 4, 12–13, 17 n. 43,
153–54, 158 n. 109, 221, 239–40
Angers: cathedral of (Saint-Maurice), 87,
137, 168, 263–67; cemetery at, 109 n.
26; episcopal court of, 120; suburbs of,
122
Angilbert of Saint-Riquier, 67–68, 72–74
Anniversaries: of the dead, 55, 64–65, 93–
97, 100, 144, 151, 158, 161–64, 173–74,
176; of the saints, 61–62, 65–66, 93–97;

solemn, 96–97, 151; use of vitae in, 96–
97, 151 n. 75. *See also* Special meals
Anointing of the sick, 39, 46
Anxiety concerning the fate of the dead,
29, 34–35, 52, 66, 70, 189, 212, 251
Appropriateness of prayer, 237–39
Ariès, Philippe, 5, 19
Associative rituals, 20, 101–2, 153–65,
172–74, 249, 251, 253
Attigny, synod of, 82, 88
Atwell, Robert, 189 n. 38
Aubrun, Michel, 201 n. 78
Augustine of Hippo, 62, 81, 90, 187 n.
30, 188 n. 35, 189–93, 195, 198, 203,
238, 257
Avranches, liturgical customs of, 72, 73

Beaulieu, monastery of, 150, 163
Bec, monastery of, 86, 130, 256
Bede, the Venerable, 18, 193–96, 198,
200, 226, 246–47
Benedict VIII (pope), 213–14, 230
Benedict of Aniane, 39 n. 57, 68, 74
Benedict of Nursia: abbot and patron saint
of Montecassino, 216; author of *Rule*
for monks, 60, 68; patron saint of
Fleury, 88
Besançon, liturgical customs of, 99
Bidding prayers, 42–43, 106, 123. *See also*
Universal prayer